DUOETHNOGRAPHY

DEVELOPING QUALITATIVE INQUIRY

Series Editor: Janice Morse
University of Utah

Books in the new **Developing Qualitative Inquiry** series, written by leaders in qualitative inquiry, will address important topics in qualitative methods. Targeted to a broad multidisciplinary readership, the books are intended for mid-level/advanced researchers and advanced students. The series will forward the field of qualitative inquiry by describing new methods or developing particular aspects of established methods.

Series Editorial Board

H. Russell Bernard, Kathy Charmaz, D. Jean Clandinin, Juliet Corbin, Carmen de la Cuesta, John Engel, Sue E. Estroff, Jane Gilgun, Jeffrey C. Johnson, Carl Mitcham, Katja Mruck, Judith Preissle, Jean J. Schensul, Sally Thorne, John van Maanen, Max van Manen

Volumes in this Series:

DUOETHNOGRAPHY

DIALOGIC METHODS FOR SOCIAL, HEALTH, AND EDUCATIONAL RESEARCH

Editors
Joe Norris
Richard D. Sawyer
Darren E. Lund

Walnut Creek, California

Left Coast Press, Inc. is committed to preserving ancient forests and natural resources. We elected to print this title on 30% post consumer recycled paper, processed chlorine free. As a result, for this printing, we have saved:

3 Trees (40' tall and 6-8" diameter)
1 Million BTUs of Total Energy
290 Pounds of Greenhouse Gases
1,312 Gallons of Wastewater
83 Pounds of Solid Waste

Left Coast Press, Inc. made this paper choice because our printer, Thomson-Shore, Inc., is a member of Green Press Initiative, a nonprofit program dedicated to supporting authors, publishers, and suppliers in their efforts to reduce their use of fiber obtained from endangered forests.

For more information, visit www.greenpressinitiative.org

Environmental impact estimates were made using the Environmental Defense Paper Calculator. For more information visit: www.papercalculator.org.

LEFT COAST PRESS, INC.
1630 North Main Street, #400
Walnut Creek, CA 94596
http://www.LCoastPress.com

Copyright © 2012 by Left Coast Press, Inc.

ISBN 978-1-59874-683-9 hardcover
ISBN 978-1-59874-684-6 paperback
ISBN 978-1-59874-685-3 institutional eBook
ISBN 978-1-61132-486-0 consumer eBook

Library of Congress Cataloging-in-Publication Data:

Duoethnography : dialogic methods for social, health, and educational research / Joe Norris, Richard D. Sawyer, Darren E. Lund, editors.
    p. cm.—(Developing qualitative inquiry ; v. 7)
 Includes bibliographical references and index.
 ISBN 978-1-59874-683-9 (hbk. : alk. paper) — ISBN 978-1-59874-684-6 (pbk. : alk. paper) — ISBN 978-1-59874-685-3 (institutional eBook) — ISBN 978-1-61132-486-0 (consumer eBook)
   1.   Narrative inquiry (Research method). 2.   Ethnology—Methodology. 3. Qualitative research—Methodology. 4. Knowledge, Sociology of. I. Norris, Joe. II. Sawyer, Richard D. III. Lund, Darren E.
  H61.295.D86 2012
  001.4'2—dc23
          2011036582

Printed in the United States of America

∞™ The paper used in this publication meets the minimum requirements of American National Standard for Information Sciences—Permanence of Paper for Printed Library Materials, ANSI/NISO Z39.48–1992.

Chapter logo by Sean Andrew Owen Barnard
Financial assistance was obtained from Brock University Advancement Fund

Contents

*Prologue written by Joe Norris

**Prologue written by Richard D. Sawyer

Foreword
Duoethnography:
Dialogic Methods for Social, Health, and Educational Research

Lisa M. Given
Professor of Information Studies, Charles Sturt University,
Australia

Few research methods texts open with Dr. Seuss setting the inspirational tone for what follows; and yet, that's where Joe Norris and Rick Sawyer begin their journey into duoethnography. And what a fitting tribute Dr. Seuss provides for this text! From page one, the artfulness and the playfulness of this work, alongside the depth and rigor expected of any volume exploring a new approach to qualitative inquiry, will capture readers.

I first encountered this methodology while editing *The Sage Encyclopedia of Qualitative Research Methods*, when Joe Norris offered to write an entry on duoethnography. He explored what he called "a relatively new research genre that has its genealogy embedded in two narrative research traditions: storytelling and William Pinar's concept of *currere*" (2008, p. 233). Where the encyclopedia entry provides a detailed overview of the approach, this new volume presents a collection of tales crafted by scholars engaged in the act itself. Edited by duoethnography's co-creators, Norris and Rick Sawyer, with Darren Lund, the book explores the "doing" of duoethnography. The end result is a text that embodies the participatory and emancipatory intentions of the methodology, where researchers co-create a narrative by coengaging in meaning making around particular phenomena.

In considering the work as a whole, I was struck by my own engagement with the book around the interplay of mind and body in conducting a duoethnography. The level of co-reflection and coactivity demanded by this methodology is what sets it apart from other tried-and-true approaches to qualitative exploration. Only too late did I wish that I had conducted my own duoethnography for writing this foreword! However, I engaged in self-talk as I reflected on each chapter in the work (uno-ethnography, perhaps?) as I found myself reflecting on the nature of scholarly writing. Here are a few excerpts presented in keeping with duoethnography's focus on writing in the form of a play script:

Lisa's Left Brain: How will I write what I feel in reading the work?

Lisa's Right Brain: Don't think . . . just write; through the act of writing, meaning will emerge.

LLB: What is the intention of a foreword? What should it do? What makes a "good" foreword?

LRB: It's all about inspiration—my being inspired *by* the book and others being inspired *by me* to read the book!

LLB: When will this get done? How will I fit this in around marking, committee meetings, etc.?

LRB: Let the writing come to you! Read. Read a bit more. Write when and what you can.

Indeed, what's most salient about this book is what it does for the researcher (and other, myriad voices) inside us. As Norris and Sawyer note in their introductory chapter to the book, duoethnography's "method creates a change in researcher perception and experience." The approach is deeply personal and introspective; each scholar pushes the other to engage critically and reconceptualize their perceptions of the world around them. Norris, Sawyer, and Lund capture the breadth of topics explored in these methodological encounters, noting that the duoethnographers in this book "are the sites of studies about beauty, power and privilege, immigration, professional boundaries, cross-cultural identity, patriotism, friendship, the act of having dangerous conversations, the hidden curriculum, postcolonialism within language arts, the curriculum of writing, male elementary teacher identity, and mathematics." For a volume to bridge so many public and private arenas is a challenge—but a successful one! And to do so in such a captivating way—presenting photographs, scripts, songs, and other modes of scholarly writing—is a testament to the duality of what can only be called the "rigorous play" at work here. In each chapter, the researchers seem to dance together, pushing and supporting each other, as they explore their chosen territories. I found myself unable to stop reading and engaging with each piece; I challenge each of you to do the same!

Reference

Given, L. M. (Ed.). (2008). *The SAGE encyclopedia of qualitative research methods.* Thousand Oaks, CA: Sage.

CHAPTER 1

Toward a Dialogic Methodology

Joe Norris and Richard D. Sawyer

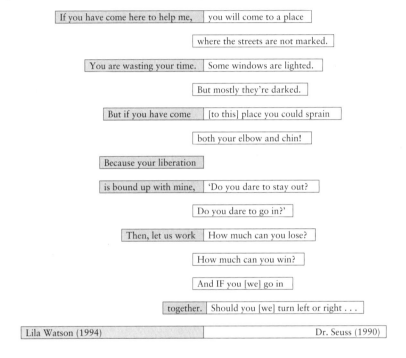

| If you have come here to help me, | you will come to a place |
| where the streets are not marked. |
| You are wasting your time. | Some windows are lighted. |
| But mostly they're darked. |
| But if you have come | [to this] place you could sprain |
| both your elbow and chin! |
| Because your liberation |
| is bound up with mine, | 'Do you dare to stay out? |
| Do you dare to go in?' |
| Then, let us work | How much can you lose? |
| How much can you win? |
| And IF you [we] go in |
| together. | Should you [we] turn left or right . . . |
| Lila Watson (1994) | Dr. Seuss (1990) |

PROLOGUE

Duoethnography (Norris, 2008; Norris and Sawyer, 2004; Sawyer and Norris, 2009) is a collaborative research methodology in which two or more researchers of difference juxtapose their life histories to provide multiple understandings of the world. Rather than uncovering the meanings that people give to their lived experiences, duoethnography embraces the belief that meanings can be and often are transformed through the research act. Readers of duoethnographers are furthermore recognized as active meaning makers (Rosenblatt, 1978) within the research text. Duoethnographies, then, are fluid texts where readers witness researchers in the act of narrative exposure and reconceptualization (Pinar, 1975b) as they interrogate and reinscribe their previously held beliefs. Duoethnographers enter the research act with multiple and often interconnected intentions. One is to learn about oneself from the "Other" (Barber, 1989). Another intention is to explore and articulate personal and collective narratives of resistance in relation to dominant discourses and metanarratives. A third is to use one's self as a site for inquiry into sociocultural socialization and inscription. In these and other cases, duoethnographers articulate their emergent thinking and changes in perception to their readers in the form of dialogic storytelling (Reason and Hawkins, 1988).

The result is not a new set of essences or theories that claim universal understandings; rather, the intent is for emergent meanings and meaning making to become dialogic within the text and between the text and the reader, problematizing reader (and inquirer) alignment with implicit metanarratives. Readers are encouraged to recall and both legitimize and question their own stories. Barone (1990) claims that a narrative is an occasion for conspiracy that invites readers to "breathe" (spire) "with" (con) parts of the text that resonate with them. Thus, readers enter the conversation rather than merely follow the lived experience of another.

During intermission and after a student-written high school performance of a collage of vignettes on "growing up," Norris (1989a) found that some audience members spoke not of the play itself but, rather, of their recollections evoked by the stories. Duoethnographies function in such a manner. The conversations of duoethnographers assist readers in recalling and reconceptualizing their own stories. As such, duoethnographies are both participatory and emancipatory because they do not strive to impose conclusions on readers; rather, they encourage readers to juxtapose their stories with the ones in the printed text. The readers' responses (Rosenblatt, 1978), albeit absent from the printed page, are present because this type of reading invites others into the research quest(ion). The duoethnographers provide theses and antitheses, and each reader will provide their own synthesis based on their unique life histories.

Like the earlier integrated poem, within duoethnographies, two or more juxtaposed texts create new hybrid texts residing within an interactive third space (Bhabha, 1994). Maruyama considers this polyocular vision, "in which the differences between images obtained from many angles enable the brain to compute invisible mental coordinates" (2004, p. 468), and duoethnography emphasizes, exploits, and celebrates the differences in point of view. Because no one meaning remains dominant, readers are released from the hegemonic expectation of aligning with a protagonist. Rather, each duoethnographer becomes the foil for the Other, challenging the Other to reflect on their own life in a deeper, more relational, and authentic manner. Similar to the initial fight scene between characters Jack Sparrow and Will Turner in Pirates of the Caribbean: Curse of the Black Pearl *(Verbinski, 2003) during which the audience is conflicted as to whom to root for (align with), so too with duoethnographies. Duoethnography's style avoids the creation of grand narrative or metanarrative, as readers find themselves alternating their allegiance among the storytellers as meanings emerge and transform. As the researcher and reader situate themselves within this process of articulated reflection and reconceptualization, they promote rigor in the study.*

Research is always a leap of faith. With autoethnography (Bochner and Ellis, 2002; Chang, 2008; Ellis, 2004; Muncey, 2010), this leap entails risk as self is revealed. Duoethnography, however, increases the risk because the researcher's current position, in the presence of the Other, becomes vulnerable. But duoethnography also has strengths. As dialogic self-study, its intent is to be critical, embodied within the researcher, and transformative. Its method creates a change in researcher perception and experience. As duoethnographers collaborate, their voices and ideas blend in unique ways. Texts merge, and through that merging, they change. New interconnections are made, and the researchers are transformed as they see themselves through the eyes of another. Duoethnography also provides a method to explore, identify, and present counterpunctual narratives (Said, 1993), narratives that contrast with more normative narratives and metanarratives. Duoethnography is soul searching, soul wrenching, and rewarding, and it is not for the light of heart.

The writers of these duoethnographies are pioneers who seek to examine lived-experiences through an emic lens. In the process, they reconceptualize their perceptions both of themselves and their cultural worlds. They present their readers with opportunities for reflective engagement. Their stories challenge us to ask, "How have we come to know the world, and after this conversation, what meanings do we wish to maintain, modify, or reject?" The topics span a range of intermingling personal and sociological constructs from beauty to patriotism, and these topics, not the individuals, are the focus of duoethnographies. Oberg and Wilson (2002) have encouraged autoethnographers to be the "sites" and not the "topics" of their research. Although identity is vital, the intersection of self with the world and how one makes and continues to make sense of that intersection underpins the quest of duoethnographers. The chapters are moments where pilgrims similar to those in The Canterbury Tales *(Chaucer, 1975) gather to reflect on the past and, based on that reflection, transform. They believe that those witnessing their discussion may vicariously learn through the stories of others (Kopp, 1972). As Maxine Greene states,*

> *Human beings who lack an awareness of their own personal reality (which is futuring, questing) cannot exist in a "we-relation" with other human beings. They cannot know what it means to live through a vivid present in common with another, to share another's flux of experience in inner time. (1991, p. 8)*

Duoethnographies inspire compassion and a sense of humanity as they call us to action. Oh! The places we'll go in quest of mutual liberation.

THE TENETS

Since its inception in 2003, duoethnography has developed into a unique qualitative research genre with its own set of principles and practices.

The methodology has emerged over time with many refinements made as the methodology's founders, Joe Norris and Rick Sawyer, examined their own studies, articulating the emergent methodological intricacies, addressing questions from conference delegates, and making suggestions to others who wished to use the methodology. Collectively, duoethnography is based on collaborative field testing by those who have written chapters in this book as well as countless, unnamed others who have expressed curiosity and interest in a research methodology that desires to be participatory, dialogic, and nonprescriptive. Although an underpinning belief is that the methodology should not dictate the form of a conversation of sentient beings in quest of meaning, a set of tenets that distinguish duoethnography from other legitimate forms of research has emerged. They are articulated here to (a) assist those interested in the methodology and/or (b) provide salient features that can be incorporated into other research approaches. Like Morse's claim that "grounded theory is not necessarily a collection of strategies. It is primarily a particular way of thinking about data" (2009, p. 14), these tenets serve as an outline of the types of researcher dispositions, principles, and foci required to undertake this work.

Currere

First, building on Pinar's concept of *currere* (1975a, 1994), duoethnography views a person's life as a curriculum. One's present abilities, skills, knowledge, and beliefs were acquired/learned, and duoethnographers recall and reexamine that emergent, organic, and predominantly unplanned curriculum in conversation with one another. Pinar defines currere as regressive, progressive, analytical, and synthetical that is "temporal and conceptual in nature, and it aims for the cultivation of a developmental point of view that hints at the transtemporal and transconceptual" (1994, p. 19). He divides the method of currere into four steps: "The first step of the method is regressive. One returns to the past" (p. 21). He labels the second step progressive; "in this phase we look the other way. We look in Sartre's language, at what is not yet the case, what is not yet present" (p. 24). His third dimension is the analytic: "Interpretation must make more visible what is lived through directly. Interpretation must not subordinate the lived present to an abstract analytical grid. One's analysis is a constituent element of the present" (p. 26). The final stage, albeit not linear, is that of synthesis. Pinar asks,

> In your own voice, what is the meaning of the present? What is the contribution of my scholarly and professional work to my present?

Do they illuminate it? Obscure it? Are one's intellectual interests biologically freeing, that is, do they permit, in fact encourage, movement? (pp. 26–27)

Currere is an act of self-interrogation in which one reclaims one's self from one's self as one unpacks and repacks the meanings that one holds. Duoethnography does this in tandem with the Other. Lévinas (1984) claims that one cannot really understand oneself unless oneself dwells in the presence of the Other. Duoethnography extends currere by inviting the Other to assist in an act of mutual reclaiming. The process can be transformative in nature as individuals change, based upon their insights. Consequently, duoethnographers do not merely repeat previously held beliefs; rather, readers witness beliefs in possible behaviors in transformation. Although therapeutic, duoethnography is not therapy because the intent is not to "cure" but to better understand oneself and the world in which one lives. Therapy's aim is "to help clients to learn more about themselves and heal or solve their problem. In autoethnography, you are expected to do that yourself, with a little help from your mentor" (Ellis, 2004, p. 296). In duoethnography, the journey is mutual and reciprocal.

Unlike currere and autoethnography, duoethnography locates the researcher differently. It is, ultimately, not about self. As noted earlier, Oberg and Wilson (2002) make a distinction between autoethnographers being either the topic or the site of research. With duoethnography, duoethnographers are the sites of the research, not the topics. They use themselves to assist themselves and others in better understanding the phenomenon under investigation. In this book, the duoethnographers are the sites of studies about beauty, power and privilege, immigration, professional boundaries, cross-cultural identity, patriotism, the act of having dangerous conversations, the hidden curriculum, postcolonialism within language arts, the curriculum of writing, and male elementary teacher identity. Although autobiographical, the focus is on how individuals experienced and gave meaning to a specific phenomenon, how these meanings transformed over time, and how this research continued the process of reconceptualization. Duoethnography is a report of a living, dynamic, and collaborative curriculum.

Polyvocal and Dialogic

Second, duoethnographies are polyvocal and dialogic. Dialogue within duoethnography functions as a mediating device to promote researchers' development of higher forms of consciousness. Promoting *heteroglossia*—a multivoiced and critical tension (Bakhtin, 1981)—dialogues are not only between the researchers but also between researcher(s) and artifacts of cultural media (e.g., photographs, songs, the written study itself). Unlike "co-constructed narratives" in which researchers attempt to "construct one story out of two" (Ellis, 2004, p. 72), duoethnographies make the voice of each duoethnographer explicit. Most coauthored texts have a solitary narrator, albeit informed by a team of coauthors. Readers follow a single perspective that has been refined by unarticulated conversations. Rather than reaching a consensus, duoethnographers make their disparate opinions explicit. Readers always know who is saying what. In the first duoethnography (Norris and Sawyer, 2004), the coauthors alternate their stories, each time labeling who is the speaker. The article is a collage of interconnected ideas that progress through time, providing insights into how attitudes toward sexual orientation were learned and relearned. Norris and Greenlaw (Chapter 4) employ more of a script format, making it more conversational, and a revised version appears in this book. Rankie Shelton and McDermott (Chapter 10) use a combination of scripts and summary paragraphs, as do Krammer and Mangiardi (Chapter 2). Breault, Hackler, and Bradley (2010 and Chapter 5) also employ a website (http://www.breaultresearch.info/methodology.html) by which readers can observe a genealogy of thought through a series of web postings. Huckaby and Weinburgh (Chapter 7) add a third voice that they call "Sojourners," through which they speak in unison, as do Le Fevre and Sawyer with the character "Both" (Chapter 12). Although styles vary, each voice/point of view is explicit.

But not all polyvocal texts in which the identity of each speaker/writer is made explicit are duoethnographies. For example, in his book *Dialogues with Contemporary Continental Thinkers*, Richard Kearney (1984) claims to have conversations with Paul Ricoeur, Emmanuel Lévinas, Herbert Marcuse, Stanislas Breton, and Jacques Derrida. In the book, he asks a series of interview questions, to which the philosophers respond. Although the voice of each participant is explicit, labeling those exchanges as dialogues is questionable as Kearney's acts more of a host than a co-philosopher expounding on his meanings as well. This imbalance is not dialogic. Nor is the piece duoethnographic, nor does it claim to be. Its value rests elsewhere. So, too, with the correspondence between Hemingway and Fitzgerald, published by Donaldson (1999). Their letters do not seek a reconceptualization of stories and beliefs but reaffirm and emphasize deeply held ones. Duoethnographies are a subset of polyvocal texts with their own unique distinctions. An explicit conversational style alone does not a duoethnography make.

Duoethnographers create heteroglossia not only by collaborating together but also by juxtaposing and interacting with pedagogies of places and cultural artifacts (Chang, 2008). These texts contribute to the polyvocal dialogues within duoethnography. Cultural artifacts, for example, tell us about our times, experiences, and history. They allow us to see a perception of an event through a critical eye (Leavy, 2009; Noe, 2000; Sawyer, 2010; Sullivan, 2005). A few examples suggest the range of artifacts duoethnographers have pulled into their studies presented in this volume as contexts of critique and interrogation. Sawyer and Liggett, for instance, examined old copies of their high school yearbooks for the sexism inherent in the photos and their educational socialization. Huckaby and Weinburgh use the old Confederate national anthem, *Dixie Land*, as a context for an examination of race and privilege in the southern United States. And McDermott and Shelton examine their high school journals, childhood photos, and their remembered childhood experiences with soap and shampoo as artifacts of their construction of a curriculum of beauty. For inclusion in their studies, these duoethnographers selected their artifacts based on their evocative power. They moved their artifacts through time and interrogated them from the vantage point of the past, the present, and the transaction between the two, and they allowed these artifacts to communicate with them.

Disrupts Metanarratives

Third, just as Lyotard (1984) questions the legitimacy of metanarratives at the cultural level, duoethnography, by being polyvocal, challenges and potentially disrupts the metanarrative of self at the personal level by questioning held beliefs. By juxtaposing the solitary voice of an autoethnographer with the voice of an Other, neither position can claim dominance or universal truth. Muncey, in her justification of autoethnography, recognizes that "postmodern world allows all points of view to be heard with no one view held as an absolute truth" (2010, p. 100). She asks, "What now forms the basis of legitimation in society if there is no overarching meta-narrative?" (p. 101) Autoethnographies exist as partial contextualized truths and, although autoethnographers often make no claim of universality, their narrative structure implies that their own stories are true. There exists a metanarrative of self that asks the reader to see through the writer's lens. Although a legitimate style, the narrative structure is a controlled framing. Duoethnography, through juxtaposition, breaks such a structure much like Brecht's (1957) breaking of the fourth wall. By being made aware that each duoethnographer is engaged in the act of construction and reconstruction, the juxtaposition acts as an "alienation-effect" (p. 9) encouraging critical thought, not alignment with the authors' stories. Such a style explicitly addresses the "crisis of representation" (Miller, 2011) as readers witness stories and meanings under construction through the dialogue between duoethnographers. No one representation holds supremacy as meanings oscillate from one to another. Duoethnographers expect and encourage the challenging of their metanarratives of self that Huckaby and Weinburgh adeptly demonstrate as they challenge each other's and their own perspectives on patriotism (Chapter 7).

In learning to read printed texts or watch videos, the spectator directly and/or indirectly ascertains the constructed narrative structure to quickly establish with whom one must align, the protagonist. Stories often proceed with the point of view of a single character through either inside or outside narration. For example, with the song *Another Saturday Night* by Sam Cooke (1963), listeners align with the singer, giving sympathy to this lonely man. Later, he is on a blind date with a female who looked like "Frankenstein." No narrative sympathy is directed toward her. In fact, she is constructed as an antagonist. In the movie *The Longest Day* (Annakin, Marton, Wicki, and Zanuck, 1962), viewers come to know many who will ultimately hit the beaches of Normandy. It is toward those that the viewers' sympathies are directed. Many more than they will and do die, but the narrative sympathy is directed toward a few. Like the running joke about those in the "red shirts" on *Star Trek* (Axe, 2008), audiences are taught that these literal cannon fodder characters might die, so one should not invest one's sympathies there.

Kurosawa's film *Rashômon* (1950) deviates from this norm by having multiple perspectives on an event. Haggis's film *Crash* (2004) goes further, making the major characters both the protagonists and the antagonists. Duoethnographers are encouraged not to place themselves as either heroes or victims but, rather, to situate themselves as pilgrims, and, like the characters in *Rashômon*, they are read as individuals trying to make sense out of past events and the stories of others.

The form of a duoethnography, by its nature, disrupts the implicit structural metanarrative of a solitary author. Readers and viewers do not witness a phenomenon as experienced by a single individual. Rather, duoethnographies present multiple points of view. Readers oscillate back and forth from one story/perspective to another, and, in the chasm/space between those oscillations, like those who observed a collage of scenes about growing up, they begin to write in and question their own stories. As a result, duoethnographers attempt to avoid creating empiricist texts that define and claim the world. They encourage "counterpunctual reading" (Punday, 2002) that makes both its form and its content problematic. It is "based on Said's belief that a text is not a simple or direct representation of the world; it is, rather, a heterogeneous mixture of unifying and disunifying elements as the text admits and denies part of colonizing life" (p. 157). Many declarative texts attempt to colonize the minds of their readers as they try to assert their particular perspective of the world (as does this particular piece of writing). Duoethnographies invite the readers into the conversation. They encourage readers, through example, to disrupt their individually constructed metanarratives of themselves and their world and make counterpunctual reading the norm. It is an ethical stance in which one recognizes that one's frame and the frames of others (Goffman, 1974) are flawed and one must act with some degree of humble uncertainty when one tells one's stories. Claiming universal truth is an act of aggression as one superimposes one's beliefs onto the Other. Although duoethnographers believe in situated or local knowledge, they also acknowledge that all knowing must be brought into question. They model a state of perpetual inquiry.

Furthermore, duoethnographies provide an opportunity for both researchers and readers to critique the relationship between personal and larger cultural narratives. Part of duoethnographer's intent is the exploration and identification of counternarratives for their own sake: to reveal them to the researcher and reader. Thus, they allow for the exposure of subjugated knowledge and texts, and although the resulting counternarratives might not decenter dominate discourses, they do offer counterpunctual narratives of experience to them.

Difference

Fourth, as indicated earlier, the difference between duoethnographers is not only encouraged but also expected. With the initial duoethnography (Norris and Sawyer, 2004) the difference was sexual orientation. Within this book, Shelton and McDermott's study on beauty focuses on difference with social class (Chapter 10). McClellan and Sader (Chapter 6) explore both class and race in their study of power and privilege and difference, and race plays a large role in Huckaby and Weinburgh's study of patriotism in music (Chapter 7). Nabavi and Lund's difference is around place of birth, as they unpack issues of immigration and identity in a multicultural country (Chapter 8). Country of residence is a factor in the types of conversations Le Fevre and Sawyer (Chapter 12) have about what they dare or do not dare to say, and Aujla-Bhullar and Grain (Chapter 9) juxtapose their concepts of self as defined in their cross-cultural work. Norris and Greenlaw (Chapter 4) compare personality types in the desire and execution of writing, and Sawyer and Liggett (Chapter 3) compare how their various life experiences have impacted the way they approach "postdecolonization" in teaching and living. Sitter and Hall (Chapter 11) juxtapose their different educational and employment histories that brought them to a similar place. Through the articulation of such differences, duoethnographers make explicit how different people can experience the same phenomenon differently.

In addition, such a juxtaposition of difference aids in keeping the text open. Readers are provided with theses and antitheses and the readers can form their own syntheses.

Duoethnography, therefore, does not seek universals. Rather, it examines multiple margins, articulating the roles each individual's unique life history plays in meaning making and behavior. Duoethnographers reconstruct their lives "alongside" (Clandinin, 2006; Clandinin et al., 2010) one another, giving space for multiple perspectives. By providing polyocular perspectives, duoethnographies present multiple positions in dialogue. They are not only polyocular but also "polytemporal" and "polygeographical" as meanings are situated by time and place.

Dialogic Change and Regenerative Transformation

Fifth, duoethnographers change in different ways and to different extents as a result of the embodied and dialogic research process. Duoethnography attempts to "turn knowledge into 'an act of unsettling its own natural condition' (conversation with Lévinas) as power and violence in order to open it to the infinity of the other who transcends every attempt to reduce him to our totalizing grasp" (Kearney, 1984, p. 49). Duoethnography recognizes the tyranny of reductionism. Wayne in *Wayne's World* (Spheeris, 1992) speaks in Cantonese with the English subtitles: "Was it Kierkegaard or Dick Van Patten who said, 'If you label me, you negate me'?" Duoethnography, therefore, makes one's current position problematic. One's beliefs can be enslaving, negating the self, but the act of reconceptualization can be regenerative and liberating. Duoethnography recognizes the need of the Other to liberate the self from the self: "The biblical and Talmudic texts, he [Levinas] claims, teaches us that the 'I' does not begin with itself in some our moment of autonomous self-consciousness but in relation with the other, to who it remains forever responsible" (Kearney, 1984, p. 48). Duoethnography, then, takes an ethical stance toward the other. It is not about telling one's stories to reify self; the duoethnographic methodology is about telling one's stories to assist both self and other in an act of "conscientization" (Freire, 1971).

Lather (1986) in her reconceptualization of validity defines the concept of "catalytic validity" (p. 240) as "the degree to which the research process re-orients, focuses, and energizes participants in what Freire (1973) terms 'conscientization,' knowing reality in order to better transform it" (p. 67). This definition is close to the stance of duoethnography, with one slight difference. A catalyst, by definition, remains unchanged. Change and transformation are integral to duoethnography. Its value rests with the degree of rigor found within the articulated conversations of inter self-reflexivity.

Duoethnographers in this book report such changes as a result of the study. McClellan (Chapter 6) states:

> I walk away from this duoethnography having experienced a deeper awareness of myself as a leadership educator/social justice educator. There is an old adage that says "understanding takes time." Having heard that for most of my childhood, it seemed like a misnomer. I knew the significant meaning of the phrase in an intellectual way. However, through this duoethnography, I've experienced the tangibility of its meaning. (p. 152)

Rankie Shelton (Chapter 10) phrased her reconceptualization in a series of questions:

> Why did I change my linguistic identity? Why did I disassociate myself from my Upstate New York identity for so many years? But this duoethnography made me realize that my conception of beauty is a different conception of self. It is completely different from my academic or linguistic self. Yet, I now see it as part of my drive to be who I am academically and linguistically. (p. 237)

Krammer (Chapter 2) reports her reconceptualization of grading within her duoethnography:

> Then the professor explained that this course would be evaluated on the basis of credit/noncredit. No traditional evaluation scheme grounded in comparative judgments; no fostering of competitive relationships; no quantification of my worth as a human being; and . . . no possibility of an A+. I was incensed: here I was about to win the ultimate prize, perfect marks in a doctoral program, and someone had the gall to change the rules of the game. . . . Today I understand my academic "game-playing" as a compulsion born of the hidden curriculum of my schooling. Many decades have passed since I first learned to equate superlative grades with academic success, and academic success with personal worth. During my master's program, I finally recognized the pernicious effects of this belief; I determined, then, to think differently. (p. 65)

These and other duoethnographers recognize that a fundamental disposition for their work is the reporting of changes in meaning throughout their life histories and during the duoethnographic process. In so doing, meaning becomes transcontextual and transtemporal.

Trustworthiness Found in Self-Reflexivity, Not Validity and Truth Claims

Sixth, due to its emergent, dialogic, and transformative nature, duoethnography makes the positivistic notions of truth and validity redundant. Readers witness the researchers trying to make sense of and transform their recalled experiences. The stories themselves are transitory as it is acknowledged that they transform over time. Cell (1984) recounts three versions of a woman telling a story three times throughout her life. Although the story remains intact, the point of view changes drastically; so, too, with all stories. Researchers, informants/participants can never really make a truth claim. Recalled stories are always susceptible; they are recollections of past events in the present (Muncey, 2010, p. 103). Likert scales obscure the opinions of past events behind the determination of the number chosen, providing a false indication of objectivity. Even videos and photographs contain points of view (Becker, 1978; Norris, 1989b) of the photographers/researchers and most often do not record the inner thoughts of the participants in vivo. To "capture," besides being a term of violence, implies that complexity can be reduced into discrete units.

Banks and Banks claim, "The opposite of fiction isn't truth but something like objectivity or actuality. Any genre or piece of writing that claims to be objective, to represent the actual, is a writing that denies its own existence" (1998, p. 13). Duoethnographies make explicit that what is reported are contextualized beliefs or "truthful fictions" (Denzin, 1989, p. 23). As Muncey asserts, "Bakhtin regards 'truth' as something that is constituted dialogically and intersubjectively, that reason is not the only way to truth; it is constituted through conversation" (2010, p. 101). With duoethnography, readers witness two or more people change over time and through the research conversation. Duoethnographies portray knowledge in transition, and as such, knowing is not fixed but fluid. Truth and validity are irrelevant. What exists is the rigor of the collaborative inquiry that is made explicit in the duoethnography itself. As Muncey has stated, "What legitimizes knowledge in the postmodern condition is how well it performs, or how well it enables a person to perform, each little story" (p. 101). Thus, the believability and trustworthiness of the research is found in the depth of researcher involvement with and accompanying praxis related to her or his study.

Audience Accessibility

Seventh, Haven believes that "people are eager for stories. Not dissertations. Not lectures. Not informative essays. For stories" (2007, p. 8). Considering the meaning of story, Ellis reminds us that "there is nothing more theoretical and analytical than a good story" (2004, p. 194). A narrative approach to research may address Leavy's (2009) call for research that is accessible to a broader range of the population than strictly academics by blending what Reason and Hawkins call "explanation" and "expression," "the two basic modes of reflecting on and processing experience. Explanation is the mode of classifying, conceptualizing, and building theories from experience. . . . Expression is the mode of allowing the meaning of experience to become manifest" (1988, pp. 79–80). Duoethnographies, then, are a form of praxis writing in which theory and practice converse.

Many new to graduate studies have commented to us, Joe and Rick, on the ease of reading duoethnographies. The unique blending of the concrete story with the abstract theory provides a complementary style of praxis through which each extends the meaning of the other. The readers report that they are also compelled to add their stories to the mix, as evoked by the stories that they read. Duoethnographies do not end with conclusions. Rather, they continue to be written by those who read them.

Ethical Stances

Eighth, due to duoethnography's dialogic nature of researching self and Other, ethical issues are somewhat different. First, by conducting research "with" and not "on" another, duoethnographers elude the researcher/ researched dichotomy that situates the Other as a subject to be talked about. Duoethnographies are conversations that position the Other in dialogue, making the status one of equals. This is not to suggest that all research "on" others is not ethical. Research review boards approve letters of "Invitation to Participate" that articulate issues of risk of harm and benefit, with those involved signing the waivers indicating informed consent. Duoethnographers agree to write joint papers with themselves as the sites of their research. A board did not review the chapters because permission is explicit with the submission of the chapter. The people who wrote them will benefit from the publication and understood the risks of harm as Le Fevre and Sawyer indicate (Chapter 12). To expect two consenting researchers to obtain permission to collaborate would, in effect, relegate all coauthored pieces to obtain ethical clearance. It is anticipated, however, that duoethnographies will move from discussions among academics to conversations with nonacademics. In these cases, reviews may be necessary as the Other participants might not be aware of potential harms, although they will benefit from the joint publication. The contracting of these "with" relationships are stories to be written, as all "with" relationships have their own unique variations. Still, the attempt to move from research "on" to research "with" does mark an ethical shift in research endeavors.

Second duoethnographers take an ethical pedagogical relationship with one another, entering into an ethics of caring (Noddings, 1984).

They regard each other as both their teacher and student, assisting the Other in the making of meaning and receptive to the Other in reconceptualizing their own meanings. Like fellow "pilgrims" (Kopp, 1972) who co-create meanings by sharing stories with one another, they recognize the power of the narrative (Barone, 1990) as they "(con)spire or breathe (with)" the stories of their writing partners. They expect to depart the duoethnography being changed by the stories of the Other, but they do not enter to change the other but to change self. Such is the paradoxical pedagogical ethical stance of duoethnography. One does not impose her/his meanings onto the other; rather, one trusts in the nature of the storytelling process, recognizing that change will emerge as deemed relevant by the Other. Each will change but not in the same way. In so doing, duoethnographers escape the potential "tyranny of consensus."

Third, this stance is transferred to the reader. Duoethnographies, unlike prescriptive studies, do not give conclusions or recommendations. The ethical stance toward the reader is one of an unknown future partner in inquiry, not a recipient of newfound wisdom. By acknowledging "reader-response theory" (Rosenblatt, 1978), duoethnographers do not try to impose their meanings; rather, they expect that by reading a duoethnography, the reader's meaning will oscillate between the stories of the duoethnographers, creating new meanings unique to the reader. As is ontologically always the case, generalizability rests with the reader, not the researcher. Duoethnographers, through juxtaposition provide theses and antitheses, leaving space for the readers to find their own synthesis. In so doing, duoethnographies disrupt the structural authoritarian stance of a single authored (narrated) text. This positions the reader, not as a spectator but a *spect-actor* (Boal, 1979), one who is an active participant in the meaning making. The style of the discourse takes the ethical stance by positioning a future present-absent Other/Reader as an implicit coauthor.

Fourth, and the most problematic, is the inclusion of others in stories of one's own. In research "on" others, the Other is typically anonymous, and when they discuss others, they too are anonymous. In autoethnographies, duoethnographies, and qualitative research approaches that reveal the identity of the researcher, others who are in relationship with the publicly known authors will also be known. Even to "bracket in," as Spradley (1979, 1980) recommends, can include information about referenced others including relatives, friends, and coworkers.

Norris, Higgins, and Leggo (2004) discuss the problematics of personal disclosure in qualitative research, taking the stance that although one has both the right and responsibility to tell one's stories, one must weigh the potential harm to the disclosed Others and the likely benefit to the larger community. Leggo explains that he received thank you correspondence regarding a story that he had published about his relationship with his father. The reader was inspired to rekindle a relationship with his own father. The perceived harm to Leggo's father was little to none, but a particular benefit was, in this case, made known to Leggo. Norris discusses a story that his father told him not to tell about a deceased uncle. Norris believed that this "minor" family secret could not harm the individuals involved but was important for the research project on human sexuality. Being asked "not to tell" reinforced the theme of "sexual secrets" and was performed as part of three scenes that dealt with masturbation (2009, p. 105).

Duoethnography, then, is one of a number of research genres in which personal disclosure is problematic, heightening the researchers' responsibilities toward those being mentioned. Two useful guidelines are to (a) just tell the story without value judgments being placed on the Other and (b) frame the individual as one constructed from your point of view, not as truth. An ethical stance is a position that requires much deliberation. In duoethnography, then, ethics lead the research process. It is not an abstract goal connected to the use of "value-free" research; it *is* the research.

Trust

Duoethnographers have reported that trust is a vital element in duoethnography. One does not want to reveal "warts and all" to an unreceptive and uncaring person. Although duoethnographers expect an interrogation of their perspectives, they expect this to be done respectfully and playfully. Without trust, disclosure is withheld, preventing a rich discussion of the phenomenon under investigation. Huckaby and Weinburgh discuss how they have come closer, respecting each other's differences as a result of their duoethnography. As they trusted, they disclosed more, and as they disclosed, they trusted more. This spiral of trust and disclosure brought them to a depth that enabled a close examination of how politically charged icons could have such disparate meaning and that through dialogue, one can keep one's own stance while respecting the Other: "We will never be able to walk into the other. But, we can approach the other get closer than we might have imagined possible" (Huckaby and Weinburgh, Chapter 7).

A REVIEW OF THE TENETS

Do all duoethnographies in the book ascribe to these tenets? To varying degrees, they do, as would be expected. Although the tenets outline a set of guiding principles and dispositions, the duoethnographic methodology does stipulate one prescriptive method to which duoethnographers must adhere. To do so would be antithetical to its dialogic nature. As Cunningham pointed out, "At its simplest, there is no group process to attend to, only the interpersonal relationship of two people" (1988, p. 164). But there are key elements that make duoethnographies distinct and strong. First, there is a focus on one's life as a curriculum, as currere. This makes it different from an autoethnography. Second, they are polyvocal and dialogic. The voices of each duoethnographer are made explicit throughout the piece. Although some joint narration may exist, the stories rest in juxtaposition. Third, this juxtaposition is deliberate, to disrupt the metanarrative found in solitary writing. This juxtaposition creates a third space (Bhabha, 1994) that invites the readers to add and rethink their stories to the ones being told. Fourth, this disruption and interrogation of stories is possible only when differences are articulated and discussed. These differences do not seek resolution. Rather, they coexist "alongside" (Clandinin, 2006; Clandinin et al., 2010) one another, with an appreciation of difference (Myers, 1980). Fifth, duoethnographies don't merely retell the past; they question the meanings held about the past, inviting reconceptualization. Although an acceptance of the coexistence of the Other is an ethical stance, so too is the inviting of the Other to shed new insights onto old stories. Duoethnographers recognize that the frames that they hold are inadequate and the Other can assist in a reconceptualization of self. They do not retell old stories; they reinscribe them. Changes in both the stories and the duoethnographers should occur throughout and be evident in the text. Sixth, universal truths are not sought. Both subjectivity and intersubjectivity provide polyocular vision on a phenomenon. Seventh, duoethnographies are a form of praxis in which theory and practice converse. This has the potential of making them of value to both academics and those in other fields. Duoethnographers believe that stories beget stories and write in such a way that invites others to tell theirs. Eighth, duoethnographers, as they attempt to enter into relationships "with" another, recognize that an ethical stance toward another is a negotiated space, one that requires vigilant deliberation. Personal stories must be told but done in such a way that the other is not reified, trivialized, vilified, or romanticized. This ethical stance is also directed on how one positions the audience by the way one tells one's stories. Finally, duoethnographies are built on a deep layer of trust that grows over time. Without it, disclosure would not be forthcoming, nor would the rigorous conversations.

THE DUOETHNOGRAPHIC METHOD

The duoethnographic method is not a fixed blueprint (Dewey, 1934) but always emergent and uncertain. Its tenets serve as dispositions to guide the research, but each duoethnography will chart its own course. To reiterate Morse's (2009) earlier citation in relation to grounded theory, duoethnography is "primarily a particular way of thinking about data," (p. 14) or, if we employ Varela, Thompson, and Rosch's metaphor, duoethnography is "laying down a path in walking" (1991, p. 236). As content (data) emerges, the methodological direction of the study will change, and vice versa. Some studies have found themselves turning to artifacts and photographs (Chapters 2, 3, 4, and 10). Others have not. Although many were face-to-face, one used e-mail (Chapter 8), one used a combination of recorded Skype conversations and e-mails (Chapter 12), and another used hypertext (Chapter 5). Three explored the influence of popular media and songs (Chapters 3, 4, and 7), and some turned a critical lens onto their schooling (Chapters 2, 3, 4, and 5). A large number reexamined their own practice as teachers and counselors (Chapters 2, 3, 4, 5, 6, 11, and 12), giving a quasi action research (Kemmis and McTaggart, 1988) focus to these studies. The following, then, does not provide a prescriptive method. Rather, exemplars are presented as possible routes to take as each research journey uniquely unfolds.

Finding a Topic and Partner

Dissimilar to issues of entry in traditional qualitative research studies in which researchers generate a research topic and then find participants, duoethnographic topics and participants, to some extent, coemerge. The first duoethnography began as an informal conversation about sexual orientation. As the discussion continued, the idea of a paper about their different perspectives based on their own histories emerged. The topic found the two colleagues based at the same university. Over a year, they met to gather their thoughts, once in a long car ride when one drove and the other took notes. They also wrote individually, meeting from time to time to refine and organize drafts to be presented at conferences. Drawing on discussions and feedback from these conference presentations, they made revisions and published in a refereed book of conference proceedings (Norris and Sawyer, 2004).

From this initial effort, both Norris and Sawyer began looking for other writing opportunities with other colleagues. In a discussion with a colleague about student writing, Norris and Greenlaw (2005 and Chapter 4) decided to conduct a duoethnography examining their own writing histories. This and a revision of the sexual orientation paper, which focused on the emerging methodological aspects of duoethnography, were presented at a Curriculum and Pedagogy Conference (Sawyer and Norris, 2005). Like the initial duoethnography, Norris and Greenlaw's partnership coemerged from an informal conversation, as did Sawyer and Liggett's (2007 and Chapter 3) research on postcolonialism.

It is no surprise that, due to its conversational nature, it was at conferences, where face-to-face discussions would take place, where the initial interest in duoethnographies germinated. Over a lunch discussion at the 2005 Curriculum and Pedagogy Conference, McDermott discussed interest with the topic of beauty emerging as one of a number of possibilities. In this case, McDermott searched for a writing partner with whom she had already established friendship and trust. She and Shelton presented a paper on the curriculum of beauty (2008 and Chapter 10).

Lund attended Norris and Sawyer's presentation (2005) at a Provoking Curriculum Conference and included its discussion in his graduate research courses. He wrote a duoethnography with a former high school student on their social activism efforts (Lund and Evans, 2006). It was a natural progression from work that they had already done. Lund and a colleague with whom he had collaborated on activism and research later wrote a duoethnography about their common interests in youth activism and issues of cultural identity (Lund and Nabavi, 2008 and Chapter 8).

Although these beginning duoethnographers found topics of common interest, it must be noted that, in keeping with duoethnography's polyocular lenses that examine differences and similarities, each duoethnographic team had dissimilar histories. With Norris and Sawyer, it was sexual orientation. McDermott and Shelton had class and urban/rural differences, and Sawyer and Liggett brought in gender. Lund and Evans had teacher and student perspectives, and differences in sexual orientation, and Lund and Nabavi focused on their differences in upbringing and countries of origin. Norris claims that his schooling made writing a chore and often painful, whereas Greenlaw took pleasure from writing. Finding a topic of common interest does not imply common perspectives. In fact, this is discouraged, as a major strength of duoethnographies is in the juxtaposition of difference.

For example, Breault, who also attended the 2005 Curriculum and Pedagogy Conference, expressed interest in duoethnography due to its dialogic nature of exploring social issues. He subsequently used the methodology as an instructional tool with undergraduates, assisting them in articulating and examining their beliefs. He also invited a graduate student to explore with him the concept of being male elementary teachers. In this case, they found that their common interest was too close with not enough difference. They invited another doctoral student, this

time a female, to provide more tension in their discussions. This was the first "trio" of duoethnographers (Chapter 5).

The next wave of duoethnographic studies was a result of workshops presented at conferences. Norris (2005) provided a workshop at the Enhancing Qualitative Understanding of Illness Processes and Prevention Conference on the methodology, and Krammer, who attended the workshop, expressed interest in conducting a duoethnographic study. She partnered with another doctoral student, Mangiardi, finding the hidden curriculum of schooling as a topic of mutual interest (Chapter 2). Norris and Sawyer (2008) provided a full-day workshop at the 9th Annual Advances in Qualitative Methods (AQM) Conference. Lund brought along three graduate students. Rapke had already begun a duoethnography exploring her teacher and mathematical selves and presented this on a duoethnographic panel (Rapke and Towers, 2008). This marked not only the first solo duoethnography, with a person exploring a concept from multiple perspectives of self, but was also the first doctoral research using the methodology.

Grain and Aujla-Bhullar (Chapter 9), two of Lund's graduate students at the University of Calgary, took part in the AQM workshop, writing a pilot duoethnography on how they learned their concept of time. From that experience, they focused on a topic of mutual interest, diversity education, exploring how both of them being second-generation Canadians from different cultures influenced their present work situations.

Although Grain and Aujla-Bhullar, and Nabavi, had conference experience, their exposure to duoethnography also came from coursework and/or conversations with their professor, Darren Lund. Such is also the case with Sitter and Hall (Chapter 11); Sitter is a doctoral student supervised by Lund, and she presented at a session at the International Institute for Qualitative Methods Conference in Vancouver, B.C., in 2010, and also took a qualitative research methods course from Lund. From Sitter and Hall's collaborative work in participatory visual media projects the theme of professional boundaries emerged, and this drew their attention. The topic and duoethnographic partnership grew from other mutual work, as is the case with many existing duoethnographic studies.

The current phase of duoethnographic studies was mostly initiated at conferences, specifically those of the American Educational Research Association (AERA). Huckaby, attending a duoethnography panel, recognized similarities between duoethnography and her published series of letters to a colleague about the song *Dixie Land* (Huckaby, 2007). She wished to refocus the issue by bringing in her colleague's voice. She and Weinburgh dug deeper exploring the roots of their emotional and political attachments and repulsions to the song (Chapter 7). McClellan also attended a duoethnographic panel at AERA and reported that she and

a teaching colleague, Sader, were looking for ways to ease their students into conversations about race. McClellan had a follow-up telephone conversation with Sawyer and received relevant literature from Norris. From this she and Sader embarked on their first duoethnography with the aim of using their duoethnographic study on racial and class differences as an example (Chapter 6) to scaffold more critical classroom conversations and writings by her students. Their mutual need and exposure to a new research methodology that models dialogue brought them to duoethnography.

Ceglowski also attended AERA sessions but was more interested in ways of having stronger engagements with children within the research process than finding a peer to explore a relevant topic. She discusses how she attempted to "develop shared meaning making with children" (Ceglowski and Makovsky, in press). In her case, she sought her co-researchers after she determined topic but was receptive to changes in direction as the conversations developed.

With the exception of Ceglowski's study, duoethnographies to this point involved peers who are also researchers, but this need not be the case. It is anticipated that, as the methodology becomes more widely known and utilized, the range of duoethnographers will expand, as will the ways individuals choose their partners and topics. The editors of this book are aware of a proposed study of a male academic writing a duoethnography with his nonacademic father. While raising new ethical issues, as discussed earlier, the desire to have dialogic relationships in which all parties are both the researcher and the researched is growing.

Dialogical Autobiographical Storytelling

Generating Stories

Simply, stories beget stories. Unlike open-ended and/or focused questions in traditional interviews, the use of natural, informal, everyday conversational structures serve as thresholds to past experiences by providing rich details to which the Other can connect. The stories themselves evoke other stories, cascading and building on one another. Some recalled stories are familiar and frequently told, but the richer ones are often forgotten, buried in the past, emerging as a particular detail in the Other's story triggers a memory. Chang claims, "Memory is not always a friend to autoethnography; it is sometimes a foe. . . . Some distant memories remain vivid while other recent memories fade away quickly" (2008, p. 72). Duoethnography, unlike autoethnography, which relies on an individual's memory, elicits stories through the listening of the relevant stories of the Other. The communal act is an integral aspect of duoethnography not only as a style of writing but as a way of assisting recall. Reason and Hawkins declare that

"storytelling has changed our approach to our work in many ways. It changes how we ask questions, how we explore sense-making, and how we tell what we know. . . . Stories also change how experience is gathered" (1988, p. 100). Storytelling, then, is not merely a form of data dissemination; it is also a form of data generation.

Although the finished product of a duoethnography has a coherent organizational structure (thematic and/or chronological), the generation of stories/data is often far from linear. Chang's suggestion of creating an autobiographical timeline in chronological order to rediscover one's stories (2008, p. 73) is a good one. Although useful and a good starting point, duoethnographic stories do not often emerge as straightforwardly as that. The process is more one of a series of declarative and interpretive hermeneutic circles through which insights and stories coemerge. Norris and Greenlaw (Chapter 4) claim, "Over a number of years, we have brought an analytical rigor to our stories and added new narratives that emerged only after our familiar stories had been articulated" (p. 91). The research brings a sensitive disposition to the material, and over time, memories of other experiences spring to the surface, are added, and redefine the piece. The beginning point of the research is not necessarily the beginning piece of the final writing.

Sitter (Sitter and Hall, Chapter 11) suggests, "Prior to immersing ourselves in a conversation about boundaries, it may be helpful to start with discussing our different educational backgrounds. I've often found myself wondering how I ended up in social work . . ." (p. 244). Later, she spirals to a family experience, "wondering how much the personal and the professional were impacted by my family and my experiences throughout life. For example, to this day I can still recall my mother teaching me that discussing family differences should always occur within the privacy of the family, not in front of dinner guests, or out in public" (p. 247).

Structuring the Stories

Consequently, there is no clear separation between data generation and writing. The sequence of the storytelling method is not linear, nor need it be. Sitter and Hall's structure follows the pattern of a natural conversation, as do most. As duoethnographers go through spirals of hermeneutic circles both in the collection of relevant vignettes and their interpretation, so too does the structure of the final text. Duoethnographies, although written as conversations, never happened in the way that they are presented. They are reconstructed text that, although dialogical, existed as fragments that were spliced together. Similar to axial coding, "whereby data are put back together in new ways after open coding" (Strauss and Corbin, 1990, p. 96), a duoethnography frames the content, as do all narrative structures. As Richardson claimed,

> Even the shape of the conventional research report reveals a narratively driven subtext: theory (literature review) is the past or the (researcher's) cause for the present study (the hypothesis being tested), which will lead to the future-findings and implications (for the researcher, the researched, and science). Narrative structures, therefore, are preoperative regardless of whether one is writing primarily in the narrative or logico-scientific mode. (1990, p. 13)

Ebert (1999), in his review of *My Dinner with Andre*, reports:

> The conversation that flows so spontaneously between Andre Gregory and Wallace Shawn was carefully scripted. "They taped their conversations two or three times a week for three months," Pauline Kael writes, "and then Shawn worked for a year shaping the material into a script, in which they play comic distillations of aspects of themselves."

The same is true of duoethnographies. They are carefully scripted to resemble natural conversations. Barbara Bowers, Kathy Charmaz, and Julie Corbin discuss the problematics of "cleaning transcripts" (Corbin, 2009, p. 54), claiming that something is lost. All editing is both subtractive and additive. Reframing brings focus but loses some of the context. With duoethnographies, restructuring in a conversational style combines the "rationality of the story and the emotion of the interview" (Charmaz, in Corbin, 2009, p. 54).

Juxtaposition and/or Conversational

The structure of duoethnographies, while dialogical, varies in relation to how the conversation is framed. In Norris and Sawyer's initial duoethnography (2004) they employ a juxtaposition style, as do Sawyer and Liggett (Chapter 3); Breault, Hackler, and Bradley (Chapter 5); and others. Their stories rest alongside one another and intertwine, with the narrative juxtapositions creating a context for the researchers to later discuss differences in content and perception. Sawyer states, "Reading Tonda's section, I began to wonder how my own cultural indoctrination played out on a deeper, more layered and contradictory way when I moved to the United States" (p. 314). These intentionally intertwined narratives create new meaning through their juxtaposition, engendering subsequent reflective discussion between the researchers.

In Norris's and Greenlaw's (Chapter 4) duoethnography, Greenlaw often speaks directly to Norris and vice versa: "Jim: It seems that your writing experiences during junior and senior high school years had some sense of audience. So did my own early writings" (p. 93). McClellan and Sader (Chapter 6) do a combination of both. Running through the duoethnography is a feeling of listening to a conversation. "Jennifer: When we were talking about this, I was a little bit . . . this could get kind of sticky and scary . . . and it seems like you have sort of parallel fears that I have" (p. 140). At times this shifts to a direct comment to the reader:

> While writing this paper, at times we each have noticed that the other person was not open enough in asking for help. We realized that we were both used to being the person who did the work in a group project, both because we weren't sure we could count on the others for help and because we liked to do things our own way. (p. 141)

They alternate between conversing with the Other to the use of "we." Huckaby and Weinburgh (Chapter 7) make the shift from talking with each other to the communal "we" by explicitly naming the third collective voice "Sojourners."

> Sojourners: We can't escape the power of words and symbols. Their meanings aren't stable and change with circumstances and the positional of the people. We embody the pain of words as weapons of patriotism. By making these weapons more public, we believe we are less vulnerable. (p. 171)

Structurally, they break the conversational point of view by explicitly labeling the voices as a collective one that directly addresses the reader. Brecht (1957) would consider this "breaking the fourth wall," reminding readers that they are consuming a constructed story. After attending a session of Norris and Sawyer (2008), Bill Pinar (personal conversation, September 2008) asked whether duoethnographers positioned their readers as voyeurs or they were invited into the conversation as a form of ménage à trois. On reflection, it is either/or and both. Readers can and do vicariously share in the stories of the writers, but the desire of duoethnographers is that readers will join in, telling and questioning their own stories, albeit to self. When readers become "alienated" from the text (Brecht, 1957), the potential for self-reflection is greater. Huckaby and Weinburgh's use of "Sojourners" does just that.

The Conversation is the Story

The structure of duoethnographies is layered. There are the stories themselves as told by the writer-researchers, but the conversation itself is also a story as readers witness the changes in the duoethnographers as the dialogue progresses. Similar to the movie *My Dinner with Andre* (Malle, 1981), readers are also engaged in the conversation. In many ways, this movie is a theatrical duoethnography as the character/actors tell semiautobiographical stories and discuss them. This double layer changes the narrative structure from merely reporting about a past experience to a constructed "real-time" event, adding to the drama. One does not know how the conversation will unfold, and in so doing, suspense and interest are generated. All duoethnographies are stories within stories.

Show and Tell

One of the strengths of duoethnographies is the power of the narrative. Readers are provided with what Geertz (1973) calls "thick description" and witness vicariously the lived experiences of another. An adage of theatre is "show; don't tell," and, partially, this is what a duoethnography does. For example, Nabavi (Chapter 8) states:

> For example, my classmates would sport sweatshirts with the different characters from a popular cartoon series at the time, the Care Bears. When asked by one classmate which character I liked best, I pointed to the character she had on her shirt, calling it by the wrong name. The student rightfully accused me of not knowing the characters, which for her made me unworthy of her friendship. (p. 179)

Concisely, she provides a critical incident of her outsider experiences as an immigrant, providing a concrete example of the phenomenon. But duoethnographies are more than stories; they also blend in analysis. This example is preceded by the comment, "I was unfamiliar with the cultural discourses of the time and would often stick out because of it" (p. 179). As cited earlier, Reason and Hawkins "see *explanation* and *expression* as two basic modes of reflecting on and processing experience" (1988, p. 79, emphasis in original). Duoethnographers, throughout their texts, work on balancing the expression (showing) with explanation (telling). Ellis (2004) subdivides explanation into thematic analysis and structural analysis. Krammer and Mangiardi (Chapter 2) have thematic sections labeled as lessons (Lesson 1: "Our Authority Is Unimpeachable," Lesson 2: "One Succeeds at the Expense of Others," etc.). Their subtitles make their themes explicit.

Transparency

Breault, Hackler, and Bradley (Chapter 5), unlike the other authors in this book, place a stronger emphasis on an audit trail that documents the data collection prior to its reconstruction. They claim:

> To accomplish our goal of creating a naturalistic and transparent presentation we decided to use the hypertext capabilities of web-based publication. All the work described below can currently be found at the *Trioethnography* link on http://breaultresearch.info. The materials included at that site are crucial to understanding our conversation and what we gained from it. (p. 126)

This website contains a discussion of the methodology, background stories, three hours of annotated transcripts, excursus that emerge from their conversations, and points to ponder. Like creators of a collage, they collectively provide a nonlinear history of the project. In so doing, the reader is made privy to the workings behind the curtain.

Although they provide a strong rationale for this approach, they deliberately fall short of making it a canon.

> None of that is to imply that we need to be suspicious of all qualitative researchers. The lack of transparency, more often than not, is due to limitations of the publication process. Online journal formats offer the potential to free researchers from some traditional publication limits but only if the new format is used in nontraditional ways. In our project we experimented with presenting our work in a way that is as naturalistic and conversational as the original dialogue. (p. 126)

Use of Artifacts and Photos

Not all but some duoethnographers turn to archived artifacts and photos as data sources and evokers of memory, some of which are included as photos within their texts. Sawyer looked at photos taken by a friend during their youth to explore how they perceived their relationship. This spurred Norris to take photos of his schools and other environments in which the curriculum of homophobia ran rampant (Norris and Sawyer, 2004). Shelton and McDermott provide pictures of their childhood homes that draw some parallels between class and beauty (Chapter 10), and Sawyer and Liggett analyze yearbooks "to examine presented norms, trends and behaviors" (p. 78, Chapter 3). Norris returned to childhood photos based on his ongoing study with Creswell on health, hospitalization, suffering, and mortality (Norris and Creswell, 2007). He found himself holding dead rabbits in one photograph and toy guns in two photographs, and his father and him holding a real rifle in another, all under the age of three. His curriculum of mortality was very much tied up with weapons, something of which he was not aware until he revisited the photos. In reconstructing one's life, photographs can play a major role.

Although photographs are relatively easy to store, even more so with the move to the digital, personal artifacts, over the years, often get filed in the trash bin. Their traces sometimes exist in photographs, but for the most part their only existence lies in the memory of the duoethnographer. Some artifacts do remain and can be excellent sources of data and evokers of memory. Norris and Greenlaw (Chapter 4) returned to their non-school-assigned writing and found pieces that were intrinsically motivated by their "muses." Norris found a Grade 12 speech that he had written for a contest in which he placed second, and Greenlaw found the memoirs he had written about his grandfather. These and other writings provided rich data for their duoethnography on the curriculum of writing. Sawyer took photographs of paintings he had that were painted by a friend (Norris and Sawyer, 2004). Krammer (Chapter 2) recalls a comment made on a Grade 12 paper. Although no longer in existence, this demonstrates the value of artifacts whether in safekeeping or recalled.

Integrating the Literature

Unlike many research projects, duoethnographies do not begin with a survey of existing literature. In fact, this is discouraged. The quest for foundational or "seminal" pieces could be considered a form of patriarchy, through which the dominant male asserts his power over his offspring/readers. What comes later is influenced by what has preceded it. Rather, with duoethnographic studies the literature is integrated as the need emerges from the conversation. As Breault and Hackler (2010) report,

> We encountered King's (1998) work after we were deep into our project and found it to be both affirming and thought-provoking. It was the single most informative source in relation to the gender-related issues that brought us to this conversation in the first place.

Duoethnographers do not reject the literature; far from it. However, the dominance of the literature, as determined by its sequence in the research process is lessened. Literature is collected as relevant. Greenlaw returns to a previously read piece that connects with Norris's and his discussion (Chapter 4):

> I am reminded of Scholes' (1985) notion of "textual power." As he points out, we comprehend the writing of others by reading "upon," "within," and "against" their texts. At times your words help to evoke in me recollections of parallel experiences that I have had in own my childhood. In the above example, therefore, I am then reading "upon" your text. Later in this chapter, as I become caught up in your stories, I am reading within your text, and I completely lose track of my own stories for the moment. Finally, at times when your experiences are different from mine, I challenge both your and my narratives and am therefore reading "against" the text. This is what I find exciting about duoethnography, as it is a transaction that leads to personal transformation. (p. 93–94)

The literature then is regarded as another partner in the conversation and provides additional perspectives beyond those of the duoethnographers themselves.

CONCLUSION

These chapters are first-generation duoethnographies. Corbin asserts in her summary of the history of grounded theory that "people change and methods change" (2009, p. 36), discussing how the works of Adele Clarke and Kathy Charmaz have "applied postmodernist and constructivist paradigms to grounded theory methodology," that take up Denzin's challenge to "move interpretive methods more deeply into the regions of postmodern sensibility" (1994, p. 37). Duoethnographies unfold as the data and the methodology co-emerge.

Our organizational structure also unfolded as we took an internal hermeneutic (Werner and Rothe, 1979) approach in determining the book's sequence. The first four duoethnographies examine culture of schools, providing a formal curriculum perspective. The next five demonstrate how cultural mores and beliefs are informal curriculums that influence one's sense of identity that can privilege and marginalize through its framing. The last two problematize professional and research relationship as duoethnographers strive to act ethically in a world full of risks.

In total, the book is a social critique through the lenses of the duoethnographers. It is also a personal critique as they reexamine how they were taught to read the "word and the world" (Freire and Macedo, 1987), personally and critically determining how one is acted upon and how, through dialogic storytelling, one can reclaim agency, authority, and authorship over one's life. In (re)presenting experience, duoethnographies (re)generate and (re)conceptualize them.

REFERENCES

Annakin, K., Marton, A., Wicki, B., and Zanuck, D. F. (Directors). (1962). *The longest day*. United States: 20th Century Fox Home Entertainment.

Axe, D. (2008). *Star Trek "Red Shirts": The harsh, statistical truth*. Retrieved from http://www.wired.com/dangerroom/2008/04/star-trek-red-s/

Bakhtin, N. (1981). *The dialogic imagination*. Austin: The University of Texas Press.

Banks, A., and Banks, S. (1998). *Fiction and social research: By ice or fire*. Walnut Creek, CA: AltaMira Press.

Barber, M. (1989). Alma Gonsalvez: Otherness as attending to the Other. In A. B. Dallery and C. E. Scott (Eds.), *The question of the other* (pp. 119–126). New York: State University of New York Press.

Barone, T. E. (1990). Using the narrative text as an occasion for conspiracy. In E. W. Eisner and A. Peshkin (Eds.), *Qualitative inquiry in education* (pp. 305–326). New York: Teachers College Press.

Becker, H. (1978). Do photographs tell the truth? *After Image*, *5*, 9–13.

Bhabha, H. (1994). *The location of culture*. New York: Routledge.

Boal, A. (1979). *Theatre of the oppressed*. London: Pluto.

Bochner, A. P., and Ellis, C. (2002). *Ethnographically speaking: Autoethnography, literature, and aesthetics*. Walnut Creek, CA: AltaMira Press.

Breault, R., and Hackler, R. (2010). *Excursus #3: Considering J. R. King's uncommon caring.* Retrieved from http://breaultresearch.info/excursus-3.html

Breault, R., Hackler, R., and Bradley, R. (2010, May). *Constructing a male teaching identity: A trio-ethnography.* Paper presented at the Congress of Qualitative Inquiry, Urbana-Champaign, Illinois.

Brecht, B. (1957). *Brecht on theatre: The development of an aesthetic* (J. Willett, Trans.). New York: Hill and Wang.

Ceglowski, D., and Makovsky, T. (in press). Duoethnography with children. *Ethnography and Education.*

Cell, E. (1984). The four kinds of experiential learning. In E. Cell (Ed.), *Learning to learn from experience* (pp. 28–41). Albany: State University of New York Press.

Chang, H. (2008). *Autoethnography as method.* Walnut Creek, CA: Left Coast Press.

Chaucer, G. (1975). *The Canterbury tales* (N. Coghill, Trans.). Harmondsworth: Penguin Books.

Clandinin, D. J. (2006). *Composing diverse identities: Narrative inquiries into the interwoven lives of children and teachers.* New York: Taylor & Francis.

Clandinin, D. J., Steeves, P., Li, Y., Mickelson, J. R., Buck, G., Pearce, M., et al. (2010). *Composing lives: A narrative account into the experiences of youth who left school early.* Early School Leavers Final Report. Edmonton: University of Alberta.

Cooke, S. (1963). *Another Saturday Night.* New York: Abkco Music.

Corbin, J. (2009). Taking an analytic journey. In J. M. Morse, P. N. Stern, J. Corbin, B. Bowers, K. Charmaz, and A. E. Clarke (Eds.), *Developing grounded theory: The second generation* (pp. 35–54). Walnut Creek, CA: Left Coast Press.

Cunningham, I. (1988). Interactive holistic research: Researching self managed learning. In P. Reason (Ed.), *Human inquiry in action: Developments in new paradigm research* (pp. 163–181). Newbury Park, CA: Sage.

Denzin, N. K. (1989). *Interpretive biography.* Newbury Park, CA: Sage.

Denzin, N. (1994). The art and politics of interpretation. In N. Denzin and Y. Lincoln (Eds.), *Collecting and interpreting qualitative materials* (pp. 313–371). Thousand Oaks, CA: Sage.

Dewey, J. (1934). *Art as experience.* New York: Minton, Balch.

Donaldson, S. (1999). *Hemingway vs. Fitzgerald: The rise and fall of a literary friendship.* Woodstock, NY: Overlook Press.

Dr. Seuss. (1990). *Oh, the places you'll go!* New York: Random House.

Ebert, R. (1999). *My Dinner with Andre: Review.* Retrieved from http://rogerebert.suntimes.com/apps/pbcs.dll/article? AID=/19990613/REVIEWS08/906130301/1023

Ellis, C. (2004). *The ethnographic I: A methodological novel about autoethnography.* Walnut Creek, CA: AltaMira Press.

Freire, P. (1971). A few notions about the word "conscientization." *Hard Cheese, 1,* 23–28.

Freire, P. (1973). *Pedagogy of the oppressed.* New York: Seabury Press.

Freire, P., and Macedo, D. (1987). *Literacy: Reading the word and the world.* Westport, CT: Bergen and Garvey.

Geertz, C. (1973). Thick description: Toward an interpretive theory of culture. In C. Geertz (Ed.), *The interpretation of cultures* (pp. 3–31). New York: Basic Books.

Goffman, I. (1974). *Frame analysis.* Cambridge, MA: Harvard University Press.

Greene, M. (1991). Teaching: The question of personal reality. In A. Lieberman and L. Miller (Eds.), *Staff development for education in the 90s: New demands, new realities, new perspectives* (pp. 23–35). New York: Teachers College Press.

Haggis, P. (Director). (2004). *Crash.* United States: Pathe.

Haven, K. (2007). *Story proof: The science behind the startling power of story.* Westport, CT: Libraries Unlimited.

Huckaby, M. F. (2007). Dear Molly: Seven letters about "Dixie." In S. Leafgren, B. Schultz, M. O'Malley, L. Johnson, J. Brady, and A. Dentith (Eds.), *The articulation of curriculum and pedagogy for a just society: Advocacy, artistry, and activism* (pp. 61–75). Troy, NY: Educator's International Press, Curriculum & Pedagogy Group.

Kearney, R. (1984). Emmanuel Lévinas: Prefatory notes. In R. Kearney (Ed.), *Dialogues with contemporary Continental thinkers* (pp. 47–48). Manchester, UK: Manchester University Press.

Kemmis, S., and McTaggart, R. (1988). *The action research planner* (3rd ed.). Victoria, Australia: Deacon University Press.

King, J. R. (1998). *Uncommon caring: Learning from men who teach young children.* New York: Teachers College Press.

Kopp, S. (1972). *If you meet the Buddha on the road, kill him.* New York: Bantam.

Kurosawa, A. (Director). (1950). *Rashômon.* Japan: Daiei Motion Picture Company.

Lather, P. (1986). Issues of validity in openly ideological research: Between a rock and a soft place. *Interchange, 17*(4), 63–84.

Leavy, P. (2009). *Method meets art: Arts-based research practice.* New York: The Guilford Press.

Lévinas, E. (1984). Emmanuel Lévinas. In R. Kearney (Ed.), *Dialogues with contemporary Continental thinkers* (pp. 47–70). Manchester, UK: Manchester University Press.

Lund, D. E., and Evans, R. E. (2006). Opening a can of worms: A duo-ethnographic dialogue on gender, orientation and activism. *Taboo: The Journal of Culture and Education, 10*(2), 55–67.

Lund, D. E., and Nabavi, M. (2008). A duo-ethnographic conversation on social justice activism: Exploring issues of identity, racism, and activism with young people. *Multicultural Education, 15*(4), 27–32.

Lyotard, J.-F. (Ed.). (1984). *The postmodern condition: A report on knowledge.* Minneapolis: University of Minnesota Press.

Malle, L. (Director). (1981). *My Dinner with Andre.* United States: Saga.

Maruyama, M. (2004). Peripheral vision: Polyocular vision or subunderstanding? *Organization Studies, 25*(3), 467–480.

Miller, J. (2011, January). *Autobiography on the move: Poststructuralist perspectives on (im)possible narrative representations of collaboration.* Paper presented at the Narrative, Arts-based and Post Approaches, Tempe, Arizona.

Morse, J. (2009). Tussles, tensions, and resolutions. In J. M. Morse, P. N. Stern, J. Corbin, B. Bowers, K. Charmaz, and A. E. Clarke (Eds.), *Developing grounded theory: The second generation* (pp. 13–19). Walnut Creek, CA: Left Coast Press.

Muncey, T. (2010). *Creating autoethnographies.* Thousand Oaks, CA: Sage.

Myers, I. B. (1980). *Gifts differing.* Palo Alto: Consulting Psychologists Press, Inc.

Noddings, N. (1984). *Caring: A feminine approach to ethics and moral education.* Berkeley: University of California Press.

Noe, A. (2000). Experience and experiment in art. *Journal of Consciousness Studies, 7*(8/9), 123–135.

Norris, J. (1989a). *Some authorities as co-authors in a collective creation production.* Unpublished doctoral dissertation, University of Alberta, Edmonton.

Norris, J. (1989b, May). *A view from inside the carriage: Ethnographic video as a methodology.* Paper presented at the International Drama Education Research Symposium, Ontario Institute for Studies in Education, Toronto, Ontario.

Norris, J. (2005, July). *From autoethnography to duoethnography: A search for the dialogic self.* Workshop presented at Enhancing Qualitative Understanding of Illness Processes and Prevention, Edmonton, Alberta.

Norris, J. (2008). Duoethnography. In L. M. Given (Ed.), *The SAGE encyclopedia of qualitative research methods* (Vol. 1, pp. 233–236). Los Angeles: Sage.

Norris, J. (2009). *Playbuilding as qualitative research: A participatory arts-based approach.* Walnut Creek, CA: Left Coast Press.

Norris, J., and Creswell, J. (2007, October). *The curriculum of health, hospitalization, suffering and mortality.* Paper presented at the Curriculum and Pedagogy Conference, Balcones Springs, Texas.

Norris, J., and Greenlaw, J. (2005). *Response to the muses: Two interwoven autoethnographic journeys of writing.* Paper presented at the Curriculum and Pedagogy Conference, Oxford, Ohio.

Norris, J., Higgins, C., and Leggo, C. (2004, April). *"Shh stories": The problematics of personal disclosure in qualitative research.* Paper presented at the Annual Meeting of the American Educational Research Association, San Diego, California.

Norris, J., and Sawyer, R. (2004, October). *Null and hidden curricula of sexual orientation: A dialogue on the curreres of the absent presence and the present absence.* Paper presented at the Democratic Responses in an Era of Standardization, Troy, New York.

Norris, J., and Sawyer, R. (2005, February). *The curriculum of sexual orientation as lived by a gay straight male and a straight gay male.* Paper presented at the Provoking Curriculum Conference, Victoria, British Columbia.

Norris, J., and Sawyer, R. (2008, September). *Duoethnography: Towards a dialogic research method.* Full-day workshop presented at the 9th Annual Advances in Qualitative Methods Conference, Banff, Alberta.

Oberg, A., and Wilson, T. (2002). Side by side: Being in research autobiographically. *Educational Insights,* 7(2). Retrieved from http://ccfi.educ.ubc.ca/publication/insights/v07n02/contextualexplorations/wilson_oberg/

Pinar, W. (1975a). Curerre: Toward reconceptualization. In W. Pinar (Ed.), *Curriculum theorizing: The reconceptualists* (pp. 396–414). Berkeley, CA: McCutchan.

Pinar, W. (1975b). *Curriculum theorizing: The reconceptualists.* Berkeley, CA: McCutchan.

Pinar, W. (1994). The method of Currere: Essays in curriculum theory 1972–1992. In W. Pinar (Ed.), *Autobiography, politics and sexuality* (pp. 19–27). New York: Peter Lang.

Punday, D. (2002). *Narrative after deconstruction.* Albany: SUNY Press.

Rapke, T., and Towers, J. (2008, September). *Tracing mathematical thinking through duoethnographic conversations.* Paper presented at the 9th Annual Advances in Qualitative Methods Conference, Banff, Alberta.

Reason, P., and Hawkins, P. (1988). Storytelling as inquiry. In P. Reason (Ed.), *Human inquiry in action* (pp. 79–101). Newbury Park, CA: Sage.

Richardson, L. (1990). *Writing strategies: Reaching diverse audiences.* Newbury Park: Sage.

Rosenblatt, L. (1978). *The reader, the text, the poem: The transactional theory of the literary work.* Carbondale: Southern Illinois Press.

Said, E. W. (1993). *Culture and imperialism.* New York: Alfred A. Knopf.

Sawyer, R. D. (2010). Curriculum and international democracy: A vital source of synergy and change. *Journal of Curriculum Theorizing,* 26(1), 22–37.

Sawyer, R. D., and Liggett, T. (2007). *A critical duoethnographic dialogue about postcolonial research and curriculum.* Paper presented at the 8th Annual Curriculum and Pedagogy Conference, Marble Falls, Texas.

Sawyer, R. D., and Norris, J. (2005, October). *Towards the dialogic and critical engagement of duoethnography for transformative curriculum: An interactive discussion of methodology.* Paper presented at the Curriculum and Pedagogy Conference, Oxford, Ohio.

Sawyer, R., and Norris, J. (2009). Duoethnography: Articulations/(re)creation of meaning in the making. In W. Gershon (Ed.), *Working together in qualitative research: A turn towards the collaborative* (pp. 127–140). Rotterdam: Sense.

Scholes, R. (1985). *Textual power: Literary theory and the teaching of English.* New Haven, CT: Yale University Press.

Shelton, N. R., and McDermott, M. (2008). *The curriculum of beauty.* Paper presented at the Annual Meeting of the American Educational Research Association, New York.

Spheeris, P. (Director). (1992). *Wayne's world.* United States: Paramount Pictures.

Spradley, J. (1979). *The ethnographic interview.* New York: Holt, Rinehart, and Winston.

Spradley, J. (1980). *Participant observation.* New York: Holt, Rinehart and Winston.

Strauss, A., and Corbin, J. (1990). *Basics of qualitative research: Grounded theory, procedures and techniques.* Newbury Park, CA: Sage.

Sullivan, G. (2005). *Art practice as research: Inquiry in the visual arts.* Thousand Oaks, CA: Sage.

Varela, F. J., Thompson, E., and Rosch, E. (1991). *The embodied mind: Cognitive science and human experience.* Cambridge, MA: The MIT Press.

Verbinski, G. (Writer). (2003). *Pirates of the Caribbean: The curse of the black pearl.* W. D. Pictures (Producer). USA.

Watson, L. (1994). *If you have come to help me . . .* Retrieved from Northland Poster Collective: http://www.google.com/imgres?imgurl=http://www.freewebs.com/edchx/liberation-poster.jpg&imgrefurl=http://www.freewebs.com/edchx/&h=485&w=300&sz=74&tbnid=VZnSTjrth0o7cM:&tbnh=129&tbnw=80&prev=/images%3Fq%3Dlila%2Bwatson&zoom=1&q=lila+watson&hl=en&usg=__IlW9cALFAA31-NeTd34WAQ2-ss0=&sa=X&ei=FMIRTY7dN8OnnQfWo4HSDg&ved=0CDMQ9QEwBQ

Werner, W., and Rothe, P. (1979). *Doing school ethnography.* Edmonton: Department of Secondary Education, University of Alberta.

CHAPTER 2

The Hidden Curriculum of Schooling:
A Duoethnographic Exploration of What Schools Teach Us about Schooling

Donna Krammer and Rosemarie Mangiardi

PROLOGUE

Duoethnography is premised on postmodern notions of identity. Such accounts view identity as culturally layered, contradictory, socioculturally based, and not stage bound. They also view identity as constantly changing, with different aspects of identity interconnected yet unfolding at different rates and even in different directions (e.g., recursively at times). Some parts of our identity resonate within larger national or international metanarratives; some within subcultural contexts, and others with personal, often submerged and liminal, narratives. Duoethnography potentially opens and promotes researcher perspective on these various narratives of experience. Researchers work to identify, expose, and describe the interplay of identity narratives. Their dialogues about these experiences—and specifically the dialectical interplay between and among them—promote researcher change and reflexivity.

This study by Donna Krammer and Rosemarie Mangiardi examines how mainstream and hidden curriculum create a context of identity formation. First, drawing from the work of McLaren (1989), they perceive the hidden curriculum as a classroom context in which students internalize assumptions of normativity. Second, drawing from the work of William Pinar (1975), they examine the hidden curriculum of our lived experience, our currere. At the intersection of these foci, currere becomes a lens with which to examine and read the hidden curriculum and a new concept, the "cryptic curriculum"; ways to read and unpack the hidden curriculum is revealed. Their study models this process of reading one's curriculum.

Through dialogue, they construct a "rhythm of duoethnography—the back and forth, inside and outside, forward and backward movements that constitute duoethnographic exploration" (pp. 44–45). To shape their direction and conceptual storytelling lens, they intentionally selected currere for its dialectical framework and reconstruct a past filtered through perceptions in the present. They interrogate, as they put it, "unanticipated points of intersection" (p. 44) until they "hit the bedrock of divergence" (p. 44). In the words of Janet Miller (2011), they create a "contingent community" for themselves. Furthermore, they moved their thinking into the future by entertaining hypothetical questions central to their inquiry. One such question was why—given their histories within institution that promote subjugation—should they become academics. They then examined their interpretations arising from these meanings. They thus attempt to create a "critically reflexive manner" (p. 44), alternating their juxtaposed narratives with self-reflective summaries organized under themes ironically referencing schooling.

In their study, they problematize the notion of research "understanding" as a positivistic term. In contrast, they highlight the concept "exposure," underscoring how duoethnography can uncover subjugated meanings and dominated memories. This process of exposure, so important to duoethnography, presents counterpunctual narratives (Said, 1993) in contrast to dominant discourses. These accounts offer the reader a new way to imagine cultural worlds.

> *The hidden curriculum deals with the tacit ways in which knowledge and behavior get constructed, outside the usual course materials and formally scheduled lessons. It is part of the bureaucratic and managerial "press" of the school—the combined forces by which students are induced to comply with the dominant ideologies and social practices related to authority, behavior and morality. (McLaren, 1989, pp. 183–184)*

> *[The hidden curriculum] posits a network of assumptions that, when internalized by students, establishes the boundaries of legitimacy. (Apple, 1975, p. 99 as cited in Pinar, Reynolds, Slattery, and Taubman, 1995, p. 249)*

As teachers, and now doctoral students, in curriculum studies, we are familiar with the concept of the "hidden" curriculum. Furthermore, we recognize, as have so many others before us (Anyon, 1980; Bailey and Smith, 1987; Flinders, Noddings, and Thornton, 1986; Gillborn, 1992; Portelli, 1993), that a hidden curriculum, once exposed, can reveal a misuse of power. We concur with those who assert that voicing what has been unspoken within school curricula is a crucial step in establishing a just classroom environment. Indeed, we have each taken that step by identifying and challenging the assumptions, values, and prejudices that constitute this hidden curriculum in our respective curricular fields—English language and literature studies and health education.

How ironic, then, given our critical proclivities and vigilance in supporting our students' interests, that we have neglected to bring that critical eye to bear upon our own role as students within the system. Only now, as doctoral students in the third year of our respective programs, do we find ourselves interrogating our beliefs about the nature and value of schooling. Only now, as we near the end of our studies, do we find ourselves questioning why we are here. What compelled us to return to school after undergraduate studies, and then again after master's degrees, to take our formal schooling to this, the highest level? What role did our elementary and secondary school experiences play in shaping this desire? To what end? For whose benefit? Finally, what injustices and abuses of power have become so naturalized within the institution's hidden curriculum of schooling that we find ourselves, only now, questioning them and our long-standing goal of earning a doctoral degree?

—*Richard D. Sawyer*

METHOD OF INQUIRY

As humans we are both storymaking beings and beings who are constituted through the act of storytelling—beings who in telling the tale, create and re-create the self, knowledge of the self, and knowledge of the world. Within educational research, this act of self-narration takes the form of autobiography/autoethnography. William Pinar's (1975) autobiographical method of *currere* (the Latin infinitive form of "curriculum," meaning "to run the course") entails that the researcher move beyond the mere recollection of a story to a reconceptualization of one's self and the world in which one lives. As Pinar et al. describe it,

> *currere* focuses on the educational experience of the individual, as reported by the individual. Rather than working to quantify behaviors to describe their surface interaction or to establish causality, *currere* seeks to describe what the individual subject him- or herself makes of these behaviors. (1995, p. 414)

Currere, it must be emphasized, is not an exercise in solipsism; it must communicate "the individual's lived experience *as it is socially located, politically positioned, and discursively formed*" (emphasis added; Pinar et al., 1995, p. 416).

Building upon Pinar's (1975; Pinar et al., 1995) method of *currere*, Joe Norris and Richard Sawyer (2004) advance a *duo*ethnographic approach to the research process (emphasis added). According to Norris (2005), when the researcher enters into a dialogical relationship with another, he or she expands the possibilities for insight. In other words, a solitary act of reflection can engender only limited understandings; but the dynamic interplay of two critically questioning minds can transform, create, and expand each participant's understanding. In duoethnography, participants employ narrative not as an organizational structure but as a communicative strategy. When researchers narrate lived experiences within the act of conversation, an *emergent* mode of communication, stories, can develop organically, take unexpected turns, and assume intriguing contours in the back-and-forth movement between participants. In this way, conversation creates its own inimitable structure. Moving in, around, and beyond the topic at hand expands the possibility for understandings. Conversational form also embodies an epistemological truth: Just as conversation is ongoing and open ended, our understandings of past experiences will always be partial and open to revision.

In the conversational telling of our stories, we have had to reveal, reconstruct, and reinterpret our memories of past events; examine the personal meanings arising from these interpretations; and then allow those meanings to be transformed in the dialogical coupling and the juxtaposition of the telling. Throughout this process, unanticipated points of intersection—similar life experiences or similar emotional responses under comparable circumstances—galvanized each teller to expand upon her story. As we unearthed long-forgotten details, we burrowed deeper into these similarities until, eventually, we hit the bedrock of divergence. In this way, we excavated each commonality to arrive at our inescapable human differences. Hence, the moments of connection and points of commonality ultimately drew our attention back to the critical points of contrast. On occasion we found ourselves manifestly in the here-and-now, discerning, and then analyzing, the language doing the telling: the words spoken, the gestures used, and the meanings implied. At other times, we brought the past into the present, scrutinizing action and motives through the lenses of present-day perspectives to explain pivotal events and understand their influence upon us. In this critically reflexive manner, we interrogated and reinterpreted our school stories. Ultimately, we came away from this duoethnographic experience with new insight into our particular school histories and our selves and with a deeper understanding of the hidden curriculum of schooling and its effect upon us.

In writing this chapter, we share that understanding and so begin a conversation with our reading audience. We hope our readers enter into this conversation by revisiting their own school narratives, stories that, when juxtaposed with our own, may transform understandings and engender new insights. As well, we wish to generate for the reader some sense of the rhythm of duoethnography—the back-and-forth, inside and outside, forward-and-backward movements that constitute duoethnographic exploration. To that end, we have deliberately disrupted the narrative at critical points to suggest the manner in which our conversation flowed from past to present, from narrative to analysis, and from self-reflection to commentary. We use this device not only to re-create the duoethnographic process as we experienced it in sharing our stories of the hidden curriculum of schooling but also to point our readers to another, equally important though necessarily embedded, tale within this telling: our story of what it means to become duoethnographers.

SITUATING THE SELF

Rose: I am twenty-nine years of age and the daughter of working-class Italian immigrants. My parents relied on the Catholic school system in Toronto, Ontario, to educate me and instill the values that mirrored their own beliefs. All my life, I have heard my father extol the benefits of education, emphasizing to my brother and me that *lavorando con la penna* (working with a pen) is preferable to *lavorando con un pala e pico* (working with a shovel and ax). My father often said that had he acquired an education, he would have had far more opportunities in life. He assured us that if we wanted to "keep on going to the very top," he would assist us in whatever way he could. Without a doubt, my parents' encouragement and assistance influenced my decision to pursue higher education; what is less obvious, however, is how the education system itself has forged my desire to succeed within its ranks. Since beginning doctoral studies at the University of Alberta, I have instructed preservice teachers in the theory and methods of teaching secondary-level health programs in Alberta schools.

Donna: I was born and raised in rural Saskatchewan, in a town where everyone knew everyone *and* their business. Though not exactly a one-room schoolhouse, we had one school housed in two buildings (one primary, the other elementary/secondary); however, our entire public school population rarely exceeded 150. My working-class parents, first-generation Canadians born to Hungarian immigrant farmers, supported postsecondary education to a limited degree. University was fine as long as it provided their children with a secure job. My initial degrees in English literature and drama caused some consternation. Eventually, I earned an education degree and entered the world of work. I have been teaching in Saskatchewan and Alberta for twelve years and am now forty-eight years old.

LESSON 1: "OUR AUTHORITY IS UNIMPEACHABLE"

Rose: I was retained in Grade 1, or, to use the vernacular . . . I failed. I remember as a child thinking that I would never make sense of the scribbles on the page. At bedtime, my mother would lie down next to me with the book of my choice and guide me as I tried to read the story it told, but before long both of us were frustrated and discouraged. Why was I not getting this reading "thing?"

One day, my father noticed a problem with my left eye. He took me to numerous doctors, who eventually concluded that my reading difficulty was the result of a lazy eye. This diagnosis helped my mother understand why reading was such a difficult task for me. She agreed with my teacher that it was better to hold me back one year than to move me on to Grade 2, where I would likely fall further behind. My mother understood that failing carried a social stigma and so insisted that I register at a different school the following September. Many years later, she explained that she wanted to protect me, to preempt teachers and students from judging and labeling me "stupid"; unfortunately, the damage had already been done. I had learned that the school imposes either/or standards: *Either* I could read like my peers *or* I could not, *either* I was deemed acceptable and worthy *or* I was not. Because I successfully assimilated this logic, the person who bullied me the most was me.

Reconstructing these memories in the context of our duoethnography, I find myself thinking of my mother. The social stigma associated with school failure affected her as well. The school system taught children and parents that to fail within its ranks was to bring shame upon one's self and one's family. I had disgraced myself; had I also disgraced my mother? Was she ashamed of me? She insisted (and still insists) that I never actually failed, that I had a "medical condition" that needed to be treated before I could advance. Why did/does she feel the need to provide this authoritative, though vague, justification for my failure? Was I an embarrassment to her? Was my mother was afraid for me? My father, who arrived in Canada from Italy when he was 20, did not read English. My mother, more than most, would have understood the difficulties and challenges associated with illiteracy. Was she worried that I might never become a skillful reader? Was she terrified of how this might impact my future?

Whatever my mother's feelings at that time, I remember only her unconditional acceptance and belief in my potential. She taught me that I could succeed at school, while my first-year experience of schooling taught me to doubt myself. In the end, I became determined to show my teachers that I could do what they were telling me I should be able to do—I could succeed by their standards.

The following September, I found myself once again in Grade 1, this time with a teacher who understood that I had a lazy eye, and by the end of that year, I had learned to read. From then on, every time that a peer asked me to explain the discrepancy in our ages, I was reminded of my failure. What could I tell them? Usually I defaulted to my mother's explanation, but when I heard the words "medical condition" come out of my mouth, I often stopped and simply said, "I failed Grade 1." "You failed Grade *1*?" The invariable tone of disbelief made me flinch. It was bad enough that I had failed a grade, but to fail Grade *1*, the easiest of all grades, was especially shameful. By the time I graduated from high school, this shame had become a part of my self. In this way the education institution explicitly structured and reconfigured my personal identity (Gubrium and Holstein, 2000). Fortunately, "the self emanates from the interplay among institutional demands, restraints, and resources . . . *and biographically informed, self-constituting social actions*" (emphasis added; p. 102). For the latter, I can thank my family. Those first two years of schooling taught me that teachers and schools were inflexible, their standards nonnegotiable. The unique circumstances of a student's life were cause for neither accommodation nor adjustment. My reality meant nothing in the face of the system's absolute authority.

Our discussion has helped me understand the ways in which schools appropriate language in order to satisfy institutional needs. The word retention *is an institutional term that serves an institutional purpose: neutralizing the ambivalence and guilt felt by teachers who must judge children adequate or inadequate, and label them pass or fail. But institutional language that achieves its intended purpose for those* inside *the institution commonly fails to achieve a desired effect upon those* outside *the institution. Bluntly stated, the abstract term* retention *does not provoke the fear and shame that I believe the institution deems necessary in order to motivate parents and students to prevent grade-failure. How does it address this shortcoming? It constructs the word* failed, *imbues it with dark and debilitating meanings, and launches it into the vernacular. In this way, the school system makes children complicit in the construction of their own painful personal realities.* Failed *is not my word; it has been imposed upon me by a rigid institution seeking order and control through the application of labels with powerful subtexts. In this case, "to fail is to fall from grace." I will never again use the word* failed *when I share this story. I refuse to perpetuate, through a thoughtless choice of diction, a value system that maintains it is acceptable to shame a child for having a physical condition that she has no personal power to alter. By rejecting the word, I release the shame.*

LESSON 2: "ONE SUCCEEDS AT THE EXPENSE OF OTHERS"

Donna: Throughout primary school, I knew nothing of the institutional reality of pass/fail and its underlying implications. From the day I entered the school system to the end of the third grade, little changed for me: I had the same teacher, the same classroom, and the same classmates. None of us seemed to move on, or stay behind, in any obvious way. Of course, I experienced the rigors of assessment and wanted to do well to please my teacher, but I did not understand that I was part of a larger system that demanded I meet acceptable standards of achievement according to a set timetable or suffer the consequences.

Schoolwork came easily to me, and with each successive year, I was able to master the required skills. For the most part, classroom activities permitted some creative input, so I was content. My teacher, responding both to the quality of my work and to my quirky imagination, showered me with praise. (I remember the day that I overheard her reading my work to her colleagues. How proud I felt.) While her lavish praise boosted my confidence, it also generated anxiety. I saw myself cast in the role of Golden Girl and felt that I must fulfill my teacher's expectations. At the same time, I knew that inevitably there would come a time when I would fail to navigate the strange rules and unending expectations of this school world.

As I moved into the elementary grades, my anxiety increased. Caught in an ineluctable bind, I responded by alternating between two unhealthy tendencies. When I could no longer tolerate the tension, I opted out: As long as I refused to try, I did not have to fear being "failed." When anxiety levels abated, I threw myself into my schoolwork, striving to be the best—not to *do* my best, mind you, but to *be* the best. This tendency grew into a painful obsession: equating academic success or failure with personal worth. In a system based on norm-referenced evaluation, I learned to value myself only to the degree that I rose *above* my peers. For the rest of my academic career, "to pass" meant to pass all other students' marks; "to fail" meant to fail to receive the highest grade of all, to fail to be the best. In this respect, I was responsible for allowing the system to quantify my self-worth.

The hidden curriculum of my schooling taught me that success is predicated upon the defeat of others; and since life, by its very nature, denies us a perpetual winning streak, I came to fear those inevitable failures. Within the classroom, this meant *not* receiving the highest mark in the class, *not* having my paper read aloud to my classmates, and *not* discovering scribbles of extravagant praise in the margins of my essays. I recognize now that my high school self thought of failure in terms of what one did *not do* rather than in terms of what one did *do*. I had overlooked a basic fact of grammar: The word *fail* is an action, not a state-of-being, verb. In other words, I regarded personal failure as a condition imposed on me from above, as simply "the way things were." What is more, I constructed success in much the same way. Rather than setting academic goals from the position of an active "I" (i.e., "This year I will . . ."), I waited for someone or something to tell "me" what to aspire to and then to hand "me" success. I was no longer the subject of my world but the object of multiple indeterminate verbs. Thus, I gave up agency for paralysis and autonomy for subjection. In so doing, I enabled the school system in its construction of an insecure and codependent student self.

For years, I saw myself as a victim and my teachers as the victimizers, but, of course, this version of events is too simplistic. I know that I also played a role in undermining my self-confidence. I do not deny my emotional investment in this value system, nor do I deny my willingness to act in accordance with it, but I do wonder at what point, and in what way, I accepted these beliefs as my own. I recall, many years ago, sitting in my undergraduate educational foundations class as the professor introduced the idea of indoctrination. Although the word was new to me, the concept was not. I knew that schools indoctrinated students; what I did not know was how and to what extent, I had already been indoctrinated, both as an elementary and as a secondary school student subjected to an institutional program of socialization and as a university student trained to perpetuate values and beliefs that assure the institution's continued existence. When I entered the system as a teacher myself, I saw that the education institution rewards teachers for enacting its ideologies—and with each dispensation, teachers offer up greater commitment and stronger allegiance. My elementary and secondary teachers were no different from myself: They were simply doing their best to carry out the duties assigned to them. I suspect few of us recognized the irony implicit in our situations: The more dedicated and conscientious we were about our work, the more likely we were to engage in practices that necessarily entailed the unjust treatment of our students.

LESSON 3: "PERFORM ON DEMAND"

Rose: Although my eye condition slowly improved, I continued to loathe oral reading. I was terrified that my peers would deride me when they realized that my reading was not up to par; at the same time, I knew that I could not refuse my teacher's request without suffering the humiliation of probing questions and, inevitably, the disclosure of my weakness. Whether I said yes or whether I said no, the outcome would be the same: public humiliation. I had learned to play the role of Good Little Girl, so even though I desperately wanted to say no, I obeyed and complied. Like a good little girl, I read, though with great trepidation, praying that I would not stumble over the long words, hoping that the end would come soon. Despite the obvious body language that told my teacher, "Forced participation is *not* improving this child's reading skills," my teacher seemed oblivious to my distress. Moreover, my classmates felt compelled to shout out the words that I was unable to decode. Since I had learned to self-evaluate my reading by comparing my skills against those of my peers, their enthusiastic corrections painfully confirmed my belief that I was a failure at reading.

Nor did this self-image improve when I entered high school. I recall that in Grade 10, my homeroom teacher, Mrs. Carmoni, required students to read a biblical passage each day of the season of Advent (a time of preparation for the celebration of Christ's birth at Christmas). She selected each reader systematically on the basis of the seating plan. Therefore, I knew the day I would be expected to read but not what I would be reading! Had I been given the passage in advance, I could have practiced and eased my apprehension. But no, Mrs. Carmoni expected students to read aloud, without preparation, before twenty-plus staring faces. On the dreaded day, minutes before the dreaded task, I asked to be excused to use the washroom. I assumed that my absence, though brief, would prompt Mrs. Carmoni to move on to the more capable student seated behind me. When I reentered the classroom, I stopped short. No one was reading. My classmates looked bored and put out. Suddenly, I was petrified. Mrs. Carmoni had waited for my return; I would have to read. I felt helpless. I could neither refuse nor swiftly offer a plausible excuse. Trapped, I shuffled to the front of the room. Timidly I began to read, my voice cracking, the paper clenched in my clammy hands. At first, my performance drew cautious snickers, but as I concluded, the classroom reverberated with laughter. When it was over, I bolted for the safety of my desk. I quickly sat down and, for what seemed like forever, listened to the laughter die away.

I cannot comprehend how a teacher of teenagers (who, we know, would suffer almost any discomfort rather than admit weakness before their peers) could miss (or, worse yet, choose to ignore) the obvious physical and verbal signs of terror. Even now I wonder what was going on in Mrs. Carmoni's mind. Did she have some misguided intention of helping me overcome my fears through enforced practice? If this were so, her desire to help implies some understanding of how emotionally devastating reading aloud was for me. Why, then, did she never speak of it? Had Mrs. Carmoni arranged for a private moment between us and shown me the least bit of encouragement, I would have dropped my defenses and admitted the extent of my fears. If this was what was needed to persuade her to excuse me from reading (or at least to allow me to practice the readings in advance), I was prepared to do it. But in the end, she never gave me the opportunity.

Of course, I am reconstructing these memories from the perspective of one who has long overcome her fears of reading and speaking in public. Perhaps I have forgotten how much this woman intimidated me. Perhaps the fact that my emotional traces are so painful and the injustice so difficult to bear proves the force of my fear and the measure of power that I perceived she wielded over me. Maybe, after all, I would have said nothing.

On that day, I learned another truth concerning the hidden curriculum of my schooling. A teacher—the person we most expect to model fairness, dignity, and respect for others—can force us to perform on demand. On that day, whether she realized it or not, Mrs. Carmoni bullied me into submission.

Yet, away from the stares and ridicule of my classmates, I gradually came to enjoy reading. Poems, brief and enigmatic, intrigued me. They elicited emotions that never surfaced when reading other forms of text. I was captivated and began writing poems in my spare time. I entered Grade 11 English eager to learn more about poetry and to share my poems with others. When my English teacher, Mrs. Remmley, asked us to compose a poem as a creative writing assignment, I was determined to create a piece that I would be proud to submit. The night before the due date, I meticulously reworked my poem. The next morning, Mrs. Remmley did not collect assignments, as was her habit; instead, she invited students to read their poems aloud. To my surprise, I felt excited about the prospect of reading my work to my peers. I immediately volunteered. That day I conquered my nervousness and fear of reading in public. I articulated each word confidently and clearly, for all to hear. But my hard-won feeling of accomplishment was short lived. A stern voice immediately asked, "Where did you get that?" Mrs. Remmely believed I had plagiarized my poem, that I was incapable of writing such a piece! I was infuriated. I wanted to challenge her assumption, but I was mute with fury. When I finally found my voice to defend myself, it was too late: Another student had begun to read.

As I reconstruct this memory, I feel anger rising once again. As a teacher now myself, I try to view this event from my teacher's perspective. Clearly, Mrs. Remmley acted upon a preconceived idea of my ability, an erroneous assumption that she failed to examine. Why? My story highlights an unfortunate tendency among educators working in our schools: a willingness to accept without question the rules, preoccupations, and obsessions of the institution for which, and in which, they work. In the end, it was more important to Mrs. Remmley to catch me cheating than it was to do me an injustice by jumping to conclusions. And because she spoke immediately, in front of the entire class, I can only conclude that it was more important to her to see me publicly humiliated than it was to preserve my dignity by arranging for us to discuss the matter privately. In that single question, Mrs. Remmley revealed a central principle of the hidden curriculum of schooling: a systemic preoccupation with what students do wrong, as opposed to what they do right. I realize now that the education system, through the multiple actions of individual teachers, can become an institutional bully.

LESSON 4: "OUR WAY IS THE ONLY WAY"

Donna: I also felt self-conscious when reading in front of the class; but for me, Rose, reading itself was a joy. I learned to read when I began to attend school. I was immediately enthralled. Reading gave my imagination free play and became a source of happiness. I discovered that I had an affinity for it, and my reading skills soon became a point of pride. During those early years of formal education, I equated school with reading. Thus, my love of reading, and my desire to impress my teacher, made me a willing and eager student.

Although learning to read the printed word upon the page came easily to me, what was far more difficult was learning to read the behavioral expectations of the system itself. I often felt that I had entered a world governed by unfamiliar and often unfathomable rules. One day in Grade 1, the phone, located in the small office around the corner from our classroom, began to ring. My teacher left, presumably to answer it. Since I sat near the door, I could not help but overhear parts of her conversation. My curiosity was piqued. As my teacher returned, I looked up at her from my little desk, smiled a friendly smile, and asked with genuine interest, "Who was calling?" I was not prepared for her brusque response: "It's none of your business. Finish your work!" It seemed I had committed some serious offense. What rule had I broken? In my home, we always asked the person who answered the phone with whom they were, or had been, speaking. I was hurt and perplexed. Although I continued to excel at my schoolwork, I became less spontaneous and more vigilant, wary of committing other incomprehensible crimes.

Ironically, as I grew older and my reading interests expanded, the curriculum became more restrictive. Students had no say when it came to the texts studied in our classrooms. Even so, I enjoyed most of the required readings in my English class. Yet, despite my interest, I was typically either behind or ahead of the teacher's reading schedule. No matter now exciting the sanctioned text, I always found a library book that was equally fascinating. Consequently, I often had three or four books on the go at once, juggling them as my mood and inclination varied. When immersed in fiction or biography, subjects such as math and chemistry held little appeal. Once, deeply engrossed in Hitler's *Mein Kampf* (cleverly hidden behind the large cover of my math text, propped up carefully on top of my desk), I vaguely registered the teacher's voice calling my name. Looking up, I saw his eyes upon me. Caught! Annoyance and exasperation in his voice: "Put that away immediately!" Too naïve to understand the benefits of *pro tem* compliance and too stubborn to give in without a fight, I protested, "But it's educational." My response only fueled his anger: "I don't care if it *is* educational; I told you to put it away, and I want you to put it away *now!*" Reluctantly, I put it away. Had my teacher somehow tried to connect the algebra of the daily lesson with my obvious interest in life stories, I might have learned how algebra could be relevant to my own life. Instead, I learned that I would need to be more cunning next time.

From then on, as class began, I would ease the book of the day out of the oversized pocket of my jean jacket and onto my lap. With the book hidden from my teacher's sight, I read as long as I dared. Every now and then, I briefly raised my eyes to the blackboard as my teacher worked through examples. But when I came upon a riveting passage, I wanted no distractions. Up went my arm. When acknowledged, I asked to go to the washroom, where, safely locked within a cubicle, I read and read and read. One day I read too long, for as soon as I returned to the classroom, the boy seated next to me hollered, "You've sure been gone a long time!" My eyes went immediately to the teacher. Caught . . . again. When the bell rang to end the period, the teacher called me up to his desk. Increasingly nervous, I walked towards him. "Seems to me you've been spending a lot of time in the bathroom lately." Panic. "Uh . . . yes . . . uh, well, I've sort of had diarrhea and. . . ." The teacher, suddenly red-faced, interrupting hastily: "Oh, well if it's a medical condition then. . . ." A reprieve! Yet as I left the room, I felt no joy, no vindication, only shame because I had lied. Surprisingly, I did learn some algebra that year, though I learned much more about deception, self-loathing, and guilt. These were the lessons of the hidden curriculum. My desires and interests counted for nothing. I could honor them only by resorting to subterfuge and lies, and in becoming a liar, I betrayed my values and my self.

A century has passed since Dewey (1916) wrote that it was possible and necessary *to make education both more sensitive to students' needs and more intellectual and rigorous. Erickson and Schultz (1982), writing in the heyday of the reconceptualist movement, made the same point with greater vehemence, implicating the institution in the schools' ongoing disregard for students' needs and interests. "The absence of student experience from current educational discourse," they wrote, "seems to be a consequence of systematic silencing of the student voice. . . . In the absence of interchange, of genuine conversation in the ways we usually teach, students are prevented from developing a voice— a critical awareness of their own ends, means and capacities for learning" (p. 481).*

The ideological foundation of our preeminently modernist institution of education makes it unlikely that students will develop such a voice. When a hidden curriculum of schooling teaches students to be compliant, passive, and tractable, no token inclusion of critical thinking in the formal school curriculum will ever develop in students the level of critical awareness that Erickson and Schultz envision. As a teacher who has worked closely with colleagues, I would say that most teachers agree with Erickson and Shultz's assertion that classroom activities aiming to promote student growth must "involve not only clear and dextrous thinking, but also passion, truthfulness, and commitment in the face of risk," for "these are all inherent in genuine learning" (p. 466). Yet, classroom practices seem to suggest otherwise. When we as teachers lose sight of what we truly believe and feel, we are set adrift from our moorings, and when our beliefs and our feelings come to belong "more to the organization and less to the self," the inevitable outcome is "burnout" and "alienation" (Hochschild, 1983, p. 198).

Lesson 5: "Perfection Is the Only Worthy Goal"

Rose: I recall one teacher who did make the effort to individualize instruction. My Grade 12 English teacher, Mr. Subbor, stressed that the mark awarded an assignment was of little value if we subsequently stuffed the paper into a binder or locker never to be looked at again. Rather, he implored his students to reexamine their essays in light of his extensive marginalia. To assist us with this task, he scheduled a fifteen-minute out-of-class meeting with each of his thirty students. I would have preferred to decipher his comments on my own. I imagined sitting next to him, transfixed by his furrowed brow as he pointed out one error after another. In fact, Mr. Subbor provided constructive criticism balanced with praise and cushioned with humor. He discussed my work sentence by sentence, attending to diction, grammar, and syntax. He showed me how I could improve my writing by helping me to revise sections then and there. I learned more about the craft of writing in that fifteen-minute workshop than I had in any previously taken English course. Mr. Subbor taught me the importance of process over product. I recall his three favorite maxims: "There is always room for improvement," "The writing process never ends," and "There is no such thing as perfection." I knew that I could never write a perfect essay, but I found it reassuring that no other student could either. Mr. Subbor taught me that a mark represents a moment in time; as one continues to write, one's skills improve, and marks change. Because marks are constantly in flux, it is meaningless to compare them. His concept of success was personal growth, and his own sense of professional success seemed predicated upon the success of *all* of his students.

In a system obsessed with product and comparative statistics (class averages, the 100 percent perfect score, the bell curve distribution), Mr. Subbor's process-oriented approach was a conspicuous anomaly. The contrast between his ways and the ways of other teachers made it clear to me that the hidden curriculum of schooling naturalizes and perpetuates competition. Prior to my experience with Mr. Subbor, I had learned to compare myself to others, to sidle up to the student seated next to me and ask, with a nonchalant air, "What did you get?" When one's primary goal is to "do better than" one's classmates, one can feel assured of achieving that goal only when one's result is "beyond compare"; that is, when it is perfect. The prevailing ethos of my school taught me that perfection was the only worthy goal; Mr. Subbor taught me that perfection was an illusion. I never completely forgot Mr. Subbor's wise words, but with each passing year they became fainter, seemingly irrelevant in the academic world of undergraduate and master's programs.

LESSON 6: "WE MAKE NO CONCESSIONS"

Donna: You remind us, Rosie, that ideological critique requires even-handedness. There will always be individuals who resist the demands and constraints that the institution places upon them in order to address the needs of students. Most of us, I warrant, can recall at least one teacher who had a profoundly positive impact on our lives precisely because s/he had the courage to engage with students as individual persons rather than as bodies and minds to be managed.

Although I enjoyed creative writing, writing an exam was another matter. My encounters with standardized testing were always fraught with tension. My introduction to the standardized test came early—in Grade 1. While I do not remember the manner in which my teacher administered the mimeographed test, nor the overall score I received, I do vividly recall one question. This test item, structured as a multiple-response question, asked simply, "What do birds do?" A detailed illustration accompanied the text. The bird depicted could have been a robin, but the diagram lacked color, so one could not be certain. There were three answer-options provided: (a) hop, (b) walk, (c) run. I remember thinking back to the birds that I knew, the birds that built their nests in our fir trees, the birds that in the spring congregated on the patch of freshly tilled earth that would become our garden. I recall whispering to myself, "Those birds walk." I circled *b*, certain that my selection was the correct response.

Later, when my teacher returned the booklet, I was stunned to see she had marked my response incorrect. But birds do walk. I knew that. Well, okay, I admit some birds do hop at times, but they do not hop all the time; sometimes they walk. But there would be no discussion: I was wrong; she was right.

I have never forgotten the injustice of that moment. In the years that followed, whenever I caught myself observing birds, I invariably noticed their movement. Were they hopping, walking, or running? Later in elementary school, when I first read about ostriches, I remember thinking triumphantly: This bird runs; it doesn't hop! As I grew older, I found myself considering the ambiguity implicit within the question: Which bird? Given what circumstances? Was the bird looking for food? Preparing to take wing and become airborne? More recently, as a teacher myself, accountable for the administration of provincial standardized multiple-choice exams, I reinterpreted my memory of "the bird-question" from a critical professional perspective: Who constructed this test item? With what species of bird was this person familiar? One thing was certain: He (or, less likely, she) was not acquainted with the birds that I saw everyday as a child—the killdeer, the sparrow, the crow—or even the birds that populated the province: the whooping crane, the Canada goose. What does it do to a six-year-old child to be told that she is wrong when she knows she is right? What does it do to a child's confidence in the system to be denied the opportunity to present her case and explain her reasoning, her rationale for her position? Quite simply, I lost faith in the value of testing and developed the unattractive habit of always needing to be right. Throughout my schooling, I remained dubious of the value of standardized test results, yet I could not entirely dismiss the voices of educational authority that pronounced their validity. And these voices, omnipotent and omniscient, as I soon came to learn, would not tolerate dissent.

LESSON 7: "SUBMIT TO OUR JUDGMENTS"

Rose: Questions—whether teacher generated or student constructed, formal or informal, written or spoken—offer critical sites for the possibility of new learning. My father believed that success in life comes to people who are forthright, inquisitive, and proactive. He taught me that it was my responsibility to ask questions if I was confused about the content of a lesson. His lesson (though I did not realize it then) influenced where I chose to sit in the classroom. I remember in Grade 11 rushing to Mr. Arddo's math class to claim a front-row seat and an unobstructed view of the blackboard. Sitting up front, I could command Mr. Arddo's attention and avoid the distractions generated by my peers. I recall thinking, "If you sit behind, you stay behind." I was determined to excel and certain that I could—as long as Mr. Arddo noted my presence and answered my questions.

And I asked plenty of questions. It was a rare day when students proceeded to seatwork without having heard innumerable questions from Rose. In fact, I became known by a question: Students referred to me as the girl who was always asking, "Sir, how did you get that?" I asked this question so frequently that Mr. Arddo began to anticipate it. When he introduced a mathematical process, he would pause as he completed each step, turn to look at me, and silently mouth the words of my question. Then he would smile. As far as he was concerned, *all* questions were valid. There were students, however, who thought otherwise. Their sighs echoed around the room as I began what they must have regarded as Rose's daily barrage of stupid questions. At times I felt that each sigh carried the same disparaging charge: "You don't know *that!*" Mr. Arddo ignored these students with their know-it-all attitudes, and I followed suit. He was exceptional at creating a warm and accepting classroom environment; other teachers, however, could leave me feeling anxious and violated. In these classrooms, I rarely asked for clarification.

Once again, the exemplary practice of one teacher throws into strong relief the institutionally sanctioned, ineffective behaviors of other teachers. For the most part, the hidden curriculum of schooling works to constrain and inhibit teachers, to force upon them behaviors that damage student-teacher relationships. For example, consider the ways in which teachers ask questions in the classroom. Many of my teachers concluded their lessons with the question, "Are there any questions?" This seemingly innocent and, one might say, commendable practice now greatly troubles me. Clearly, these teachers wished to identify students who had failed to grasp the concepts of the lesson. But trying to achieve their goal in this manner placed students in an extremely vulnerable position. To ask students after the lesson has ended if they have any questions is to dare them to admit that they "didn't get it," that they "failed" the lesson. To ask the teacher after the lesson has ended for clarification or reiteration is tantamount to announcing one's "stupidity" to everyone in the room. It is not surprising that no one had any questions. Did my teachers not understand this? Or did they recognize the fear in the silence?

I wonder if, perhaps, these teachers had another motive. Were my teachers seeking validation when they asked us if we had questions? Did they reason, "There are no questions; this means that all students have understood the lesson; ergo, I taught a perfect lesson." Perhaps our silence confirmed in their minds their prowess and expertise. Perhaps the hush in the classroom became, for them, a form of indirect praise. Did my teachers assume that they were being judged positively while their students sat in fear of being judged negatively?

When students voiced questions during the lesson, my teachers often prefaced their response with the judgment, "Oh, that's a good question!" Sometimes teachers responded to my questions in this way; other times, they did not. Sometimes they were sincere in their praise; other times, they were not. When a teacher judged my question "good," I believed s/he thought the question sophisticated and me, intelligent. Conversely, when my teacher said nothing, I assumed s/he thought my question elementary and me, stupid. Yet, I could detect no difference between the questions judged "good" and the questions not overtly judged. I was confused: What was it that distinguished a good question from a bad? Conceivably, a good question would provoke a thoughtful response. In this case, a teacher's silence could be a compliment. My teachers, however, had little to say on the value of thoughtful silence, the importance of quietly processing ideas. Therefore, when I asked a question and they said nothing, I could only assume the worst. Or perhaps when my teachers voiced the words, "That's a good question," they were stalling while furiously constructing an adequate answer. Perhaps they felt constrained by our expectation that they know all things. Perhaps they feared that students would judge them "stupid" if they thought too long about the question. I reiterate: Conceivably, a

good question would provoke a thoughtful response. Why were
we both, students and teachers, afraid of the silence?

LESSON 8: "NO AUTONOMY ALLOWED"

Donna: Rarely did I ask questions in class. Ostracized by my peers and
ignored by my teachers, I reacted by refusing to participate in
classroom discussions. Instead, I remained wary and silent,
afraid of making myself vulnerable to ridicule and disparage-
ment. In my final year of high school, one teacher did encourage
me to speak up and speak out; but by then vigilance had become
so much a part of who I was in school that I could not muster
the courage to change, and so I continued to keep my questions
to myself. Besides, given their nature, I thought it unlikely they
would be welcomed. It had become clear to me that the questions that popped into my head were nothing like those raised
by my peers or formulated by my teachers. My questions were
typically tangential and, so I believed, likely to be judged unim-
portant. I had already learned that teachers rarely tolerate an
irrelevant question (there was, so we were told, a curriculum to
get through).

The questions that I asked were never formulated in class;
instead, they bubbled to the surface as I read about interesting people, unfamiliar things, and intriguing places. One summer I became
preoccupied with Greece. My questions were endless. What would
life be like living on the shores of the Mediterranean Sea? Why
didn't Odysseus just keep his mouth shut as he sailed away from
Polyphemus? How did the people on the islands get their houses
so white? I found it gratifying whenever I was able to find an
answer to a question, but the questions for which no answer could
be found—for which, perhaps, no answer existed—those were the
questions that challenged my thinking and teased my imagination.
Books set me sailing on a vast sea; they stimulated my curiosity and
introduced me to new worlds and understandings. Classrooms, in
contrast, were arid, salt-encrusted seabeds with neither jetsam nor
flotsam to excite my imagination.

Imagination, creativity, and autonomy were not valued in
my high school classrooms. Time and time again, as I began
work on an assignment, I found myself taking an approach or
developing an interpretation that deviated from the norm. At
times—but not always—my way did not meet with my teachers'
expectations, and my teachers, mistakenly believing that equity
arises out of uniformity, were consistent in identifying my

way as wrong. I recall one Social Studies 30 paper in which I both deviated from the required sequence of subtopic headings and experimented with an unconventional script. My teacher scrawled his feedback on the back of the final page: "Your handwriting is bee-yoo-ti-ful! This report does not meet my expectations. Hence, your mark (Such is the price of such strong independence.)" A mixed message, indeed! Even when I was certain that I *had* followed the rules, I soon discovered that, according to my teacher, I had not. Was I, on some subconscious level, refusing to compromise?

Only once during my four years of high school did a teacher permit me to attack a problem in my own way. I was in Grade 11 chemistry, working through a problem as part of a lab assignment. As I considered how best to solve the problem, I experienced a flash of insight that led me (as I later discovered) to an unconventional method. Granted, it was a roundabout way of arriving at the answer, and it required an elaborate setup, but it was my way and it made sense to me. Fortunately, my teacher provided the necessary equipment and allowed me the time to explore. I remember the rush I felt as I put *my* ideas and *my* procedures into effect: For the first time in twelve years of schooling, I could actually imagine myself as a scientist—this because one teacher abandoned traditional teaching methods in a sincere effort to honor a student's natural curiosity and individual meaning making.

If, as Gubrium and Holstein (2000) tell us, institutions are "relatively stable, routinized, ongoing patterns of action and interaction" (p. 102), then the agents who perform these actions, and initiate and manage these interactions are vitally important to the institution's survival; indeed, they determine it. In the school system, these agents are teachers. When I first began to teach, I stepped into a preexisting matrix of expectations, duties, and allegiances. As a neophyte I found it easier to slip into the groove prepared for me than to create my own niche. Besides, there was something comforting about this institutional orderliness, something reassuring. It took some time before I understood that the system was at work winning my allegiance and constructing my identity to satisfy its own needs—and what it needed was an institutional soldier, a champion to secure and uphold the ideologies underpinning the structure.

Today, I cringe at the thought that I inculcated in my students values that worked to undermine their feelings of self-worth, and I shudder when I think that, driven by my own inadequacies and desire to please the people positioned above me in the institutional hierarchy, I worked diligently to do so. But these thoughts accomplish nothing: It is far more productive to understand the "hows" than to lay blame upon the "whos." This duoethnographic process has shifted my attention from the question of responsibility (the "who") to the substance and manner of transmission (the "what" and the "how"). Today, rather than dwelling on who should be held accountable for the construction of my neurotic student self, I ask, "How did the institutional 'discourse-in-practice' construct me as the 'troubled' student self that the institution needs to justify its work?" (Gubrium and Holstein, 2001, p. 16) And instead of allowing guilt and self-recrimination to taint my memories of my work as a teacher, I ask, "How did the institution construct me as the 'troubled' teacher self that it needs to do its work, that it requires to put its discourse-into-practice?" If we hope to change schools for the better, we need to understand these processes.

REENTERING THE LIVED PRESENT

Rose: As I turn my attention to the here and now and the educational problem that prompted this duoethnography—the question of how the lessons of the hidden curriculum of my schooling have influenced my decision to do doctoral studies—I recognize that the duoethnographic process has helped transform my understanding of "success." Success, of course, is a fundamental concept in education, implicit in any discussion of students and schooling. Yet, despite its prevalence and significance, educators and students rarely discuss its meanings and their ramifications. As a result, teachers send students contradictory messages about success. On the one hand, my teachers assured me that I would be successful as long as I worked hard. Effort, they said, would bring the intrinsic rewards of satisfaction and pride. Subtext: You are in control of your own school success. On the other hand, the school system valorized its role as judge and benefactor, bequeathing the material markers of achievement: honor roll placement, certificates, diplomas, awards, and scholarships. The subtext here: We determine, legitimize, and rank your school success. By the time I moved from high school to university, it had become clear to me that intrinsic satisfaction meant little in an institution geared towards the production and propagation of extrinsic rewards. Thus, despite the occasional comment from an instructor or professor acknowledging the importance of *intrinsic feelings* of success, the institution's priority was (and continues to be) the *extrinsic* system-generated *markers* that certify success.

I had been led to believe that success in school guarantees success in life. I wanted a successful life, so I decided to comply with the education system's expectations, procedures, and rules. My description of a successful life is fairly typical: a stimulating career, a comfortable home, a solid marriage, healthy children, and an income high enough to make all of this sustainable. These were my life goals, the rewards that would come at the end of my schooling. In the meantime, I would do what was necessary to move me closer to that end point. As a high school student I followed directions, listened attentively, and completed assignments. I performed when my teachers commanded it, worked tirelessly to achieve the highest marks possible, and accepted the judgments of teachers regarding my skills, intellect, and potential. When I entered university, I brought with me the same modus operandi. By then, I had learned that I needed the system—its approval, judgments, and markers of success—if I was ultimately to garner the credentials that would proclaim my worth and value to the world. But I was confused: What credentials were needed? How many degrees were necessary?

My parents taught me that education would open career doors; my schooling taught me that *more* education would open *more* doors. In this way, I was led to believe that the more degrees I earned, the more career opportunities I would find in the "real" world. By accepting this logic, however, I became dependent upon the system. Intent upon increasing my options, I reasoned that I would need to continue my studies beyond an undergraduate degree and perhaps even beyond a master's. At the same time, I learned that the markers of school success were not simply a means to an end but significant in and of themselves. Degrees, so the institution taught me, were intrinsically valuable, for they conferred academic status and prestige. With this added incentive, I extended my studies determined to work through the multiple levels of the postsecondary system. I became an excellent client: By remaining in the system, I bolstered student enrollment (which serves to justify the schools' existence) and provided revenue in the form of tuition (which enables universities to maintain and sustain themselves). For decades I had acquiesced, complied, and conformed, but I believed the sacrifice worthwhile. I also believed that now constraints would be relaxed and independence granted. I was mistaken. I had made it to the "very top," but I was still bound by the system's barriers, restricted by its rules, and constrained by its curriculum. I felt inhibited by the rules, frustrated with the procedures, and limited by the curriculum. After almost a lifetime in this system, I have come to understand that "the beliefs and attitudes that undergird this [modernist] view of education amount to a lie: Despite the slim chance it [education] can make you 'successful,' it cannot make you free" (Smith, 2000, p. 12). What *has* set me free is critical critique and the layered understandings that it engenders. Today, with insight into the nature of the hidden curriculum of schooling and its impact upon me, I begin a new journey to a place where I am finally in control of my learning. I refuse to compromise any longer.

Donna: As an elementary and secondary student I was too naïve, and too well indoctrinated, to question school authority. It was unthinkable to blame my limited success on the mandated curriculum or the institutional structure. Instead, I blamed myself—my individual circumstances (the clannish nature of my rural school, the mediocrity of my teachers) and/or my personal shortcomings (my obstinacy, my laziness). According to Paul Watzlawick (1984), this is how ideology works. The system masks the lie at the heart of the ideology—in this case, school omnipotence—by creating the impression that all within its ranks happily accept its authority, judgments, and values. Thus, we are led to believe that "whoever does not feel this within himself [sic] had better recognize that something is wrong with him [sic] and not perhaps with the official definition of reality" (p. 233). When I completed high school, I reasoned that if I was the problem, then I had the power to fix that problem. I believed that if I "pulled myself up by my bootstraps," I could move onward and upward in the world. The painful irony of my situation eluded me: While the school system rendered me virtually powerless, the hidden curriculum taught me that only I had the power to change myself. As a result, I succumbed to the false promises of individualism and to the myth of meritocracy (Briskin, 1994). Thus, I convinced myself that education at the postsecondary level would a far more positive experience.

As I moved from high school to university, I embraced the doctrine of perfection; that is, the one who achieves perfection is the "best," and only the best are deemed worthy. I reasoned that perfection could be achieved in the classroom by earning perfect marks. Thus, I regarded A+ grades as the central product of my efforts in that domain. As my postsecondary education proceeded, I deduced that perfection could be achieved within academe by acquiring a complete set of degrees; in other words, one degree at each of the three levels offered in the postsecondary system: baccalaureate, master's, and doctorate. Thus, I came to regard degrees as the ultimate products of my labor within the institution. Given this perspective, doctoral studies became an especially critical endeavor, an opportunity to (finally) achieve perfect grades *and* a perfect "set" of postsecondary degrees. As I began the final course in my doctoral program, it appeared that I might finally achieve the most enduring of my goals, perfect grades. Then the professor explained that this course would be evaluated on the basis of credit/noncredit: no traditional evaluation scheme grounded in comparative judgments, no fostering of competitive relationships, no quantification of my worth as a human being, and . . . no possibility of an A+. I was incensed: Here I was about to win the ultimate prize, perfect marks in a doctoral program, and someone had the gall to change the rules of the game. The intensity of my response forced me to admit how completely I had internalized the doctrine of perfection as taught within the hidden curriculum of my schooling, and the degree to which I had been living a value system that I claimed to detest.

Today I understand my academic "game-playing" as a compulsion born of the hidden curriculum of my schooling. Many decades have passed since I first learned to equate superlative grades with academic success, and academic success with personal worth. During my master's program, I finally recognized the pernicious effects of this belief; I determined, then, to think differently. And yet, on an unconscious level, it retained its hold on my imagination. Despite my genuine love for learning, my fledgling attempts at resistance, and my determined efforts as a teacher to "do it better," I harbored an ineradicable need to be validated by the system. Although I did not realize it at the time, I began my doctoral degree still clinging to the hope that I could win the competitive game of academics and, by winning the game, win the approbation of the classroom demigods I had constructed. My desire was deep seated, and irrational, for it makes no sense to seek validation from a system that is deeply flawed, nor from professors who are co-constructed by what is plainly another version of the hidden curriculum of schooling, the university's hidden curriculum of faculty. What does make sense is to recognize, understand, and resist the forces that construct students in self-serving ways. After much soul searching, I have decided to complete this doctoral degree, though not for the reasons I would have given prior to our duoethnography. As I work toward that end, I will think of my story as "a narrative of resistance, not a lament over the state of the . . . [schooled] self in contemporary life" (Gubrium and Holstein, 2001, p. 4), for it is in resistance that I will find the strength to begin the difficult process of reconstructing my schooled self.

METANARRATIVE: DECODING THE CRYPTIC CURRICULUM

Every study is limited in some respect; therefore, one must always identify and acknowledge limitations when assessing the value of one's work. The researcher who studies what is hidden takes on a difficult task. When the "object" of study is a *hidden curriculum*, the task is particularly challenging. Here, the researcher must go in search of attitudes, values, and routinized practices, none of which are easy to "find." Often we hardly think to look for them. Caught up in the pell-mell of contemporary life, we race through our day, rarely pausing to consider how the people around us influence our beliefs. When, for some unaccountable reason, we do pause and reflect upon the attitudes and values of acquaintances and friends, and their possible influence on us, we are apt to end up more frustrated than enlightened. Complex by nature, belief systems are difficult to anatomize. Attitudes and values, and the practices that ensue from them, are often internally inconsistent and made manifest in a farrago of antithetical speech and action that frequently defies analysis. Given this messy context, one so inclined can easily disguise and perpetuate self-serving beliefs and practices. Many are deeply invested in doing just that, for hidden curricula perform ideological work: They present and naturalize a social order in which those with power persuade those without to accept and sustain their own subjection. Should the veil be rent and all disclosed, this order would collapse, and the powerful would become powerless. This they cannot risk. Hence, they do their utmost to disguise the indoctrinatory lessons that make it possible to secure control. Although we have uncovered eight principles embedded in this hidden curriculum of schooling, we suspect that we shall, over time, discover many more. Thus, our understandings, though important and useful, are limited in breadth. We must also point out that they are open to revision. All meanings are historically situated, conditioned by the place and time of their construction and, therefore, contingent. As our lives move on and we evolve, the meanings we have constructed as a result of this duoethnographic inquiry will change, and our understandings of who we were, who we are, and who we will be will be transformed. Succinctly stated, the understandings we have generated are both partial and protean. We encourage our readers to take this into account when evaluating the potential value and broader implications of our study.

Nevertheless, the duoethnographic process has enabled us to construct deeper understandings of the nature of our hidden curricula of schooling and the ways in which they have shaped our school identities. We now see more clearly what we were taught, what we have resisted, and what we have internalized. Today we understand this curriculum in terms of several distinct and treacherous principles: reverence for school authority, glorification of competition, preeminence of performance, insistence upon conformity, a standard of perfection, infallibility of teachers, naturalization of acquiescence, and demand for compliance. What is more, we recognize that these ideologies also permeate the institution of our educational present. Even at the doctoral level, we find a hidden curriculum against which, in many respects, we are compelled to react. As well, we have gained invaluable insight into our "selves," both the student selves of the past and the schooled selves—both student *and* teacher—of the present. Gubrium and Holstein (2000) argue that a personal self, if such a thing exists, is "not a distinct private entity so much as it is a *concatenation of traits, roles, standpoints, and behaviors that individuals articulate and present through social interaction*" (emphasis added; p. 100). We now recognize the traits (e.g., Donna's stubborn resistance and Rose's determined perseverance), the roles (Golden Girl versus Good Little Girl), the standpoints (one seeking emotional validation, the other seeking success), and the behaviors (Donna's sporadic opting out and Rose's *pro tem* compliance) that have come into play in the construction of our schooled selves. Most important, we have come to realize that the process of constructing an institutional self is profoundly complex. Understanding it requires more than recognition; it requires thoughtful interpretation. In this institutional context, no trait, role, viewpoint, or behavior is necessarily what it seems. Does one read Donna's stubborn resistance as defiance or simple self-preservation? Or both? Does one interpret Rose's lengthy compliance as submission or sagacity? As the transformation of one into the other? Or as a vacillation between the two? Moreover, we must never forget that an institutional self is always a *co*construction: The institution imposes upon us attributes, roles, viewpoints, and behaviors that serve institutional needs, but we also bring aspects of our out-of-school selves into the construction.

While "the circumstances of [institutional] self-construction play a pivotal role in how we view ourselves, they do not dictate identities nor construct selves outright" (Gubrium and Holstein, 2000, p. 19). Finally, we must acknowledge that teachers as well are constructed as institutional selves. If education institutions are, indeed, "relatively stable, routinized, ongoing *patterns of action and interaction*" (emphasis added; p. 102), then student-teacher interactions lie at the heart of an indoctrinatory curriculum. This fact gives us hope, for we have both witnessed and experienced how critical awareness and insight can transform individual beliefs, value systems, and perspectives and, subsequently, our ways and means of interacting with others.

Most important, our duoethnographic inquiry has taught us that it is never enough to expose a hidden curriculum; we must also understand *how* that curriculum accomplishes its ideological work. We must go beyond exposure and aim for comprehension. When we identify what our hidden curricula have taught us, we take only the first step. We take a second step when we recognize the institutional selves formed by those lessons. But it is only when we comprehend *how* the lessons have been presented and the ideologies transmitted that we are able to apply our research and are empowered to instigate change. How, then, do curricula teach these ideological "truths?" They do so by concealing them in customary practices and reinforcing them through regulation and routine. We have elected to refer to this process as *encoding*. In other words, the researcher who successfully uncovers the content of a hidden curriculum must still contend with— and decipher—an encrypted "lived" curriculum, a *cryptic curriculum*. The encoding of ideological "truths" occurs in the embodied interactions between students and teachers. If we are to successfully decode a cryptic curriculum, we must enter into "the 'messy' details of actual lives [lived] *through talk and interaction*" (emphasis added; Gubrium and Holstein, 2000, p. 17). Each individual is unique; that being so, his or her interactions with any one person must also be unique. This means that each student's experience of the encoding process will be unlike any other's. We must "enter the lived present," as Pinar (2004) would say, and observe this dynamic interplay between student and teacher as it unfolds, as each constructs and reconstructs the other. It is only in studying the lived relationship between the two, the precise details of speech and behavior that constitute their interactions, and the way in which each uses space and time to frame those interactions, that we can eventually break the code of a cryptic curriculum. Only then, when we have come to understand how the lessons of a hidden curriculum have been encoded in the daily interactions between students and teachers, will we be able to select and implement effective strategies for intervention and reconstruction—we will have gone beyond description and begun to take action. So our inquiry into the hidden curriculum of schooling and its influence upon us must go on, the conversations resume, and the duoethnographic process continue if we are to eventually understand the interplay between the institution's ideological discourse so cleverly disguised within the lived curriculum of the classroom and the individual's capacity for resistance and self-invention.

REFERENCES

Anyon, J. (1980). Social class and the hidden curriculum of work. *Journal of Education*, *162*(1), 67–92.

Bailey, G., and Smith, N. (1987). The rural school administrator's role in achieving sex equity of curriculum. *Rural Educator*, *9*(1), 1–6.

Briskin, L. (1994). Feminist pedagogy: Teaching and learning liberation. In L. Erwin and D. MacLennan (Eds.), *Sociology of education in Canada: Critical perspectives on theory research and practice* (pp. 443–470). Toronto, ON: Copp Clark Longman.

Dewey, J. (1916). *Democracy and education: An introduction to the philosophy of education*. New York: Macmillan.

Erickson, F., and Schultz, J. J. (1982). *The counselor as gatekeeper: Social interaction in interviews*. New York: Academic Press.

Flinders, J. D., Noddings, N., and Thornton, J. S. (1986). The null curriculum: Its theoretical basis and practical implications. *Curriculum Inquiry*, *16*(1), 33–42.

Gillborn, D. (1992). Citizenship, "race" and the hidden curriculum. *International Studies in Sociology of Education*, *2*(1), 57–73.

Gubrium, J. F., and Holstein, J. A. (2000). The self in a world of going concerns. *Symbolic Interaction*, *23*(2), 95–115.

Gubrium, J. F., and Holstein, J. A. (2001). Introduction: Trying times, troubled selves. In J. F. Gubrium and J. A. Holstein (Eds.), *Institutional selves: Troubled identities in a postmodern world* (pp. 1–20). New York: W. W. Norton.

Hochschild, A. R. (1983). *The managed heart*. Berkeley: University of California Press.

McLaren, P. (1989). *Life in schools: An introduction to critical pedagogy in the foundations of education*. New York: Longman.

Miller, J. (2011, January). *Autobiography on the move: Poststructuralist perspectives on (im)possible narrative representations of collaboration*. Keynote address presented at the meeting of the Narrative, Arts-based, and "Post" Approaches to Social Research, Tempe, AZ.

Norris, J. (2005, May). *From autoethnography to duoethnography: A search for the dialogic self*. Paper presented at the Thinking Qualitatively Workshop Conference of the International Institute of Qualitative Methodology, Edmonton, AB.

Norris, J., and Sawyer, R. (2004). Null and hidden curricula of sexual orientation: A dialogue on the curreres of the absent presence and the present absence. In L. Coia, M. Birch, N. J. Brooks, E. Heilman, S. Mayer, A. Mountain, and P. Pritchard (Eds.), *Democratic responses in an era of standardization* (pp. 139–159). New York: Educators' International Press.

Pinar, W. (1975). Currere: Toward reconceptualization. In W. Pinar (Ed.), *Curriculum theorizing: The reconceptualists* (pp. 396–414). Berkeley, CA: McCutchan.

Pinar, W. (2004). *What is curriculum theory?* Hillsdale, NJ: Lawrence Erlbaum.

Pinar, W., Reynolds, M. W., Slattery, P., and Taubman, M. P. (1995). *Understanding curriculum*. New York: Peter Lang.

Portelli, J. (1993). Exposing the hidden curriculum. *Journal of Curriculum Studies*, 25(4), 343–358.

Said, E. W. (1993). *Culture and imperialism*. New York, NY: Alfred A. Knopf.

Smith, D. G. (2000). *Trying to teach in a season of great untruth: Globalization, empire and the crises of pedagogy*. Rotterdam: Sense.

Watzlawick, P. (1984). Components of ideological "realities." In P. Watzlawick (Ed.), *The invented reality* (pp. 207–247). New York: W. W. Norton.

CHAPTER 3

Postcolonial Education:
Using a Duoethnographic Lens to Explore a Personal Curriculum of Post/Decolonization

Richard D. Sawyer and Tonda Liggett

PROLOGUE

Archived personal photographs are temporal cultural markers, making them ideal for duoethnographic research. One can look at past events from the vantage point of the present, recalling the meaning and feelings of the time, as evoked by the pictures, and then analyze them from present cultural perspectives. Self is juxtaposed with another temporal self among two or more time periods. One's hidden and null curriculums become evident through temporal lenses. Both Liggett and Sawyer examine and provide photographs as a means of (re)presenting the past and understanding their curriculum of, in this case, colonialism. As Liggett remarks,

> *Going back through my own yearbook clarified and rearranged my memories: a backward and forward movement of memory, a critical engagement with my personal mythology, particularly realizing the influence of my Eurocentric curriculum. (p. 81)*

The duoethnographic process is one of critical juxtaposition, and photographs provide one means of doing just that.

But this is not just done individually. Sawyer claims that, "Reading Tonda's words make me wonder how the curriculum that I have been exposed to has been inscribed by cultural norms" (p. 82). Self is also juxtaposed with the Other, and through listening to the Other, each duoethnographic partner can view oneself partially through the lens of the Other. As the Other's themes emerge, one searches for similarities and differences in their own life histories. As Greene (1973) suggests, becoming strange to self, broadens one's perspective. Liggett claims, "As I began writing, I realized that a significant turning point in my life hinged around my undergraduate semester abroad" (p. 79). For Liggett, understanding takes place in the "face of the Other" (Hendley, 2000). She became a stranger through her travels, and in duoethnography, she became anthropologically strange to self as she became aware of Rick's lenses. In

71

duoethnography, one's fellow research partner is an "interlocutor" (Hendley, 2000, p. 71).

But duoethnographies are not static pieces. Duoethnographers not only make new meanings of past events, they also make plans for action. Sawyer concludes the chapter with a challenge to himself, Liggett, and their readers: "However, by attempting to deconstruct and then reimagine our own educational histories, we can begin to construct new learning spaces for our students . . ." (p. 87). In keeping with one of the tenets, this chapter exemplifies the role of duoethnography in personal and social transformation.

—*Joe Norris*

DUOETHNOGRAPHY IN SEARCH OF POSTCOLONIAL PEDAGOGY

Although the two of us work in different areas of educational research, we are both committed to teaching in ways that do not privilege one particular group over another, both on a local level within our own classrooms and on a larger, more systemic and global level. As our schools become increasingly diverse, our teaching force is becoming increasingly less diverse (Natriello and Zumwalt, 1994). Working with students from different cultural, language, class, and sexual orientation backgrounds calls on us as educators to recognize and build curricula from students' diverse perspectives.

The attempt to teach in ways that respect the voice and democratic inclusion of different cultures and people is not a simple process (Brettschneider, 2001; Gutmann, 1999; Henderson and Kesson, 1999). As teachers, we are each positioned differently in relation to schools, subjects, students, and communities. Part of this process necessitates our understanding and critiquing of our own educational histories in an honest and complex way. To engage in substantive teaching change, an initial step is working individually and communally in examining our cultural imprints. Individuals who identify strongly with their own classroom teachers may internalize teaching strategies, for better or worse, from these teachers and, perhaps unknowingly, use these strategies as a basis for their teaching (Lortie, 1976). Perhaps even more subversively, even teachers who may be "counteridentifiers" and who wish to change the system might still unknowingly teach in the very ways that they disliked as students—ways that still support a sense of oppression and marginalization—in their view of students and other countries and cultures (Apple, 1979; Skeggs, 2008).

In this chapter, we engage in a duoethnography about a teaching and research topic that is mutually important to us, postcolonial language arts curriculum. As we reflect critically on the process of coming to understand our educational histories, both as students and then as teachers, we try to unpack some of the social, cultural, and geographical underpinnings of our respective journeys of teaching language arts.

PART 1: ON THE OUTSIDE LOOKING IN

The Early Years: Identity Formation, Becoming Gendered

Tonda: As the firstborn granddaughter in a combined line of eight aunts and uncles on both my mother and my father's side, the moment was not to be lost. My mother dressed me up in frilly frocks and bonnets until I was old enough to voice my dissent. I reflect on a photo that shows me alongside my brother in front of Snow White's house (Figure 3.1).

It is a small, wooden A-frame about four feet tall. A few of the dwarfs are behind me. My brother smiles shyly at the camera, and I look uncomfortable in my bonnet. Years later when I enter elementary school, I shed my bonnet and competed with the boys on the playground in football, running races, baseball, basketball, snowball throwing, etc. Being able to beat them

Figure 3.1 A fairytale childhood.

was important to gaining acceptance in the many new schools I entered during that time. In second grade, my mother, brother, and I lived downtown, which meant in one of the Black neighborhoods of the city. This was my first exposure to African Americans. I don't remember it being something that was talked about or acknowledged in any way. The German neighbors seemed more remarkable as they spoke a different language, linguistic difference trumping any racial defining that took place for me then.

By this time, in the early 1970s, the Civil Rights movement had caused transformative change and raised awareness about marginalization not only for African Americans but also for women (Kesselman, McNair, and Schniedewind, 2003) and homosexuals (Nelson, 2006). I don't remember any protests or commentary on it. Perhaps this is part of the legacy of colonialism, not hearing about conflict or the messy part of social revolution, the demand for shared wealth, equality, representation, and access (Narayan, 1997). Even in high school, while there were many clubs and organizations, there was no rallying around anything political, and notions of diversity at my school meant the French and Spanish language clubs. This provided fertile ground for shaking me to my very core as I stepped into the taxi queue outside the Nairobi airport. Thus began the slow process of deconstructing my own legacy of what it meant to be White.

I spent the semester abroad living and traveling throughout Kenya, walking among the Masai tribe on the edge of the Rift Valley as one of a small group of college students venturing out to learn about orienteering, biology, history, and the culture of this new environment. No longer could I rely on my background information to give me an advantage in this learning situation. In small villages, people came up to me and asked questions about my life, where I was from, what the United States was like. In answering, I realized I was pressed to respond for all Whites—a representative of my race—something I discuss now with my students when we address the deconstruction of racial identity and the ways that colonialism plays out today. In speaking for my country, I was speaking as racial minorities are often called upon to do in classrooms across the nation.

How could my small experience speak for such a wide range of people, as there are many influential factors that contribute to one's sense of identity: race, ethnicity, culture, class, gender, sexual orientation, religion, physical ability, age, and so on? In studies of

American mainstream teachers and the factors that influence their pedagogy, White racial membership and the cultural positionality that this inherently implies has been shown to have implications for teacher-student interactions in ways that limit minority student academic achievement (Delpit, 1995; Ladson-Billings, 2001; Sleeter, 1996). This situation is further complicated by the embedded nature of racial and cultural assumptions, making it difficult for teachers to know the extent to which their own ideologies are influenced by the assumptions they make of people from different backgrounds (Hinkel, 1999). This semester abroad, I discovered, marked the beginning of an awareness about colonization, its legacy, and the ways that post/decolonization was apparent not only in my own personal identity but also in my teaching and in language arts curriculum.

From the 48 Club to the 50 States: Acts of Destruction, Reconstruction, and Deconstruction

Rick: My father was in the U.S. Army when I was young, and I spent the first four years of my life on an army base in Germany in the late 1950s. In Germany at that time, I witnessed an American message that announced no longer just the end of a war but, rather, the dawn of a new reality, one mirrored in an ideal portrait of America itself. I'm not sure if or how this message was directed toward Germans, but I did encounter it directed at me.

One way that I have tried to uncover these early cultural messages is by examining an interesting souvenir my father got in Berlin at the end of the war. The souvenir, a photo album put out by the U.S. Army, is a short promotional booklet of the new military enlisted men's club in Berlin, called the "48 Club." My purpose in examining this artifact is to try to understand its messages not so much on the Germans but, rather, on myself, as to how I was socialized into being an American on foreign soil.

The cover picture of this black-and-white booklet is exceptional—modern (almost postmodern!) and clever with overlapping titles, angular framing, and an interplay between text and image (Figure 3.2).

On the cover in the left margin is a narrow column with the names of the then all forty-eight states in the Union. This column borders a photo of the building that the club was housed in. The right border itself is stark white, in contrast to the opposite border, and acts as a statement of the future, of the unknown.

Figure 3.2 The U.S. border with Berlin.

The photo of the building in the center is taken from an inside wing and lends a gay tropical touch—with a miniature palm in the foreground—to the southern Florida design of the building. The title of the booklet, *Berlin 1945/47*, bridges the photo of the building and the blank right border. Although the title suggests the booklet is about Berlin, it is not. It is about America, and it frames the future.

There are approximately twenty-five photos in this booklet, and they each represent a different aspect of the Americanization of Germany at this time period. For example, the caption to one photo is "Coca-Cola, milk shakes and ice cream are served at the Coke Bar." The photo of the Coke Bar shows a streamlined art deco dream, commercial, clean, and shiny. In no way a warm image, this photo announces that American efficiency and organization will be served with sweet Cokes, milkshakes, and ice cream. One of the more interesting photos in the book is of a German musician. The caption reads, "Berlin's Tommy Dorsey 'Kurt Widmann' and his band." We see him standing in front of an oversized American flag, this German Tommy Dorsey. The message is clear: American culture, as well as its military, won the war. Other photos in the book show how the walls of the dining area are decorated with images of modern American cities—skyscrapers announcing the superiority of American business and know-how and the Statue of Liberty announcing its freedom.

On the military base in Germany, I had lived in a very well-defined world of rules, ranks, and propaganda. When I returned to the United States just in time to enter elementary school, I found that the rules of public school, although just as entrenched as those of the military, were harder at first to read: No one gave me a manual. Going from my home on the base to the old brick school in Seattle, I learned initially that the world off the army base was just as rigid—although in a different way—as the world on the base. For me, it was interesting to develop a dual lens. Like other military kids, I became socialized in both settings and learned to code switch.

Given my military past, I initially made an easy transition to the regimentation of school life. We stood in line to go to the cafeteria, sat in neat rows in class (in which the teacher could "hear a pin drop"), played gender-specific games at recess, and worked industriously as every second hand of every electric impulse clock in every room clicked in unison. I loved raising my hand and being called on. But slowly and with stealth, a sense of violation crept in: The rules were to control, not to support.

I learned in class that my teachers did not appreciate "difference." For example, I wrote a short story about being trapped on an island. The story included elements of magic realism. The teacher informed me that one object could not transform into another object and very publicly failed me. I didn't care about the grade so much as a sense of suffocation and near panic at feeling, in the third grade, that I was a failure in life. It would have been unheard of for me to try to explain why I constructed my story as I did; there was no student negotiation of, only negation in, the curriculum. Instead of contributing to the curriculum, I learned about the inevitability of the Manifest Destiny, how Native Americans in Washington State lost their land, and how "No taxation without representation" came to be a powerful rallying cry.

I learned in class there were identity markers that contributed to the receipt of classroom rewards or punishments. The list included but was certainly not limited to the following: gender, ethnicity, obedience, parents' occupation, ways of arriving at school, past and assumed future grades, appearance, ways with words, ways with prior and sanctioned knowledge, types of friends, numbers of friends, friendliness of parents, reading skill, home neighborhood, and, my favorite, number of Valentine's Day cards. The actual hierarchy of these items shifted from teacher to teacher and year to year. Students without status, knowledge, and privileges of birth were outsiders and knew it.

Once I made it to high school, I found that a core group of these items remained while new items were added, such as intelligence quotients, letterman jackets, busing, and guidance counselors. As a way to become reacquainted with my old high school, I, like Tonda, recently examined my high school yearbook to examine presented norms, trends, and behaviors. A contrast of two photos on opposite pages of the yearbook—the "men's club" and the "girl's club"—speaks volumes. The seventeen-year-old male students in the men's club photo pose in what appears to be in a cocktail lounge, dressed for an outing with Frank Sinatra and other members of the Rat Pack, even though the photo was taken in the post-Beatles era. The other photo is of the girls' club. How the school had the nerve to contrast "men" with "girls," even in the early 1970s, is beyond me. As can be seen, the "girls" stand wearing matching stewardess-like outfits, cool, calm, and collected. In the yearbook, there are many photos of athletes, but with the exception of the girls' volleyball team, the photos are only of boys. I remember that in my last year, I was lucky enough to be able to find sanctuary in the Black Student Union during lunch every day. Interestingly enough, this group, formally recognized by the school, is not even mentioned in the yearbook. Even though the nation was fighting the Vietnam War at this time, there is not one mention of politics.

This yearbook is indeed an artifact of what the school was about (Flinders, Noddings, and Thornton, 1986) but, in retrospect, perhaps not what the yearbook adviser might have intended. The story of the yearbook is found in its message of what is valued or not—what is worthy of inclusion or not. Yes, there are the obligatory photos of the student body, but the real story is in the other photos: the lack of gender recognition, the lack of diversity, the lack of student controversy, the lack of student voice and debate, and the lack of any sort of world or global context. The neat world of the school, and its amazingly provincial worldview are all that matters. If something didn't fit, it didn't exist.

The curriculum of this school, a proud representation of my country during the Vietnam War, ran parallel to that of the elementary school, only instead of writing a paper about a lumber town, I wrote a paper about the Marshall Plan. Instead of writing fantasy short stories, I did Dada photography, much to the bewilderment (and scorn) of my photography teacher. In health class, we were told about the horrors of homosexuality and the importance of personal hygiene. In English, we got Steinbeck and Hemingway, not Plath or Baldwin. History was told from the perspective of White victors, and math was taught through rules and formulas. Someone from the 1890s could have entered the math class and—if he didn't glance at the looming Space Needle at the bottom of the hill—feel right at home. Again, we sat in neat rows. I had a friend who, out of desperation, drank whiskey every day before going to English class. One day the teacher smelled it on his breath and sent him to the counselor.

Dialogue: The Early Years

Tonda: Through our duoethnographic inquiry on postcolonialism, I began to reflect critically on the background experiences that have influenced my teaching and thoughts about learning. Engaging with Rick in such dialogue, I was pressed to reconsider past memories and critically analyze them in relation to Rick's. I read a rough draft of Rick's initial paper, which provided a starting point to organize mine. I wrote according to the topics he had addressed (early years, high school yearbook, becoming a teacher, etc.). As I began writing, I realized that a significant turning point in my life hinged around my undergraduate semester abroad. I thought about the influence that living in a new culture had on me at that time, the overwhelming newness of it all. Fast-forwarding to the present, I began to make connections to my work and teaching, which focus on aspects and issues of racial and cultural identity and their impact on teaching and learning. Even though my most poignant memories did not include high school or the yearbook, my conversations with Rick compelled me to dust off my old yearbook and take a look. Going through these pages proved to be instrumental in clarifying the cultural orientations that were the backdrop to this semester abroad, as they highlighted the stark absence of alternative perspectives besides the majority White, middle-class one represented throughout the pages. This underscored the reason why my semester abroad had made such an impact as I, for the first time, was immersed in a culture with which I was not familiar and surrounded by people that were not of my racial identity. This looking back, prompted by my discussions with Rick, caused me to examine a deeper layer of my experience with new eyes—a critical investigation into how my life has been situated socially and culturally. In this sense, the dialogue that

Rick and I had engaged in created critical tensions, insights, and perspectives.

The topic of race is uniquely the focus of much scholarly work in the United States, as it is one of the key defining colonial marks that the legacy of slavery retains and weaves through our social, political, and historical context (e.g., Goldberg, 1993; Krysan and Lewis, 2008; Morrison, 1992). That I have come to such a focus in my work today makes the journey back through my formative years that much more enlightening. I look back through the reflective mirror of race in a way that I never did when I was twenty years old. As I do now, however, I find it ironic that one of my life-changing events took place in the previously colonized country of Kenya, with the British relinquishing their power the same year I was born, 1962. My awareness of race, culture, and linguistic difference was imprinted on me as I looked around Nairobi and realized that I was, for the first time, a minority. I describe the years before my Kenya experience and then afterward, using my experience there as a midway point in this essay interaction, looking back and then forward. I conclude with the impact this experience has had on my curricular choices, course design, and overall professional inquiry.

Rick's commentary on how his alternative approaches to the language arts curriculum through magical realism and Dada photography indicate, in these early years, the confines and normativity of a postcolonial curriculum. This backdrop underscores the impact that our experiences abroad had on us. Both Rick and I have defining elements in our lives shaped by our participation in a culture other than our one of origin. Rick spent his first four years in Germany, then moved to the U.S., where his lens is framed by his particular involvement with German culture and U.S. military culture, a straddling and reconfiguring of two worldviews. Similarly, my entry into Kenya caused a reordering of my own previously constructed notions of race, culture, ethnicity, and language. My semester abroad represented a foundational shift in my worldview as a racial and cultural minority.

As Rick and my discussion unfolded, it included not only a give-and-take of comments and responses but also an internal criticality of our past in relation to postcolonialism. This critical tension enabled us to mediate a higher level of consciousness. The process offered me the chance to better understand why my Kenya experience was such a turning point and how the experience compelled me to continue to examine the ways that race, culture, and language play out in different contexts. Reading and dialoguing with Rick about his personal reference points made me look back with a new perspective, noticing elements in our discussions and considering how they might apply to my own experience. Going back through my own yearbook clarified and rearranged my memories: a backward and forward movement of memory, a critical engagement with my personal mythology, particularly realizing the influence of my Eurocentric curriculum. With this lens, I was able to better understand that my postcolonial education was the educational format for my generation. What have I done and what was I doing to decolonize it? In our attempts to answer these questions, I have realized the dynamic nature of this form of researching and writing, remembering in a nonlinear, sometimes circular, most often abstract way a connection made that was hard to determine for even myself, perhaps from a hint of memory, one still influential.

Rick: Reading Tonda's section, I began to wonder how my own cultural indoctrination played out on a deeper, more layered and contradictory way when I moved to the United States. She mentioned a number of ironic situations from her life that suggest a dialectical relationship between being on the border between colonizer/colonized. For example, her being in Kenya put into relief her own cultural identity, her Whiteness, allowing her to deconstruct her identity from a new perspective while at the same time asking her to translate examples of United States culture. Her thoughts push me deeper into an analysis of my own story. I wondered about the dichotomies in my own life. When I came from Europe as a child, I was a little confused about who I was. While I may have heard stories about patriotism, freedom, and duty as a young child, I now realize that these homilies had a hollow, disingenuous ring. As a child I sought connections, not abstractions. Back in the U.S., I found that I was placed in a shifting landscape of new and rather confusing sociocultural constructions. Learning in class was a process of cultural indoctrination. From the first grade, I learned in competitive and individualistic ways. I lived in fear of the spelling bee and came to dread the oral report. What we read reinforced a view of the inevitability of America's place in the world (although threatened by Sputnik), leaving me feeling strangely anxious. In class, instead of feeling connected by the curriculum, I felt as alienated by it as I did by the hollow abstractions of my life on the military base.

We all have multiple layers to our cultural identities. But to go back three decades, my public schools had a much more singular cultural focus. Language, behavior, power, and merit revolved around a particular cultural standard, one that privileged White heterosexual (and affluent) males. Students in the school who couldn't connect to this standard were alienated and labeled. People around the world who were different from this standard have been both culturally and physically displaced. Reading Tonda's words make me wonder how the curriculum that I have been exposed to has been inscribed by cultural norms.

PART 2: ENTERING THE CLASSROOM AS TEACHERS

Becoming a Teacher: Tonda

Tonda: My first teaching experience was in Quito, Ecuador, where I walked into an English language school and was given a job. In Ecuador an American English accent was desirable and native speakers were in short supply, so despite having no teaching experience, I suddenly had a class. As I reflect back on this introduction to teaching, I recall an acquaintance I had made, a British woman who also taught English language learners (ELLs), one of the few Black travelers I had seen throughout my time in Ecuador. She had been applying to various jobs around the city, and when I ran into her one day after teaching for a few months, I told her that I had just gotten a new position at the Catholic University (*Universidad Catolica*), a better situation with a substantial salary increase. She was surprised and slightly exasperated (it seemed), for she had just applied for the same position and had much more experience. I glossed over her reaction, however, because I was happy about my new situation. I reasoned that my advantage was an American accent, even after meeting one of my White male colleagues who had a British accent.

It wasn't until I began studying about Whiteness and White privilege years later that I reanalyzed this distant memory and understood that it wasn't my accent at all. Peering through a postcolonial lens and, thus, a racialized socialization, my skin color most likely rewarded me with this unearned advantage (Kailin, 2002; Liggett, 2009; Rothenberg, 2002). I felt slighted with my education at that point because I hadn't learned about such advantage earlier. I know now that the relatively unexamined culture of the self is important to address in order to confront the underlying issues of power that work to sustain certain knowledge forms and to solidify the positionality of the White race in the context of teacher education.

As an elementary English language teacher, I often read stories to my young students and tried to locate books that reflected their culture as well as the various cultures represented in the U.S. This was often not possible, however, as resources were limited for me as well as for the general education teachers whose material I borrowed. I think back on these readings and wonder if my language was inclusive enough to make up the gap in their cultural and linguistic nonrepresentation in the curricula (Norris and Sawyer, 2004). This situation is not unique, as resources and funding are limited, but I still wonder what impact this has made on these children. What would my life be like if I, as a child, did not see my race or culture represented in the books my teachers read in class? What if American history only included a White perspective? I continued as an English language teacher working with adult ELLs, where I gained heightened awareness of the ways language proficiency put into question these students' cognitive ability.

Becoming a Teacher: Rick

Rick: Time moved on, and as a high school English teacher I tried to teach in ways that embraced the different cultures of my students in terms of both the pedagogy and the content of my curriculum. However, as I now examine my teaching in relation to my own history as a student, I see that I approached this goal of making a culturally inclusive curriculum with uneven results. A deconstruction of one of my assignments that I was proud of at the time shows the challenging nature of this process. I called the assignment a "slang/formal English dictionary." Considering myself a bridge between the world of my students and that of "formal society," I had my students take the everyday slang that they used and translate it into formal, perhaps exaggerated "Standard English" and use both forms in a story. For example, "get ghost" meant to vanish, the "rollers" were the police, and "tags" were personal identification symbols. Other terms were more graphic and connected to poverty, drug violence, and gender violence. One student wrote these two stories:

Yeah, homes, I was chilling with the beat, just kickin it down on two-four when I seen Grizz from the crew. She said, "Hey cuz, got a square?" I said, "don't mess with it, babe." "Why don't we stop off at

Mickey D's and get some grub?" asked Grizz. I said, "Na, let's go score on some steers."

Translation:

Yes, my friend, I was calmly sitting listening to the radio, just relaxing down on Twenty-Fourth Street, when I saw Grizz from the gang. She said, "Hey, you got a cigarette?" I said, "I don't smoke." "Why don't we go to McDonald's and get something to eat?" asked Grizz. I said, "Na, let's go get some beer."

In many ways, this assignment represents an improvement from the more decontextualized and test-framed curriculum then found at the students' school. It also recognized students' more personal language and encouraged them to construct a story from it, possibly for the first time in their student lives. However, there are some things that I would change if I were to repeat this assignment. In this duoethnography, I have noted that colonial notions framed some of my earlier perceptions, symbolized by the brochure from the 48 Club in Berlin. What I found fascinating in doing this duoethnography was that I discovered that a similar "red-white-and-blue" border framed some of my teaching. In teaching writing, for example, I framed authentic student voice with the dominant discourse. The fact that I isolated the students' language with quotation marks and called it "slang" represented a privileging of Standard English. And while the activity was fun to do in class, the not-so-hidden message suggested that the students' language needed to be translated, not the other way around. I ask myself if this, then, becomes an act of colonization.

Another imbalance of privilege in this assignment may be found in the grading process. While all students who did this assignment received maximum points for doing it (an "A"), students who didn't do it were marked down. But can I really blame some of them for resisting what they may have considered an act of appropriation in the pairing of their personal language with Standard English, a language that privileges some (Christensen, 2009) and condemns others? I now think that an improvement to this assignment would be to use it as a means to examine the overall framing of power and privilege in language in general, and in Standard English in particular. How did it become the standard? Who was the agent? Why? Christensen echoes this concern as she reflects on her own teaching:

Without examining the legacy of language supremacy, I maintain the old world order because I haven't explored why. Standard English is the standard and how it came to power, and how that power is wielded to make some people feel welcome and others feel like outsiders. (p. 209)

As I reflect on this assignment, I now question the extent to which larger structural issues framed it.

DIALOGUE ABOUT TEACHING

Tonda: Rick's questioning of his "slang/formal English dictionary" assignment in relation to the overall framing of power and privilege in language so accurately underscores the relationship of language to power. Foucault (1972) says that the set of factors that directly generate the discursive field take place at the preconceptual level, at a level that is barely recognizable, even subconscious. One social consequence of this discursive field is the establishment of a hierarchy of humankind where racial classification—the ordering of human groups on the basis of inherited or environmental differences—implies that certain races are superior to others (Goldberg, 1993). Postcolonial education necessitates teaching practice that dismantles and works to break down preconceptions in established discursive fields, broadening notions of what counts and doesn't count as valid and important to school curriculum and inquiry.

Being put in the position to speak for my race or explain culture in the U.S. has made me rethink where I fit in—moving within stereotypes of "mainstream" America, moving away from being defined by them. I have come to better understand my own culture through the lens of the cultures where I have lived or traveled and have deepened my understandings through reading and researching topics (Greene, 1973) of race and other social factors. As a teacher educator, I try to create shifts in perspective through course readings, media, and activities geared toward evoking transformative experiences, shifts that uncover culturally nuanced values and expectations that inform teaching—in a sense, a hidden cultural curriculum that can disadvantage students who are not members. Even as I work toward deconstructing dominant cultural assumptions in my classes, I catch myself making assumptions about my students, colleagues, friends, family, and the various people I encounter throughout my day. This process of deconstruction is slippery; it takes constant vigilance.

Rick: As a new teacher, my intentions were good. I knew that I didn't want to teach in the same ways I had been taught—committing little acts of emotional violence against my students—but I had to learn about trying to teach in noncolonial ways through a process of trial and error (and the errors involve lives). Engaging in trial and error, I often fell back on my old ways of knowing language, subject matter, and forms of assessment. My perception of my students' conceptual worlds was normative and often seen as a point of departure in teaching, not arrival. It is easy to fall into the trap of thinking that we are operating in our classes within a "culturally neutral" model. But of course we are not. Attempting to create a respectful classroom space in a vacuum is both an act of cultural genocide and a subtle guarantee of the dominant narrative since it is not critiqued and remains hidden. The dominant culture can become so normative that it is difficult to even see it, making the process of deconstruction nearly impossible.

CONCLUSION: A DIALOGIC, CRITICAL VIEW OF THE CONSTRUCTION OF A COLONIZING CURRICULUM

Tonda: In the writing of this paper, I have come to recognize how racial, cultural, and linguistic hierarchies have woven through all of my formative conceptualizations of self and my views of the world and that even as I have constructed this way of ordering life, I work to deconstruct the categories and systems that are, by default, ingrained in my approach to teaching, curricula, and scholarly writing. How does such ordering play out in the everyday? How can I make the insidiousness of such constructs more apparent in my teaching? How can I use language that works to dismantle the "us vs. them" model that is reinforced throughout the political arena, in multicultural policies, in "English only" initiatives, and in classroom texts, the media, newspapers, and advertising? This act of deconstruction is a constant thought process, a filter that needs to reorder what has previously been unjustly ordered. It is seemingly a necessary response to dismantling hierarchies that limit access and opportunity.

Multicultural education has attempted to address issues of cultural difference in schools and classrooms; however, these approaches have varied greatly over the past decade, highlighting the need for critical strategies and alternative methodologies to evolve beyond content alterations and slight changes in pedagogy to include teacher reflection and critique, examinations of identity in curriculum, and representation of diverse ways of knowing within classrooms.

Rick: Writing this chapter proved a more complex and dangerous process than I had initially expected. In the first draft,

I presented a cover story (Connelly and Clandinin, 1990) of my life. It was hard for me specifically to problematize the initial period of my life in Germany. I wished to present it through the slogans of freedom, patriotism, and capitalism. While resisting the dominant narrative, I presented it. I liked telling the story and got caught up in it. As a young child, I lived a life with happiness, anxiety, and promise. The clichés and slogans decorating the backdrop to my life were not my life. Tonda's more analytical narrative helped me to recognize that these slogans were less important to me in the past than in the present. As could be seen from my narrative, at times they began to frame my life.

To teach language arts in a way that engages and captivates our students, we must create spaces within our classrooms and our lessons to allow our students to expose and explore their cultural identities. The way we structure the interplay of educational form, content, and academic language, as well as the way that we allow students ownership of the curriculum, will all influence how our students learn in the classroom. Without, and often even with, examining ourselves deeply and critiquing our own beliefs in relation to our educational histories, we can easily create classroom spaces with conflicting cultural meanings. However, by attempting to deconstruct and then reimagine our own educational histories, we can begin to construct new learning spaces for our students that can clarify, rather than confuse, our students' learning experiences.

REFERENCES

Apple, M. W. (1979). *Ideology and curriculum.* New York: Routledge.

Brettschneider, M. (2001). *Democratic theorizing from the margins.* Philadelphia: Temple University Press.

Christensen, L. (2009). Teaching for joy and justice: *Re-imagining the language arts classroom.* Milwaukee: Rethinking Schools.

Connelly, M., and Clandinin, J. (1990). Stories of experience and narrative inquiry. *Educational Researcher, 19*(5), 2–14.

Delpit, L. (1995). *Other people's children: Cultural conflict in the classroom.* New York: The New Press.

Flinders, J. D., Noddings, N., and Thornton, J. S. (1986). The null curriculum: Its theoretical basis and practical implications. *Curriculum Inquiry, 16*(1), 33–42.

Foucault, M. (1972). *The archeology of knowledge* (A. M. Sheridan-Smith, trans). London: Tavistock.

Goldberg, D. (1993). *Racist culture: Philosophy and the politics of meaning.* Oxford, UK: Blackwell.

Greene, M. (1973). *Teacher as stranger: Educational philosophy for the coming age.* Belmont, CA: Wadsworth.

Gutmann, A. (1999). *Democratic education*. Princeton, NJ: Princeton University Press.

Henderson, J. G., and Kesson, K. R. (Eds.). (1999). *Understanding democratic curriculum leadership*. New York: Teachers College Press.

Hendley, S. (2000). *From communicative action to the face of the other: Levinas and Habermas on language, obligation, and community*. Lanham, MD: Lexington Books.

Hinkel, E. (Ed.). (1999). *Culture in second language teaching and learning*. New York: Cambridge University Press.

Kailin, J. (2002). *Antiracist education*. Lanham, MD: Rowman & Littlefield.

Kesselman, A., McNair, D., Schniedewind, N. (2003). *Women, images, and reality: A multicultural anthology* (3ʳᵈ ed.). Boston: McGraw-Hill.

Krysan, M., and Lewis, A. (Eds.). (2008). *The changing terrain of race and ethnicity*. New York: Russell Sage Foundation.

Ladson-Billings, G. (2001). *Crossing over to Canaan: The journey of new teachers in diverse classrooms*. San Francisco: Jossey-Bass.

Liggett, T. (2009). Unpacking white racial identity in English language teacher education. In R. Kubota and A. Lin (Eds.), *Race, culture, and identities in second language education* (pp. 27–43). Mahwah, NJ: Lawrence Erlbaum Associates.

Lortie, D. C. (1976). The balance of control and autonomy in elementary school teaching. In A. Etzioni (Ed.), *The semi-professions and their organization* (pp. 1–53). New York: Free Press.

Morrison, T. (1992). *Playing in the dark: Whiteness and the literary imagination*. New York: Vintage Books.

Narayan, U. (1997). *Dislocating cultures*. New York: Routledge.

Natriello, G., and Zumwalt, K. (1994). Challenges to an alternative route for teacher education. In A. Lieberman (Ed.), *The changing context of teaching: Ninety-first yearbook of the National Society for the Study of Education* (pp. 59–78). Chicago: University of Chicago Press.

Nelson, C. (2006). Queer inquiry in language education. *Journal of Language, Identity, and Education, 5,* 1–9.

Norris, J., and Sawyer, R. D. (2004, January). *Hidden and null curriculums of sexual orientation: A dialogue on the curreres of the absent presence and the present absence*. Paper presented at the Fourth Annual Curriculum & Pedagogy Conference, Decatur, GA.

Rothenberg, P. (Ed.). (2002). *White privilege: Essential readings on the other side of racism*. New York: Worth.

Skeggs, B. (2008). The problem with identity. In A.M.Y. Lin (Ed.), *Problematizing identity: Everyday struggles in language, culture, and education* (pp. 11–34). New York: Lawrence Erlbaum Associates.

Sleeter, C. (1996). *Multicultural education as social activism*. Albany: SUNY Press.

CHAPTER 4

Responding to Our Muses:
A Duoethnography on Becoming Writers

Joe Norris and Jim Greenlaw

PROLOGUE

Although we have discussed in this book the tenets of duoethnography as individual components, in practice the tenets work together. Duoethnographers combine and find synergy among the tenets as they engage in storytelling about their currere. The concept of currere, which calls for a temporal and conceptual analysis and synthesis of one's curriculum of experience, provides a framework for inquirers' construction of deeply meaningful polyvocal texts. These texts promote the exposure and reconceptualization of perceptions of experience.

Joe Norris and Jim Greenlaw playfully examine contexts of their becoming writers within an exploration of their currere. They study their currere as if through a kaleidoscope, juxtaposing and creating complex reflections between different images and time periods. Using these juxtapositions as the basis for discussion, they become the form and content of their emergent dialogic texts. Although they have clearly organized their discussion in their chapter, it is important to note that their discussion emerged from a recursive and cyclical process. For example, although they begin their written presentation of their study by giving research questions, in actuality, they surfaced these questions within their dialogue, shaping them as emergent guidelines for their recursive storytelling.

Their dialogue creates a dialectic that promotes analytical self-perspective. In this chapter, they spiral through specific themes, presenting them initially as individual stories. An example of how this process generated layered stories may be found in the passage on the role of audience as they learn to write: Norris and Greenlaw first tell their own stories of audience in learning to write and then juxtapose and intertwine these stories. They raise and respond to each other's questions about their stories and discuss insights based on these questions and juxtapositions. And they weave theory (or a theoretical lens) (e.g., Scholes' 1985 notion of "textual power") through their narratives. Throughout, there is an explicit articulation of borders, gray zones, and overlaps among the stories. These layered narratives create the dialogic tension with the piece and form the basis for a restorying process—a goal of duoethnography. They present this complex process playfully, creating an integrated text (intertwining process and product) in a seemingly spontaneous way.

In their stories, Norris and Greenlaw present and discuss a range of cultural artifacts—journal writings, poems, early prose, pictures of actual writing notebooks, images of early written pages—through which they show how they both conceptualize and reconceptualize their perceptions of their writing currere. They lay this process out so the reader can see the changes happening as they emerge. This "rich data" allow readers and audience members to transact with their text and create a new text. To add a layer of analysis, they present a table that shows which themes of reconceptualization have emerged within the study. By making their thinking process explicit (showing their changes in perspective), Norris and Greenlaw promote a sense of "rigor" within their study.

—Richard D. Sawyer

Jim: What drives us to write?

Joe: Where do we find our sources of inspiration?

Jim: What makes us want to record our inner thoughts for ourselves and for others?

Joe: What impact did the school system have on our ability to write and our attitudes towards writing?

Jim: What role did our informal writing play on our interest in writing?

Joe: Do different people answer such questions differently?

Jim: By addressing these questions through an exploration and interrogation of our writing histories, we may enable ourselves and other teachers to understand how their students approach writing . . .

Joe: . . . and provide possibilities of how they may structure their writing assignments to build upon varying students' needs and talents.

Jim: Due to its dialogic nature in examining life histories, we decided to use duoethnography (Norris, 2008a; Norris and Sawyer, 2004; Sawyer and Norris, 2009) to address these questions.

Joe: In 2003 Rick Sawyer and I began to discuss our diverse histories of sexual orientation. As the conversation unfolded, I found similarities between our conversation and Bill Pinar's (1975) concept of *currere* (i.e., the curriculum of the lived experience) and suggested that we turn our discussion into a paper. Our chronological stories converged and diverged, producing multiple perspectives of how attitudes about sexual orientation are learned.

Jim: The approach that Rick and you took brought together two stories that were quite different in style and content. Rather than striving for homogeneity of voice, the duoethnographic methodology juxtaposes stories in such a manner as to resist falling into the metanarrative that an autoethnography often produces. It is appropriate that we use this design to explore the intertextuality of our curreres as developing creative writers given our shared belief that writers have many learning styles (Myers and McCaulley, 1985) and multiple intelligences (Gardner, 1996). We need to recognize that research "cannot be construed as monological, as the authoritative statement about, or interpretation of, an abstracted, textualized reality. The language of ethnography is shot through with other subjectivities and specific contextual overtones" (Clifford, 1988, p. 42), so we have chosen duoethnography as our research methodology to enable us to tease out our parallel and diverging contexts and experiences as lifelong learners of the writing process.

Joe: As Richardson claims, "Whenever we write science, we are telling some kind of story, or some part of a larger narrative" (1990, p. 13). Researchers influence their studies by the media that they choose and the styles that they employ.

Jim: And as Clifford might argue concerning the relationship between the researcher and his or her research participants, "mutual construction must be at work in any ethnographic encounter, [even though] participants tend to assume that they have simply acquiesced to the reality of their counterpart" (1988, p. 43). Traditional ethnographic authority is difficult, if not impossible, to achieve because the researcher is attempting to work across cultures while at the same time striving to maintain objectivity. In duoethnography, the researchers are also the research participants. They are both the investigators and the subjects under investigation. Thus, by conducting this duoethnography, we are aware that we have chosen to use a necessarily subjective or, I should say, intersubjective research approach.

Joe: While we cannot achieve nor do we wish to claim objectivity, we have been rigorous. We now (2010) find ourselves rewriting this piece after a series of conference presentations (beginning in 2005), a number of revisions, and one journal submission that reviewers liked but rejected because they found it inappropriate for their readership. While the initial substance remains intact, through revisiting it over a number of years, we have brought an analytical rigor to our stories and added new narratives that emerged only after our familiar stories had been articulated.

Jim: Our dialogue about our emergence as writers differs from, say, the collection of letters written between Fitzgerald and Hemingway (Donaldson, 1999). Like us, they were friends, but they were also in competition with each other. Their epistolary dialogue, which took place over several years, was written for the benefit of themselves as writers. In contrast to their dialogue, our conversation is intended to reveal the insights that we have each gained about the inspirations for our writing processes so that we can share these revelations with our fellow educators. As Barone (1990) claimed, narratives should assist readers to (con)spire, or breathe with, the text. So we hope that our readers will find a resonance with our narrative conversations in order that they, too, can experience some of the same magic of the writing process that we have enjoyed discussing with each other. So, tell me, Joe, when did you first discover the mysterious pleasure of being a writer?

Joe: I would say that I wrote my first authentic piece of writing in Grade 7. I use the term *authentic* in a political sense in that the root of *authorship*, *authority*, and *authentic* means s/he who brings about (Klein, 1966). Up until that time, I felt that writing was always done for others. There was one moment in Grade 2 that I recall which gave a hint of the importance of the personal in writing, but for the most part, when I wrote, I wrote because people "told" me to.

Grade 7 was slightly different as there was a bit of "play" in the assignment. Yes, the writing was assigned, and, yes, the topic was predetermined, but within the topic, there was latitude in which I could enter my own writing. "The adventures of a dime" and "What I would do with $1000.00" were two of the topics that I remember writing on. I enjoyed them, and the words flew from an unknown place deep within me.

That summer I read two of my "compositions" at a public speaking contest and won. I was appointed the "Prime Minister" of all Halifax city playgrounds, and I actually read my speech to Robert Stanfield, the premier of Nova Scotia (see Figure 4.1). This experience, which gave me a glimpse of the power of words, was short lived. I enjoyed writing an advertisement and recording it on a tape recorder in Grade 8, but, for the most part, throughout junior and senior high school I wrote for others. There was no passion, no muse to evoke my words from another place.

Near the end Grade 12, I did find another opportunity, again through a public speaking contest. I turned a Grade 11 paper that I wrote, entitled "Canada, the Steps to Confederation via Revolution" into a speech called, "The Right of Change" and read it to a large high school audience (Figure 4.2). I was first runner-up.

Jim: It seems that your writing experiences during junior and senior high school years had some sense of audience. So did my own early writings. Joe, as I comment on what you are writing (or saying, because we are discussing this jointly over a keyboard), I am reminded of

Prime Minister Norris delivers his speech in the Red Chamber. (Halifax Photo Service, Ferris)

Premier Stanfield Meets The 'P.M.'

Premier Stanfield met the "prime minister" yesterday — Joseph Norris, 13, of 2692 Gladstone Street, Halifax.

They chatted for five minutes in the province's Red Chamber, and Joseph, smartly dressed in a sports jacket, explained some of his political theories to Mr. Stanfield.

Joseph, recently elected "prime minister" of the city's 12 playgrounds put forward a three point program for the consideration of the premier.

Figure 4.1   Joe wins public speaking contest.

Scholes' (1985) notion of "textual power." As he points out, we comprehend the writing of others by reading "upon," "within," and "against" their texts. At times your words help to evoke in me recollections of parallel experiences that I have had in own my childhood. In the above example, therefore, I am then reading "upon" your text. Later in this chapter, as I become caught up in your stories, I am reading within your text, and I completely lose track of my own stories for the moment. Finally, at times when your experiences are different from mine, I challenge both your and my narratives and am therefore reading "against" the text. This is what I find exciting about duoethnography because it is a transaction that leads to personal transformation.

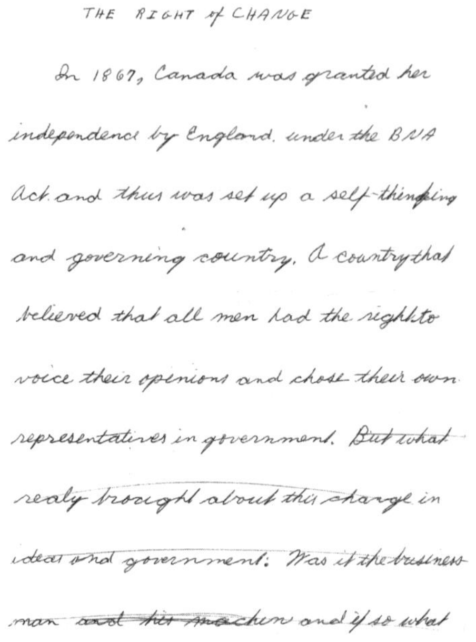

THE RIGHT of CHANGE

In 1867, Canada was granted her
independence by England. under the BNA
Act. and thus was set up a self-thinking
and governing country. A country that
believed that all men had the right to
voice their opinions and chose their own
representatives in government. But what
realy brought about this change in
ideas and government. Was it the business
man ~~and his machen~~ and if so what

Figure 4.2   Text of another of Joe's public speaking contests.

Joe: Ironically, by reading "against" my text, you are working "for" and "with" me. Such is the power of collaborative writing.

Later, in my master's program, I began to understand that part of my writing was based upon my learning style. I am an "extravert" (Myers and McCaulley, 1985) and think best with my mouth open. A sense of audience provided me with a communal context, and it was to that context that I wrote. As an extravert, I found being alone and private to be painful. My sense of audience eased that pain, enabling me to relax and my muse to speak.

Jim: It's interesting, Joe, that you needed an audience and you needed to feel comfortable in order for your muse to speak to you when you were an emerging writer.

Joe: Actually, Jim, I think my muse spoke "through" me rather than "to" me. Was your experience similar or different from mine?

Jim: I think my experience with writing emerged not from the need to write but from my response to the writing of others. I was an avid reader when I was a boy. I did not consider myself to be a writer until I reached my early teens. I suppose you could say that my favorite authors at that time, such as Ray Bradbury and Charles Dickens, were my muses; I wanted to be able to write like them. So they spoke "to" me rather than "through" me. However, I think that my grandfather had an even more important influence on my writing when I was in my early teens than did these writers. He spoke both to me and through me. Pappy would sit beside me watching his smoke rings float up the chimney of his fireplace as he told me many wonderful tales about his life as a carpenter in Ireland. I eventually wrote some of these stories down for him in a book that we called *Memoirs of an Irish Rogue*. He was a vivid storyteller, and I was inspired by him to craft my own writing so that it would move people in the same way that his words moved me. I had a brand new small cassette tape recorder, and I was fascinated as I recorded Pappy's answers to my questions about doing carpentry work on the *Titanic* in the Belfast shipyards.

Joe: Sounds like your early roots of being a qualitative researcher.

Jim: Yes, I guess so. Like you, Joe, I wrote speeches in junior high school. At the beginning of Grade 8, I wrote a speech to persuade my fellow students to vote me in as the president of the students' council. As I wrote the speech, I imagined what it would be like to grab the audience's attention with some outrageous campaign promises, and it made me feel excited to think that they would be interested in what I had to say. The contest was a stimulant for my creativity. It was my muse. I wanted to make my audience laugh. I wanted to persuade them. I wanted them to see me as a leader. And I believe that they, in turn, wanted to laugh, to be persuaded, and to have a leader. I won the race and became president of the students' council, and I have loved the risks involved in writing ever since. The element of risk stimulates my muse. Although I did not realize it at the time, the pleasure that I derived from writing Pappy's memoirs and those speeches probably fueled my desire to write other pieces throughout my life. So I believe that during these early experiences when my muse spoke to me, it was telling me to enjoy the contest of writing and to enjoy moving others with my words.

Joe: Unlike you, Jim, I had no early exemplars. Reading was not high on my list, and most of the stories that I was told came from the television. I did not learn how to use words to evoke inner visualizations and auditory experiences. Television left little to the imagination. It wasn't until my first year of university that my muse came to me.

I had stayed up late one night and found the three-hour wait between my two classes a long one. After lunch, I made way to the student lounge (also known as the "purple passion pit") to have a nap. I settled in and found myself waking from a deep sleep around 4:00 PM.

Jim: "We are such stuff as dreams are made on and our little life is rounded in a sleep" (Shakespeare, 1972, p. 1563). Sorry, Shakespeare is one of my muses.

Joe: It was a peaceful, euphoric awakening, and while a fleeting panic of missing my English class crept in, the feeling remained. I felt a magical power of freedom and imagined that I could leave the fourth floor through the concrete block walls and drift off into space. While I sniffed the room for smells of secondhand substance-banned smoke, I knew that the state of euphoria came from deep inside. Eventually the guilt of missing my English class returned, and I abated it by writing my first muse-evoked poem.

> We (meaning the community of me) is a prisoner.
> A Prisoner within itself,
> Of its movements, time and god:
>
> The thought in me, it wants to be free,
> To soar, experience and know.
> But I so weak cannot travel there
> To what the latter was like and the future will go . . .

I passed the complete poem in with my verbal excuse, and I received positive feedback. But it wasn't the external reinforcement that drove me to write again but the thrill of that euphoric state . . .

Jim: Like one's first kiss . . . the challenge of pulling words magically out of my head and the results they produced. It was *that* day that I learned to write. I learned to write for me, and others, simultaneously. Although term papers came and went, the writing experiences that I longed for were those that came from this inner state. Again like you, Joe, I, too, found that poems came to me when I was passing from sleep into wakefulness. I remember, for instance, waking from a nightmare one night when I was seventeen and being too petrified to move. When I eventually settled down, I went to my desk, and the dream spilled out on the page without any effort on my part. Several times throughout my life since then poems have come to me, apparently out of thin air. As I look back on those experiences when the writing was relatively effortless, I realize that books that I was reading at the time or encounters with people and places had often stimulated me subconsciously. In the case of my nightmare poem, I had been reading Edgar Alan Poe's "Fall of the House of Usher" (1962) in bed just before I went to sleep, and I suspect that this tale frightened me more profoundly than I realized at the time.

The nightmare poem came to me when I was in Grade 11. I was fortunate that year to have a very good English teacher named Doug Frame. Until then, I had not connected my love of reading with school, but in Grade 11 my private interest in writing and my school life suddenly and irrevocably came together thanks to the kindness and skill of this English teacher. Mr. Frame had been teaching us to read a series of poems and to write personal responses to them, but he had removed the title and author's name for each professionally written poem. Years later, I realized that his methodology was influenced by I. A. Richards' (1929) practical criticism and Louise Rosenblatt's (1968) reader response approach to teaching poetry.

Because I was interested in some of the poetic devices that we were encountering in the poems, I wrote a poem of my own and decided to show it to Mr. Frame, who treated my work with respect. He asked me if he could remove the title and my name and have the class respond to it. I was thrilled to have the students analyze the poem as if a seasoned poet had written it, and I was surprised to see the variety of interpretations that emerged from their readings. After that, I was hooked. I wrote poems for the school magazine, for the yearbook, and for anyone else who was willing to listen to what I had to say. I took my craft seriously and appreciated the chance it gave me to express my feelings.

Joe: It was an inner state that hooked me, and throughout my undergraduate years I searched for and found it. I wrote unrequited love songs that may have been therapeutic. I also wrote a poem about an argument that I had with my father that was more than therapeutic. I presented it to him as a form of an apology. He accepted it and seemed to understand the gesture, if not the poem. I also had the thrill of writing poems on napkins at parties for those who requested them. I was the poet laureate at a particular group of get-togethers. The following is the only such poem that I kept.

R O A D S
HIGHWAY, BY WAY, SKY WAY, NO "MY WAY"
L O V E
MY WAY, YOUR WAY, THEIR WAY, NO "OUR WAY"
T R U T H
THEIR WAY, MY WAY, YOUR WAY, NO "GOD'S WAY"
HAPPINESS
LOVING ROADS FULL OF TRUTH
CONFUSION
EVERYONE'S WAY

LONELINESS
FOR YOU . . . YOUR WAY
FOR ME . . . MY WAY
FOR THEM . . . THEIR WAY
FOR US . . . NO WAY

I had found the pleasure of writing, and while I had not taken the next step to submit any for publication, I took pride in the fact that a few people placed some value on my playful voice. Writing was becoming a part of everyday living.

During that time, I would also recount the dreams that I had to a few close friends. They were amazed at their complex story lines and well developed characters. I can remember one friend stating that I was writing screenplays in my head. Unknowingly, I was becoming a storyteller.

Jim: And a playwright.

Joe: Upon conducting this 2010 rewrite, I recall another series of past writing experiences that are relevant but only now recalled due to a recent one. It could be said that since 1970 I compiled digital stories. A group of friends and I would take popular songs, go through collections of slides, sequence them to the music, and compile performance pieces for social, church, and educational events. We always received rave reviews, and the use of music and image evoked many deep responses from our audiences. This dated back even before music videos. I wrote with sound and image to the music of Carlos Santana and Neil Diamond. At the recent Visual Culture of the Americas Workshop (Norris and Mirror Theatre, 2010), I compiled a series of slides on the Niagara region and presented it with music. My daughter works with digital stories, and as a result, I have recently recognized this as a legitimate form of writing. While informal at the time, throughout my undergraduate years I did write with image and sound.

Jim: In 1977, I encouraged my students to set slides to music, as well, in my drama classes, not realizing that this activity would become a popular pastime thirty years later. I remember one student showing slides of the Holy Land set to the music of the movie *Exodus*.

Joe: We were waaaaaaaaaay before our time, Jim! I did the same thing with my junior high English classes. We taught them how to write using different "multiple intelligences" before the term was invented.

Jim: But while I have written some film and website reviews, most of my creative and scholarly writing has been focused on printed texts rather than visual images. As an undergraduate student of English and philosophy, I often digressed from my required course work to enjoy reading books and to write poems on the side. On one occasion, I had been studying the work of Alexander Pope in an eighteenth-century literature course, so I decided to write a 100-line satire on education. (This was another example of a poem coming to me in a dream. I woke up at 2:00 in the morning and finished it by dawn.) In it, I complained about how we spend all of our time in university English classes sharpening our critical faculties instead of learning how to write poems ourselves. After that, I entered a phase of writing poems in imitation of the works of writers I admired. I learned a great deal more about the workings of poems by studying them in a writerly way than I had ever learned before by simply reading poems as if I were a literary critic. I also came to enjoy the reading of poetry much more than before because I could appreciate more fully the great skill and craft of the writers, having struggled myself with various forms and techniques in my own poems. My muses at this stage in my life were other poets. I was interested not only in the forms of their writing but also in the way their poetry sprang from their lives.

Joe: Increasingly my muses sprang from my dreams. In the wee hours of the morning, I would suddenly awake to find a complete story in my head based upon the dream that had just occurred. I wasn't as concerned with the mechanics of my words as I was with recording the adventure for future use. Sometimes I would outline the dream; sometimes I would record character lines and short descriptions. I wrote so that I would remember. They were stories to come back to. In my twenties, I would jot down notes in a small black book that I still have (Figure 4.3), but by my mid-thirties, the computer became my template.

As an aside, I cannot overestimate the power of the computer on my writing. My handwriting is poor, and I was often criticized at school over my penmanship. In the era of the typewriter, I made too many mistakes as my typing could not keep up with my thoughts. Word processing has enabled me to get my thoughts out for a later edit. I am convinced that I would never have obtained a master's degree, let alone a doctorate, had it not been for the computer.

To date, I have a *Star Trek* episode, a postmodern screenplay on point of view, a short story on camping, and a few poems, to list some creations that were inspired by my dreams. But the discipline of follow through had not caught up with my muse as I moved on to something else before I polished my work. I have returned to certain pieces over the years, and one story was written down approximately twenty years after the dream. Such was the power of the one about camping conflicts called, "Intense, in Tents."

Figure 4.3   Joe's writer's notebook.

Editing, for me, is a painful process. It lacks the excitement of emerging ideas, and while I know that this impedes my public voice, I find that writing for self is often all that I require. My academic papers sap all of that type of energy, leaving my creative writing wanting.

Jim: As a teacher, Joe, I have marked and edited many thousands of pages of student writing, and while I enjoy reading their work, the effort that it takes to work through thousands of pages of student writing each year has certainly sapped my creative energies, too. However, I find that when I edit my own work, I do not seem to resent the time that I spend as I like to see the improvements that result.

Joe: Actually, Jim, since our first draft of this, I have come to enjoy editing more. I have my first solo book published (Norris, 2009a), and I relish the craft of phrasing. So editing now is far less painful. I also appreciate that we were able to meet in person once again to bring this chapter to fruition. The immediacy of response feeds my muse.

Jim: I became a high school English and drama teacher in 1976, and I also found that I enjoyed the opportunity of working alongside students as they wrote their own poems, plays, and novels. As an early advocate of the writers' workshop approach, I realized that most adolescents enjoyed working with their peers on writing tasks and that the writing process need not always be a solitary one. In 1980, several students in my school's writers' club decided that they wanted to write a group novel together. They came up with the title, *I Was a Teenage Witch*. I wrote the first chapter of the book to get them started, and then each student in turn contributed a chapter to the book. In the end, we sold all 100 copies of the book in the school cafeteria (see Figure 4.4). From that day to this, I have derived great pleasure from encouraging students to express themselves and to have fun with creative writing, and I have written along with them to model the writers' workshop approach. In this case, the members of the writers' club served as muses for each other. We fed off of each other's ideas and enthusiasm.

Joe: I have also found that my muse is often active when I work with others. One of my areas of expertise is the collective creation, a theatrical genre in which a group of actors collaboratively write plays. Over the years, I have directed over thirty shows, touring them and performing them as keynotes at conferences. My extroverted side is

Figure 4.4   Cover of Jim's students' coauthored text.

stimulated and gives me the energy to privately record and edit the scripts that the cast members improvised (Norris, 2009b). Michael Ondaatje, author of *The English Patient* (1992), began his writing career with collective creations.

When we think of writing, we usually think of it as a private activity. Research with the Myers-Briggs type indicator (Myers and McCaulley, 1985) claims that seventy-five percent of our population is extroverted, that they learn best with their mouths open. In my work in playbuilding, I find that my ideas are stimulated by the thoughts of others and vice versa.

The genuine need to communicate with another is one key to my muse's door; another is the co-creation of anything with another. In a real sense, Jim, you are my muse for this piece. From a psychoanalytical perspective, perhaps duoethnography, for me, is a kind of talk therapy that may be more based upon my need to commune than any deep epistemological concept. That is, unless we believe that all epistemology is psychologically rooted.

Jim: And just as our dialogue together has brought to my mind many episodes in my life as a developing writer, Joe, the opportunity to look at pictures from my past has opened up an internal dialogue in which my younger selves have reminded me of the pleasures I derive from creative writing. So we are communing not only with each other in this process but with the theater of selves that we carry within.

Joe: And not only do we commune but we rewrite our past and present selves in this dialogic process.

Jim: Said (1978, 1993) describes the juxtaposing of texts as "contrapuntal reading," and it seems to me that in this duoethnography we have been conducting a contrapuntal reading of both our writing processes and our products.

Joe: So, for a seventh inning stretch, let's recap our insights thus far, itemizing our writing similarities and differences through the following.

Jim: In 1985, when I first moved to China to teach writing at a university in Changsha, I wrote many letters to my friends and extended family. I wrote journals about the people, places, and experiences that fascinated me. The following passage, for instance, is a brief excerpt from my journal about my visit to Lhasa in July 1986.

I was awakened at sunrise this morning by the sound of ceremonial horns. Outside the windows of my hostel, a rooster crows, cows moo, and dogs bark. A monk can be heard repeating a chant as he walks past in the street below. As I look down through my window into the red ornate interior of a Tibetan apartment, a woman throws a basin of water out her window to splash on the cobblestones.

Table 4.1 Juxtaposition of Experience

Joe	Jim
Wrote at the request of others Extrinsic motivation	Wrote because the stories of others beckoned him Intrinsic motivation
Found writing painful	Found pleasure in writing
Evoked by dreams	Evoked by dreams
Wrote for an audience Wrote for self Wrote for needs of others	Wrote for an audience Wrote for self Wrote from exemplars
Articulation of ideas, not polish	Enjoyed the craft of writing
Inspired by television	Inspired by books

The sound of the horns must have come from the Jokhang Temple that I visited yesterday afternoon. I was there during a ceremony that had the building overflowing with visitors. As I approached the temple, I could see the spires and dragons' heads ornamenting the golden tiled roof. In front of the entrance were two forty-foot poles covered in brightly colored papers with handwritten prayers on them. Between these poles was a large vase-shaped furnace in which herbs were burning that provided a mystical fragrance. A woman was sitting on the ground at the base of the furnace chanting prayers and working a string of beads through her fingers as the smoke wafted past her wrinkled face.

As I entered the inner courtyard of the temple, the dazzling Himalayan sunshine revealed hundreds of pilgrims gathered before a statue of Buddha. The ceremony had not yet begun, so I followed others and circumnavigated the inside of the temple in a clockwise direction. Many hundreds of candles and yards of red silk lined the passageway. On the walls were painted hundreds of images of Buddha that had been gazing down upon the devoted pilgrims for the past 1,400 years. Long rows of golden upright cylinders were kept spinning by the pilgrims. These prayer wheels produced a pleasant purring sound. When I returned to the inner courtyard, monks dressed in red robes were ringing hand-held bells and chanting in unearthly deep voices in front of the main statue of Buddha. I stood entranced by the sound for a long time until some twelve-year-old monks broke the spell by asking me in perfect English if I could give them a picture of the Dalai Lama. Several other monks passed me and smiled in a curious way, but then one old monk with a wide powerful face stopped and stared at me with his head tilted on an angle. There was no doubt in my mind that his expression was scornful, as if he were looking at some clown. He seemed to me to be saying with this glance, "Why are you intruding upon our sacred place?" His gaze still haunts me this morning as I prepare to leave for Golmud.

The sights and sounds of places where I have lived and worked such as rural Canada and China have fired my imagination to write poems and journals over the years. And it is the work of travel writers such as Paul Theroux (1988) that has attracted me the most strongly as a reader. In short, the world and its inhabitants are my muses. I learn about the world and its people and cultures by living in and traveling through different places, and I am inspired to write by the images that these landscapes present to me in passing. Both the real and armchair varieties of traveling have shaken me out of my taken-for-granted assumptions about life, and in the resulting unsettled state, I feel the need to put pen to paper to interpret my experiences.

Joe: Like you, Jim, traveling is another state that beckons my muse and pushes me to the core of self. Like Maxine Greene's concept of "teacher as stranger" (Greene, 1973), I find that when I am out of my element, off guard, decentered, confused, or half awake after a dream, my senses are tuned to a different frequency. I call this space my "twilight zone." The clutter of everyday life disappears, and my creative energies are tapped. My muse ventures forth unabashed and takes over. I just sit back and enjoy the ride.

I have written pieces while in the air, traveling to and from destinations, and while on the ground in a hotel room, reflecting on the events of the day. As an extrovert I find myself alone when I travel and am compelled to have a conversation with someone,

Figure 4.5 Jim in Bhutan.

even if that someone is myself. Through my writing, I keep myself company.

Cooped up on a plane for hours forces this hyperactive person to displace his energies elsewhere. After a long dry spell in my writing, I found myself on a plane. Awakening from a short nap, I wrote this:

LOST AND (in)JOYing IT
sur(PRIZE)ingly (A)LIVE in a POST MODERN ERA

Slowlllllllllllllly
the "screws"   (you dirty rat)
which fastened the hinge   (me)
to the frame   (Goffman)
loosened.   (Trust/Risk)

To my sur(prize)   (not really)
I did not (plume)t to the earth
but floated
in space
along side of the frame.

Like an astronaut in space
I drifted
Watching (the) world, (my) world,
(Your) world
Float lost beside me.

Joe: In writing this paper, I now notice the parallel between this poem and the one I wrote in the "purple passion pit." They are similar in both evocation and content. After a sleep, I sometimes wake to a euphoric state with the feeling of freedom. This sense of freedom demands a response, and, in turn, I relax and let the words flow. I have had a few experiences that called, no, *demanded* that I write. While waiting to board a plane, I was attracted to a striking woman who I hoped beyond hope would sit next to me. She didn't, but I decided to have the conversation anyway. Here is the beginning.

The attraction was uncanny. Clearly there were at least thirty years separating us when I first noticed her at the airport, but the attraction was too strong to ignore. I knew somehow that we were destined to meet. And while a degree of uncertainty lingered, I was confident that she would be boarding the same flight as I and that the fates would give us some opportunity to interact. This was both my destiny and my calling.

She was my senior, and I chuckled that, as a middle-aged man, it would be she that would entice me. The cliché would have it that I be drawn to someone of a lesser age than I, but here was a woman with presence. A woman whose manner spoke of a life well lived. Perhaps it was . . .

There are times in my life that I find that the experience is too powerful to keep bottled up. When that happens, I have to write. This was one such time. The wonder and awe of people awakens my muse.

Jim: Over the past twenty-five years since I first taught in China, I have gone back there many times to lecture at various universities, to observe my Canadian student teachers teach in Chinese schools, and to write an English textbook series that is used in rural schools throughout the country (Greenlaw, 2004). Recently I tried to capture in a poem inspired by the Tang Dynasty poets how I feel about the changes that are taking place there.

Reflections on Weiming Lake

It's 8:00 AM,
and, in the streets
beyond the gates of Peking University,
car horns honk and tires squeal
as frantic citizens
cram onto crowded buses,
or dodge their way to work
on noisy motor scooters.

But in the relative tranquility
of the university's gardens,
where I sit on this breezy summer morning,
the modern metropolis of Beijing
seems to disappear.
Here I view the reflection of Boya Pagoda
as it glistens upon the jade green waters
of Weiming Lake.
At the water's edge
weeping willows dip their delicate leaves
beneath the surface
to slake their thirst.
Overhead dragon kites are flying,
while artists sketch a marble boat.

On a nearby path,
sequestered under shady pines,

and oblivious to the outside world,
retired scholars perform tai chi
in this timeless place.

Jim: In the world of educational publishing, I am often forced to deal with writing problems in a hurried and businesslike fashion when, instead, I want to enter into a dialogue with the words on the page and with the teachers and students who will eventually read the books that I write. Thus, the tone that I adopted in this poem was the result of my muse, in this case the world of the ancient Chinese scholars, telling me to step back from the noise and confusion of my everyday curriculum writing and to think for a minute about the higher calling of the writer.

Joe: Some of my poems were inspired not by places or the imagination per se but by ideas. I believe that traditional research is too restricted in form and thought. At an action research workshop that I attended, all participants were asked to write a few summary notes. This is part of the poem that I wrote which became my first juried publication.

> I look at my reflection in the mirror
> I smile
> The Reflection changes . . .
> . . . I frown
> And the Reflection changes.
> I begin to play in the mirror
> The mirror in me
> Me in the mirror . . .
> Norris (1993, p. 255)

Since then I have had other poems published (Norris, 2007, 2009a). But for the most part, my creative writing had not been published or submitted for publication until recently, after this duoethnography began. I have written a children's story to address epistemological territoriality, as I am convinced that epistemology is taught at an early age. My story was written to address it indirectly by demonstrating territoriality on a beach, with the sand of time acting as a metaphor. This story was read at a curriculum theory conference.

So if I were to summarize my writing experiences under one theme, it would be that of displacement. I find that I write best when I am off guard either by being half awake or in a foreign land. Perhaps my mind is too busy in the waking hours or while in familiar territory to allow my creative side to emerge. So I have become aware of the importance of the "twilight zone" or "half-sleep" of writing. For me, writing cannot be forced but must flow from an unknown place (Harman and Rheingold, 1984). The writing is recursive; as I write it, it writes me.

I have used this awareness in my teaching. While I recognize that not everyone has the same routes to lure the muse from the labyrinth of the subconscious to the printed page, the easel, a lump of clay, or an improvised drama, I know that putting my students to sleep is a pedagogical act. I use guided imagery and/or soft music to lull them into a state of relaxation, a state of disorientation where the busy-ness of rational thought melts away and the creative spirit is freed. This is the curriculum of writing to which I aspire.

Jim: If I were to summarize my writing experience, Joe, I would have to say that I have not had one muse but many different muses to inspire me in the various writing projects that I have attempted. Sometimes, my muses were real flesh-and-blood people. Occasionally, they were the places I visited or books that I read. Sometimes, they caused me to write work that surprised and impressed me. At other times, they encouraged me to reject a piece of my writing and to take a new direction. But, in the end, I believe that writing for me, like you, is a magical and mysterious affair. So when I teach my students to write, I know that I must be careful never to silence the muses that inspire them to write.

Jim: We can add these new themes to our juxtaposition table:

Joe: Both of us have found that travel displaces us, creating a sense of isolation and aloneness. Our pen/paper/keyboards became our travel companions, and we explicitly conversed with ourselves, recording our acts of meaning making. Courtney (1980) claims that we are all playwrights reliving and preliving scripted drama in our heads as we imagine what could have or might happen. Since we have no one to talk to, our writings become our imaginary friends.

Jim: And our surroundings. . . . When I am alone, the landscape, architecture, and people take on a greater significance. My senses

Table 4.2 Second Juxtaposition of Experiences

Joe	Jim
Displacement through travel as muse	Displacement through travel as muse
Importance of the twilight zone	Sacred places and encounters
Creative writing mostly private Three (academic) poems published Academic writing published	Read poems at conferences Academic writing published

become acute, undistracted by the presence of an other with whom I am obliged to converse. I experience wonder and awe and have to write it down.

Joe: I guess that is another dimension of what I call my "twilight zone." My mind is uncluttered by the minutiae of the day, and little things take on greater significance due to the intense focus. I believe that I write better in the morning before I am awake to the day. My inner world of thoughts and ideas takes precedence. As you said earlier, I "step back from the noise and confusion." Knowing that I am writing for myself also helps. While I tend to write to a particular audience, I also ignore them. Nachmanovitch (1990) claims that the fear of the judge can block creativity. My twilight zone keeps them in silhouette, on the other side of the stage lights.

Jim: But eventually we bring them to a public by reading our creative works at conferences and/or by submitting them for print.

Joe: Yes, Jim, but these I consider another form of writing. Based upon the above chart/conversation, would you regard your academic writing as muse inspired?

Jim: Some of my academic writing is literary critical, some of it is philosophical, and some of it is pedagogical (as in the case of the textbooks that I have written). In each of these types of writing, I have been inspired by my mentors (the professors who have taught me) or by the teachers and students who have used my textbooks. Writing involves communicating with colleagues and students. So, yes, I would have to say that my academic writing is inspired by many different muses, just as my creative writing has been inspired by traveling, reading writers of fiction, and remembering my grandfather. How about you, Joe?

Joe: I'd have to admit that I much better enjoy writing evocative metaphorical texts full of ambiguity and plenty of style. I still haven't warmed to the expository form that many academic circles expect, although I have published quite a bit. I also enjoy devising plays with students, colleagues, and members of the community. We discuss topics of interest and explore them through improvisation. Such work feeds my extraversion.

Over the past number of years, I have become an advocate for arts-based research (Norris and Buck, 2002) and pedagogy (Norris, 2008b) primarily because I don't believe that these two types of writings are as separate as they are made out to be. Saks (1996) asked, "Should Novels Count as Dissertations in Education?" I agree, and so did the University of British Columbia. Both Rishma Dunlop (1999, 2002) and Pauline Sameshima (2006, 2007) wrote their dissertations as novels and later had them published. As you said earlier, Jim, you better understood the mechanics of poetry by writing poems than by analyzing them, and through this conversation, it now becomes explicit that I preferred creative writing during my schooling to the hegemonic expository paragraph. While I do believe that there are distinctions to be made, it is more like a Venn diagram. We are moving into an era of hybridity. Duoethnography, at least, can contain a bit of both, so it addresses my extraverted style and the way I prefer to represent the world.

Since this study began, I have taken a creative writing course, attended workshops, joined a provincial writing organization, partaken in a writing group, entered writing contests, and submitted some works for publication. Through these, I have written new poems, revised old short stories, started two novels, and completed an assortment of other writings. These fed my inner being as I wrote completely for myself, albeit in the company of others. I am convinced that it has also assisted me in my expository writing. I now appreciate the value of drafts and the process of word craft. There has been transference.

Unfortunately, such writing has been put on the back burner. I have just finished one book that needed my writing energy focused elsewhere and have three new academic book contracts that will require a more expository style. I will return to these lost but not forgotten friends once these three projects reach fruition. Hmmm, "reach fruition." Before the creative writing sojourn, I probably would have said, "are finished." This duoethnographic endeavor has increased my sensitivity to the choice of word and styles of expression.

So, Jim, besides fostering our friendship, how has this research process changed you?

Jim: Until you invited me on this exploration of our parallel lives as developing writers, Joe, I had not given any thought to where I have found the inspiration for my writing. Watching you puzzle over your muses enabled me to identify mine more clearly. This process of shifting from parallel to dialogic self-discovery also caused me to think more deeply about the notion of "the muse" and to recognize the debt I owe to my teachers, my students, and my favorite authors as I have explored ideas in collaboration with them. This project that you and I have shared has helped me to see that just as I have served as your muse and you have served as mine, perhaps generally muses are beings with whom the writer exists in relationship. Coaxing and guiding each other on this pathway, Joe, I think that you and I have both understood more profoundly than before the power of sharing experiences with a fellow researcher.

Perhaps my way of defining duoethnography, then, is "to research common interests with a kindred spirit."

Since this study began, like you, I have had to put my creative writing on the back burner, in part because I have become rather busy as an administrator. Recently, the academic writing that I have been producing has been in the area of the philosophical foundations of e-learning. As the dean of a Faculty of Education that offers a master's in education and digital technology, I write these days about the uses of the Internet in teaching and learning, and I enjoy talking with my colleagues about the issues that they and their students are grappling with as they think about the nature of the classroom of the future.

When I invited you last spring to give a keynote address at my Arts and Technology: Creativity and the Millennial Student Conference, you captivated the participants' imaginations with a multimedia presentation that took them through your fascinating history of the relationship between technology and the arts. Not surprisingly, your muse for that talk was the television show *Star Trek*, and my muses for writing about the moral issues associated with digital pedagogy were the books of two cultural critics, Neil Postman (1995) and Pierre Levy (1999). And, yet, the direction and nature of our arguments about the arts and technology in education converged at that conference in many ways. I have to conclude that despite the differences in our various muses, you and I have grown closer together over the past five years in our thinking because of our ongoing dialogue about what we value in our work as writers and educators. Thanks, Joe, for inviting me to join you in this conversation and for reminding me that there are good reasons why we both love to write and to encourage others to write, too!

REFERENCES

Barone, T. E. (1990). Using the narrative text as an occasion for conspiracy. In E. W. Eisner and A. Peshkin (Eds.), *Qualitative inquiry in education* (pp. 305–326). New York: Teachers College Press.

Clifford, J. (1988). *The predicament of culture: Twentieth-century ethnography, literature, and art.* Cambridge, MA: Harvard University Press.

Courtney, R. (1980). *The dramatic curriculum.* New York: Drama Book Specialists.

Donaldson, S. (1999). *Hemingway vs. Fitzgerald: The rise and fall of a literary friendship.* Woodstock, NY: Overlook Press.

Dunlop, R. (1999). *Boundary bay: A novel.* Unpublished doctoral dissertation, University of British Columbia, Vancouver, BC.

Dunlop, R. (2002). A story of her own: Female bildungsroman as arts-based educational research. *Alberta Journal of Educational Research, 48*(3), 215–228.

Gardner, H. (1996). *Intelligence: Multiple perspectives.* Fort Worth, TX: Harcourt Brace.

Greene, M. (1973). *Teacher as stranger: Educational philosophy for the modern age.* Belmont, CA: Wadsworth.

Greenlaw, J. C. (2004). *Project English.* Beijing, China: Renai Education Research Institute.

Harman, W., and Rheingold, H. (1984). *Higher creativity.* Los Angeles: Jeremy P. Tarcher.

Klein, E. (1966). *A comprehensive etymological dictionary of the English language.* New York: Elsevier.

Levy, P. (1999). *Collective intelligence: Mankind's emerging world in cyberspace.* (R. Bononno, trans.). Cambridge, MA: Perseus Books. (Original work published in 1997.)

Myers, I. B., and McCaulley, M. (1985). *Manual: A guide to the development and use of the Myers-Briggs type indicator.* Palo Alto, CA: Consulting Psychologists Press.

Nachmanovitch, S. (1990). *Free play: The power of improvisation in life and the arts.* Los Angeles: Jeremy P. Tarcher, Inc.

Norris, J. (1993). Adulthood . . . lost: Childhood . . . found. *Educational Action Research, 1*(2), 255.

Norris, J. (2007). Dependence day. *Journal of Curriculum and Pedagogy, 4*(2), 6.

Norris, J. (2008a). Duoethnography. In L. M. Given (Ed.), *The SAGE encyclopedia of qualitative research methods* (pp. 233–236). Los Angeles: Sage.

Norris, J. (2008b). A quest for a theory and practice of authentic assessment: An arts-based approach. *LEARNing Landscapes, 1*(3), 211–233.

Norris, J. (2009a). On the phenomenology of truth. *Educational Insights, 13*(3). Retrieved from http://www.ccfi.educ.ubc.ca/publication/insights/v13n03/toc.html

Norris, J. (2009b). *Playbuilding as qualitative research: A participatory arts-based approach.* Walnut Creek, CA: Left Coast Press.

Norris, J., and Buck, G. (2002). Editorial. *Alberta Journal of Educational Research, 48*(3), 203–205.

Norris, J., and Mirror Theatre. (Director, coauthor, actor, and joker). (2010, April). *Traces.* Closing keynote performance at the Visual Culture of the Americas Workshop, St. Catharines, ON.

Norris, J., and Sawyer, R. (2004, October). *Null and hidden curricula of sexual orientation: A dialogue on the curreres of the absent presence and the present absence.* Paper presented at the Democratic Responses in an Era of Standardization Conference, Troy, NY.

Ondaatje, M. (1992). *The English patient.* New York: Knopf.

Pinar, W. (1975). Currere: Toward reconceptualization. In W. Pinar (Ed.), *Curriculum theorizing* (pp. 396–414). Berkeley, CA: McCutchan.

Poe, E. A. (1962). *Tales of mystery and imagination.* London: Oxford University Press.

Postman, N. (1995). *Technopoly: The surrender of culture to technology.* New York: Random House.

Richards, I. A. (1929). *Practical criticism.* New York: Harcourt Brace Jovanovich.

Richardson, L. (1990). *Writing strategies: Reaching diverse audiences.* Newbury Park, CA: Sage.

Rosenblatt, L. M. (1968). *Literature as exploration.* New York: Noble and Noble.

Said, F. (1978). *Orientalism.* New York: Random House.

Said, E. (1993). *Culture and imperialism.* New York: Alfred A. Knopf.

Saks, A. L. (1996). Viewpoints: Should novels count as dissertations in education? *Research in the Teaching of English, 30*(4), 403–427.

Sameshima, P. (2006). *Seeing red—A pedagogy of parallax: An epistolary bildungsroman on artful scholarly inquiry.* Unpublished doctoral dissertation, University of British Columbia, Vancouver, BC.

Sameshima, P. (2007). *Seeing red—A pedagogy of parallax: An epistolary bildungsroman on artful scholarly inquiry.* Amherst, NY: Cambria Press.

Sawyer, R., and Norris, J. (2009). Duoethnography: Articulations/(re)creation of meaning in the making. In W. Gershon (Ed.), *Working together in qualitative research: A turn towards the collaborative* (pp. 127–140). Rotterdam: Sense.

Scholes, R. (1985). *Textual power: Literary theory and the teaching of English*. New Haven, CT: Yale University Press.

Shakespeare, W. (1972). The tempest. In S. Barnet (Ed.), *The complete Signet classic Shakespeare*. New York: Harcourt, Brace, Jovanovich.

Theroux, P. (1988). *Riding the iron rooster: By train through China*. New York: Ivy Books.

CHAPTER 5

Seeking Rigor in the Search for Identity: A Trioethnography

Rick Breault, Raine Hackler, and Rebecca Bradley

PROLOGUE

Researcher trust is a central feature of a duoethnography. Trust promotes duoethnographers' sharing, disclosing, and interrogating personal aspects of their histories. But in duoethnography, researcher trust applies not only to their joint creation of a safe place for storytelling. It also applies to researchers' responsibility to facilitate each other's critical stance to deconstruct and reconceptualize their narrative perceptions. Duoethnographers working together thus enter into a relationship as critical friends, keeping the process critical and limiting their co-researchers' reification of their values, beliefs, and perspectives.

Rick Breault, Raine Hackler, and Rebecca Bradley illustrate this process of critical trust in their study of perceptions of the construction of teaching identity among male elementary teachers. Their study is noteworthy for how they explicitly examine and discuss the critical nature of their work together. Early in their work together, Breault notes that they are "engaging in a less than critical exploration," finding more commonalities than contrasts in their construction of their narratives. This process reinforced rather than expanded their initial perspectives. They then added methodological questions to their inquiry: "How can conversation partners avoid convergence—the mutual construction of a shared master narrative?" And, "How do we more transparently represent the insights gained as a result of a complex interplay of dialogue, introspection, reflection and consideration of the research literature" (p. 121). This simultaneous emphasis on the study of gender identity and method gave a particular focus to their use of reflection in their study, making it more explicit as a dedicated process in their work. This reflection led them to then ask Rebecca Bradley to join their study to add a contrasting perspective to their study.

Bradley entered the study as the third participant motivated to examine questions about issues of elementary male-teacher quality. Her own research question, then, acted as a counterpoint to that of Hackler and Breault. With Bradley's addition, they then renew their process of storytelling. Working together, they encounter an early dilemma between keeping their research process transparent by including considerable unedited transcripts of their conversations and keeping their study short, concise, and more thematically focused. They resolve this dilemma by placing the transcripts of all their conversations online. As part of this openness, they actually invite readers to discuss their conversations as part of their online "blog."

An additional step in their method was to organize their long conversations into more concise narratives. These narratives are followed by reflective summaries—in which they engaged in critical discussions of key themes from their narratives. They situate themselves in these summaries in terms of personal accountability and self-reflexivity. As they engage in these conversations, they discover that they focus changed from that of perceptions of gender construction in male elementary teachers to that of the role of personality traits to effective teaching.

Noteworthy is how they expose and clarify their thinking to the reader (and each other). For example, Bradley states in her reflective essay, "These personal changes [her views of male elementary teachers] will invariably affect my professional practice, as I will view others, especially males, through a new and expanded lens. This growth opens doors to new learning experiences that would not have been possible in the past" (p. 133). What appears to change in the course of this study is not necessarily her views of teachers per se (the teachers she described are probably still reading those newspapers) but rather her self-understanding about this topic. Breault in his reflective essay writes that this study has given him more questions than answers. These questions are about teacher identity construction and the relationship between authentic curriculum and the influence of testing and accountability on students. And in his reflective essay, Hackler makes potentially emancipatory connections between the world of a sensitive and intelligent childhood and ways that schools can become personally meaningful and respectful places for both students and teachers.

Their study is important in how it models unrelenting researcher trust, and even honesty, in research. This honesty led them down unexpected pathways in their work together. Given their generation of new questions as well as their study's implications for their practice, theirs is a living study that will continue to evolve.

—Richard D. Sawyer

EARLY EXPERIENCES AND FUTURE CHOICES

Since at least the early to mid-1800s, teaching has been predominantly a women's field (Perlmann and Margo, 2001). As such, it has an organizational culture characterized by the "absent presence" of gender (Sargent, 2001, p. 90), where many gender-based traits are implicit and all the more powerful for being taken for granted (Hansot and Tyack, 1988).

Moreover, many of the prerequisite characteristics and requirements are ones for which men are considered to be deficient (Jacobs, 1993; Reskin, 1991).

Anticipatory Socialization

These are not natural deficiencies but the result of a cumulative disadvantage of a lifelong series of socially prescribed experiences that prepare men and women for the roles they are expected to fulfill as adults (Jacobs, 1993). If this is true, one reason men tend to not consider elementary teaching as an option is that they are typically excluded from nurturing child-care routines—babysitting, physical contact with children, and so on—through most of their formative years. Serving in a child care role is simply not something they see as within their abilities. Janet Lever calls this "anticipatory socialization" (1978, p. 485). Others have suggested that this early socialization might be more than just benign exclusion and that many young boys and men are made to feel that they do not belong in K to 12 education by being dehumanized, alienated, demoralized, and threatened.

"Symbolic Violence" and Gender Formation

This is especially true in cases where there is a policing of male affection, compassion, and sensitivity toward children. Schools often systematically prevent boys from merging schooling with their personal identity because the methods and motives of schooling are feminine and to be successful in school requires being less masculine, less active, and less in charge (DeCorse and Vogtle, 1997). Gosse, Parr, and Allison argue that this "symbolic violence" can even extend to teacher education: "When viewed as a . . . trespass into women's space, this kind of symbolic violence may take the forms of being ignored, inadequately mentored, or deprived of knowledge one needs to succeed" (2008, p. 65). For young men from working-class backgrounds, integration into a largely middle-class profession, with its expectations of linguistic and cultural capital, can be particularly difficult. For them the question becomes, "Had the expectations of their youth and adulthood as males, generated from self, family, teachers, friends, community and pop culture . . . inhibited the nurturing of 'the right stuff' to navigate through teacher education?" (p. 65). Or, in the case of Rick and Raine, the two men involved in this duoethnography, had those same external influences actually planted the seeds of the right stuff that grew into later success as elementary teachers?

In examining our own lives, we look at the possibility that our early socialization contributed to our success in an atypical field. Although we do not view our past experiences as having nurtured some natural tendency toward teaching, they did, especially for Raine, contribute to a sense of injustice and dissatisfaction with existing schools that made the profession an appealing choice. More important, in relation to the question that motivated this study was the possibility that early experiences among friends and family might have anticipated the skills and perspectives we needed to succeed in the feminized culture of teacher education and teaching.

BEGINNING THE CONVERSATION

The guiding question for the duoethnography was, What is the role of early male identity construction in negotiating one's place in a predominantly feminine work setting, such as the elementary school? However, Rick was also curious as to the nature of the influence of the work environment on continuing construction or reconstruction. Therefore, a second question emerged: What is the nature of the influence of a predominantly female professional school culture on male identity construction?

Rick's Story

It is a weekend in the late spring of 1967, and a ten-year old boy sits on the porch of his home in suburban Chicago. Surrounding him today, instead of G. I. Joes or Matchbox cars, are his six-year old sister and two of her girlfriends. They are all playing some family-centered game of make-believe. When summer comes, in between invading Nazi strongholds as a British commando with his friends and constructing fortresses for his toy soldiers out of Styrofoam and cardboard, he'll spend many hours with his mother, shopping, overhearing conversations at the hair salon, helping hang laundry on the line to dry, and engaging in long talks with her while she irons clothes or tucks him into bed. Rick has a good relationship with his father, who works long hours, sometimes at a second job on the weekends to make ends meet so Rick's mom can be home with the kids. His father isn't like other working-class dads of the time in that he exhibits unconditional love, supports Rick's interest in music, has minimal interest in sports, goes to church with the family, listens to a wide variety of music, and never uses profanity in the home. Rick will learn from his father how to work on cars and do home repairs, the value of hard work, and (for better or worse) to be contrary for the sake of being contrary to popular opinion. These lessons will serve him well in the future, but it is his hours with his mother, sister, grandmother, and aunts that will teach him how to listen and to enter the world of his future colleagues and students.

Since at least high school, with a few exceptions, Rick has enjoyed his time around the girls and women in his life more than time spent with his own sex. The long conversations, relative maturity, and absence of pretense, posturing, and sports talk that characterized his female friendships were more comfortable and natural for him. So the path to this project should not be surprising.

Rick: When I grew up, my social circle was actually my younger sister and her friends. I had male friends, but they lived farther from where I lived, and my parents didn't really let me go there as an elementary child. I couldn't go far distances to play with them or get chauffeured everywhere. So I ended up by default playing with my younger sister . . . four years younger than I am, and some of her friends. So I started to wonder, well, to what extent did those interactions start to prepare me to work in a female environment? Did I start to hear the conversations and the priorities and the way girls think and . . . was that a factor? So those kind of things . . . looking at some autobiographical factors and how my other interests and so on might have shaped some of that. And rather than just making it a singular internal process, I thought it might be kind of interesting to hear somebody else who's in the same situation, someone who's male, who's also experienced some success as a male elementary teacher, and maybe draw each other out like that (Transcript, Hour 1, p. 1).

INVITING A CONVERSATION PARTNER

During Rick's four years in Georgia, he had not yet met a male elementary teacher, and the few he had known during his own elementary teaching career were no longer available. The potential intimacy of the topics also required that conversation partners establish some level of trust and safety. As a result, he put aside the possibility of a duoethnography until a serendipitous conversation with his wife who taught educational policy at another university. During that conversation, she suggested Raine, one of her former students, whom she saw as being articulate, open, insightful, and passionate about teaching, as a possible duoethnographic partner. He had also been named Teacher of the Year for Atlanta Public Schools. This presented what seemed to be an optimal situation. We could enter the project with the blank slates, lack of preconceived notions, and curiosity of a new relationship and also enter the relationship with some level of mutual respect and trust that came with being brought together by a trusted intermediary.

Our initial conversation was not directly related to the project and, therefore, not transcribed or considered in the research. We used that time to clarify the purpose of the project and duoethnographic process and to explore how compatible we might be, the level of shared and contrasting experiences, and our general ideas about teaching, students, and schooling.

Raine's Story

Across the rolling prairie foothills of southern Alberta, Canada, in the shadowy lap of the Rocky Mountains, a 12-year-old boy writes, "I live in a town that's two blocks wide. Two blocks wide, and who am I?" As he listens to his parents' collections of 1970s albums sprawled out on the shag carpet, he feels a tingle in his fingers and restlessness in his feet knowing that his life will always have a love affair with music and movement. The Chinook winds howl relentlessly outside as he plans his weekend endeavors: a hike on foot to his uncle's farm with his younger friend from across the street, a horseback ride with a girl who lives a few blocks away, and hanging out in a nearby fort with his younger friends, mostly girls, while his brother and dad go fishing. He knows that the only way to combat the boredom of a small prairie town is to escape into a world of creativity and invention, music and dance, truth or dare, hide and seek. Little does he realize that the path he has constructed before him will not run parallel to any he will cross in his life.

Difference within Similarity

One tenet of duoethnography is that the conversation partners bring differing experiences, meanings, and points of view to shared phenomena. In this project, Raine and Rick share the experience of being men in elementary education. As such, they are both part of a minority group within the predominantly female profession. Both are White and were raised in communities that were not very racially or ethnically diverse. They taught similar grade levels, had a variety of international experiences, and do not differ widely in age. However, they bring differences to the dialogue that appear to be especially relevant and crucial in relation to the topic.

Rick grew up in a mostly working-class urban/suburban area of Chicago whereas Raine grew up in a largely agricultural area of Alberta, Canada. In several important ways, the surrounding culture that influenced each young boy was very different. Most significantly, given the nature of this exploration, is the fact that Rick is straight and Raine is gay. Surprisingly, none of those factors resulted in the difference in perspective that we anticipated. In fact, the similarities threatened to overwhelm what we hoped to accomplish in that we quickly began constructing a master narrative that would steer the conversation.

Raine: I think what's amazing to me is every time I talk with you is that . . . and it's so refreshing . . . we have so much in common . . . is that our experiences growing up and I'm, you know, and I ended up being [slight pause] gay and you're not. [Both laughing]. And that's really great for me . . . your lifestyle . . . because it brings another dimension of normality into my own identity. I'm selfish to say that, but it makes me feel that, "Yeah, you know, what if all those things [referring to experiences around elementary age students] were also not necessarily because I was gay." 'Cause I didn't even know I was at that time. I just knew I liked fun things. I liked to laugh. I loved the youthfulness (Transcript, Hour 1, p. 8).

Rick: In our last conversation, Raine and I probably put a pretty positive construction on men who go into teaching. And reflecting on our own experience . . . it really put ourselves in a pretty positive light (Transcript, Hour 2, p. 1).

The realization that we were headed toward a less than critical exploration led to the first of two questions related to difficulty of seeking some level of rigor in duoethnography.

- How can conversation partners avoid convergence, the mutual construction of a shared master narrative?
- How do we more transparently represent the insights gained as a result of a complex interplay of dialogue, introspection, reflection, and consideration of the research literature?

TOWARD A HYPERTEXTUAL TRIOETHNOGRAPHY

As our conversations proceeded, we found that the preoccupation with method began to trump insights into gender construction. We did not see this as problematic because we believed that any insight gained into gender construction would have been questionable if we did not reconcile them with our concerns about their trustworthiness and meaningfulness. This was especially the case for Rick, whose postpositivist epistemological leanings often clash with his belief in the value of naturalistic methods. The challenge this apparent contradiction posed was to increase the rigor of the process in ways that would remain true to the dialogic, naturalistic character of duoethnography. Although our general concern about rigor was not new, the question about increasing the transparency of the conversations for a larger audience was more complicated. First, however, we chose to address the problem of an emerging master narrative.

Becoming a Trio

One tenet of duoethnography is that the method must remain open to avoid becoming prescriptive. Joe Norris (2008) reassures future duoethnographers that, although he and Rick Sawyer initiated this method, they lay no claim of proprietorship and that researchers can adapt the method to their unique circumstances.

As described above, early in our conversations, we discovered that despite the differences in our early backgrounds, the men we had become were very similar and had become distracted by the similarities instead of interrogating the differences. Moreover, because we both experienced a good deal of success as teachers, we began spending much conversation time building an increasingly positive construction of men who go into elementary teaching, especially ourselves. Reading the self-congratulatory tone of the early transcripts made us skeptical of our ability to honestly investigate our own development, and we ran the risk of what Norris and Sawyer have warned against: the possibility that the writers end up creating a "hero or victim saga." When this happens, the storytellers tend to be—or at least appear to be—unlikely to undergo the transformation of perspective that underpins duoethnography. As the project developed, Rick also had an experience that threw an element of necessary disequilibrium into the process.

REBECCA'S CONTRIBUTION

In talking to women who were students in his graduate classes, all practicing teachers, about the research, to a person they said they had never had a positive impression of the few male teachers with whom they worked. Although duoethnography is not about generalizing findings to a larger population or comparing oneself to some control group, because there are so few men in teaching and the experiences we shared seemed to differ so radically from those of the men Rick's students describe, they felt that this issue had to somehow enter into the dialogue. The point was not to look into the backgrounds of those other men but to use the other teachers' perceptions of men in elementary teaching to disrupt the conversation they were having and, by doing so, more critically examine their own reflections and challenge their notions of their own effectiveness. At this point, we decided to add Rebecca to our conversation.

Rick: In our last conversation, Raine and I probably put a pretty positive construction on men who go into teaching. . . . But I know in the past you've not been as impressed with some of the men that you've seen teaching.

Rebecca: I feel that the majority of the men that I have seen in teaching have been doing so in an effort to move towards administration [Raine nods in agreement] . . . where I'm very passionate about curriculum. I think oftentimes my opinion of other teachers is based on . . . that drive toward the betterment of the curriculum and teaching practice. . . . Unfortunately, what I see many times . . . I've seen men sitting back and reading the paper [all laughing] while their kids are doing work. Also, many of them carry that disciplinary role. . . . Many times they're more in rows . . . didactic teaching. . . . I'm not saying that there aren't any good teachers that are men. Just the men I have come in contact with have left me [slight pause] . . . wanting more [all laugh] (Transcript, Hour 2, p. 19).

Rebecca's Story

On any given day you could find Rebecca, a young girl from a small South Carolina town, traveling from one home to another. With each home came a different set of activities, values, and ideals. In the evenings, when she was not studying the bones of the body and various other biological topics with her young single mother putting herself through nursing school, you could find her seeking out friends of various ages to talk with. In this home, Rebecca was treated not as a daughter but as a friend and was encouraged to thoughtfully consider her situations, choices, and actions. She was expected to take on as much responsibility as possible at any given age. On Friday evenings, you could find her enjoying the carefree, playful environment of her father's home. Any outings included multiple conversations with various individuals, as in her father's eyes there were no strangers.

Although there was a strict traditional set of rules, Rebecca was encouraged to look for the best in people and love them and life unconditionally. During the rest of the weekend and each afternoon, you could find her at her paternal grandparents', who were self-made owners and managers of several small businesses, including a child care center. In this home, Rebecca was taught the importance of hard work and perseverance, the joy and value of serving others, the positive effects of encouragement, and that true learning experiences come from asking questions. Regardless of the differences in these homes, one message rang true in each: "Rebecca, you can not only be anything you want to be, but you will be a success in anything you choose." All of the lessons and beliefs melded to create an individual with varied and unique perspectives that have served her well in both her personal and professional life.

Rebecca—a straight, married White woman—is an elementary school science specialist and one of Rick's doctoral students. Although her work in an elementary school is the most obvious point of similarity within our inquiry, in previous unrelated conversations she had mentioned that she perceived herself as being different from most of her female colleagues. She saw her assertiveness, strong will, and sense of professionalism as not typical "teacher-y" characteristics. She had also pointed out that she seldom took part in teacher lounge griping, gossip, or relational tensions. So although we originally conceived of Rebecca's role as one of challenging and deepening Raine and Rick's inquiry into male identity construction, we could just as easily have shifted to a trioethnography—or multiple, intersecting duoethnographies—that looks at a sense of difference among elementary teachers.

Rebecca also contributed important differences to the conversation. She brought a woman's insight into the outward manifestations of masculine identity and behavior in the world of the elementary school. Unlike Rick and Raine, who are transplanted Northerners, she was born and raised in the South. She also followed a more traditional path toward teaching in that she knew from an early age that she wanted to be a teacher.

The Roles of a Third Partner

The third person, at least in a case like ours, can provide a corrective point of view and challenge the current direction and unquestioned assumptions. Raine and Rick had quickly created a master narrative for their investigation that limited critical probing and insight. The third person provided a necessary antithesis to this thesis. This role might not be necessary in other investigations that are conceived as duoethnographies. The need for a third person would depend on the partners, the topic, and what the researchers want from the project. Therefore, at this point we are not ready to recommend that trioethnography be a starting point. Instead, we see it as an accommodation when it seems necessary, much as a researcher might add a new interview source to a case study based on the recommendation of other participants.

The third person did more than just disrupt or deconstruct a comfortable conversation. The infusion of new questions and lines of thought played a *re*constructive or revisioning role. Rebecca brought new energy and imagination to the line of inquiry. The way Rick described it was as though a new, more topological perspective had been introduced. He chose that term because topological representations force us to see common objects in unusual ways and expose surfaces in ways we usually do not see them. In our investigation, the introduction of perspectives that blurred lines between what we had assumed were based largely in gender and sexual orientation raised some new questions about the nature and influence of gender in the elementary school setting.

Considering a Silent Partner

After adding a third partner, it might be said that we added the perspectives of one more "partner" who, although not the same in substance and form as the original three, played a crucial role. We are referring to the research literature on the role of gender in elementary teaching. This literature might be considered a third party because, unlike most traditional research projects, we did not immerse ourselves in that literature before beginning the conversations. Instead, after we were several hours into the project, we began reading the literature, and as each new source was considered, it was inserted into the conversation as though the authors were adding his or her perspective when and where it was relevant. Although the literature did not inform the original topic or initial questions, it did shape subsequent questions and perspectives.

The addition of research literature also completed another part of the triadic, interactive rethinking of our duoethnographic approach. The conversations obviously serve as the central focus of the inquiry, but they would be just so much "navel-gazing" without careful pre- and postconversation reflection. During those periods, the previous conversation was analyzed and interpreted, and the next step was determined based on insights and new questions developed out of the reflective process.

Transparency in a Complex Conversation

Unless they saw the small tape recorder in the middle of the table, other patrons in the coffee shops where we held several of our conversations could be forgiven for thinking we were just three friends chatting. They could not know that embedded in that "chat" was a significant amount of ongoing reading, numerous e-mail questions and answers, personal introspection, conversations with family members and former students, and postconversation reflection. Even in the best of journal articles, the notion of transparency within conversational or narrative forms of research does not go much beyond a few extensive quotations from an even more extensive transcript and the author(s) insights and conclusions. Typically, the reader must trust that authors have honestly represented hours of dialogue in the selected quotations and that reams of field notes, participant reviews, and researcher notes indeed are reflected in a few pages of conclusions.

None of that implies that we need to be suspicious of all qualitative researchers. The lack of transparency, more often than not, is due to limitations of the publication process. Online journal formats offer the potential to free researchers from some traditional publication limits but only if the new format is used in nontraditional ways. In our project, we experiment with presenting our work in a way that is as naturalistic and conversational as the original dialogue.

INVITING OTHERS INTO THE CONVERSATION

To accomplish our goal of creating a naturalistic and transparent presentation, we decided to use the hypertext capabilities of Web-based publication. All the work described can currently be found at the *Trioethnography* link on http://breaultresearch.info. The materials included at that site are crucial to understanding our conversation and what we gained from it. This is especially true because in this chapter we focus more on the process and method of our study than on the content related to gender construction. Therefore, we strongly encourage you to open the website as you read this chapter and find examples of the documents being discussed. We also hope you will do so as a way of becoming part of the conversation. Not only will you be able to scrutinize our "data" in a way seldom possible in quantitative research, but you can also contribute to the blog in which we solicit your questions, critique, or stories about experiences related to men in elementary education.

Description of Format and Content

The main or home document is the transcript of the interviews. One tenet that is crucial to duoethnography is that each voice be made explicit. Related to that is the importance of undergoing and demonstrating a change of perspective. To highlight individual voices, most of the text in duoethnography is written as a conversation or play script that helps the reader distinguish who is saying what. This approach also encourages readers to form their own synthesis out of the dialogic process of the researchers. Another tenet—that a change of perspective results from the methodology—suggests that if there is a measure of rigor for the duoethnographic process, at the center of it will be transparency and explicitness. The reader wants to and should be able to witness the transformation of the researchers as it occurs, not just be told of it in a section of conclusions. Ideally, the reader will see that a transformation has taken place and might even pinpoint when, where, and how it happened, perhaps better than the researchers themselves.

The hypertext format allowed us to provide the reader with easy access to the complete and generally unedited transcripts of our conversation. Although few readers will have the time or desire to read so many pages of conversation, those who may wonder about or dispute our conclusions can now follow the lines of thinking that led to them. Ideally, full access to our words and reflections will make this an open-ended project in which readers can raise questions and add opinions or suggestions on the blog that accompanies the research.

Some minor editing was done on the transcript for the sake of readability and focus. Whereas Rick typed and did the initial editing of the transcripts, Raine and Rebecca reviewed the original for accuracy. The editing process also included the initial placement of tentative links to other documents. Those other links fit into three categories labeled *Contextual Information, Intraconversational Extensions*, and *Extraconversational Links*.

Contextual Information

The documents included in this category provide some of the information that would typically be included in a traditional research report format and that some readers will find helpful. They are not critical, however, to understanding the insights from the transcripts themselves. The *Prologue* provides an introduction to and context of the study in general and a brief review of literature related to male identity in elementary teaching. The *Method* is what you are now reading. *Biographical entries* are included to help the reader gain a more vivid and intimate sense of the participants. An *Epilogue* is also included to provide each participant an opportunity to discuss the influence of the project on their own perspectives and to draw some insights and conclusions for the trio as a whole. Some of that document is included.

Intraconversational Extensions

These links allowed us to extend discussion of issues that were raised in the original conversations. The entries take the form of brief reflective essays on things that were said during the conversations but that the participants thought about after reading the transcript or written side conversations between participants in which specific questions are raised and answered.

Extraconversational Supplements

The content available in these documents links the reader to scholarship related to male gender construction in elementary schools. One type of link is to specific articles and quoted material that sheds light on or that informed some aspect of the main conversation. Another provides what we are calling an excursus based on synthesis of other research or scholarly thought that speaks to a particular area of interest in the conversation.

Some Final Thoughts about Rigor

Some fellow duoethnographers disagree with the need for so much attention to validity, but we were sensitive to early critique of duoethnography, even from a number of fellow qualitative researchers, who kept asking, "So what?" and "Isn't this really just a long conversation?" We do not feel it is necessary for anyone to justify their approach to or the meaning of their research, especially if it provides insight into their practice or helps their own development as persons, scholars, and teachers. We do worry that without sustained and deliberate attention to the rigor, however defined, techniques like duoethnography or any other autobiographically based or self-study inquiries run the risk of becoming introverted rather than introspective. Moreover, we agree with Bullough and Pinnegar's caution regarding any self-study research:

> In order to assert any authority, a study must do so from the frame or frames of the borrowed methodology as well as from the virtuosity of scholarship established in the piece of writing itself. . . . A claim to be studying oneself does not bring with it an excuse from rigor. (2001, p. 15)

THE TROUBLING ROLE OF MEMORY

Honore:	We met at nine.
Mamita:	We met at eight.
Honore:	I was on time.
Mamita:	No, you were late.
Honore:	Ah, yes, I remember it well.

In the lyrics from *I Remember It Well*, in the 1958 musical *Gigi*, Alan Jay Lerner and Frederick Loewe used a lighthearted and romantic approach to explore the subjectivity of memory and truth. Honore remembers meeting at nine and Mamita at eight, both claiming that they "remember it well." Although the implication is that Honore does not recall the early days of their romance as well as his longtime companion, Mamita, we do not actually see those early days, so it could well be that Honore is correct or that neither remembers the way it really happened. Early in our conversation, Rick added a reflective essay titled "Revisionist History," in which he began to wrestle with the veridicality—the truth content—of the recollections he brought to the project.

Creating Fictive Memories

One of the key experiences that prompted the study was Rick's recollection of the time spent playing with his sister and her friends when they were young children and his speculation that these ongoing experiences played a crucial role in helping him feel comfortable and effective in predominantly female settings such as elementary teaching.

Rick: So I ended up by default playing with my younger sister . . . four
years younger than I am and some of her friends. And so I started
to wonder well, To what extent did those interactions start to prepare me to work in a female environment? Did I start to hear the
conversations and the priorities and the way girls think, and . . .
was that a factor? (Transcript, Hour 1, p. 1)

After checking the dates of various related experiences, such as the
airing of television shows that prompted some of the imaginative play,
he found that the relatively short span of time involved and the age of
his younger sister at the time made it unlikely that those play experiences
could have been as influential as he remembered them. In this case, the
recollections were not necessarily false memories because other participants or observers will verify that the play situation occurred. Instead,
what seems more likely is that Rick has, over time, attached more substance and significance to the events than is warranted by the events
themselves. So the problem that arises in this and any other autobiographical account is "that the subject may find it difficult to be objective about him/herself and, in viewing ourselves from the perspective of
the present, it may be difficult to create oneself as one was in the past"
(Clements, 1999, p. 24).

In Rick's example, Conway's (1990, 1995) observation that we
remember things differently from how they actually occurred to enhance
our own self-image is especially relevant. Rick entered this project with
the assumption that he generally communicates effectively with female
colleagues, students, and friends and that the conversation would help
reveal autobiographical events that nurtured that ability. Therefore, it is
likely that events and relationships were selectively recalled to suit the
purpose or, if not deliberately recalled, that they were reconstructed and
reinterpreted so as to make them sufficiently profound.

> In every case we remember our past today rather than in the past itself and
> we must therefore necessarily remember with the benefit of hindsight . . .
> and with the various pieces of intellectual and emotional baggage we have
> accumulated over the intervening years. (Clements, 1999, p. 26)

What can result is a fictive memory—true memories that may
in fact be false or recreated purely through our own perspectives or
interpretation of them after time (Clements, 1999). If left unexamined,
such memories might be of little use, but it is also possible that "these
thought processes may, by their very academic slovenliness . . . show
what presuppositions have been made in constructing narrative and the
values which may emerge through the research" (p. 30). What happens,
though, when those thought processes intermingle with those of one

or more additional autobiographical accounts in the duoethnographic conversation?

Cointerpreting Memory

The potential for fictive, biased (Conway, 1990, 1995; Kennedy, Mather, and Carstensen, 2004), or false memories (Loftus and Loftus, 1980; Loftus and Pickrell, 1995) seem to suggest the need to rigorously interpret autobiographical recollections in a duoethnographic conversation. But is that the role of the participants? Do they have an obligation to interrogate or challenge one another's memory, or is it enough to help each other explore, clarify, and find meaning in recollections? Although increasing the rigor of the method, the former could lead to an unproductive questioning of every recollection to the point of inaction or, in the extreme, an undermining of trust and intimacy. In the latter approach, however, duoethnography might result in no more than two or more largely fictional characters co-constructed to reinforce what was already believed.

In our own project, we did little to challenge the recollections and self-perceptions each of us brought to the table. We took at face value each other's perceptions of teaching effectiveness and descriptions of past events. The addition of Rebecca's perspective helped shift Raine's and Rick's skewed perception of men who teach elementary school, but it did not necessarily challenge their self-perceptions. At no point did we question the veridicality of our stated autobiographical influences. Of course, none of us were present at each other's childhood events—which will probably be true in most duoethnographies—so, unlike Honore and Mamita, there could be no direct contradiction of remembered events anyway. However, neither is there any evidence in the transcripts or supplemental documents that any of us questioned each other's recollections and interpretations based on our present knowledge and perceptions of each other. A preoccupation with the subjectivity and accuracy of memory remains an important topic in the discussion of methodological rigor, but in our case, the veridicality of our recollections appeared to have little influence on our conclusions. In the end, our trioethnography was the merging of the stories of three elementary teachers and what those stories have meant to the students in their charge. Tim O'Brian described this phenomenon in *The Things They Carried*, a fascinating blend of memoir and fiction about the impact of the Vietnam War on its participants.

> And sometimes remembering will lead to a story, which makes it forever. That's what stories are for. Stories are for joining the past to the future. . . . Stories are for eternity, when memory is erased, when there is nothing to remember except the story. (1998, p. 38)

So What and What Next?

Our project is far from over because we continue to find additional questions to answer and avenues to explore. Moreover, as we write this chapter, all of us are preparing for new professional directions. Raine is beginning his first year as principal of a charter school. Rebecca will continue teaching elementary school science but is in the research phase of her dissertation and considering a move into higher education. Rick has taken a position at a different university. Each of these new opportunities may put a new spin on how we use what we took from our trioethnography.

Refocusing the Role of Gender

As our conversations drew to a close, we found that our individual stories and recollections had become less about individual insights than creation of one fictive teacher. What started as an exploration of early influences on gender construction in male elementary teachers had moved toward the notion that there are experiences or early personality traits that might lead to becoming an effective elementary teacher. Had we stayed with our original conversation, Raine and Rick might have concluded that early nontraditional gender conditions were largely responsible for their elementary teaching experiences. Rebecca's contribution challenged that conclusion. What seems more likely is that the personality traits and early life experiences of some individuals who choose elementary teaching contribute to becoming a certain kind of elementary teacher.

Gender seemed to be only tangential to the traits that made Rebecca, Raine, and Rick the teachers they are. All were comfortable with or adapted to being different or outside their most likely peer groups. They all have a wide range of interests, including the arts. Each was given significant freedom and support to become what they wanted to be from parents or other family members. Each retained a degree of childlike appreciation of life and sense of self longer than might be typically expected. Each developed a sense of passion and tenacity in their commitment to something larger than their immediate teaching. In each person, gender-based expectations and interactions might have facilitated the development of these traits: Raine's rejection of western Albertan prairie machismo as he became increasingly aware of his gay identity; Rebecca's home life, in which "one message rang true"—"You can not only be anything you want to be, but you will be a success in anything you choose"; and Rick's extended time with female friends and family. But as each story developed, the gender identities they have constructed appeared to be the result or expression of other personality traits and not determiners of them.

Thoughts about Meaningfulness

Factors related to geographic, professional, and family commitments have kept us from being in the same place at the same time for quite a while. As a result, all of our postconversation reflections have been on our own or, at best, via e-mail. Although they have been helpful, they lack the dynamism and intimacy of the personal conversations. Even if that conversation never happens, though, each of us has taken away some insight, application, or challenge that we believe would have been much less likely without the trioethnography.

Raine: A Personal and Professional Journey

As I listened to the stories, reflections, and questions of the two of you, I began to understand and validate the relevance of events in my own professional and personal journey. This was particularly signified by the focused exchange about our influence on our students (and our students on our own lives) through the lens of our sexualities, social identities, and deeply rooted philosophies. Having the opportunity to explore these questions in a risk-free setting (coffee shops, hosted kitchens, hotel lobbies) proved to be invaluable. The evolution of information that we shared unraveled the way it did because of our mutual agreement upon authenticity and transparency.

The questions we answered through this process—about ourselves, our practice, our rationales and justifications for who we are as practitioners and people—inadvertently cultivated newfound questions that took us each in new directions. I realized, for myself, for example, that the profession did not just find me but, rather, that I found what I needed within the craft to evolve as a human being. Perhaps by living vicariously through the journeys of my students, I was able to better understand what happened to me as a young man. Perhaps by squeezing my feet back into those once-worn shoes, I allowed myself another opportunity to question, through adult eyes, the norms and rituals of our classrooms and society that may or may not have had a positive or detrimental effect on who I am today.

As I looked back, I realized I was profoundly affected by my experiences in school, particularly the elementary landscape. Of course it was a socializing process, but moreover, it became a place where I was able to discover myself through the recognition and validation of those I honored, trusted, respected, and admired. It didn't take long for me to connect with my authentic instructors and avoid those less transparent. Kids have this intuitive nature in them, an ability to sniff out advocates as opposed to adversaries. I knew which teachers I liked, and I gravitated toward them, investing more effort into my work and more energy into my personality/character development in their classes.

I know now that at some point, even though I might not have agreed with most of the norms and standards set by the school culture that surrounded me (a rather redneck-meets-construction-worker-meets-farmer kind of atmosphere), I would at least endure, knowing that certain educators whom I respected and whom I knew accepted me for who I was were there for me, like oxygen, aligned with the truth of what I perceived as my own reality and identity. I believe now, more than ever, that most of them knew, even before I did, my unfolding sexual orientation.

Loners need validation and recognition, just like anyone else, and as an adult teacher I carried with me the irrefutable knowledge that if such students in my own class were not recognized and supported, they risked terminally dissolving into the surrounding colorless brickwork.

The process and content that we visited as a "three" transformed how I see explorative learning today. As I sit here now, in a newly unwrapped "principal's" chair for the first time in my life, I catch myself carefully constructing opportunities for my brand-new staff to explore, encouraging them to question and challenge the processes they have become a part of before, rather than after, they consider replicating such perspectives, behaviors, values, and paradigms in their daily professional and personal lives.

Rebecca: Changing Notions of Teacher Quality

This process was insightful for me because it challenged my somewhat negative perceptions of male elementary school teachers. My past interactions with male elementary school teachers have left me with an impression that is less than stellar. I have viewed these men as users of the system, who were looking for an easy job that provided a flexible schedule and a noncompetitive work environment. Many times I also resented them because others feel as if they are "needed" as strong examples. I believe that women are multidimensional and capable of providing both the strength and the structure that many children need. Through this process, I have begun to see an alternate role for male elementary school teachers. Evidentially, they can and sometimes do provide a nurturing relationship that builds a safe environment that allows expression and growth for students. These personal changes will invariably affect my professional practice, as I will view others, especially males, through a new and expanded lens. This growth opens doors to new learning experiences that might not have been possible in the past.

Our conversation also brought into relief that teachers are human beings—dynamic, complex, and sometimes mysterious creatures. In society, we have the habit of categorizing or stereotyping individuals based on a few surface features and our past experience, which is often quiet limited. This practice unfortunately blinds us to reality and possibilities.

Had I encountered Rick or Raine in the classroom setting prior to this research experience, I might have viewed them in a limited manner. Each small detail or action that confirmed my previous definition of a male elementary school teacher may have blinded me from seeing their pedagogical strengths and belief in a dynamic and lived curriculum. It may have constrained my desire to understand them, which in turn would have limited my opportunity and capacity toward learning and growth.

This experience has also caused me to further question the idea of a quality teacher. I have wrestled with the question, Are quality teachers born or shaped? The question boils down to nature or nurture. This experience has pointed out environmental factors that shape one's identity that in turn affects one's identity as a teacher. Are there experiences we should look for when attempting to identity effectiveness in future teachers? Are there types of environmental factors and experiences, beyond the technical training often employed, we should promote in preservice teachers that will promote effectiveness? I believe that the ideas unearthed in this study offer food for thought that could enhance our understanding of teachers, their multiple personal identities, and how those affect their self-perception and contribute to their effectiveness as a teacher.

To that end, this process has made me, as someone who hopes to move into the role of teacher educator, want to explore how we might come to understand teaching candidates in the same manner that we came to know each other. I believe that we need to tap into these deeper, more meaningful identifying features to identify as early as possible the potential strengths and weaknesses that determine and promote effective teaching.

Rick: Still More Questions

I enjoyed this process immensely and found the listening to be personally enriching. I knew my stories and some of the meaning I had given to them but had never examined them in light of other people's stories. I enjoy introspection and had revisited the stories I shared in our trioethnography hundreds of times in my own mind, often reinterpreting their meaning to suit my latest need. Telling them publicly stripped away the glossy finish I had put on them. Hearing them in relation to Raine's strikingly similar yet significantly different stories and in light of Rebecca's disarming critique and probing questions made my stories less self-serving and more powerfully reconstructive. Beyond whatever personal benefit the new perspectives lent to my stories, it was also intriguing to watch those stories become part of a larger collective story. Each of our stories had been intimate possessions, but as we shared them, they seemed to take on lives of their own as they reached out to and were drawn in by the other stories. In the end, the process resembled some Tolkien-esque fantasy in which three characters must tell one part of an ancient story for their essences to join and to overcome some malevolent force. However meaningful our stories might have been on their own, it was only in their conversational retelling that they took on significance for a larger audience.

I also found this to be a frustrating process. I did not want the conversations to end and continually found new directions to explore. Finding a logical stopping point in this process is not easy. Maybe there is none. At this point, though, I have more questions as a result of our project than answers. Some of those questions relate to the systemic, cultural nature of schools that I did not have before. For example, while conventional wisdom—as well as the research on the profession—generally depicts the elementary school as a feminized workplace, our discussion has raised the possibility that in reality schools represent a distinctive, hybrid, institutional gender on the order of what we suggested of individual teachers in the first question. And now, as state and federal agencies continue to strip away teacher autonomy, standardize the process of learning, and increasingly demand that success be defined in terms of measurable productivity, what will remain of the "feminine?" How will a feminized work culture respond to the imposition of such masculine, factory-like demands? Will the elementary school become a more comfortable place for career-driven men?

Other questions are of a more conceptual or methodological nature. We have already written a little here about the concern over the role of memory in autobiographical recollection. At an even more fundamental level related to this research is my skepticism about the question itself. I wonder if gender construction as related to something as specific as career choice and performance can really be determined through self-exploration, except in cases where outright gender-based discrimination clearly limits entry or opportunity to prepare for a profession. This process, for whatever other insights it has brought to our self-understanding, has also led me to wonder if we really have or can come to any understanding of our gender development through conversations like this. As we heard each other's stories and identified so many different paths to similar results and so many similar paths to different outcomes, we came to wonder whether any of our insights were really related to gender, or was there some other difference.

Finally, there are questions that have direct implications for my teaching such as, If elementary teaching and teacher education are as hostile to young men as some of the research seems to say, do I have any special obligation to the few men that sit in my classes? Or if what Rebecca and other female teachers have pointed out is true—that very few men have stood out as effective elementary teachers—maybe I should be holding those who do enter teacher preparation to a higher level of scrutiny. What are the implications, if any, for my interactions with and preparation of female teacher candidates? How do they view me as a former male elementary teacher? Am I viewed as a former elementary teacher at all or as just another man teaching at the college level? These are all questions I hope to explore as this process continues. Anyone interested in a duoethnography?

References

Bullough, R. V., Jr., and Pinnegar, S. (2001). Guidelines for quality in autobiographical forms of self-study research. *Educational Researcher, 30*(3), 13–31.

Clements, P. (1999). Autobiographical research and the emergence of the fictive voice. *Cambridge Journal of Education, 29*(1), 21–32.

Conway, M. (1990). *Autobiographical memory.* Milton Keynes, UK: Open University Press.

Conway, M. (1995). *Flashbulb memories.* Mahwah, NJ: Lawrence Erlbaum Associates.

DeCorse, C. J. B., and Vogtle, S. P. (1997). In a complex voice: The contradictions of male elementary teachers' career choice and professional identity. *Journal of Teacher Education, 48,* 37–46.

Gosse, D., Parr, M., and Allison, J. (2008). Researching the halted paths of male primary school teacher candidates. *Journal of Men's Studies, 16*(1), 57–68.

Hansot, E., and Tyack, D. (1988). Gender in American public schools: Thinking institutionally. *Signs, 13*(4), 741–760.

Jacobs, J. (1993). Men in female-dominated fields. In C. L. Williams (Ed.), *Doing women's work: Men in nontraditional occupations* (pp. 49–63). Newbury Park, CA: Sage.

Kennedy, Q., Mather, M., and Carstensen, L. (2004). The role of motivation in the age-related positivity effect in autobiographical memory. *Psychological Science, 15*(3), 208–214.

Lever, J. (1978). Sex differences in the complexity of children's play and games. *American Sociological Review, 43,* 471–483.

Loftus, E. F., and Loftus, G. R. (1980). On the permanence of stored information in the human brain. *American Psychologist, 35*(5), 409–420.

Loftus, E. F., and Pickrell, J. E. (1995). The formation of false memories. *Psychiatric Annals, 25*(12), 720–725.

Norris, J. (2008). Duoethnography. In L. M. Given (Ed.), *The SAGE encyclopedia of qualitative research methods* (pp. 233–236). Los Angeles: Sage.

O'Brian, T. (1998). *The things they carried.* New York: Broadway Books.

Perlmann, J., and Margo, R. A. (2001). *Women's work? American schoolteachers 1650–1920.* Chicago: University of Chicago Press.

Reskin, B. (1991). Bring the men back in: Sex differentiation and the devaluation of women's work. In J. Lorber and S. Farrell (Eds.), *The social construction of gender* (pp. 141–161). Beverly Hills, CA: Sage.

Sargent, P. (2001). *Real men or real teachers?* Harriman, TN: Men's Studies Press.

CHAPTER 6

Power and Privilege

Patrice McClellan and Jennifer Sader

PROLOGUE

Patrice McClellan and Jennifer Sader's chapter emulates the book's opening poem on liberation. McClellan, a Black woman, and Sader, a White woman, have the courage to enter into what they call "sticky and scary" (p. 140) conversations about race relations and how they experienced lessons of difference in their upbringing. Their aim is to learn from each other and, through articulating such learning, liberate themselves from past experiences by dismantling "a wall of resistance to work interracially and a willingness to take a risk in order to honestly discuss race, power, and privilege" (p. 140). They recognize that, although others may identify with particular sections of their duoethnography, the duoethnography is contextual. Their intent is to be open, avoiding prescription. Their desire is not to reify their stories, but, rather, "re"story them through dialogue with the Other.

McClellan and Sader effectively intersperse their stories with analytical interludes, providing an example of a writing style that can both show and tell. In so doing, they exemplify reflexivity as they dialogically reexamine their lives. They make explicit the tacit points that, through their articulation, assist themselves and their readers to make sense of their experiences. Ultimately, they model such reflexive conversations so that students in their diversity courses can witness such conversations as possible and necessary.

Trust is foundational to all duoethnographies, and this chapter exemplifies this tenet. McClellan and Sader knew little of each other before their study began, but because of their mutually perceived necessity of such research for their students' sakes, they embarked on the journey. They claim that they felt safer once the conversation began, that the "skeletons in our closet seemed less threatening when we could talk about them" (p. 153). We witness the healing and transformative nature of duoethnography as they demonstrate that our liberation is bound with theirs.

They also demonstrate self-reflexivity, the act or acknowledgment of personal change grounded within the real world. For claims of reflexivity in research to be believable, the process of reflexivity needs to be apparent in the study. And McClellan and Sader show—through transparency and rich description—an embodied engagement in praxis and conceptual change. First, they position themselves within all aspects of their research text, not outside of it. They begin with a clarifying statement:

> *In order to gain a deeper understanding of classroom dynamics around power and privilege, we, a Black woman (Patrice) and a White woman (Jennifer), revisit our lives . . . to uncover invisible barriers (such as fear of betrayal, feeling protective of family and friends, concerns about the proper role of self-disclosure, and students' resistance) that impact honest discussion of diversity and social justice issues in leadership education. . . . As leadership educators, we challenge ourselves to engage rather than deny or repress differences that emerge at the dynamic intersections (Asher, 2007) of power, privilege, difference, and/or equity. (p. 139)*

Thus, they examine themselves within their inquiry as a means of engaging rather than denying difference.

—Joe Norris

INTRODUCTION

Norris and Sawyer's article on the hidden and null curricula of sexuality asks, "How does one go about creating a safe space in the classroom?" (2004, p. 158) Building upon their research, we employ duoethnography (Norris, 2008) to reflect on and interrogate how discussing privilege in leadership education affects our pedagogical approaches, influences our interaction with learners, and forces us to confront our own biases when discussing power, privilege, and equity. To gain a deeper understanding of classroom dynamics around power and privilege, we, a Black woman (Patrice) and a White woman (Jennifer), revisit our lives as sites of research (Oberg and Wilson, 2002) to determine if our tensions around this topic influence discussions in class. Our goal in this duoethnography is to uncover invisible barriers (such as fear of betrayal, feeling protective of family and friends, concerns about the proper role of self-disclosure, and students' resistance) that influence honest discussion of diversity and social justice issues in leadership education. We see duoethnography as an ideal method to engage a critical dialogue.

In this chapter, we use an alternative and progressive stance on advancing the teaching of leadership and being inclusive to diverse perspectives. As leadership educators, we challenge ourselves to engage rather than deny or repress differences that emerge at the dynamic intersections (Asher, 2007) of power, privilege, difference, and/or equity. The insights gained through this process will help us and our colleagues to create a safe space in the classroom through an examination of power and privilege in our own lives. In the following sections, we define and detail the use of duoethnography, outline the themes that arose during our research conversations, express the lessons learned through discovery, and discuss implications and future directions for this line of inquiry.

METHOD

In keeping with William Pinar's concept of *curerre* (Norris, 2008; Pinar, 1975), this duoethnography traces our learning process instead of presenting our new understanding as a polished, monolithic finished product. This allows readers to learn along with us by examining how we have acquired new understandings that influence our actions and the meanings we give them (Norris, 2008; Sawyer and Norris, 2009).

Duoethnography has five tenets that are central to the methodology (Norris, 2008). However, we focus on three that are central to our collective exploration and recollection of our life lessons on race, power, and privilege. The first tenet is that methodology must remain open to avoid becoming prescriptive. In doing so, we express our experiences not as a prescription for others' behavior but as an example of the learning process we have experienced while discussing race, power, and privilege. The second is that each individual voice is made explicit. We are very specific in the stories told who is speaking so that the reader can make connections of meaning and understand the context of the conversation. The third tenet is that a change of perspective is central to the methodology. We show what we have learned from our experience but do not attempt to present our experiences as universal or even typical. We open up our learning process to readers and show how this dialogue has informed our perspectives (Norris, 2008). By listening to each other, we've not only learned about ourselves in relation to others, but we also have a new understanding of our professional selves in relation to our students.

Therefore, we have explored our personal stories and recollections of past events in the contexts of power and privilege that have shaped and continue to shape our personal as well as professional lives. This duoethnography between two female faculty members, one Black, the other White, is a process of examination through which we make meaning out of our particular experiences with power, privilege, difference, and equity in an effort to prepare us to be better educators for our students.

FEAR OF BETRAYAL

Building lasting relationships with people whom we've recently met or are acquainted with can be a daunting task. One of the most difficult things to do is speak honestly and share intimate thoughts about race, power, and privilege. Most often those conversations are held in strict confidence with family, friends, or loved ones. Even to consider having these conversations in an intercultural or interracial space breaks many taboos or unspoken norms. However, as colleagues and evolving friends, we have taken on the challenge. In the following excerpt, we discuss Patrice's fear of betrayal, marginalization, and invisibility (Stanley, 2006). The power of a few words highlights the complexity of the lived experiences and historical memories Black women have regarding academic abuse by colleagues. During this conversation, we overcame resistance to working interracially and accepted the risk to honestly discuss race, power, and privilege.

Jennifer: When we were talking about this, I was a little bit . . . this could get kind of sticky and scary . . . and it seems like you have sort of parallel fears that I have.

Patrice: Yeah . . . with my girlfriends, we're all Black. We all have similar stories of a collaboration between a Black scholar and a White scholar where the White person shoots off like a rocket, leaving the Black person in the dust. When I talked to my girlfriends, they were skeptical and said, "I don't know, Patrice. This is your idea?" With my girlfriends, I don't have that fear with them. We talk about race and all of the other *isms*. You know, Black people and Latinos have been doing critical race theory and stuff for years, but the minute a White person does it, it's like, "Oh, great." Somehow their (White scholars') presence is deemed more important and valuable and our voice is silenced. But that speaks to privilege.

Jennifer: But I feel like this is central to your scholarship, and this is sort of a sideline to the kind of thing I wouldn't normally do. I don't see myself as really—as this being the direction I'm going to go. I think you have the established credentials in this field, not me. And I really don't want to steal your ideas. But I think the bigger fear that we kind of both have is, What if they see what I'm really like?

While writing this chapter, at times we each have noticed that the other person was not open enough in asking for help. We realized that we were both used to being the person who did the work in a group project, both because we weren't sure we could count on the others for help and because we liked to do things our own way. Another kind of trust we had to learn was that we could really lean on each other to get the work done.

ROLE OF FAMILY

Both of our families talked about race but really didn't talk about race. As children, we learned about race from family conversations. One of Jennifer's aunts warned her more than once when she was a child to be careful because someone had just seen a Black woman trying to kidnap a White child at the mall: "She was in the bathroom, cutting the little girl's hair when the police caught her." When she was older, she was warned to look under her car when she was shopping alone because Black men would hide under women's cars and grab them. Jennifer never took it seriously and often wondered about the strange details in the stories. Why the hair? Why under a car instead of in it? How could anyone get out from under a car fast enough to hurt someone? None of the adults listening openly questioned the underlying assumption that Black people were dangerous, though. At the same time, Jennifer's parents let her and her sisters stay up late to watch *Roots* on television and explained that slavery and prejudice were wrong. The whole family read *The Color Purple* in 1985, the year the movie came out. There were a lot of mixed messages.

We also learned from our families' values about life (espoused and in use) and interactions with others (verbal and nonverbal cues). Through our socialization processes, we picked up coping strategies that continue to help and those we continue to unlearn. Upon reflection, we believe the primary sources from whom we learned were well intended. Our parents taught us to "treat everyone with respect" and "all people are created equal," but what we learned and now interrogate are those espoused ideologies. We now understand that, depending on your social status as a member of a targeted or dominant group, the meanings of those infamous quotes vary greatly. In other words, some of us are subjected to scripted responses and meanings based on appearance, perceived difference, and/ or ability (Baraka, 1997) We see this ourselves as diversity teachers. As McIntosh stated, "Many, if not most, of our white students in the U.S. think that racism doesn't affect them because they are not people of color; they do not see 'whiteness' as a racial identity" (1997, p. 297). Like them, Jennifer thought only racists thought about "White identity" until she took her first diversity and social justice course in graduate school.

Patrice: So our parents talked about race. I didn't talk about my parents because, wow, I can't. I didn't/don't want to air any family business without asking permission.

Jennifer: But you should have. If I'm going to be honest, you have to be also. It's not easy to admit to these things.

Patrice: But some of the stuff I learned at home from my mom. My dad was really good; he grew up in Jim Crow south Alabama, but he never was angry, which always made me angry that he wasn't angry. He was very political and believed in the political process, sometimes a bit too much. He made sure we knew the importance of voting and the responsibility we owed to those who died for our rights. He voted every time, as did my mom. He made sure he stayed abreast of what was going on in schools. I guess you can say my father embraced working-class values because he would've been first generation, whereas, my mom went to private school in the 1960s. She was more middle class and was privileged in that regard. She was sheltered in some ways yet also isolated at school. She went to school with the children of some influential families. She always has nice things to say about some of the children/teenagers she went to school with, but in some form or another, she's angry about the way she was treated during those years by some of the White children. She's talked about some of the incidents, but some I know she has kept to herself. I often wonder how she felt; then I realize that I already know. I, too, was one of a few Blacks in my AP classes in high school. It can be an isolating experience.

Jennifer: It seems like both of you were interacting with especially privileged groups of Whites. This might have exposed you to more opportunities, but it might also have put you into situations where there would be a more than average sense of competitiveness and cliquishness.

Patrice: Yeah! As I got into graduate school and started reading about race and how it all played out, I realized how my mother articulated her privilege of income and education, through class distinctions. Even now, I can see that and understand her position. I mean, that was her experience and has been mine to an extent. It surprises me how shocked people are that I am not a first-generation college student and have had a different life than what is portrayed in media. We were not the Huxtables, but it felt as if we were. For example, my first semester teaching at a university I had a White female student who happened to be first generation ask me how I coped being a first-generation college student and if I could help her. I have to admit I was upset and mad at the assumptions she made about me. I assumed she made the assumption because I was Black. I held it together and told her I was not first generation but that I was third generation. I gave her the appropriate resources and university contacts. Unfortunately, she could barely make eye contact with me after that incident. I didn't know whether she was embarrassed because of her assumptions, or she was upset because what she thought or learned about Blacks was untrue at that particular moment. In my opinion, teaching this diversity course, or any other for that matter, is about the entitlement and broad assumptions that come with privilege that I think our students don't recognize. That gets under my skin, but it is also the nature of the work. Looking at my mom and how she articulated her class privilege, especially when I was a little girl, makes sense. I'm sure that if I ask her, she will say that she was giving me coping strategies that would help me navigate the world as well as shield me from various forms of stereotyping and/or profiling. No matter how many coping skills I have, I am still subjected to the negative attitudes and meanings associated with my Blackness, and it's disappointing. Using my class privilege to navigate racial boundaries is not right because it potentially marginalizes others, but it's one way of coping with hostility, tension, and unspoken silences around race and power in the environment.

Jennifer: Just having been a target doesn't mean you don't target others. I don't think people apply it to themselves. That was what I was trying to say. As Italian immigrants, my grandparents were discriminated against in the 1930s and 1940s. They bought a house because they couldn't find anyone who would rent them an apartment, but they were still okay with saying, "They're no good" when talking about African Americans. They were amazingly kind and loving people, but they had their own limitations. That's what made it difficult to write about some of this stuff. It's not like only "bad people" perpetrate racism or any of the other *isms*. Just like we teach, it's a rotten system, and everybody gets burned by it somehow. When I was growing up, my parents didn't make racist comments, but a lot of my family members did, and my parents never said anything about it. So when my aunt or my grandmother would say that Black people were dangerous, I thought my parents agreed. They probably just didn't want me to question adults, but by not saying anything, they were giving their tacit agreement. When I was five or six years old, I was riding in the car with my mom, dad, and sister. The car ran out of gas, and we were getting ready to walk to the gas station. A car pulled over with a Black family in it: a mother, a father, and a boy a few years older than I was. My dad knew the father from work and told us to get into their car. I completely freaked out, but my parents made me get in. I sat in the back seat between the boy and my younger sister, keeping an eye on him and making sure that I kept my distance, and he looked back me with what was probably disgust. I remember being really angry with my parents about it: Either they were making me do something that wasn't safe or they hadn't told me the truth. I am still embarrassed now when I think about this incident. I probably feel the way a lot of our White students do.

WHO CAN OR SHOULD TEACH DIVERSITY?

One thing that came up in our discussion is the assumption that a Black faculty member is a more logical fit to teach a diversity class than a White faculty member. Many people on campus seemed surprised that Jennifer rather than Patrice would teach the diversity class. The assumption was that because Patrice is Black, she has either more responsibility to teach diversity or more knowledge of it, borne of her experiences as a Black woman. To be fair, teaching the class was not easy for Jennifer. She was new to teaching diversity and expected to have some rough patches but was very upset when she got very positive reviews from a small, all-White, partly online cohort and very negative reviews from a more diverse cohort. These responses made her question whether she was presenting the material fairly, but she did not—and does not—feel that she should take the easy way out and give up teaching diversity.

We understand that Jennifer can't fully understand what it is like to be Black, but assuming that Patrice is somehow an "expert" in diversity just because of her standpoint as a Black woman is to essentialize her unfairly and discount her scholarship in this area. As Collins rightly pointed out, "Despite the common challenges confronting African-American women as a group, individual Black women neither have identical experiences nor interpret experiences in a similar fashion" (2000, p. 27). Patrice's expertise in social justice comes from her study of the issues and theory, not just from experiences. The point of this class is to initiate conversations around privilege and power and their relationship to race, gender, sexual orientation, religion, and other sites of prejudice. We couldn't give the sense that we agreed that the problem of confronting racism belongs to Blacks and that Whites have no responsibility to start and participate in these conversations. Neither of us wanted to be complicit in a system that models passive acceptance of privilege and oppression by agent groups.

Patrice: Another thing here. You know how you were talking about your reviews with the mixed-race class as being bad but the all-White class being good: I was like, "At least she got good reviews." For me, this class is always the lowest score.

Jennifer: I have never taught a diversity class before. My other course evaluations were always good. So the reviews that I got for that class are typical of what you get all the time in diversity courses?

Patrice: Yeah, because the content isn't so emotionally charged in other classes.

Jennifer: I really took it personally. I just thought that I screwed up. That's just the content?

Patrice: It's just the content. We always say that if they're not bad, we didn't do something right.

Jennifer: But see, if I opt out and say, "Diversity class is too hard; I'll just let Patrice do it," then I could have better reviews. However, with the content of the course, you don't feel like you could do that the way I might. I feel like that's really unfair. When they look at evaluations for promotion, Black faculty would be at a huge disadvantage for teaching these tough classes.

Patrice: Yeah.

Jennifer: I do feel like, when I talked about teaching the class, everyone said, "Really? You're going to teach it?"

Patrice: I remember seeing that. I don't know where we were. We were at a meeting, and I remember one of the administrators saying, "You're teaching diversity?" Like, how dare you even teach it or something? Or, "What do you have to say as a White person about diversity?"

Jennifer: But before they hired [a Black adjunct faculty member], I think it was always taught by White faculty.

Patrice: Yeah.

Jennifer: So maybe it's now that we have a Black faculty member . . .

Patrice: YOU will teach . . .

Jennifer: . . . why did we hire her if we're not going to have her teach diversity?

A related phenomenon is called "cultural taxation" (Padilla, 1994, as cited in Stanley, 2006), a term used to describe the expectation placed on faculty of color to handle minority issues and/or affairs. What Jennifer is speaking to is the assumption that Patrice is "required" or "expected" to teach the diversity course.

Safe Space

The main focus of this investigation was to attempt to answer Norris and Sawyer's (2004) question, "How does one go about creating a safe space in the classroom?" (p. 158) This question drives our desire to create an inclusive, equitable, or democratic learning environment. Most of our students come into this class in the "Passive Acceptance" stage (Hardiman and Jackson, 1997, p. 25). They want to believe in a fair world and don't like talking about privilege. The first assignment, an autobiography that explores the messages they received about race when they were growing up, elicits vague idealized statements like, "My parents taught me to treat every person with respect." This lack of awareness was not surprising but made for a difficult class experience. We could not talk about how to combat discrimination and prejudice when students refused to see that these problems still exist.

We realized through our conversation that Norris's directive to autoethnographers to see themselves as the "site of investigation" rather than the "subject of the investigation" (2008, p. 234) could be applied when we asked students to disclose their experiences and might help break down some of these barriers. Students could start to see that the real point here was not "getting off the hook" (Johnson, 2006, p. 108) and proving that they had a race-free upbringing but was instead in investigating how their experiences might reflect the larger issue of how we are all socialized around race. We are now reexamining the autobiography and exploring other possible ways that we can introduce our exploration of this socialization that might help students to feel safer.

Patrice: "How does one go about creating a safe space in the classroom? Is it even possible?" (Norris and Sawyer, 2004, p. 158) I think we should open up the article as a response to this question. This question drives our desire to create an inclusive, equitable, or democratic classroom. Our desire to create a safe space in the classroom is the reason we are doing this duoethnography and having these conversations. We want to enhance our teaching strategy. We want the students to walk away with an understanding of themselves as a site of investigation of issues of race, gender, all those -isms, and we want them to start with themselves. Just like we have to start with ourselves.

Jennifer: Maybe unpack those assumptions they have that they don't realize that they're holding and see how they operate. I think something that has come to me with all this reading: When I felt like I couldn't speak in the class, I think it was that combination of shame about things that I felt weren't right in my past and fear that somehow I'd be exposed as a bad person. I liked when Sawyer and Norris (2009) reported that Joe heard negative messages about gays all of his life and had this null curriculum that homosexuality was wrong, but he didn't internalize it. He started to question it a lot, and those questions led to other questions. I grew up with this myself. My aunt's crazy stories were so crazy that as I grew older, I couldn't figure out how anyone could believe them. There were enough messages in the popular culture that racism was wrong—this was in the 1970s, after all—that I felt right to question not only the truth of those stories but the assumptions upon which they were based. As I got older, I wanted to think I was different, but I also had this fear that I was just like her, especially when I heard people tell racist jokes or stories and didn't confront them, even if I didn't laugh along. I think all of our students are probably falling somewhere on that spectrum, but because they feel they're not completely and totally on the side of "the good," they're secretly bad, and they don't want to expose themselves.

Patrice: That's a good point. I've never thought of it that way.

Jennifer: I don't know what imagined perfect racial upbringing I was thinking that people should have, but I know I didn't have it. But I think I questioned a lot of things as I was growing up.

Patrice: Remember when you said one time that you're trying to get students to realize, the White students, that just because they didn't grow up around Black or Latino or whatever type of people doesn't mean that their environment was race free? Maybe that "secretly bad" is a form of White guilt.

Jennifer: I think it's completely White guilt. I walk around with it, and I know what it looks like. The feeling that there is something bad in my background or, worse, that I have internalized those negative messages. Even you expressed it. You were afraid to do this because you didn't want me to know that you might have a problem with White people. Both of us sort of felt that maybe if we just didn't talk about this, it would be easier.

Patrice: Yes. Because we can just pretend.

Jennifer: Yeah. The students who claim that they just never heard about race growing up: I just don't believe that. But I'm thinking,

Who had the ideal upbringing where they heard nothing but good messages, and everything was positive, and everything was rosy, and they never had a bad thought, and they never did anything . . .

Patrice: . . . mean, or thought it . . .

Jennifer: . . . were never the agent of oppression in some way? [laughs]

Patrice: Yeah, who had that?

Jennifer: Who's that person? That's probably why I think all of us are afraid to have this kind of conversation because we talk about things in terms of good and evil.

Patrice: Yeah, everything is good and bad. We're taught that as kids. We're never taught gray; it's black or white. Nothing's ever in the middle. You're right or you're wrong.

Jennifer: I think people in general have the feeling that if anybody found out what they were really like, no one would want to be around me or like me, but in terms of race especially, because it's such a charged issue.

SELF-DISCLOSURE

For most faculty, including us, disclosing personal information and personal stories can bring on feeling of anxiety, tension, and strain. When disclosing personal information within the classroom, one constantly wonders where the boundary begins and ends. According to Griffin and Ouellett (2007), facilitators of social justice-related courses need to choose carefully when to expose personal stories and/or reactions to material that encompasses issues of race, power, and privilege. They also suggest being clear and transparent about the purpose of the disclosure and how it relates to course content. As we have learned, there is a delicate balance that we as faculty are sometimes not aware of. Through our personal narratives, we discuss the effects of disclosing too much and not disclosing enough. In our "aha" moments, we have realized that we made a few mistakes about faculty self-disclosure. However, through this duoethnographic process, we seek to remedy our mishaps by learning as we go and continuing to grow through the discomfort.

Patrice: I was thinking about something you said when you were teaching diversity class and you said something like, "Class is not about me. I don't want to be one of those professors who just talks about me." I thought about that, and I went back and I looked at one of my evaluations, and one of the comments was, "Talk about yourself less." I wrote a little note for myself because I really thought about that. For me, that would be a change of perspective because I thought I was modeling self-disclosure. If I can talk about myself, even though I'm uncomfortable, but I'm still sharing with you all, shouldn't you guys feel comfortable to talk, too? I thought I was modeling, and then when I just go deeper, yeah, some of it was modeling and teacher ego, but when I really got down to it, I was trying to prove that I'm not the stereotypical Black person that I feel many students expect to see.

Jennifer: So it was more about you.

Patrice: So it was more about me.

Jennifer: But I think my reluctance to talk about myself was, obviously, defensive, too. I didn't want to talk about myself because it's uncomfortable. I think probably both of us need, that may be the one place where we need, to shift our perspective. Add ourselves as a site, but not the subject matter (Oberg and Wilson, 2002).

Patrice: I was like, "Oh, wow, that's it." We then become—I think Antoinette Oberg says it—the site of the research and not the focal point of it. Finding that healthy balance that doesn't overshadow what we want to do in the classroom. That was my "aha!" I get it. This is what we want to do is figure out what all our life history stuff has to do with the classroom. For me, that brought it all together. I think if we can just let them be the site of and not the focal point . . .

Jennifer: Looking back on our experiences and how they shaped the development of our identity and how they're affecting our classroom behavior, it's not just unearthing the past; it's making new meanings out of what happened. "Telling tales and exposing that which would otherwise remain hidden as well as invisible and taken for granted. . . ." I think that's one of the things we were trying to do, get students to tell some of their tales.

Patrice: Yes.

Jennifer: Maybe the reason that they're reluctant is because they're not sure what we're going to do with that. If they tell their stories, what are we going to do with those stories? Again, if we could get them to understand, we're going to ask them to use their own experiences as the site of research/pedagogy. We're not interested in so-and-so's grandfather was racist. We're interested in, What did that teach you? What does that teach other people with similar backgrounds to you? How does this help us to understand how race operates in this country?

No Such Thing as Value-free Facts

Learning about social justice is a lifelong process (Griffin and Ouellett, 2007). As leadership educators, we want students to walk away from our courses with a new understanding of how race, power, and privilege play an integral role in the daily lives of leaders. We also want the knowledge blockers of privilege to be removed so that they can learn through the discomfort. Learning about one's privilege is challenging, emotionally taxing, and unnerving. However, this learning process involves students' thinking and talking about their experiences and feelings in relationship to race, power, and privilege as they explore different perspectives and challenge their own understanding, attitudes (Griffin and Ouellett, 2007, p. 89), and leadership praxis. Therefore, according to Norris and Sawyer (2004), there are no such things as value-free facts or value-free judgments. The value we espouse in this process is to model the way (Kouzes and Posner, 2002) and push our students to process, explore, and learn through the tensions around race, power, and privilege.

Jennifer: One thing that's hard, I think, about teaching diversity is that in a lot of classes you're opening up a discussion, and you want the students to take the discussion wherever it goes. But we can't help but want them to take a certain message away, which I think makes it feel to students sometimes that we're indoctrinating them.

Patrice: Pushing an agenda.

Jennifer: I don't know how to do that in another way. I don't want them to think that it's okay to go through this and conclude that being a racist is all right.

Patrice: There was one . . . in Norris and Sawyer's (2004) duoethnography, there's an example of a meeting about the sex-ed program. Joe says, "There is an agenda here. Your agenda may be different from mine. It's funny how the majority are blind to the fact that their choices, values, etc., are also an agenda" (p. 153).

Jennifer: The "null curriculum" (Flinders, Noddings, and Thornton, 1986) thesis is that "there are no value-free facts" (Norris and Sawyer, 2004, pp. 148–153).

Patrice: I think that's the invisible barrier. Teaching diversity, that's the invisible barrier that we fight against. We try to say, "Oh, we're just trying to talk about it, there is no agenda." But really, there is. We're trying to get people to realize the way racism, sexism, all the *isms*, how they operate. It's wrong. And we want students to realize it's wrong so they don't perpetuate it.

Jennifer: What would be interesting, though, is—I don't even think we can articulate really easily. Even with all this theory, what are we exactly fighting against?

Patrice: Yeah, it's this invisible force. Because we can't say who the originator was, we can't pinpoint a location, we can't . . . so yeah, we're fighting a sort of age-old monster.

Jennifer: The sort of underlying prejudices, ideas, assumptions people make without realizing they're making them. I don't even know that the students know that they're doing it. The coded language that I hear about, "I have to lock my car because I'm going to a bad neighborhood," and all that.

Patrice: Right.

Jennifer: In the Norris and Sawyer duoethnography, Joe talks about how even though he thought sexual orientation issues were important, he didn't talk about them because he didn't want his kids to think they were a big deal (2004, p. 148). I think that's what our generation's parents were doing. Don't talk about it; if we pretend it's not a big deal, it won't be a big deal.

Patrice: Yeah, because as Joe says, "My silence was problematic."

WHAT ARE THE REWARDS?

An "unhomely moment" is "a disruption of the façade of normalcy can allow us to get past cultural relativism to learn through conflict" (Bhaba, 1994, cited in Asher, 2007, p. 71). Breaking through students' resistance and confronting the ways that race still operates in our lives is a distinctly unhomely experience, one that can be painful, even for teachers of diversity and social justice courses.

The immediate "rewards" of teaching diversity might be a difficult class experience and negative evaluations. Neither of us finds teaching diversity to be a fun experience. We both feel committed to it because we want the topic to be honestly addressed in a way that promotes social justice. We are also going to try to bring in more voices to the discussion by inviting guest speakers to talk about different aspects of diversity and the way they intersect. We don't know whether our actions will have an effect, but we feel a responsibility to try. In his book on privilege, Johnson quoted Ghandi as saying, "Nothing we do as individuals matters but it's vitally important to do it anyway" (2006, p. 132). We are hoping that even introducing a crack into students' denial and resistance, we will have a long-term impact, even if we never know that we did.

Jennifer: I think it's a hard topic because there isn't a really good way to wrap it up and answer the question.

Patrice: I think "such a disruption of the façade of normalcy can allow us to get past cultural relativism to learn through conflict" (Bhaba, 1994, cited in Asher, 2007, p. 71). By the nature of this topic alone, we have to break down barriers but also learn through the tension and the conflict. It will be an ongoing process; it's not something that will happen the first time they encounter it.

Jennifer: It would be interesting to follow up with students a year, two years after they leave the class and see what they took away from it.

Patrice: See if they've changed any.

Jennifer: I think when the teacher of the diversity class was an adjunct, it was too easy for students to dismiss the class. Now that we're full-timers teaching the class, it will be different, I hope. Always handing a class off to an adjunct sends a message that it's irrelevant.

Patrice: Yeah. It is a supposedly core class, and then they ask, "When are we going to talk about leadership?"

Jennifer: My two topics that I'm researching right now couldn't be more different. I'm doing a project on assessment with another faculty member, and I'm doing this project on diversity. In both of them, there's the sense of faculty thinking it's important, but they don't want to do it, and they don't know what they will get out of it.

Patrice: Like Asher says, "Such pedagogical work is demanding, even draining, and the rewards are few and far between."

LESSONS LEARNED

Patrice: I walk away from this duoethnography having experienced a deeper awareness of myself as a leadership educator/social justice educator. There is an old adage that says, "Understanding takes time." Having heard that for most of my childhood, it seemed like a misnomer. I knew the significant meaning of the phrase in an intellectual way. However, through this duoethnography, I've experienced the tangibility of its meaning. To understand myself in the reflection of Jennifer was a vulnerable feeling. At times, I wanted to quit for fear of the unknown and many questions that followed, such as, What would our relationship be like after this process as colleagues? What if I share too much? What if she doesn't share at all? And when will the process of discovery end? But I was able to learn through the dissonance and discomfort, as Griffin and Ouellett (2007) suggest, and began to experience comfort in the relationship that I was building with Jennifer.

I also walk away from this process having grown as an educator. I've come to vocalize and admit to myself as well as Jennifer the hot buttons or triggers that I continue to work out in regard to race, power, and privilege. It's inappropriate for me as an educator in social justice and leadership to work out my issues during class with my students. If I am emotionally overcharged in class, the atmosphere to learn and grow through the tension is forever lost. I must be an example of how to have the difficult conversation without losing control of who I am. In essence, as a leader in the classroom I must model the way (Kouzes and Posner, 2002). However, that does not mean I will put on a façade. It just means that I am aware of my triggers and respond (or maybe not) in a respectful manner that does not disrupt the learning environment of the course. Although this concept of knowing your triggers is widely known and accepted in the social justice leadership literature, there are times when my head has been overruled by the emotions of my heart. I thank Jennifer for helping me walk through the myriad of emotions and conflicts that arose this past year while teaching this course.

Jennifer: One of the primary lessons we learned from this investigation is that even though it is natural to avoid talking about or examining our own internalized racism, we both felt safer once we had opened the lines of communication. Initially, both of us had felt the need to hide the negative attitudes that were passed along to us by our families, explicitly or implicitly. These skeletons in our closets seemed less threatening when we could talk about them.

Our first step toward this project was our discussion of the fears we each had about doing it. Realizing that Patrice shared my fears helped. I learned that both of us had guilt and shame about things we had heard, said, done, or thought around race. I realized that this guilt and shame was what was sticking in my throat and preventing me from speaking in class at times. It was also what kept me from intervening quickly enough to prevent one of the Black students got out of line and ended up saying something that deeply hurt and offended another student, also a Black woman. This wasn't the kind of comment that can promote better understanding or healing; it was just a personal attack. It was an instance of not listening to my instincts because I was concerned about possible racial overtones to my reaction.

I think I also projected some of my problems onto a few of the White students. The result was that I thought they were not taking the class seriously. I didn't see resistance as a natural part of the process; I saw it as my own failure. It isn't surprising that I had bad evaluations in that class. My own self-evaluation of my performance was worse than the students', and I found myself going over and over things that were done and said in the classroom, trying to see how I could do things differently. This experience has helped me to understand better the feelings behind students' resistance.

This project has reminded me that theory can provide guidance on how to handle difficult classroom experiences. I also believe that by this open examination of my own experiences and hidden curriculum, I have made peace with the lessons of my past. I am hoping that I can model this to students the next time I teach a class on diversity and social justice issues.

CONCLUSION

The learning facilitated in our duoethnographic process is an ongoing journey. Through duoethnography we have gained some insight into each others' lived experiences and how each incident described affects our perception of each other, our students, and our teaching. This chapter is a beginning, as we seek ways to improve strategies to teaching a graduate course on diversity and social justice. Our experiences with this assignment have not only given us new insights into student resistance and the ways to make students feel safe in the classroom; they also suggest new pedagogical strategies. We have a new awareness of the importance of including a variety of voices in our conversations about diversity. Team teaching our courses might not be practical in a small program like ours, but looking for opportunities to bring in guest speakers with a variety of experiences seems essential. We need to open up the conversation. To facilitate student dialogues, we are developing a duoethnography assignment to replace the autobiography we have used in the past. We think that pairing students up and having them write in concert about their different experiences will help make the theory we teach in this class more real.

Our initial goal of this project was to uncover tensions about race, power, and privilege in the context of the classroom setting. We wanted to see if our resistance, tension, and/or anxiety had an adverse reaction in the classroom. This continues to be a goal because we are the sites of the research. However, we walk away with not only a sense of urgency to change individual comfort levels with the topic but also a desire to change structural dynamics within the academy that hinder productive learning and conversations around race, power, and privilege.

We are fully aware of our positional power within the academy hierarchy as junior faculty; however, our commitment to break down barriers that fuel structural inferences in regard to race, power, and privilege within the academy does not dismay us. We also seek creative ways to strategize and galvanize those who rarely have a voice. In doing so, we feel that our conversation is only the beginning. We've pondered our next steps and implications for this line of inquiry.

We adamantly believe that the student voice is important as we seek to have difficult conversations about race, power, and privilege. Much has been written about classroom environment, multicultural education, and equity in teaching and learning (Brooke, 1999; Chesler, Alford, and Young, 2007; Cohen and Lotan, 2004; Holton, 1999; Pope, 2005; Tiberius and Flak, 1999). However, there is a paucity of information written from the learner perspective, especially the graduate student learner. By including student voices, we feel that we will learn their needs and help us better prepare curriculum that meets those needs so that the conversation can move from theory into practice. Our thinking is grounded in the work of many social justice educators that posit that what we do (or don't do) translates into actions in our communities, schools, and organizations (Cambron-McCabe and McCarthy, 2005; Johnson, 2006; Ladson-Billings, 1995; Lindsey and Terrell, 2009; Rusch and Horsford, 2008, 2009).

REFERENCES

Asher, N. (2007). Made in the (multicultural) U.S.A.: Unpacking tensions of race, culture, gender, and sexuality in education. *Educational Researcher, 36*(2), 65–73.

Baraka, J. N. (1997). Collegiality in the academy: Where does the Black woman fit? In L. Benjamin (Ed.), *Black women in the academy: Promises and perils* (pp. 235–245). Gainesville: University of Florida Press.

Brooke, C. P. (1999). Feelings from the back row: Negotiating sensitive issues in large classes. *New Directions for Teaching and Learning, 1*(77), 23–33.

Cambron-McCabe, N., and McCarthy, M. M. (2005). Educating school leaders for social justice. *Educational Policy, 19*(1), 201–222.

Chesler, M., Alford, A., and Young, J. (2007). Faculty members' social identities and classroom authority. *New Directions for Teaching and Learning, 1*(111), 11–19.

Cohen, E. G., and Lotan, R. A. (2004). Equity in heterogeneous classrooms. In J. A. Banks and C.A.M. Banks (Eds.), *Handbook of Research on Multicultural Education* (2nd ed., pp. 737–750). San Francisco: John Wiley & Sons, Inc.

Collins, P. H. (2000). *Black feminist thought: Knowledge, consciousness, and the politics of empowerment.* New York: Routledge.

Flinders, D. J., Noddings, N., and Thornton, J. S. (1986). The null curriculum: Its theoretical basis and practical implications. *Curriculum Inquiry, 16*(1), 33–42.

Griffin, P., and Ouellett, M. L. (2007). Facilitating social justice education courses. In M. Adams, L. A. Bell, and P. Griffin (Eds.), *Teaching for diversity and social justice* (2nd ed., pp. 89–113). New York: Routledge.

Hardiman, R., and Jackson, B. W. (1997). Conceptual foundations for social justice courses. In M. Adams, L. A. Bell, and P. Griffin (Eds.), *Teaching for diversity and social justice* (pp. 16–29). New York: Routledge.

Holton, S. (1999). After the eruption: Managing conflict in the classroom. *New Directions for Teaching and Learning, 1*(77), 59–67.

Johnson, A. G. (2006). *Privilege, power, and difference* (2nd ed.). Boston: McGraw Hill.

Kouzes, J. M., and Posner, B. Z. (2002). *The leadership challenge.* San Francisco: Jossey-Bass Publishers.

Ladson-Billings, G. (1995). Toward a theory of culturally relevant pedagogy. *American Educational Research Journal, 32*(3), 465–491.

Lindsey, R. B., and Terrell, R. D. (2009). *Culturally proficient leadership: The personal journey begins within.* Thousand Oaks, CA: Corwin Press.

McIntosh, P. (1997). White privilege and male privilege: A personal account of coming to see correspondences through work in women's studies. In R. Delgado and J. Stefancic (Eds.), *Critical white studies: Looking behind the mirror* (pp. 291–297). Philadelphia: Temple University Press.

Norris, J. (2008). Duoethnography. In L. M. Given (Ed.), *The SAGE encyclopedia of qualitative research methods* (Vol. 1, pp. 233–236). Los Angeles: Sage.

Norris, J., and Sawyer, R. D. (2004). Null and hidden curricula of sexual orientation: A dialogue on the curreres of the absent presence and the present absence. In L. Coia, M. Birch, N. J. Brooks, E. Heilman, S. Mayer, A. Mountain, and P. Pritchard (Eds.), *Democratic responses in an era of standardization.* Troy, NY: Educator's International Press, Inc.

Oberg, A., and Wilson, T. (2002, December). Side by side: Being in research autobiographically. *Educational Insights, 7*(2). Retrieved from http://ccfi.educ.ubc.ca/publication/insights/v07n02/contextualexplorations/wilson_oberg/

Pinar, W. (1975). Curere: Toward reconceptualization. In W. Pinar (Ed.), *Curriculum theorizing.* Berkeley, CA: McCutchan.

Pope, R. L. (2005). Faculty and curriculum: Examining multicultural competence and inclusion. *Journal of College Student Development, 46*(6), 679–687.

Rusch, E. A., and Horsford, S. D. (2008). Unifying messy communities: Learning social justice in educational leadership classrooms. *Teacher Development, 12*(4), 353–367.

Rusch, E. A., and Horsford, S. D. (2009). Changing hearts and minds: The quest for open talk about race in educational leadership. *International Journal of Leadership in Educational Management, 23*(4), 302–313.

Sawyer, R. D., and Norris, J. (2009). Duoethnography. In W. S. Gershon (Ed.), *The collaborative turn: Working together in qualitative research* (pp. 127–140). Rotterdam: Sense Publishers.

Stanley, C. (2006). An overview of the literature. In C. Stanley (Ed.), *Faculty of color: Teaching in predominantly White colleges and universities* (pp. 1–29). Boston: Anker Publishing Company, Inc.

Tiberius, R. G., and Flak, E. (1999). Incivility in dyadic teaching and learning. *New Directions for Teaching and Learning, 1*(77), 3–12.

CHAPTER 7

Alleyways and Pathways:
Our Avenues through Patriotic Songs

M. Francyne Huckaby and Molly Weinburgh

PROLOGUE

Drawing from the work of Bakhtin (1981), duoethnographers structure dialogic situations to promote imagination and multiple perspectives. Although these dialogues are almost always between at least two researchers working together, they are also between the researcher and additional texts, such as cultural artifacts. These texts promote inquirers' interactions among their currere (e.g., their analysis and reconceptualization of personal histories and interpersonal relationships) within their cultural worlds. Examining themselves as the site of their inquiry, they focus on how the cultural tools and symbols that populate their lives mediate their experiences. This process ideally promotes the agency of inquirers within their cultural worlds.

*Francyne Huckaby and Molly Weinburgh's study about patriotism in the southern United States exemplifies the use of dialogic texts to promote new perspectives. In their study, they juxtapose their presentation and discussion of two songs—*Dixie Land *and* Lift Every Voice—*as cultural contexts of analysis. They examine these songs as cultural artifacts with which to explore personal and societal "issues of worth, dignity, power, and position" (p. 159).*

As readers of their study, we (Rick and Joe) immediately recognized how we have deeply embodied associations to music, associations that can trigger profound emotions. The associations and meanings that these songs evoked within Huckaby and Weinburgh deepened the embodied nature of their inquiry into power and patriotism. Juxtaposing these songs, they created a dialectical structure of analysis, delineating their overlaps, differences, and gray zones. The research topic itself—patriotism within a landscape of complex inequities—is relatively inaccessible to many other research methods. On one level, they explore in various contexts the meanings they have made and are continuing to make in relation to the songs. For example, Huckaby shares these thoughts:

> *I responded to* Dixie *as though it were an attack or at least a potential attack on my person—my black, Southern person. The song created a visceral and emotional self-protection response for me. The option of considering what the person mentioning it, singing it, or honking it might mean did not enter my considerations. (p. 162)*

Weinburgh, discussing with Huckaby how the meaning of the song Dixie *may have shifted to become a de facto flag for the Confederacy, states that*

> *the shift can be gut-wrenching for some. You can hear where I am—with both sides I become insecure because either threatens who I am and where I'm positioned. I do NOT want white supremacy. I don't want this supremacy thing to take on any force and potential at all. Though I side with the other way more intellectually, my gut says, but where does that leave me? I'm in that unusual position where I certainly don't want to go where the song* Dixie *seems to be leading. But it is unsettling to think about all of the things that I have taken for granted, things that would change if we restructure—even if we restructure the way I'd like us to restructure—life's not going to be the same way it was, or is, or would continue to be. (pp. 173–174)*

As the above passages suggest, dialogue in duoethnography can promote researcher dedication to honesty and at times a destabilizing process of disclosure. Personal contradictory meanings emerge from the fabric of these embodied disclosures. And on another level, as the song Dixie *is loaded with shared local and national cultural meanings, Huckaby and Weinburgh use their personal analysis as a lens for a broader survey of the racial landscape in the United States from the Civil Rights movement to the present. Furthermore, as they deconstruct their relationship to the historical, racial, and geographic contexts of these songs that are well known at least throughout the United States, they encourage the readers to do so as well.*

Huckaby and Weinburgh's study demonstrates how dialogue in duoethnography promotes a critical, yet embodied growth in perspective toward a topic, as well as a level of catharsis through a greater awareness of our symbolic landscape. Part of what their study shows is that some research questions benefit greatly from dialogic study.

—*Richard D. Sawyer*

Patriotism

In this duoethnography, we walk parallel paths that honor and expose our experiences, which are valid and reasonable despite their differences. In this telling, we restory earlier experiences and events as we reflect on later ones (Connelly and Clandinin, 1990; Pinar, 2004). We know restorying shift our stories with time, and we see distinctions with each retelling. We have listened and given stories back to the other with interpretations from our outsider perspectives; transforming our thoughts with each elucidation. We create a new story within this text that is the moving forward and rethinking of both our experiences. Framed around a year of conversations that we recorded, transcribed, revisited, and restoried, our writing is authentic, real, and incomplete. Neither experience negates the other but instead complicates it. We now question whether we are in any way representative of our groups or merely two individuals sharing our experiences.

OUR AVENUE OF TRANSFORMATION

This journey began in a song. As two Southern women—friends, academics, spouses, and nonparents—we have continued our sojourn not just with a song but with songs: songs we have known, loved, hated, embraced, found, and jettisoned. Songs that we now know have shaped us, strengthened us, and failed us. Songs we have sung with pride and pain as well as with enthusiasm and embarrassment. Songs that have brought, and still do bring, a mixture of emotions. With our story, in the form of a conversation, we invite you to join us in thinking about issues of worth, dignity, power, and position. We begin by sharing two of the songs with selections of the lines most influential in our lives.

Song of the South	*Negro National Anthem*
I wish I was in the land of cotton . . .	*Lift ev'ry voice and sing . . .*
In Dixie Land where I was born in,	*Sing a song full of the faith*
Early on a frosty mornin'	*that the dark past has taught us*
Away, away, away down south in Dixie.	*Sing a song full of the hope*
(Emmett and Hobbs, 1860)	*that the present has brought us.*
	(Johnson and Johnson, 1900)

We are bookends of the wave of the Civil Rights movement enacted during the mid-twentieth century that sought legal equality for African Americans.

Molly: I lived it. Not like those who marched or put their lives on the line, but with the adult decisions about integration, my life changed. As a late teenager, I was fearful of the ramification of state-mandated desegregation. These were turbulent times in my small town. My parents discussed sending me to a private school, which would have been one of the most upsetting ramifications. We had a huge debate over several weeks, and the stance of our family was that I would stay in public school as it desegregated.

Fran: Were you involved in this decision?

Molly: Yes, I was a part of the decision. I lived desegregation in a way that you did not, partly due to your being younger and growing up in Houston. But I remember the closing of the African American school in my town. All the students were required to go to school in the building that had housed only white students the year before. I found it terribly sad that the African American students had to give up all the artifacts associated with a school: their school colors and mascot, trophies won, pictures of graduating classes. The students moved into the white school as if they had no prior life or identity.

Fran: I wasn't alive during that time. By the time I came, desegregation had started doing some things.

Molly: I was sixteen when you were born.

Fran: Sixteen years can make a difference. Not that the arguments were quieted, but the laws and the actions changed the land-scape enough that I went to integrated schools from preschool to graduate school. The schools were differently integrated depend-ing on whether the school was parochial, public, magnet, or pri-vate; where the schools were located; and the years I attended the schools. I also grew up in a family raised by my grandmother, who consciously avoided situations that would limit her choices and dignity. She preferred to walk or to ride with somebody she knew and refused to step onto a segregated bus. I benefited from being born into such a family.

Born in Athens, Alabama, Molly was fourteen years old during the 1965 Freedom March from Selma to Montgomery. Aware and sympathetic of the movement, she was not an active participant in any of its public manifesta-tions. Her mother was a vocal supporter and advocate for civil rights, her father a silent supporter. Fran was an infant in Houston, Texas, two years after the Freedom March. Local leaders (white and black) quietly desegregated the city, businesses, and schools to comply with federal nondiscrimination laws and to desegregate without public disturbance to acquire NASA (National Aeronautics and Space Administration) and the Astrodome (Lawson, 2008; Moss, 1997). Unaware of the newly acquired possibilities for her life in her early years, Fran grew up in a family that believed change would come through education and purposeful resistance to quotidian inequities.

Table 7.1 Juxtaposed Voices of *Dixie Land* and *Lift Every Voice and Sing*

The part of the United States known to many as *Dixie* was my reality. *Dixie* was the feel of red clay as it stuck to my shoes after a rain and covered the surface of cars during the long hot summer. *Dixie* was the smell of insecticide sprayed on cotton fields and the sweet mix of privet and honeysuckle on a summer night and wood smoke from the fireplace in winter. *Dixie* was the sight of a dormant field waiting for spring planting. *Dixie* was waterskiing and fried chicken, Christmas pageants and fruitcakes, hot nights and fireflies.	*Lift Every Voice and Sing* is belonging, whether standing with childhood neighbors in pews, friends and colleagues in January or February, or strangers at a community event. *Lift Every Voice and Sing* is memories recalled and retold of suffering, struggling, and overcoming; a call—from elders, adults, and youth for justice, humanity, and education—asking each of us to join the song and the work to improve our lives. I am a quieter South of negotiated rights, history lessons, civil rights stories, new opportunities, and lingering limitations.
I am *Dixie Land*, the song of the South.	I am *Lift Every Voice and Sing*, the Negro National Anthem.

PATHWAYS OF TWO PATRIOTIC SONGS

Molly: After one of our conversations, I talked with Cecilia, our colleague from Columbia, about patriotism. I told her I feel apologetic for feeling more loyal to the region than to the country as a whole. She indicated that the Spanish language has two concepts, *patria grande* and *patria chica*. You were expected to be a patriot of your city or township (*patria chica*), your state, and your country (*patria grande*). These Spanish expressions allow you to be patriotic to both township and country, and nobody thinks it's unusual because you used the correct term for the level of patriotism. But I have always felt that we are expected to be more patriotic to our country than to our local community. English doesn't have the kind of language that shows these levels.

Fran: We have *patriotism*, one word only and can use it to exclude: You are a patriot if you show it this way, but not if you act another way. I also feel that U.S. local and national patriotism exist in tension; states' rights are an example.

Molly: There is that—states' rights verses U.S. rights. Also, we use the word *expatriate* for people who may not be away from the country forever.

Fran: Ironically, I was an expatriate as a U.S. Peace Corps volunteer. Were you considered an expatriate when you were in Zimbabwe?

Molly: No, I was only there for a summer, but people talked about the expats living there. The "ex" for us is derogatory, so the "ex" means that you no longer are, yet while living in Papua New Guinea, you carried your passport and identity. As I think about language a little more now, I find English to be a restrictive language.

Fran: I suppose all languages open up some possibilities and restrict in other ways, but we don't think about it much when we are *in* the language.

I think forms of competition are within patriotism, as you compete against something or someone to show how patriotic you are. How that competition plays out depends on who you are. If you are someone who "looks American," your possible plays are very different than if you don't "look American." Looking a certain way, of course, has nothing to do with your choices or feelings but with the way others read you. I have thought of *Dixie* as part of that competition: Which camp are you in? The setup is adversarial.

Molly: As in: "If you are not with me, you must be against me."

Fran: In fact, our initial conversations about *Dixie Land*, which I captured in writing "Dear Molly: Seven Letters About 'Dixie'" (Huckaby, 2007), illuminate how I responded to *Dixie* as though it were an attack or at least a potential attack on my person—my Black, Southern person. The song created a visceral and emotional self-protection response for me. The option of considering what the person mentioning it, singing it, or honking it might mean did not enter my considerations.

Molly: I also came to a similar conclusion; otherwise, I would not have felt the need to give *Dixie* up. If I do not want others to see me in the stereotypic idea of *Dixie*, I had to give it up.

Fran: We entered these conversations about *Dixie* after you said you were sad about not being able to sing *Dixie* in public.

Molly: For fear of being labeled a racist.

Fran: Yeah, I had a hard time reconciling my view of people who would sing *Dixie* and the person I knew you to be. Your affection for *Dixie* did not fit my conception of you as a person willing to challenge racism and seek social justice. I began to wrestle with understanding your experiences with *Dixie*. I am appreciative of your willingness to talk with me about *Dixie* over a year, to read my reflective writings after our conversations, and to trust me as I published these writings as a series of letters to you, "Dear Molly" (Huckaby, 2007).

So here we are, two Southerners
On a journey with songs
One that Fran does not want
One Molly chose to give up
Position & Justice

Sojourners: The song becomes a place symbolic of the struggle but not itself the struggle. Just because we silence a song doesn't mean we rid ourselves of the underlying adversarial stuff. No it does not, because the underlying stuff is the way we treated other human beings at particular times and in certain places; in this case, the U.S. in the late 1800s, when *Dixie Land* was written and performed in minstrel shows, which were considered an appropriate entertainment venue. Therefore, the song carries the baggage of its own beginnings. But when Molly sang the song as a child, she did not know this. In her *patria chica*, *Dixie* was simply representing home: the roots and hard work of her ancestors captured in visions of cotton fields, sweet tea, and rocking chairs.

BETWEEN PRIVATE AND PUBLIC

Fran: I remember our conversation in the bagel shop last fall, Molly. You told me about your early memories of *Dixie*—hearing lines of it sung in your Alabama home by your mother as she mopped the floor, by your grandmother as she kneaded bread, by your father as he fixed your bicycle. You never heard or sang all verses of the song in any public venue. Instead, you sang or hummed lines of the song as your family had in your home. The intimacy of your experiences as you grew up with this song surprised me, maybe even shocked me.

    In my experience, *Lift Every Voice and Sing* is a communal, if not public, song, but its public nature, as I have come to know through our discussions, is not public for all Americans, even though its first singing was in the White House for Lincoln's 100th birthday celebration in 1901 (Bond and Wilson, 2000; NPR, 2002; PBS Video, 2010). James Weldon Johnson (1935) explained the song's genesis:

> A group of young men in Jacksonville, Florida, arranged to celebrate Lincoln's birthday in 1900. . . . I wrote the words and [my brother] wrote the music. Our New York publisher . . . made mimeographed copies for us and the song was taught to and sung by a chorus of five hundred colored school children.
>
> Shortly afterwards . . . the song passed out of our minds. But the school children of Jacksonville kept singing it, they went off to other schools and sang it, they became teachers and taught it to other children. Within twenty years it was being sung over the South and in some other parts of the country. Today, the song, popularly known as the Negro National Hymn, is quite generally used. (cited in Bond and Wilson, 2000, p. 3)

    Exposure primarily within the African American community protected the song, which was adopted by the NAACP (National Association for the Advancement of Colored People) as the Negro National Anthem, from broader public scrutiny. *Lift Every Voice and Sing* occupies a hybridized space of privacy and protection from the broader society while remaining public and shared within the community. *Dixie Land*, as you have shared, seems both intimately private and publicly exposed, at least in the South. How interesting are the ways both *Dixie* and *Lift Every Voice* are private *and* public songs and unlike the very public national anthem, *Star-Spangled Banner* (Key, 1814). I have to say, I considered *Dixie* a public song that expressed the ideology of its singer. Before our conversations,

I had not considered *Dixie* in the private realm as an expression of familial intimacy.

My naïve thinking about *Dixie* was that there was only one stance for loving *Dixie*, and not that there could be some variety. It's really interesting because I thought that I had learned my lesson through "Dear Molly" (Huckaby, 2007), but as we talk, I'm noticing nuances in this lesson.

Molly: Me too, very much so for me; I'm learning lessons, too. What was around me in the South in the late '50s and early '60s looked normal, even if it was not. It looked like what I wanted it to be rather than what I would not have wanted. I'm noticing how easy it is to romanticize something so that it doesn't look so bad.

Fran: Right.

Molly: The kinds of things that epitomized the "South," like picking cotton: When you romanticize them, you forget that it's in the middle of the hot summer and it's smelly, hard work. It rips your hands apart; you know nobody wore work gloves. It didn't bring much money, so that huge burlap sack gets full and you've made a dollar and a half. That's not romantic; that's not wonderful. When we've made it that way, we've changed it in some way. It's interesting to me how we do that, make something seem more elegant than it is.

I guess *Dixie* was that way for me. The phrase "live and die for Dixie" meant something different for me. But now, knowing who wrote it, when it was written, how one dressed in blackface to sing it, the vernacular that made it what it is: These things make the song different for me; it is about not home but servitude. When I sang *Dixie*, I did not mean that I would die for slavery, but I would die for Dixie—my *patria chica*.

In reverse, *Lift Every Voice* is more a song about bursting into freedom. I can read the letters in "Dear Molly" (Huckaby, 2007) and know where you are coming from. I'm beginning to understand why you wrote in "Dear Molly" about getting joy from the act of singing *Lift Every Voice and Sing* as well as the words. I can understand why these words, even though I didn't know the tune, were written to be uplifting and give you the sense of "knowing the words intellectually, feeling them soulfully, and singing them viscerally" (p. 66).

So here we are, two academics
Discussing our sojourns with songs
One that Fran would never want

And Molly chose to give up
Another Molly can't claim
And Fran knows proudly
Power & Position

Sojourners: The public representation isn't really the same as the private experience as we've both seen in these songs and the Southern experience. Isn't it interesting that a discussion of songs can carry us into deeper understandings?

MOVING TOWARD THE PUBLIC

Molly: Thank you for sending me that link (see http://video.pbs.org/video/1410865290/ chapter 16 of 16). I have now heard *Lift Every Voice and Sing* sung at the White House by a chorus of well-known artists (PBS Video, 2010). It tells us something that I, as a white person, never thought, that *Lift Every Voice* would be included on the program for Black History Month.

Fran: I knew immediately. When I heard the news announcement on the radio, I knew they're going to sing *Lift Every Voice*—it's going to be sung there—and I just had to share it with you! After all, with current technology unavailable at the turn of last century, this second singing in the White House would be more broadly available for the public.

Molly: And it was just the opposite for me. If someone said, "Which songs do you think are going to be there?" I have to think—two or three really good spirituals, probably . . .

Fran: . . . some good civil rights songs . . .

Molly: . . . maybe some working songs. But I might never have gone to *Lift Every Voice* . . .

Fran: . . . this might be about positionality (Kincheloe, 2001).

Molly: Exactly. What one would expect . . .

Fran: . . . what knowledge we can and cannot access. I think it speaks to this notion of private and public. I have a more private knowledge and could say: "Well, yeah, of course."

Molly: *Lift Every Voice* is more public now. That one act of showing it is very different from being in a private large congregation or at Carnegie Hall.

Fran: It's on the Internet with American celebrities singing it.

Molly: What a great cast of people. You're looking at all of these artists and going: Whoa!

Fran: I'm sure it's going to be on DVD and played on national TV.

Molly: I think at the end of the month.

Fran: I marked it on my calendar just to see it on TV, you can see it on the Web, but I would like to see it on TV.

Molly: *Lift Every Voice and Sing* wasn't what I expected.

Fran: So, what did you expect?

Molly: I couldn't tell you exactly what I expected. Hearing the song just wasn't what I expected. I now know the words because I've read them often enough in "Dear Molly" (Huckaby, 2007), so I anticipated the way it was going to unfold, and I really liked hearing it. I was just very conscious that it didn't quite sound . . . I don't know.

Fran: I am used to being within a group of people who are singing the song, and it was interesting watching people sing it. Additionally, the credits started rolling after the first verse, making the song the ending instead of the experience. Our talking about *Lift Every Voice* has been so much about it being the experience. I was really struck by the difference of seeing it on a screen and hearing it through speakers as opposed to being among bodies singing it—being part of it.

Molly: I would think it would be because you begin swaying—most of us can't sit still to music—so you get not only the hearing of it but the full movement of it. Dixie makes me want to march in place.

Fran: I don't think it's a song that begs you to move to it.

Molly: It didn't! And that may be the strange part: I thought it would be more like a spiritual that got you to . . .

Fran: It's more like a standing song. You just stand to it; it doesn't ask you to move at all. The only part of it that has a catalytic rhythm did not come out very strong. But if you are in a place experiencing it live with some good baritones around you, a couple of lines go bass:

Sing a song full of the faith that the dark past has taught us
Sing a song full of the faith that the present has brought us

But the deep tones of these lines were not expressed in this higher octave version. But *Lift Every Voice and Sing* doesn't call you to move. [laughter]

Molly: I guess that is what I expected—something that was much more physical.

Fran: *Dixie* calls you to move much more, there's a little catch to it. Interesting that *Lift Every Voice is* not what you thought it would be.

So here we are, two women
Exploring our paths with songs
One, Molly, hums under her breath
Another, Fran, sings openly
Dignity & Humanity

Sojourners: Once again, the songs have given us a route to talk about difficult topics, but the conversation itself is filled with laughter and learning as we share private insights with each other.

WEAPONS OF PATRIOTISM

Fran: I've thought about the public/private and power/freedom parts of our conversations, although I may go in a different direction on power than you would, but that is absolutely okay. Maybe I've approached the power around *Dixie* with too many limitations. Relations of power (Foucault, 2000; Freire, 1989) necessarily imply freedom. Freedom, then, is having a field of possible actions while relations of power are actions upon another's actions that limit the field of possibility (Foucault, 2000). So maybe my responses to *Dixie* have been an example of how the song has governed and limited freedom; at least in my case, I only reacted to it in one way. I do have to be careful here, for *Dixie* has not been just about a song, and I am certain the anxiety and self-protection response has been about preservation, and while this is clearly not necessary with you, it may be the case in other circumstances. I'm considering the question: How might we respond to the *governmentality* (Foucault, 1997) of something like *Dixie* without limiting our freedom? In doing so, how can we continue to protect ourselves when necessary? I think these issues of freedom and protection are very real for both of us, but in different ways. DiFranco, in "My IQ" (1993, track 9), sings:

Every tool is a weapon if you hold it right.

I realize that any tool, even a song like *Dixie*, can be experienced as a weapon, even when it is not held as one.

Molly: Every tool can be used as a weapon, even a song.

Fran: I love "My IQ" because I was introduced to the song at a time when I was trying to figure out who I am and how I could be in the world; how could I be, as a young woman in the world, when the world didn't want the kind of young woman

I was becoming? How do I fight for my self-formation without wounding myself or others? What kinds of tools are appropriate for such a struggle? As I was reading our work, DiFranco's idea turned on itself. A tool can become a weapon because it is experienced and perceived as being used as such, even when an individual use of it may be benign . . .

Molly: . . . designed for one purpose but used for another. It's that same idea that knowledge itself is not moral or amoral but changes with how you choose to use the knowledge. "Every tool is a weapon if you hold it right." Occasionally, I hear a little clip like this, and I wish I had said it.

Fran: And she's talking about words. She's a songwriter talking about her songs.

Molly: If her words delivered in song can become a tool or weapon, then the words of other songs can, too. Tools and weapons have power. Foucault's idea of power as the implication to freedom verses power as the thing that stifles freedom reminds me that power is different depending on which side of the coin you are looking at and how you are using that tool.

One of the things you did in the "Dear Molly" letters (Huckaby, 2007) was to say that you were going to try to do a mind experiment. I think that is really powerful in the letters. You asked, "What if I were not me? What if I were the other? (de Beauvoir, 1989; Husserl, 1991). What does that do for what I think about the other? What does that do for what I think about myself?" If we do a reverse of that, is it possible for me to imagine a world in which I was not me: How would it be different . . .

Fran: . . . if relations of power and privilege reversed your positionality?

Molly: What would that have done? What would a song like *Dixie* say to me if I had not been me, if I had been other? That's terribly hard, and it can only mean something if it is contextualized. It has to pull up some kind of prior knowledge, feelings, or something, or it would just be a song. What in the song would I have known or not known?

Fran: The way I started the thought experiment was not so much with the song, but I tried to locate historical markers that I knew, and I thought, "Well, let's just imagine the world as different and I am connected to this song through my community, but my community was positioned in the world very differently." So, what if it were my song and I were positioned dominantly in society, where I didn't have to worry, were more likely safe, likely to have access to more resources, coming from ancestors that were not slaves but slave owners? I tried to imagine, as much as I could, realizing that I can't do it completely. I started thinking what it would mean today if I came from generations that had such experiences; if I looked around a society, at the TV, in the museum, how might they be different? Who would be represented, respected, honored? I tried to recognize all of that and then imagine what *Lift Every Voice and Sing* might mean if it could remain tied to me.

It was hard to let go; I could go to a point but not further, because I got nervous thinking I could feel entitled: "Well, so what if I am here and others are not? My family earned this." I could go down that road.

Molly: *Dixie* was intended to be sung in dialect and with blackened faces, so for me to say, "What if I were not a privileged one? What if my people were being portrayed this way? What would I feel about the 'land of cotton, old times there are not forgotten' if my skin were black?"

Fran: Well, *Dixie* is a subordinated song in some ways, isn't it? I mean the South lost. So in one way *Dixie* is subordinate (North/ South), but in another relationship (owner/slave, white/black) it's dominant.

Molly: You're right. So if thought about it in terms of North/South conflict, definitely it is the song of those who did not conquer. It is more likely to be thought of as the song of the people who were conquerors in the sense of being slave owners, and what can be more conquering than taking ownership of another human being?

Fran: I'm wondering if it becomes a song that is so incredibly charged because of the vulnerability of a people who have lost and also had a degree of power over other people. Is there something more charged about being in this sandwiched position as opposed to being in the position say of *Yankee Doodle Boy, popularly known as Yankee Doodle Dandy*? (Cohan, 1904) I do not have the same reaction to this song. Why is that?

Molly: Yeah, yeah. [silence] And boy, talk about a foot tapper; that one is. [joint laughter]

Fran: Do we miss the overarching dynamics because it is easier to target a group that is above us but still below something else? "This one is dangerous to me immediately, but that one up there may not be as directly or personally dangerous." Is this about a hierarchy? Is this about being Southern? Is it just about *Dixie* because the South is my home and *Dixie* as a song of the South and *Yankee Doodle Dandy* is from far away or neutralized by its Americanization?

Molly: Also, *Dixie* has physical things attached, like a flag and rednecks.

Fran: Well *Yankee Doodle Dandy* has Yankees and the Union flag, right?

Molly: But I don't feel that connection. I get images now when you start talking about *Dixie* of the rebel flag and being . . .

Fran: . . . this flag is intimately connected to *Dixie* . . .

Molly: . . . waved back and forth and a swept yard with a vehicle up on blocks, sort of the redneck image, which I don't get with any other songs. Most songs don't carry such a secondary artifact with them.

Fran: *Lift Every Voice*, I picture black people and more likely church-going black people . . .

Molly: . . . and I don't have an image. I just wondered why anyone else would need a song when we have a perfectly good national anthem.

Fran: It's just that *Lift Every Voice*, in its contemporary use, is sung in black communities and has not been sung in other communities, even though it débuted in the White House.

The rebel flag, the Confederate flag. . . . My spouse and I were living in an apartment while we tried to figure out where we wanted to live in Austin. We visited this new suburban community, which was a bit more affordable than some of the other neighborhoods and still close to the city. We could afford to live there while I was a graduate student. We looked in the model homes, walked around the neighborhood, and were excited about the place as a possibility. For some reason, we walked to the corner of one street, and a family was living in the house. You know how the address numbers are painted on the curb? Well there was a Dixie flag—I mean a Confederate flag—painted on the curb. I thought, "I am not moving to this neighborhood." That was too much; the flag was too much. I don't know about the family. They might have been nice people, and it might not have been a problem, but I was not willing to take the chance of moving into the neighborhood.

Molly: And the country of that flag is no more. *Dixie* became the unofficial song of the Confederacy, but then the Confederacy no longer exists. Supposedly, Lincoln loved the song, and at his request it was sung before crowds at the White House to soften the pains of the Civil War (National Public Radio, 2002). The South has as many really wonderful people as it has had really horrible people. Some Southerners didn't own slaves and considered themselves an Alabamian or a Mississippian, so the flag is a piece of cloth, but it is so often used for ill will. I would have felt the same way you did. The truth is that if I had seen a rebel flag displayed rather prominently, I would have thought it was a bigoted neighborhood, and I wouldn't have wanted to live there either, and yet I very much associate in many ways that very symbol.

> *So here we are two learners*
> *Restorying our herstories with songs*
> *Ambling onto public pathways*
> *After walking through alleyways first*
> *Our passages converge*
> *Worth & Power*

Sojourners: We can't escape the power of words and symbols. Their meanings aren't stable and change with circumstances and the positionality of the people. We embody the pain of words as weapons of patriotism. By making these weapons more public, we believe we are less vulnerable.

MOVING TOWARD THE PRIVATE

Fran: So what does it mean for you, what is it like for you—I don't even know how to word the question—where something of your history gets used in the public often in negative ways, is cursed publicly, if cursed is a good word?

Molly: That's right back to that very first conversation that we had. It's sad. It's painful to know that certain artifacts of my family's history are now cursed, symbols of things that I would never want to be associated with, and yet the other side is that they are symbols of who I am and where I come from and the people that are my people. So unlike *Lift Every Voice*—unless we have some huge change in society . . .

Fran: . . . like a black president in the White House?

Molly: That's not a big enough change, I don't think. There will never be anyone who—well, that's wrong of me because for someone it may. There may be someone right now who may say *Lift Every Voice and Sing* has become an embarrassment—I don't think that will happen.

Fran: Oh, I see. I wasn't looking at it in that direction.

Molly: You see, *Dixie* is an embarrassment for me. A part of me wants to hold it, but the bigger part of me is embarrassed that it hurts people that I like, that it's associated with rednecks, with poor "white trash," with bigotry. It would even make me uncomfortable if I heard a group of kids walking down the mall singing *Dixie*; I would not be comfortable. I would particularly be uncomfortable if they were waving the Confederate flag. Talking about being conflicted, because instead of saying, "Aren't those good, patriotic Southerners," I'm thinking they are trying to put a message about who should have power that I don't believe.

Fran: The list that you gave, at least in some ways in our society are markers of a marginalized group. To label people as "white trash" is clearly a tactic of marginalization. We have this highly charged song that's associated with a marginalized group. Is it scary because it's associated with a marginalized group and history? It's an interesting dynamic, and I have to say I have not really thought of *Dixie*—or people connected to *Dixie*—in that way before our conversations. It was purely a song that indicated a potential threat for black people.

Molly: And it's probably because of these things I am talking about, because it is not sung in safe places any more by people who believe in social justice. It is usually sung in little enclaves of people who are a threat. They are as big a threat to me as they are to you. So it is a song that carries the connotation that you are a racist that you are hoping to create much more power for the group you are . . .

Fran: . . . at the expense of others . . .

Molly: . . . and a group that is not very tolerant. For me, this group doesn't understand diversity and restrict themselves by not reaching out to others. This image of *Dixie* is the picture opposite of *Lift Every Voice*. It's not a song that more and more people are enjoying and that more and more people engage in public places that are respectable public places. *Dixie* is going more and more underground.

Fran: While *Lift Every Voice and Sing* may be. . . .

Molly: . . . coming above ground. . . .

Fran: . . . or at least in the recent White House concert.

Molly: So if we are talking about public and private, and about power, even for people who might feel a connection to *Dixie*, they may feel an aversion to it because it implies the desire for power in a "the way it used to be, good old days" way. Although we know the "good old days" were a romanticizing of an era when we had power and when white Americans could do what they wanted to do and didn't have to go by the rules. So it's scary. [silence]

Fran: Earlier you talked of feeling bothered about *Lift Every Voice* because people were singing it in secret and needing their own national anthem, that the *Star-Spangled Banner* did not suffice. I'm hearing the same concern with *Dixie* . . .

Molly: . . . as it is becoming more and more private . . .

Fran: . . . and the potential of the intentions of that group and what it might mean for others.

Molly: Pathways are public and alleyways tend to be private . . .

Fran: . . . and dangerous, right?

Molly: Yes, and often an escape route. When something is public it belongs to all and when private it belongs to a select group. What does being public or private do? How do the public and the private carry power? One would think that if it is public then it would have more power—like a public pathway. I'm suspecting that things that are private may have potential for a lot more power . . .

Fran: . . . danger, escape . . .

Molly: . . . like an alleyway . . .

Fran: . . . more potential to change the way power currently works. What is scary about such privacy is that if enough people with enough whatever are brought together, getting organized, and beginning to act because of a particular song or the ideology the song represents, they could shift the dynamics more broadly.

Molly: The shift can be gut wrenching for some. You can hear where I am: With both sides I become insecure because they threaten who I am and where I'm positioned. I do *not* want white supremacy. I don't want this supremacy thing to take on any force and potential at all. Though I side with the other way more intellectually, my gut says: But where does that leave me? I'm in that unusual position where I certainly don't want to go where the song *Dixie* seems to be leading. But it is unsettling to think about all of the things that I have taken for granted, things that would change if we restructure. Even if we restructure the way I'd like us to restructure, life's not going to be the same way it was, or is, or would continue to be.

Fran: Right. In some ways we are inevitably on that path of changing. We might want things to be familiar, but there is change; but some changes or the potential for change is scarier than others. This is interesting: the use of the public as a way of diffusing and thus possibly defusing or at least diluting, making something less scary, less catalytic.

Molly: There are so many hidden things about what you do in public and what you do in private. So many things like organizations that have private handshakes and you have to be invited in to be part of the group. If you're not a member of them, you might question them. I think of the Knights of . . .

Fran: Columbus is it?

Molly: . . . yeah . . .

Fran: . . . the Masons, Skull & Bones, and others I don't even know to name . . .

Molly: . . . because they are so private and secretive. You think, "Who are these people?" They may be totally innocent and harmless, but when they close that door, we don't know what they are doing. So a song that is going underground and becoming more and more associated with a private kind of group begins to make me uncomfortable. It wasn't that way in my youth with *Dixie*. It was a song that a lot of people hummed, and almost any collection of Southern songs would have included it.

> *So here we have two songs*
> *Both sung privately*
> *Both sung publicly*
> *One becoming more private*
> *Another becoming more public*
> *Worth & Power*

Sojourners: But if one song is more about reaching out to that which *can be*, versus let's go back to the way it *used to be*—that is a big difference between the two songs. But the idea that makes them scary is that they are exclusive to a group: You have to be in the clique. We wonder, Does becoming public move it to being a song all can sing? Will *Lift Every Voice and Sing* always be the Negro National Anthem, just as *Dixie Land* will be the song of the South? Does *Lift Every Voice* get more or less power as it becomes public?

RESTORATIVE STEPS

> *So here we are two Friends*
> *Like Janus, trying to understand in bifurcation*
> *Bookends marking spaces in herstory*
> *were born*
> *into the groups that*
> *sing and claim these songs*
> *So here we are two seekers of wisdom*
> *Transforming and reforming as we*
> *See power in songs*
> *Seek freedom through songs we've lived*
> **Worth, Justice & Humanity**

Sojourners: As we try to answer all these questions posed and even those left unstated, we find they only lead to more questions, layered like an onion. We've been trying to figure out a metaphor for these conversations because we've been under the illusion that at some point this might get to something. And we've gotten to many things, some of which are in this text. Could it be like the mathematical one half, where there will always be a half that we cannot traverse, Zeno's paradox. It's just always half, half, half; no matter how close we get or how many steps we take, if we take half steps toward each other, we will always be taking half steps; if we do it by halves, we will never be able to walk into the other. But, we can approach the other get closer than we might have imagined possible.

Justice—Worth—Position—Power—Humanity—Dignity

REFERENCES

Bakhtin, N. (1981). *The dialogic imagination*. Austin: The University of Texas Press.

Bond, J., and Wilson, S. K. (Eds.). (2000). *Lift Every Voice and Sing: A celebration of the Negro National Anthem*. New York: Random House.

Cohan, G. M. (1904). The *yankee doodle boy*. Sheet music, Performing Arts Encyclopedia. Library of Congress, Washington, DC.

Connelly, F. M., and Clandinin, D. J. (1990). Stories of experience and narrative inquiry. *Education Researcher*, 19(5), 2–14.

de Beauvoir, S. (1989). *The second sex*. New York: Vintage Books.

DiFranco, A. (1993). My IQ. On *Puddle Dive* [CD]. Buffalo, NY: Righteous Records.

Emmett, D. D. (Writer), and Hobbs, W. L. (Composer). (1860). *I wish I was in Dixie's land*. New York: Fifth, Pond.

Foucault, M. (1997). Technologies of the self. In P. Rabinow (Ed.), *Ethics: Subjectivity and truth: Essential works of Foucault, 1954–1984* (pp. 223–251). New York: The New Press.

Foucault, M. (2000). The subject and power. In J. D. Faubion (Ed.), *Michel Foucault: Power* (pp. 326–348). New York: The New Press.

Freire, P. (1989). *Pedagogy of the oppressed* (M. B. Ramos, trans.). New York: Continuum.

Huckaby, M. F. (2007). Dear Molly: Seven letters about "Dixie." In S. Leafgren, B. D. Schultz, M. P. O'Malley, L. A. Johnson, J. F. Brady, and A. M. Dentith (Eds.), *The articulation of curriculum and pedagogy for a just society: Advocacy, artistry, and activism* (pp. 61–75). Troy, NY: Educator's International Press, Curriculum & Pedagogy Group.

Husserl, E. (1991). *Cartesian mediations: An introduction to phenomenology*. (D. Cairns, trans.) Dordrecht, Netherlands: Kluwer Academic.

Johnson, J. W. (Writer), and Johnson, J. R. (Composer). (1900). *Lift every voice and sing*. Retrieved from http://www.poets.org/vicwmedia.php/prmMID/15588

Key, F. S. (1814). *The star-spangled banner*. Lyrics, American Treasures of the Library of Congress: Memory, Library of Congress, Washington, DC.

Kincheloe, J. L. (2001). *Getting beyond the facts: Teaching social studies/social sciences in the twenty-first century*. New York: Peter Lang.

Lawson, B. (2008, March 14). *Interview with Reverend Bill Lawson.* Interview by J. Ely [Video recording]. Houston Oral History Project, Houston Public Library. Houston Public Library Digital Archives, Houston, TX.

Moss, S. L. (1997). *NASA and racial equality in the south, 1961–1968.* Unpublished master's thesis, Texas Tech University, Lubbox. Retrieved from http://etd.lib.ttu.edu/theses/available/etd-01292009-31295012200167/unrestricted/31295012200167.pdf

National Public Radio. (2002). *Dixie.* Retrieved from http://www.npr.org/programs/morning/features/patc/dixie/index.html

NPR (2002, November 11). Present at the creation: Dixie [Radio broadcast episode]. In B. Gordemer (Producer/Director), *Morning edition.* Washington, DC: National Public Radio.

PBS Video. (2010). *In performance at the White House: A celebration of music from the Civil Rights Movement.* Retrieved from http://video.pbs.org/video/1410865290/

Pinar, W. F. (2004). *What is curriculum theory?* Mahwah, NJ: Lawrence Erlbaum.

CHAPTER 8

Tensions and Contradictions of Living in a Multicultural Nation in an Era of Bounded Identities

Maryam Nabavi and Darren E. Lund

PROLOGUE

Exploring difference is a major tenet of duoethnography, and Nabavi and Lund's duoethnography makes the exploration of difference problematic. In investigating power and privilege, they can potentially cast one duoethnographer as representative of the perpetrators and the other as representing the victims. As Lund reports, "My own childhood memories are infused with incidents that are now painfully embarrassing . . ." (p. 180). As someone who was born in Canada, he defines part of his early curriculum as racist. However, due to the nature of the duoethnographic method, he moves beyond such casting by juxtaposing his former self with his present self through the addition of the phrase, "and even shocking to my current self" (p. 180). Duoethnographers are not the topics but the sites of their studies, and ultimately readers witness Nabavi and Lund, not as victims or perpetrators but as different individuals trying to make meaning of their life histories and then reconceptualizing those meanings. Lund has the courage to make explicit some of his curriculum of racism, as did Norris in his articulation of his curriculum of homophobia (Norris and Sawyer, 2004). These and all duoethnographies portray researchers in flux, documenting the emerging and changing meanings, particular to the point of time of the writing.

There are also differences within differences as when Nabavi and Lund examine race within the construct of immigration. While Lund reports that "the narrative in my own family was around being the proud children and grandchildren of these hardy Danish immigrants who struggled to make a living in Canada in their early years" (p. 185), Nabavi claims that "in my case, I feel that my experiences of belonging within the social and cultural milieu of Canada would have been far different had not just my skin and culture practices been similar to what was considered mainstream at the time, but also how I spoke" (p. 181). Through their juxtaposition, they discover that not all experiences of immigrants are the same, that other factors can and do come into play. One of the strengths of a duoethnography is in the way it makes difference explicit.

In addition to difference, inclusion is also made problematic. In their discussion of school programs, Nabavi reports:

> *A number of events in my early years as a child immigrant resulted in my feeling unsat-isfactorily different. First, I remember being taken out of class three times a week to the school's storage room to have an ESL (English as a second language) session; this repeated exercise was damaging to me in that it drew further attention to my stark difference as the girl who neither spoke, dressed, nor looked like others. (p. 178)*

And later Lund responds: "There is a kind of paternalism at play and an assimilative function that underlies even the best of these programs. A driving motivator seems to be the notion that the faster these kids 'fit in' to 'our' culture, the better off they'll be" (p. 184).

Duoethnographies, due to their nature of examining difference and different perspectives of difference, move research to a place of ambiguity in which multiple meanings can be celebrated for their unique contributions in understanding and improving the human condition. Readers, then, are not provided with conclusions that focus their thinking from the perspective of the metanarrators. Rather, they can choose from a polyphony and cacophony of ideas, including their own, and con/spire or breathe/with (Barone, 1990) the insights of their own choosing. Duoethnography marks a turning point in research in which the hegemony of a unified narration is replaced with multiple forms of thought that do not seek convergence but celebrate diversity.

—Joe Norris

Maryam: I'd like to begin our conversation about multiculturalism, the nation, and identity with a reflection of my earliest memories. As a child immigrant to Calgary, Alberta, Canada, in the mid-1980s, I quickly learned that I was different and that my differences made a difference to others and consequently to how I experienced the world. A number of events in my early years as a child immigrant resulted in my feeling unsatisfactorily different. First, I remember being taken out of class three times a week to the school's storage room to have an ESL (English as a second language) session; this repeated exercise was damaging to me in that it drew further attention to my stark difference as the girl who neither spoke, dressed, nor looked like others. There are numerous models of specialized instruction for ESL students in Canada, such as in-class, being pulled out of class, or mainstreaming, which integrates students into regular classroom instruction (Ashworth, 2000). Research in the area suggests that ESL students who are pulled out of class for reasons not necessarily related to their academic success face social stigmatization and withdrawal (Derwing, DeCorby, Ichikawa, and Jamieson, 1999; Watt and Roessingh, 2001).

Second, I was unfamiliar with the cultural discourses of the time and would often stick out because of it. For example, my classmates would sport sweatshirts with the different characters from a popular cartoon series at the time, the Care Bears. When asked by one classmate which character I liked best, I pointed to the character she had on her shirt, calling it by the wrong name. The student rightfully accused me of not knowing the characters, which for her made me unworthy of her friendship. The absence of cultural capital (Waters, 2006) was traumatizing, and I would often run home from the school bus in order to watch TV and educate myself on the shows that my classmates would ultimately make reference to. So being taken out of class as others watched not only drew attention to how I was different but also negated my efforts to learn the culture of my peers and fit in.

Thirdly, I experienced humiliation when teachers spoke exceptionally louder than normal when addressing me, as if raising their voice would help me understand what they were saying. My feelings of insecurity triggered by my developmental stage and emphasized by my cultural ignorance often left me feeling paralyzed when I was spoken to in class, and the teacher speaking perhaps in a more directive manner and what seemed much louder reinforced my feelings of inadequacy. And finally, schoolgirls would pull my curly hair in efforts to make it straight, like theirs. This accumulation of experiences quickly schooled me to draw a clear boundary in how I articulated (or silenced) my immigrant identity in the social and institutional sites in which I participated. For example, I would not discuss the experiences I had with my family over the weekends, such as our communal outings to the grocery store, where simply witnessing the diversity of food served as a sort of leisure activity that I knew other students would find difficult to understand.

Darren: Your recollections here of early memories as an immigrant to Calgary are troubling, as I have known you for years but have never heard these specific stories before. As a member of the dominant group of locally born Canadians whose actions helped script these negative experiences for you, I am led by your stories to question how I positioned myself then. Our family had its own narratives and rituals that placed us in the center of our community and "foreign others" at the margins. Through some very direct teaching, I learned that I belonged here and "they" didn't. From so many around me as a child, I learned a lot of negative lessons about specific ethnic groups such as Chinese, Pakistani, and Black people that I am not comfortable repeating here. In my youthful past—albeit a decade or two earlier than yours—I stood on the other side in many ways, smug in my unexamined status as a Canadian "insider" and eager to think up humorous ways to marginalize those who were seen as cultural or racialized outsiders.

My own childhood memories are infused with incidents that are now painfully embarrassing and even shocking to my current self. I remember telling so many terrible "Paki" jokes and always finding a receptive audience, even with some of my own family members. My father, who recently passed away, was the son of relatively poor Danish immigrants. Dad used to love the character of Archie Bunker on the TV show *All in the Family* (Lear and Yorkin, 1971–1979), but not as a focus of derision for his obviously exaggerated narrow mindedness. Rather, he saw Archie as a straight-talking and hilarious role model! My father had gone from working the oil rigs to being a downtown city cop, and the curriculum of our nightly dinner table included listening to a wide range of off-color stories he would bring home from his eventful shifts in downtown Calgary. Many of his tales featured the First Nations people he encountered during the day, and I couldn't help but have my own values shaped by these lessons. We touched on this past a bit in our recent collaboration (Nabavi and Lund, 2010).

Maryam: Both our above reflections demonstrate the role that cultural identity plays in determining processes of inclusion and exclusion. Our cultural context can certainly be affirming of parochial values and ideals, as you emphasize regarding your upbringing, while at the same time exclude those who are not privy to the nuances, as in my case. While our identities are made up of different cultural, social, and migratory histories, both our repertoires are rich with nationalities, belongings, and identifications. It seems that in your case, while your father's experiences with immigration were not that long in his past, his status as a White Canadian trumped his status as an immigrant.

Darren: I think you're right, as my immigrant ancestors never had to face racism based on their visible ethnic identities. Still, at the same time, we knew we were different from British norms of "proper" Canadians. Our proud Danishness set us apart in some significant ways from those who "settled" this colonized land prior to our arrival, and even though the Scandinavians were considered "preferred" immigrants, my parents and grandparents still held to imported ethnic traditions—including our pickled herring and Akvavit breakfasts on special occasions and the ubiquitous blue Danish plates on our walls. However, even as immigrants, my family enjoyed a kind of racialized similarity to mainstream White British Canadians. I believe my ancestors looked enough like the dominant culture to escape the experiences of marginalization that befell other immigrant groups. This came to the fore in my grandmother's journal from when she and my grandfather first arrived by boat from Denmark back in 1926. She described how the Danish settlers stopped at the "Chinaman's" for some pie and soon complained that they were not getting a good deal; after just days in the country they already knew who the "other" was in the pecking order of immigrants here.

Maryam: In my case, I feel that my experiences of belonging within the social and cultural milieu of Canada would have been far different had not just my skin and culture practices been similar to what was considered mainstream at the time, but also how I spoke. Auditory differences can be as explicit as visible ones. My early experiences of discrimination vis-à-vis culture and social protocol were punctuated by my limited vocabulary and accented English. Even as a child, I was aware that speaking English with an accent was equally excluding as skin color. Neither of my parents spoke English when we first moved to Canada. I recall my mother, with great frustration, stumbling to pronounce a word clearly on the telephone as she attempted to make a doctor's appointment. Without success, she passed the phone to me so I could repeat the word for the person on the other end of the line; I was immediately understood. My mother's inability to communicate effectively was not because of incorrect pronunciation, but, rather, a thick accent that did not align with the Anglicized point of reference for the person on the other end of the line was the cause of the loss in communication. This and other similar incidents have afforded me an understanding that our *multiple* social identities dictate how we are positioned within the nation.

Darren: I think you've touched on a particular kind of discrimination that features a harsh narrow mindedness around accents, another hierarchy of acceptability of differences. A thick Scottish brogue or a distinct Irish lilt have a vastly different and invariably more positive connotation—and often evoke a different emotional reaction—than accents originating further from the British Isles. Coupled with deeply held notions of cultural superiority, I believe the mainstream Canadian response to accents is often intertwined with the various subtle forms of racism. Our complex notions of citizenship and belonging have many layers, but often these are unspoken and unexamined; even this conversation feels strained and discomforting.

Of course, I also remember more overt expressions as well. Along with singing all of the racist songs and children's games (it wasn't "catch a tiger by the toe" we played, and we never called a particular candy a "licorice baby"), many of us kids became adept at remembering and retelling racist jokes. I can't fully explain it now, but there was something pleasurable about feeling superior to other groups that were clearly the "other" in our small world. Lots of kids in my working-class neighborhood chanted racist sayings as part of our daily routines and games. Many of the racist songs and stories of my youth had a morbid, cruel, or scatological basis, and I can still remember most of them. Perhaps most awkward to me now is the absolute immunity and guilt-free way I remember feeling when telling them—whether at school, with friends, with new acquaintances, or with my family.

Only a few rare times do I remember stopping to think about the impact my words might have on others. Once I was in a restaurant with a few friends, and I was telling distasteful "Paki" jokes and then realized there were a few people behind me who I believed were of Pakistani origin, and we laughed awkwardly. I felt self-conscious for a moment but never gave a thought to the dehumanizing impact of this kind of humor. I am often reminded of these cruel jokes, sometimes in subtle and unexpected ways, as I parent my own children. Just the other day one of them came to mind when I was driving with my teenaged daughter, but I choose never to share these "jokes" or my personal history with telling them, even with those closest to me. I remain deeply ashamed of the person I was, and I wonder if there is an ongoing effort to assuage my lingering (White) guilt embedded in the work I now do for a living. In many ways, I feel damaged by this kind of behavior—not to minimize the subjects of racism, but I know that there are many victims of oppression, *including* the apparent perpetrators.

Maryam: As we question the contexts and conditions that drove those early experiences for both of us in order to generate new meanings and insights, we also recognize that they inevitably have informed how we now engage with issues of social and political justice. We share a common bond in our commitment to transform, reform, and reinscribe our interpretations of pejorative acts we were each subject to and perpetuators of. In my case, it's been twenty-five-plus years since those initial experiences, and the rise of "ethnic" migrants to Canada, the cultural and social dimensions of globalization, and ensuing policies have informed a much different reality for the newest generation of youth.

Recently, I was part of collaboration between a Vancouver-based community organization and a university research project wherein we worked with a group of newly immigrated youth to unpack their experiences in Canada (Wright and Nabavi, 2010). We engaged in a number of theater-based projects with the participants in which they reflected on different dimensions of their status as an immigrant youth. In one case, I was teary eyed when one participant shared the ways she and her family experienced blatant racism in Canada and that, while she found solace in supports such as with the social worker that an immigrant-serving agency had set up for her and the program through which I had met her, she remains a victim within institutional structures that racialize her. Additionally, the participants of the project would discuss with great pride the number of countries and languages represented in their schools and the countless projects catering specifically to immigrant youth.

While experiences of discrimination continue to be present, newly immigrated youth have outlets that were not present when I immigrated to Canada. While I think this is great, it troubles me that the key positive experiences for these youth are in programmatic and institutionalized spaces, such as an immigrant club, for them to feel like they belong. Such spaces not only perpetuate differences based on language, culture, and country of origin but also send conflicting message of the nation's "multicultural" identity, which emphasizes difference regarding integration and belonging. The challenges of how immigrants fit into the boundaries of the nation need to be troubled. While government funding to support new contexts exists, the broader structures underpinning the liberal-democratic ideologies of Canada shape the discourse and practice of the multicultural nation.

Darren: I appreciate your raising this troubling aspect, as my usual response when I learn of these kinds of opportunities for young immigrants, and children of immigrant and indigenous families, is to *feel good* about my community. I've spent a number of years on various committees trying to coordinate the services available for young people who may need some cultural and linguistic bridging, but, as you suggest, these are almost always funded through government grants. There is a kind of paternalism at play and an assimilative function that underlies even the best of these programs. A driving motivator seems to be the notion that the faster these kids "fit in" to "our" culture, the better off they'll be.

Maryam: As helpful as these supports are, they are not quite enough, and we must remain critical of how much the margin is shifting in relation to the center. Although my status as an immigrant and racialized woman continues to position me on the margins of social identity, I have found comfort on the margins. Now my intellectual and political pursuits are largely dedicated to shifting the margin in relation to the center. I do this by refuting the image of binaries—I am either an immigrant or a Canadian, either I am a person of color or I am not—and identity as a fixed social category rather than as a whole and complicated set of criteria that positions me as an immigrant, intellectual woman of color whose Canadian and global identity is complicated by my intellectual and political commitments to shifting the margin. Like many immigrant intellectuals of my generation, who have developed much of our thinking and training in a hypervigilant, "surveillance," and xenophobic post 9–11 Western context, I find it necessary to trouble the waters of what is considered the margin. For example, in the early years after 9–11, I was unable to enter the U.S. without being questioned and fingerprinted; in one instance, I was asked what my relation was to the several other people with the same last name as mine. A couple of weeks ago, upon entering the U.S., I was asked questions about the frequency of my visits to Iran. While I recognize that these are questionable, problematic protocols and that I have no reason to be fearful, they ultimately continue to position me as an "other" within the Anglo-mainstream that maintains power and privilege within social, cultural, and political realms of the state.

Darren: As someone who came late to the field of equity and social justice, I began only as a young adult to question my own identity as a Canadian citizen. The narrative in my own family was around being the proud children and grandchildren of these hardy Danish immigrants who struggled to make a living in Canada in their early years. My White Danish grandfathers both arrived speaking English, and so held both racialized and linguistic privileges as "preferred" immigrants, yet in my family's narrative these were ignored; accounts of our family's experiences collapsed our "immigrant" identity with those groups facing serious racism and xenophobia in the 1970s. For example, I have honestly never heard an offensive joke that dehumanizes Danish or other Scandinavian people. I know firsthand that many people immigrating to my city from India and Pakistan faced racist slurs and exclusion from me and the other "locals." I heard (and expressed) criticism for their failure to assimilate as well as "our own people" had. I remember one South Asian fellow who sat in front of me in my high school chemistry class; I never knew from which country he had emigrated, but I remember teasing him about his accent. Another boy and I kept on bothering him until he got angry, but he kept repeating, "I am a peaceful man," to which we laughed derisively. Remembering it now, I think I'd rather cry. I feel ashamed even telling you this now. In my family's curriculum at that time, obvious discrepancies of unearned advantages of particular immigrants—those surrounding language, accent, and skin color—were never talked about. It wasn't until well into my adult years that my activist students helped me replace this curriculum with one that felt more humane.

Maryam: While your story makes me cringe with the feelings of oppression your classmate must have felt and the shame you feel almost four decades later, I acknowledge that we are all a product of the familial, popular, and peer culture of our time. Your grandparents seem to have had a "We made it, so should they" attitude, which negated the social identity, cultural, and political contexts of individuals as well as the national policies that maintained institutionalized forms of discrimination. However, there is also another force that interlocks with our identities and the nation, and that's the centrality of class. Your family's working-class background was muted by your racial privilege, which you clearly used as your trump card. In my case, it was slightly different. I remember taking the school bus, which in many ways was where the social, cultural, and economic status of students was punctuated by the enclosed space from which we could not escape for thirty minutes each morning and afternoon. The students, including me, would incessantly taunt a young boy whose family members were caretakers on a farm at which the bus would drop him off, en route to the socioeconomically advantaged neighborhood where we were all lived. We made fun of this boy for his unkempt hair, the same clothes he wore daily, and that he smelled like horses. We never directly brought attention to the fact that his family was poor and, for many on the bus, theirs were not. I reveled in the opportunity to be like the other children, taunting rather than being taunted. Like you, it was a desire to belong within my peer culture and have others like me, in spite of an astute awareness of how much it must have stung to be that boy and that once he got off the bus, I could be the next target. It did not matter, and I savored the experience of my socioeconomic likeness as a weapon against my racially marginalized immigrant status.

The poignant experiences that made up much of early memories have impacted me emotionally, psychologically, culturally, and socially. I think it is these informal experiences that shape our identities and inevitably propel us to make the links between the different aspects of ourselves (emotional, psychological, etc.). For me, my steadfast commitment to antioppression work was a constructive response to the injustices that I experienced, and through that work I was able to understand the deeper structural and cultural underpinnings of what made up my experiences.

Darren: Reliving these moments also reminds me that these are just snapshots of personal examples of oppression. The much more insidious systemic racism and institutional barriers go much deeper than these lived experiences. In my case, I only began becoming aware of this other level after taking part in the progressive activism of a group of high school students I was teaching in the mid-1980s who decided to form an antiracism action group in the heart of conservative Alberta.

Our small classroom English language arts project happened when a poetry lesson I was trying to teach went off the rails. My "nonacademic" students responded to a metaphorical poem I had written about racism, and talk quickly turned to the Aryan Nations that had set up a training camp in nearby Caroline, Alberta. One student shouted, "Let's form our own group against racism!", and suddenly the students had formed an activist coalition! Our Students and Teachers Opposing Prejudice (STOP) project gained immediate support within the school, attracting dozens of students and getting coverage in the local television and national news. Soon STOP became a regular school program. It went on to last two full decades, tackled a wide range of issues related to discrimination, and garnered some national recognition and awards. The collaborative efforts fired my own engagement in the field, and eventually I realized I could learn more about this through my doctoral program.

But now, even looking at my work with those students, I was so often lauded for "leading" students with this project that I rarely found occasion to trouble and question my own latent assumptions and unearned privileges. Living my life as a "normal" Canadian, I was never directly challenged to understand the implications of my White, straight, able-bodied male identity. Even being in this field of study, I am rarely invited to implicate my own identity in my work. As a cultural insider, I never have my *Canadianness* questioned, and my sense of belonging, citizenship, and entitlement seems quietly affirmed. Unlike your more fluid and shifting identities, mine remains fairly fixed in my community and academic work.

Maryam: The ways our social identities intersect our scholarly and community work are certainly complicated by our understanding of and experiences in Canada. My scholarly commitment is to explore the "messy" intersections in the context of the tensions that arise for immigrant youth living on the margins of a multicultural state; I explore this in relation to their non-national experiences and specifically how that informs their location in relation to the margin.

A number of the participants in my study are involved in the Green Movement, which aims to bring awareness to and challenge the hegemonic structures of the Iran's political regime. One participant, who has lived in Canada since she was six years old and has always worked to align herself with the mainstream Anglo-European culture, though often unsuccessfully, tells me that she got involved in the Green Movement as it's *finally* a forum where in she can fight for something she believes in. Her story, like many others in the study, sheds light on how young immigrants, while they are "multicultural," are caught seeking a space to express their multiculturalism in a way that is meaningful for them. In other words, she was not interested in expressing her Iranian identity through the superficial dimensions of the multicultural; rather, she wanted to be aligned with others fighting for rights. I think this is largely because the discourse and practice of multiculturalism is not speaking to the nuances of her national and political affiliations. In this context, I think it's not only useful but necessary to interrogate how the articulations and on-the-ground manifestations of multiculturalism in Canada inform our subject location and how, in effect, we can advance discussions about the multicultural nation using our diverse subject locations. As my commitment to this type of work is so intertwined with my personal context, in my role as an educator, teacher, and researcher I provide personal vignettes of my experiences, as we've been doing here, as a means to connect to the larger discussion of the tensions and contradictions of living in a multicultural nation.

Darren: This makes a lot of sense to me, as I have been working for the past twenty-plus years within a field that has been shifting at a rapid pace over those few decades. The political and social "experiment" of multiculturalism only came into being in the early 1970s, and the early manifestations of it would be considered fairly conservative and even archaic by today's standards, focused as they were more on cultural retention and celebration, leaving issues of power and privilege untouched. My earliest work with the national leaders in this field came when I was invited to document the STOP program and present my work at a gathering of top scholars from across Canada. At that time, the raging debate was between the mainstream work of veteran multicultural educators such as Keith McLeod (1992), John Friesen (1991), and Jack Kehoe (1994), among others, and the upstart "antiracism education" movement inspired by leftist theorists and critical movements taking place in the UK. There was a proverbial changing of the guard, and I found my own work initially straddling these two conceptually and theoretically oppositional poles of the same progressive movement to promote the value of diversity within Canadian schools. My public work has included attempts to chart this contested field (Lund, 2006) and to outline some of the pitfalls (Lund, 2008), and this dialogue is an attempt to look more critically at how our personal identities both inform and complicate this work.

Maryam: In their taxonomy of multiculturalism and multicultural education, Kincheloe and Steinberg (1997) create a useful framework for understanding how the different waves of multiculturalism in Canada (see also Kymlicka, 2007) have informed commitments to social justice by ways of education, community activism, and policy interventions. Critical multicultural scholars from south of the border (e.g., Giroux, 2006; McLaren, 1997; Sleeter and Bernal, 2004) have provided a rich theoretical landscape for representing Canadian discourses of multiculturalism, between inclusion and exclusion, and reveal the slippages between noncritical theoretical discourses and the ways people experience their lives. While there has been a wide spectrum of grounded intervention, to which you earlier referred, critical discourses that you and I are committed to fail to speak to the ways social justice activism in multicultural Canada, by necessity, intersect the nation and our own identity formation, as we've been discussing.

Darren: I find the critical pedagogy literature, including the work by the scholar/activists you note above, so compelling as a way to ascribe radical politics to my own activism, and to name the politicized nature of so much of our social justice work in schools and communities. However, I'm also conscious that the work I have done in collaboration with young people has been very tentative and rather limited in some ways. For example, our long-standing STOP youth activist group never became part of the school's or the school district's organizational structure, and we never forced these institutions to question their own policies or practices in any sustained way. The grassroots projects and events we organized to raise awareness of racist practices, homophobia in the school, sexism, unfair international development work, and other issues were mainly directed at changing individual attitudes. Even our letter writing campaigns, our protesting, and our lobbying of provincial and federal government seem rather limited and even timid in light of the sweeping transformations called for in most leftist critical literature toward progressive social change. I'm left wondering if I *ever* stepped over the line of a typical liberal White male who believes he's a radical at heart. My critical multicultural work may be conservative multiculturalism in disguise, through efforts that leave power structures and privileges fairly intact.

Maryam: The impact of your work is perhaps more significant than you might imagine. Tackling racism in the 1980s on the heels of the trial of James Keegstra and the growth of the Aryan Nations in Alberta was radical in its own way. Likewise, your human rights efforts around gay and lesbian students were groundbreaking, and the community and legal activism you have done have proven to be precedent setting in terms of limiting hate speech in Canada.

Darren: Thanks for saying so. I think that when I stood up to that homophobic "pastor" who wrote a hateful letter to the editor of an Alberta newspaper in 2002, I may have been taking my critical work to another level. My educational efforts in schools and now with teacher preparation are important, but it seems crucial to stand up to bigotry wherever it emerges. I filed a human rights complaint a few weeks after the letter was published and a local gay-bashing had taken place. The next several years would be spent defending against a nuisance lawsuit, numerous hateful e-mails and letters, and at least three death threats. I eventually won the rights complaint but lost on appeal. With the support of a local lawyer who is working pro bono, I am currently presenting my case to the Alberta Court of Appeal. It has gone on a long time, but I believe it will set an important precedent to limit hate speech and discriminatory violence in Canada.

Do you see any parallels with your work with other marginalized and "minoritized" groups?

Maryam: In many ways, there are complex links between so much of our antioppression work. I think we are currently experiencing a greater gap in the ways that the discourse of multiculturalism works on the ground than in any other period since the inception of formal multicultural policies by Prime Minister Pierre Elliott Trudeau in the early 1970s. Canadian national identity is shaped by a multicultural identity, which is seemingly inclusive of all nationalities. This view of the nation moves beyond traditional conceptions of a nationalist citizen, which has pejorative connotations (e.g., racist, xenophobic) and antithetical to core Canadian values. Thus, for immigrants to Canada, adhering to multiculturalism suggests a progressive view of national identity and rejection of the "backward" national context from which they have arrived to Canada. At the same time, to refuse to adhere to the Canadian multicultural model suggests a noncommittal view of the nation or, in other words, that one is a guest in Canada and rejects Canadian core values. This idea is reflected in discourses of "citizens" and the "nation." While some scholars suggest that we live in a postnational world (Soysal, 1998) and nationalist discourses are not useful, others suggest that the needs and interests of a nations diverse population—as hailed in discourses of diaspora, cosmopolitanism, and transnationalism—is driven by cultural, political, and social contexts (Anthias, 2009; Cohen, 2010; Werbner, 2002), and the argument is that these versions are incongruent with linear nationalist policies such as multiculturalism. Have you found this tension riddled in your own work?

Darren: I believe that may be a helpful analysis of what I'm seeing and feeling. In any work I do or read around citizenship, I feel an inevitable tension. The underlying intent in the discourse seems to be around finding ways to allow the "other" to feel like a full citizen in Canada rather than crafting a more robust and complex notion of citizenship that includes all of us. I am currently doing some collaborative work with a group in Sweden, where their scholars and government officials are grappling with these very notions of citizenship within a pluralist nation-state. Their strong historical notions of Swedish national identity are tied directly to their racialized identity as Nordic people. Immigrants are always the "other" in this framework. According to my colleagues collaborating on an international project on "cultures in exile," to be Swedish is something historically linked to a certain White identity, and non-White "outsiders" remain unable to attain the status of those who are seen to "belong" there. A new national narrative is needed in order to avoid the radical shift to xenophobic and exclusive government policies.

In many ways, this discourse also exists in Canada but seems far more carefully coded and suppressed, perhaps mitigated by a growing acceptance of ourselves—and of our official constitutionally entrenched status—as belonging to a smugly tolerant multicultural nation. As a White person who celebrates diversity as part of the teaching and activist work I do through the university, I may feel better about myself knowing that my country is "officially" accepting of difference, even despite the daily conflicts I may see and experience. Yet, the painful moments you recounted above are emblematic of millions of other individual and group experiences of exclusion and oppression.

Maryam: This smugness of many White Canadians seems to permeate not only the public discourse around cultural difference in Canada but also the personal narratives we script for ourselves as actors within this nation-state. While traditional Canadian practices of multiculturalism remain committed to apolitical cultural diversity, such as the Four D's of multiculturalism—dress, dance, dialect, and dining—and critical discourses are committed to changing social, cultural, and institutional structures (Kincheloe and Steinberg, 1997), we must also consider the ways that "new identities," as Hall (1992) compels us to think about, are implicated in these "new times." So what are these new times? And what does that mean in the context of *nation*?

Darren: Finding a new way to talk about difference within a multicultural nation will require some very difficult and even painful soul-searching on the part of individuals and complex dialogue and consensus building across a complex fabric of intersecting and often contradictory sets of identities and privileges. Hybrid identity formations and shifting national, global, and cultural allegiances will characterize the new times in which our notions of self and citizens of Canada will undergo a tremendous rupturing. I don't think most White Canadians are ready for this direction, but perhaps we need to get ready to open up this dialogue. Just a few weeks ago, I was invited to contribute my ideas to a series on CBC radio, entitled "Being White in an Increasingly Diverse Calgary." I was asked to comment on a "shocking" statistic that the City of Calgary is facing exponential growth in its non-White population and that eventually White people could become part of the new "visible minority," as we already are in Toronto. Rather than feeding a public fear of this change, I shared my views on the need to stake out a new notion of citizenship that can somehow embrace this demographic shift in a way that defuses White fear. These views emerge from my ongoing work on White privilege with my colleague Paul Carr (Carr and Lund, 2007; Lund and Carr, 2010). Something tells me that our young people—both Canadian born, and second- and third-generation immigrant—already have a different sensibility about their identities that will allow for an attitudinal flexibility to keep notions of diversity threaded comfortably within conceptions of national identity and citizenship. We need to know more about how this is working. Does your current research with young people show any evidence of this?

Maryam: Yes and no. As I suggested earlier, I have found that while there are clear expressions of the meanings of and attitudes toward national and cultural identity, there exist many tensions and contradictions. In a case that sticks out, a participant was struggling to articulate why she didn't feel Canadian. While earlier she had expressed her positive sentiments toward multiculturalism as all-inclusive and embracing of multiple cultures, and that she was both Canadian and Iranian, she later provided a list of reasons why she wasn't Canadian; for example, that she didn't go to bed at 10:00 and didn't watch hockey. This was followed by a several examples of her cosmopolitan identity: that she had traveled extensively and felt more comfortable in big cities like New York. This was a case in point of the ways participants negotiate their citizen identity between national and global contexts and the conditions in their lives. Their experiences with international migrations in general and, more specifically, the socioeconomic, political, and cultural conditions of migration yield a tug and pull of managing multiple allegiances within the boundaries of a multicultural nation.

Participants also expressed experiences of inclusion and exclusion simultaneously. Within the context of national identity, their shifting subject location (as both/either Iranian and/or Canadian) reveals their ambiguous position within multicultural Canada. They discuss the ways that global, cultural, and multicultural discourses and experiences inform the tensions and contradictions associated with the values and belongings of their national identities. For participants of this study, belonging is not just about membership to a nation or identification with a particular national group but is also about the ways social and institutional sites intersect with their self-identifications. The participants in this study are building what I am calling an "immigrant youth citizen identity." In other words, their citizen identity is rooted in the multiple processes of citizenship learning and, in effect, how they express or perform their citizenship. While I recognize that the process of citizenship learning for this population is, by and large, informed by their subject location, a call for an "immigrant youth citizen identity" is contingent on moving beyond binaries, or us/them and oppressor/oppressed, and, rather, recognizing that inclusions and exclusions operate simultaneously, as I've been discussing, and our multiple and intersecting identities and geographies position us *all* between inclusion and exclusion.

Darren: This actually sounds exciting and promising. I think it's remarkable how young people can negotiate the social world in some very creative and flexible ways. There is a cultural malleability or mutability that allows them to self-identify in ways that make sense to them and that defy the borders and names ascribed by history and the adults around them.

Maryam: While I agree that there is attitudinal flexibility with notions of diversity, the ways this flexibility emerges is the result of building an immigrant citizen identity that is a response to the dominant discourses in their lives, such as in their schooling experiences or an identification with their parents' systemic exclusions. Have you had similar experiences in your earlier research projects with immigrant youth?

Darren: I think that you're naming what I have been seeing in a lot of the data from young people in my research; that is, an earnest and innovative grappling with identity in these new times. Young people don't seem to be finding useable identifications of citizenship and belonging from their own first-generation parents, nor from the outdated materials in existing school textbooks on Canadian identity. With the burgeoning use of social networking across national boundaries and the shrinking of the global world, these young people daily redefine what it means to be a citizen of this place and also a citizen of the world. For socially conscious students, this means crafting a new notion of engagement and commitment that goes beyond traditional notions of simply voting in elections or learning to access government services. I believe we are seeing this new generation really learning to live out a new and vibrant kind of "cosmopolitanism" as originally articulated by Kwame Appiah (2006).

Maryam: As educational researchers committed to social equity, we have learned a lot from the informal experiences of young activists we have engaged with our research (Lund and Nabavi, 2008) and use these understandings toward the reform of formal education. Through the process of understanding the trajectory young activists took to engage in various issues and the extent to which their commitments were fueled by personal experiences, it gave me the opportunity to reflect on my position as a young activist, often not that much older than the participants in our study. I realized that my intellectual and political commitment to the issues enabled me to shift the focus of my early experiences of feeling victimized to giving me the tools to enact change. This change was at a personal level, wherein it began the shift in feeling like a victim to one of the intricacies of the relationship between oppression and resistance. The change was also at a professional level, where I felt like I was making a modest contribution toward building knowledge and awareness of issues. My current commitment to this is to explore how the informal curriculum of learners can be embedded in their experiences of citizenship, as it is currently absent in the formal curriculum (Nabavi, 2010).

Darren: Isn't this really the core of our current collective project of nation building? I mean, you and I both grapple with our own personal and academic understandings of living fully and freely in this changing Canada and finding ways to craft and articulate our own complex notions of citizenship in an ethical manner. In many ways, our very different racialized identities and our disparate personal histories reflect part of the wide range of ways of being Canadian. Likewise, I hope our dialogue here, and our ongoing efforts to honor principles of social justice and inclusion in our work, may serve as an encouragement for the opening up of more such conversations across Canada and beyond.

Maryam: While I fully acknowledge that part of the project of nation building is working through the tensions and contradictions of what it means to be a citizen in this nation, we need to reach a point where such expressions move beyond personal and intellectual conversations. We must continue to challenge historical and contemporary meanings and values of citizenship that, at the current moment, require interrogating the troubling aspects of the multicultural liberal underpinnings of this nation. This can inform practical approaches to and expressions of citizenship that may be better aligned with the multiplicity of shifting identities of the very people contributing to the project of nation building.

REFERENCES

Anthias, F. (2009). Thinking through the lens of translocational positionality: An intersectionality frame for understanding identity and belonging. *Translocations: Migration and Social Change, 4*(1), 5–20.

Appiah, K. A. (2006). *Cosmopolitanism: Ethics in a world of strangers.* New York: W. W. Norton.

Ashworth, M. (2000). *Effective teachers, effective schools: Second-language teaching in Australia, Canada, England and the United States.* Toronto: Pippin.

Barone, T. E. (1990). Using the narrative text as an occasion for conspiracy. In E. W. Eisner and A. Peshkin (Eds.), *Qualitative inquiry in education* (pp. 305–326). New York: Teachers College Press.

Carr, P. R., and Lund, D. E. (Eds.). (2007). *The great white north? Exploring whiteness, privilege and identity in education.* Rotterdam: Sense.

Cohen, R. (Ed.). (2010). *Global diasporas.* London: Routledge.

Derwing, T., DeCorby, E., Ichikawa, J., and Jamieson, K. (1999). Some factors that affect the success of ESL high school students. *Canadian Modern Language Review, 55*(4), 532–547.

Friesen, J. W. (1991). Multicultural education in Canada: From vision to treadmill. *Multiculturalism/Multiculturalisme, 14*(1), 5–11.

Giroux, H. (2006). *The Giroux reader.* London: Paradigm.

Hall, S. (1992). New ethnicities. In J. Donald and A. Rattansi (Eds.), *"Race," culture, and difference* (pp. 252–259). London: Sage.

Kehoe, J. W. (1994). Multicultural education vs. anti-racist education: The debate and the research in Canada. *Social Education, 58,* 354–358.

Kincheloe, J. L., and Steinberg, S. R. (1997). *Changing multiculturalism.* London: Open University Press.

Kymlicka, W. (2007). *Multicultural odysseys: Navigating the new international politics of diversity.* New York: Oxford University Press.

Lear, N., and Yorkin, A. (Producers). (1971–1979). *All in the family* [Television series]. Hollywood, CA: Columbia Broadcasting Company.

Lund, D. E. (2006). Waking up the neighbors: Surveying multicultural and antiracist education in Canada, the United Kingdom, and the United States. *Multicultural Perspectives: The Official Journal of the National Association for Multicultural Education, 8*(1), 35–43.

Lund, D. E. (2008). Harvesting social justice and human rights in rocky terrain. *The Ardent Anti-Racism & Decolonization Review, 1*(1), 64–67.

Lund, D. E., and Carr, P. R. (2010). Exposing privilege and racism in the great white north: Tackling whiteness and identity issues in Canadian education. *Multicultural Perspectives: The Official Journal of the National Association for Multicultural Education, 12*(4), 229–234.

Lund, D. E., and Nabavi, M. (2008). Understanding student anti-racism activism to foster social justice in schools. *International Journal of Multicultural Education, 10*(1), 1–20. Retrieved from http://ijme-journal.org/index.php/ijme/issue/view/4

McLaren, P. (1997). *Revolutionary multiculturalism: Pedagogies of dissent for the new millennium.* Boulder, CO: Westview.

McLeod, K. A. (1992). Multiculturalism and multicultural education in Canada: Human rights and human rights in education. In K. A. Moodley (Ed.), *Beyond multicultural education: International perspectives* (pp. 215–242). Calgary, AB: Detselig.

Nabavi, M. (2010). Constructing the "citizen" in citizenship education. *Canadian Journal of New Scholars in Education, 3*(1). Retrieved from http://www.cjnse-rcjce.ca/ojs2/index.php/cjnse/article/view/135

Nabavi, M., and Lund, D. E. (2010). Youth and social justice: A conversation on collaborative activism. In W. Linds, L. Goulet, and A. Sammel (Eds.), *Emancipatory practices: Adult/youth engagement for social and environmental justice* (pp. 3–13). Rotterdam: Sense.

Norris, J., and Sawyer, R. (2004). Null and hidden curricula of sexual orientation: A dialogue on the curreres of the absent presence and the present absence. In L. Coia, M. Birch, N. J. Brooks, E. Heilman, S. Mayer, A. Mountain, and P. Pritchard (Eds.), *Democratic responses in an era of standardization* (pp. 139–159). Troy, NY: Curriculum and Pedagogy.

Sleeter, C. E., and Bernal, D. D. (2004). Critical pedagogy, critical race theory, and anti-racist education: Implications for multicultural education. In J. A. Banks and C. A. McGee Banks (Eds.), *Handbook of research on multicultural education* (2nd ed., pp. 240–258). San Francisco: Jossey-Bass.

Soysal, Y. (1998). Toward a postnational model of membership. In G. Shafir (Ed.), *The citizenship debates* (pp. 189–217). Minneapolis: University of Minnesota Press.

Waters, J. (2006). Geographies of cultural capital: Education, international migration and family strategies between Hong Kong and Canada. *Transactions of the Institute of British Geographers, 31*(2), 179–192.

Watt, D., and Roessingh, H. (2001). The dynamics of ESL drop-out: Plus ça change . . . *Canadian Modern Language Review, 58*(2), 204–224.

Werbner, P. (2002). The place which is diaspora: Citizenship, religion and gender in the making of chaordic transnationalism. *Journal of Ethnic and Migration Studies, 28*(1), 119–133.

Wright, H., and Nabavi, M. (2010, September). *Immigrant Canadian new youth: Expressing and exploring youth identities in a multicultural context.* Paper presented at the 4th Global Conference on Multiculturalism, Conflict, and Belonging, Oxford, UK.

CHAPTER 9

Mirror Imaging Diversity Experiences:
A Juxtaposition of Identities in Cross-cultural Initiatives

Sonia Aujla-Bhullar and Kari Grain

PROLOGUE

While these duoethnographers employ the pronoun "we" in the opening paragraph, focusing their attention toward the readers, whose presence is implied, Sonia Aujla-Bhullar and Kari Grain quickly shift into a style that brings the reader into their pursuit of understanding, identity, culture, immigration, nationalism, and race. This duoethnography predominantly reads like a conversation, and readers sit back and watch/listen the story unfold as the duoethnographers talk with one another, trying to create new meanings about past events. As Kari concludes: "It's almost as if talking about it with you has pulled those past experiences into the present and repositioned them in my adult frame of reference. Then to juxtapose all of this with your narratives of learning . . . it's kind of enlightening" (pp. 220–221).

But such conversations cannot exist without a strong degree of trust. Kari also claims, "But because we're friends and this duoethnographic format has been fairly casual, I feel comfortable sharing these narratives and tracing my learning to certain moments and specific types of curriculum" (p. 220). Undertaking a duoethnography requires willingness to tell one's vulnerable stories and half developed thoughts with a companion who will share that journey toward new meanings, with care and compassion. Kari has such a writing partner in Sonia who says, "It's been a change for me as well to really listen and take in the challenges that you've experienced" (p. 220).

Together they explore perspectives on difference. They blend their stories and the literature to portray the complexities of "minoritization." Sonia explains that although she is in the majority in a school that is largely Indo-Canadian, it "doesn't take away from being minoritized by the curriculum and the institution of education" (p. 210). Throughout this chapter, the literature is intricately woven into the dialogue as they draw ideas from the works of others. Duoethnographers do not reject the literature but deny its value as a seminal text because texts have valuable perspectives regardless of their historical placement. Thus, the literature became part of the conversation.

Ultimately, duoethnography is about transformation. If a duoethnographic study merely reifies existing meanings, it is hollow. The (re)search is about (re)looking, and though this (re)examination, readers witness a progression in the duoethnographers. Duoethnographies are stories in and of themselves with a collage of other stories embedded within them. In conversation, Sonia and Kari claim:

Sonia: *This is a continuous journey, and our interactions with the world and others will add to how I speak to and for the curriculum of diversity. How I navigate and negotiate my own identity will always impact my work and learning.*

Kari: *This conversation has in many ways been cathartic for me because I'm beginning to realize how much these stories, which I thought were random, have actually been quite pivotal in the formation of my worldview. It's helping me understand how I have created my idea of normalcy or even just my idea of who I am. (p. 220–221)*

—*Joe Norris*

Kari: Building upon the work of Norris and Sawyer (2004) and Sawyer and Norris (2009) and a workshop on duoethnography that we took with them in 2008, we embarked on a duoethnography exploring our identity formation and how it seems to impact our work in education and issues of diversity. Recognizing our differences and similarities as second-generation children of immigrants, we still enter into conversation from two very different subject positions. Sonia, why don't you begin by telling us a little about who you are?

Sonia: Sure . . . I am a lot of different things . . .

Kari: Yes, you are.

Sonia: But I think that in the past year especially, working on research and looking at more complex ways of identifying myself, I've really come to be critical of how I define myself. The basis of how I would explain myself to someone else is, first and foremost, a woman of color, East Indian, Indo-Canadian, second-generation immigrant born to parents who were born in India, in the northern region of Punjab. I'm also a teacher working with minority-identity students for the most part in a high-needs area of Calgary. And I am a graduate student studying forms of multiculturalism in Canada. In past few years, especially, I've really come to see my identity as being more complex than just referring to myself as an East Indian Canadian woman.

Kari: It's interesting hearing you say that you've explored more complex ways of identifying yourself because I feel like since I started research as a master's student, I've become less oriented in cloudy, detailed identity markers and more oriented in markers I would consider more simple or blunt. Whereas before I might have described myself, my occupation, and my traits, I have begun to use markers that, while complex in theory, are simple and short in practice. They're blunt in the sense that I identify myself as a woman, like you. But now, with a mind that is slowly becoming more critical, I always think of the fact that I am White because I am starting to see that that my Whiteness has aided my success in ways I have never been conscious of. I remember reading Kendall's (2006) work about Whiteness as the norm to which everything is compared and the privilege involved in having the same skin color as people who run the institutions. My first thought was: "Hey! I never received handouts or any money for my education from my parents, and I definitely was never spoiled. I worked for what I had." As I spoke to more people in the community, including academics and students, I began to understand that I've been privileged in areas other than money. In one piece that George Dei (2007) wrote, he talks about Whiteness as currency, which I think is apt. Being an educator, doing interfaith work, and facilitating dialogue on identity, it's been a really interesting journey to try to do that effectively when you realize: "Hey I am educating young people about diversity, but I am White." So where does that leave me? Actually, I take it back; it's not simple at all.

Sonia: Yeah, I know we've talked about it in the past, and we wanted to write this duoethnographic piece to challenge ourselves, to really interrogate one another's stories (Norris, 2008), urging the other to go further in how we think and approach our work, both academically and professionally. Do you think we've had similar experiences of frustration in the past year working as new scholars and as educators in the area of cultural diversity? We both talked about how frustrated we've been at times.

Kari: Yeah, at times we seem to find solace in sharing our challenges with one another. With this methodology we can focus on how we have both developed individual perspectives on the phenomenon of identity (Norris and Sawyer, 2008). I think it will allow us to explore where we are present at in negotiating our voice in this field and learn more critically about where we are now and to enrich and deepen these understandings.

Sonia: And right now you're saying that it's difficult to navigate being White and having a critical mind in the field?

Kari: Yeah. I feel like I have colonialism following me around and nipping at my heels because I'm always cognizant of the fact that anytime I teach, it's almost like I have that whole cloud over my head of . . . colonialism, and this "White is right" attitude, even when I completely disagree with it. And then, to take this a step further, when I teach or try to facilitate on topics around diversity, I sometimes catch myself thinking, "Who the heck do I think I am talking as a White person about diversity?" And I think your experiences, from what you've told me, seem to mirror my own in that we understand each other's frustrations but only through being on the opposite sides of the mirror.

Sonia: Yeah, and for me, if I talk about diversity, then it's like "tooting my horn" as a visible minority, or I'm communicating in a "White" way, right? So it's as if I can't win. I'm talking to the "White privilege," "Whiteness," "oppression," or "colonialism," whichever you want to say. I find it frustrating because it's really putting my experiences out there for everyone to see . . . and sometimes, if I can be completely honest, I feel like, "What if I'm exaggerating what it's like to be me?" Or I question whether I should even talk about these things because I might be giving the audience ammunition to judge my culture. It's being in this third space of living between cultures (Bhabha, 1994; Dunlop, 1999).

Kari: Tell me a bit more about that.

Sonia: To a degree, it feels like my identity is so embedded in every single thing that I do that there's no room to really step out of it and just . . . be me. But I think that's a part of being a minoritized person in Canada. We're very multicultural in the sense that it is almost synonymous with defining how we are Canadian, "proud" to be Canadian. We are all of these things that we are supposed to be proud of, but is it ever truly that? How does Canadian nationalism tie into the experiences of minority persons? I mean, participation in society is talked about with multiculturalism legislation but can you really ever be yourself, or are you always out on the table, talking about your experiences . . . talking about what it's like? Even talking about others' experiences and empathizing with them and at some point asking, "Wouldn't it be nice to go in a corner and just not . . . be under that spotlight?"

Kari: Or wouldn't it be nice to present at a conference without having people look at you and assume they know something about you based on your appearance? I remember asking a professor what type of clothing I should wear to my presentation at a conference, and he said that some female colleagues had vowed to never wear "sharp" professional outfits again. According to his colleagues, especially in the social sciences and education side of academia, audience members may be more aggressive toward you or critical of your work if you wear clothes that appear too expensive or attractive; they judge you as rich or sexualized if you pay too much attention to your wardrobe. That's just one example. So it would be interesting to just erase your visual identity from what you're saying while you present.

Sonia: But don't you feel that everyone is entrenched in that? Even if you were in the dark, wouldn't they want to know where you're coming from? When I'm reading anything or analyzing any research articles, I always check to see who the author is, and I have been dismissive of some things; I have tired of certain ideas or attitudes. For example, there are articles that discuss "Indian women" in India and the oppressive cycle, and it's similar in all of these publications and has been critiqued by many as well (Bannerji, 1993; Mohanty, 2003). When I first started my undergrad, that's all I read about: the oppression in rural villages, for example. In my development studies classes, it was always talking about how to be free from that, and as much as we wanted to be sensitive around those issues, I still felt that I was that person in the book even though I wasn't. I am from a middle-class household, a second-generation immigrant here. But I couldn't relate to anybody else in the class talking about this issue. Even though I'm passionate about certain things, I don't know who to talk to about it or how to move forward, other than being the one who explains or offers my perspective as an "Indian woman" (Sheth and Handa, 1993). So never mind reading; how can I write something and critically look at it without worrying about who's reading it or who's looking at it? I am always conscious of who the audience will be.

Kari: I find that so challenging when I write anything; whether it's around antiracism or multiculturalism or more critical theory, I feel like my background comes under scrutiny. Something that caught my attention when you spoke was when you said you're from a middle-class home and a second-generation immigrant. I see how our duoethnography helped me tease out layered ideas because that made me realize something; I guess that's where I'm at, too. I am a second-generation immigrant from a middle-class home, but because my background is Norwegian, it's been a totally different experience, obviously. From what I know about you based on our friendship, we have enjoyed similar access to resources in that our parents always put food on the table and had a car to drive and a roof over our heads. It's funny how we can match up those pieces of our identity, and yet we have had such distinctive experiences within that realm. You have had a minority experience, from what you tell me, and yet I haven't.

Sonia: I wonder: Did you grow up feeling like a second-generation immigrant? By this I mean that even though my parents have a distinct Canadian experience in integrating as immigrants (Handa, 2003), it is different from being born in Canada and being a second-generation Canadian. Did you have a distinct feeling of being a child of an immigrant parent?

Kari: Only in the sense that my mom always talked about how she didn't have enough to eat when she was little, and I guess economically we never threw anything out. We reused every last scrap of food until my Mom put it in a big stew, basically; not that we ever went hungry. It is more so in my Mom's stories and the values that my parents have passed on to us. She always recalled narratives of being poor and not being able to speak English when she came to Canada . . . and how her parents built—just from working random construction jobs—a whole life for their entire family. I guess in this way, my parents' stories have served as a sort of curriculum in my childhood and even now as an adult. The stories stay the same, but they continue to reinvent themselves as I encounter new challenges and phases in my life. But I'll be clear on this: I wouldn't say that I've felt *minoritized*. I think there's a difference between feeling like a second-generation immigrant and feeling minoritized. I think that could be really different.

Sonia: Yeah, because I'm thinking back to when I was a child. One of the most poignant memories for me was when I was in Grade 5 or 6. We were in a field, and there was a group of us playing soccer or some sort of a game. There was this East Indian woman that walked by. She looked like my grandma, you know, with the outfit, the pyjami or salwar suit and with a covered head and everything. She walked past our game, and it was interesting because the people I was playing with were all White, but all my friends started talking among themselves and saying, "I'm not a racist or anything, but there's getting to be way too many of them here." And I remember someone else saying, "Yeah, that's what my mom says too. We don't have anything against them, but there are too many here."

I think that really . . . it hurt me, but at the same time I was scared because I didn't want them to see me like that. I was embarrassed because that was me, and I didn't know what to say. I remember going home and just wondering, "Are there too many of us? Am I one of the 'us'?" They didn't look at me like that, but why were they playing with me? I started thinking of that, and I still remember that day very clearly. I'm still feeling that sick feeling to my stomach that I didn't say anything. I should've stuck up for myself and . . . and my culture. I'm so embarrassed about that still. I reflect on it now and see how it affected the construction of my identity, how others perceived me, and how I perceived myself (Kelly, 1998).

Kari: That's so interesting. And it's almost—the word *invisibility* keeps coming to mind just because that part of you was invisible for them. You enjoy that as a child, you almost enjoy that ability to see people with stripped-down honesty and also to be seen with stripped-down honesty. Those kids knew "Sonia" for Sonia, but they didn't know that woman except for how she looked. And as a child, I guess you don't really have a voice to rationalize it or talk about it.

Sonia: Yeah. I suppose that's why I was asking you how you felt growing up. Your experiences are kind of inside the home whereas mine are out in the world and display vulnerability because it's part of the public experience.

Kari: Your poignant narrative and that sense of shame remind me of something that transformed me, and my thinking around racialized identity, when I was in high school. I was sixteen years old, and I should have had a stronger sense of when and how to stand up for something. I had some friends over, and we were sitting out in the backyard with three popular guys in my high school and a few girlfriends. This one guy, Aden, was a bit of a bully. He was also the jokester, the class clown, a bit of a jock, and a lot of the girls liked him. But he started making racist jokes, and I was clearly disapproving of them. He saw it in my face, but he kept going and went on to a second joke. I will never forget it: "How are . . ." I'll never forget this: "How are an 'n-word' and an apple the same?" He looked right at me, as if to challenge me, and he said, "They both look good hanging from a tree." It's like he was saying to me, "What are you gonna do about it?"

And, honestly, I was sick to my stomach, and I got up and walked inside. I felt paralyzed, and I didn't know to tell him to "get the f- out of my house." I was so angry and upset, especially since it was in . . . my territory. It was in my family's space. And this is a spiritual space, in a sense; it's a space where you're secure and where you practice your own beliefs and live out your own values. And everything he had just said and done went against that value system.

I felt so violated, and I didn't know how to ask him to leave because I was scared. I was scared he would yell at me or embarrass me in front of all of our friends. That incident has haunted me because I was a coward. I often think, "Man, I wish he would've pulled that now."

Sonia: But I don't know why you're embarrassed. You walked away. You didn't approve it. How many times have you heard of people telling stories where they laughed along with it, or even if they knew it was wrong, they're like, "Awww, don't say that." But you kind of physically left that space. That's something . . .

Kari: Yeah, it's something, but it's not enough. I feel like it was more of a cowardly thing to do than say, "Hey, that's not okay in this space," or make him feel embarrassed somehow. I keep thinking, "If I knew then what I know now . . . ," and I would love the opportunity to go back and educate him.

Sonia: Do you mean just voicing it? Yes, same with me. I still played with them, those kids in the field. It became a choice between fitting in and being left out, a choice that I regret to this day.

Kari: Exactly, and it's interesting that your experience of regret comes from failing to defend your own culture whereas my experience of regret comes from failing to defend someone else's. I could choose to be a coward without my own identity being questioned, but regardless, both groups looked at us kind of like we were White, I think. Right? The perpetrators, I guess you could call them, looked at us both as being "White," or one of them.

Sonia: I wonder how much they thought of me as White or whether they thought of it as, "Oh, she's different, though. She's a different kind of 'Indian,' not like the other ones." You know how people justify that, right? I know I've heard that: "I have this Black friend" or "I have a Native friend, so I know I'm not a racist." I wonder how many times that's referred to?

Kari: Oh, that comes up so often!

Sonia: Actually, I was thinking about this during this past week at work. How often do you think that comes up for me as one of the few visible-minority teachers at my school? You know, I've become the unofficial multicultural liaison/expert person to approach with diversity concerns. Frideres (2007) talked about how White people never have to represent the "White perspective," so why do I have to represent the "Brown perspective?!" I'm passionate about the work, but I wonder how isolating it is for the staff members when they don't get to know the larger picture than just me and my perspective. Because I know one staff member said that it was great that I was willing to talk about these things because she "would never feel comfortable asking anyone else." We were talking about going to the mosque, the temple. But then I wondered, "Am I stopping people from going because they feel satisfied with just having enough information from me?"

Kari: Oh, interesting. I don't know. I suspect that any perspective other than that dominant, White, Christian viewpoint is educational for your colleagues. Sure, you can only speak to Sonia's worldview based on your intersecting identity markers like gender, religion, socioeconomic status, and the like. But allowing others a glimpse of the world through your particular lens is certainly more informative than if they had been too uncomfortable to ask a stranger the question.

Sonia: And then I have my own experiences where I want to have my voice heard. I have a lot of ideas, but I'm wondering if people want to hear it.

Kari: Yeah, exactly. If people want to hear it and whether they will think it's valid.

Sonia: Mine is maybe too valid. It's too much of a *given*, as if they're saying: "That's what Sonia said, so it must be right." But it shouldn't be a given, right? Should it?

Kari: I have no idea. On the one hand, it is more valid because you have this authentic voice, and then, on the other hand, what makes it authentic?

Sonia: It shouldn't be just taken for granted. I say yes or no to someone's question, and people view it as the final answer.

Kari: Yeah, *you* are the bottom line.

Sonia: It makes me question how different points of views can be meaningful and yet contradicting. My perspective is an account coming from within the culture . . . my being within that culture: the *emic* side (Headland, 1990). It can be really problematic.

Kari: But it's flattering in some ways, is it not? People ask you questions not just because of who you are but also because of what you do and because of your special knowledge surrounding diversity topics. I struggle with that because I have sometimes felt that *who* I am does not exemplify diversity, even if my knowledge and skill set can speak to those things. It's odd sometimes when people approach me as a cultural liaison.

Sonia: Well, you are a cultural liaison. And with your knowledge and understanding you're able to describe and apply a perspective to other cultures. It's the *etic* side of things where there is an attempt to be culturally neutral (Headland, 1990).

Kari: Yes, in some ways I am. But, I can't get away from feeling like an imposter. You know, equity and social justice are such worthy pursuits, and they come from the core of what I believe, who I am, and my experiences traveling and interacting with people. But the color of my skin still tells me that I, for example, can't stand up at an academic conference and voice my opinion on racism or privilege. I still feel so vulnerable, especially in those circles where there is that critical piece. And I wonder if it's something that I'm ever going to get around.

Sonia: But what about your work with [a multicultural agency]? You were working with those focus groups and running all sorts of workshops. Did you feel under that critical spotlight?

Kari: Not at all. I only feel that in academic circles. I feel really respected in my position as a workshop leader, but the majority of what I do isn't necessarily teaching; it's facilitating dialogue. But I guess good teaching is essentially the facilitation of critical dialogue. Nonetheless, I definitely don't feel such tension in that role, although I wonder if it's because of a lack of critical voice. Even when I was running workshops in [a Canadian city], we had a very diverse room filled with forty students, faculty, and staff from a major university, and I never felt that my being White was under scrutiny. Even when I was facilitating a day-and-a-half-long workshop on diversity and leadership, I certainly never felt like my White skin was being held against me. But here's what perplexes me: I feel uncomfortable with that criticism, but think it's needed. When I hear or see White diversity workers and educators and scholars, my first thought is, "Is this another well-meaning White person?" Is that weird?

Sonia: You know, if I hadn't known you and the work you do, I probably would've taken one glance at you and said, "Okay, it's coming from that perspective, and it's nothing that's going to further my own knowledge or where I want to go," you know? I hate saying this, but . . . "I've been there, done that." It's kind of like those multicultural workshops or ESL workshops for students. They are talking to the room as if no one knows what diversity is. And I'm sure that's there, but they don't know how to confront it. But I live it. So it's kind of like if I didn't know you and how passionate and critical you were about this work, then I would probably look at those workshops and say, "Oh well, that's typical."

Kari: Oh, and I fully look at it that way. So few organizations really give you the space to be critical and disrupt the status quo. If you get too "radical" in any workshop or presentation, you're out of a job, or your organization isn't welcome in a given arena. I remember doing a diversity workshop in a Catholic high school, and we were having a brainstorming session on ways that people can be different. Nobody would say "sexual orientation" or "sexuality," and when I began hinting at it, a quieter guy in the class finally said, "You can be gay or straight," and three confident boys in the class began snickering. One of them said, "I don't wanna see fags around here," and I asked him, first, to change his language and, second, to imagine how he would behave toward a person he knew was gay. He said, "I'd punch him in the face." That might have been the most challenging position I've experienced in a diversity workshop, knowing the more conservative views that Catholic institutions possess around homosexuality. Yet I was aware of my obligation to gay and straight students alike.

     As a workshop facilitator for a diversity organization I had a goal to break down the barriers between different people and help individuals understand the poorly informed roots of their discriminatory attitudes. But I knew that my employer could not and would not ever fault me for discussing LGBTQ issues, especially in an environment that often lacks such discussions. So I was able to have that discussion with the class and help them arrive at the understanding that there is nothing *wrong* or *bad* about being gay or straight or whatever. I could facilitate that discussion because my organization had a positive reputation and a clear stance on issues like that one. But had I been a teacher in that school, who knows if I could have had that discussion without fear of being reprimanded for "radical" views?

     And even within that, I think organizations and businesses want to hire "visible minorities" partly because they value their input and also because it makes them look good, but they often stop short if someone wants to bring in ideas that aren't in line with a more conservative view on multiculturalism. And what do you end up with? More White people in those positions because White people think they can afford to remain neutral and just "celebrate our differences!"

Sonia: Like Nancy Fraser's (2003) and Alex Honneth's (2003) "recognition versus redistribution" debate, where recognition is great, but let's actually *act* on our ideas of equity. There has to be more of critical lens on "diversity." How we pursue meaningful change that works toward equity is what needs to be challenged.

Kari: Yeah, and it's funny; I feel uncomfortable saying these things because it seems like such a sham, trying to reconcile these critical thoughts with my White identity.

Sonia: It's healthy, though, to have those thoughts and share them in a context that is safe and trusting.

Kari: Yeah, definitely. But going back to what I said before about having never experienced *minoritization*, I think it's relevant to contrast that idea—minoritization—with being a visible minority. The term *minoritized* speaks to more than just a racial representation and actually encompasses the systemic implications of being marginalized from people in positions of power and privilege (Waterfall and Maiter, 2003).

Sonia: Because you can be a minority, right? A visible minority, for example, in a setting where you look different and you are not part of the majority. However, minoritized—and I'm relating directly to where I am right now in my career—is a completely different situation. I'm in a school where, being Indo-Canadian, I am definitely a majority, visibly, if you count the students and the teachers all together. The vast majority of our student body is composed of East Indian students, specifically Punjabi-speaking students. But that doesn't take away from being minoritized by the curriculum and the institution of education (Majhanovich and Rezai-Rashti, 2002). Most of my students and I are minoritized within the institution of education while being part of the visible majority in that school.

Kari: That's interesting because you can look at the idea of being a minority in all sorts of layered groupings: within your school, within the northeast quadrant of [a Canadian city], [a Canadian city] itself, and beyond. A lot of my passion for this kind of work came from my early traveling experiences and feeling like a minority for the first time. I remember feeling so visible to everyone for the first time in my life.

When I was fifteen, I went to Japan. I was walking down the street in Tokyo, and I remember seeing a sea of black-haired heads and everyone just stared at me. I was only 5 foot 9 inches, but I was literally looking down at everyone, feeling like an awkward Goliath. And then one of my high school teachers, who was 6'3", was just walking down the street, and locals asked if they could take photos with him. That was the first time I ever remember thinking, "Wow, I thought I was normal, but maybe I'm not." Ha ha! For me this was a parallel to Carl James (2007) writing about Whiteness being assumed as the "basis of comparison" for everyone else in Canada. I always thought I was the "normal" way to be and then realizing that, no, I've just been told by the Canadian powers-that-be that I am the norm in that I am a White person of average Canadian height. And to continue that idea, the kindness that people showed me when I was the minority made me wonder why we don't treat minorities this well in Canada.

Sonia: Yeah, it was about understanding Canada as not being very welcoming, right?

Kari: Right. When I go traveling, I definitely feel like a minority, but I don't feel minoritized because there is so much privilege emanating from my skin.

Sonia: Your travel experience reminds me of when I went to India for first time. I went without my family because I was doing a semester at a university close to Mumbai in the city of Pune, which is far from my roots in India. India is very diverse, and one area may be totally different from another, like a different country. It was very interesting because the students that I went with were all Canadian students, and the majority of them were White. Out of the total, there were five East Indian or Indo-Canadian girls who went.

But it was interesting; the first day we got there, we got the dorm assignments, and everyone picked their rooms and we randomly picked our room, my friend Milan and me. We knew we wanted try and be next to each other since we didn't know anyone else on the trip, and it turned out that in one wing, four out of the five of us were East Indian girls. Kari, you wouldn't believe this, but we heard afterwards that people were upset, and there were two girls in particular who started saying, "Of course they are all going to stick together because they know what it's like here." And that was really . . . heartbreaking because I . . . first of all, it was my first time in India!

Kari: And you weren't even cognizant of it. It wasn't even purposeful.

Sonia: No, I didn't even know these girls, but it was threatening, right? I think this spoke to how they felt threatened by being a visible minority, where they were looking at us and saying, "Hey, you blend in." But in actual fact we were all just as terrified, just as unsure about being away from home. We weren't there with our families; we didn't know the language, as the local dialect was completely different from what most of us East Indian girls spoke. The friend that I'm referring to is from Fiji, so that added a piece to how she identified with India and how the language wasn't even acknowledged; she was a threat because of her India/nness (Sheth and Handa, 1993). I speak only Punjabi. None of us spoke or really understood the local dialect, Marathi.

The experience overall was a negative one at the time, but as our trip went on, I came to reflect on how important it was to me to have other Indo-Canadian girls to talk with and share our experiences . . . you couldn't have the same depth of conversation with someone who wasn't from a similar background. Our identity was suddenly thrown in our face and we were like, "Wow, okay we're in a position that can be seen or perceived as privileged."

Kari: Oh wow. And what a shock for you?!

Sonia: It was a total shock, and it didn't stop there. It continued. There was a basketball game, and it was Canadians versus Indians because we had a lot of friends there. It was a shared hostel with other foreign- and Indian-born students. And one of the White girls from Canada says, "Well you're on the Indian team," to my friend Milan. She said, "But I'm not. I'm not on the Indian team because none of them wants me there, and they told me to go to the Canadian team." She was telling me afterwards that it was so funny because she felt like a tennis ball going back and forth . . . she thought, "What side do I belong on?"

And just to wrap that piece up, when we came back, we had had this long, crazy flight. It took us two days longer to get back to Canada. When we finally arrived in the Montreal airport, one girl turned around—I don't think she realized or was aware of what she was saying, especially to me—and she said: Oh, it's so nice to be back where I see people like me or people that I recognize.

My first experience in India was beautiful, and I felt so much like I belonged, more than I've ever felt anywhere else, but to have that said to you when you come, and you know it's true . . . like it's true! Of course it's true; she felt happy that she wasn't standing out any more. And being in India, for me, was the first time I've sort of felt that relief of fitting in and belonging to a group where religion, culture, language are all "givens" rather than being on the margins.

Kari: It's so mind blowing that something I've just felt my whole life, that sense of belonging that I didn't even know I felt until I went traveling, was = −w— something you didn't experience until you went to India. I guess this speaks to the curriculum of travel. I can identify with that girl's experience in a sense because when I taught in Africa and then backpacked around for six months, it's a vulnerable position. You probably understand this on a much more regular basis than I do, but I felt so vulnerable. I remember getting to South Africa, where there are far more White people than in other countries. One White woman walked up to me, and she must have been asking me directions or something in Afrikaans. I just looked blankly at her and said, "Sorry, I speak English," and it was this weird sense of confusion, for both of us I'm sure. Seeing her, though, I had this strange sense of . . .

Sonia: Home?

Kari: No, not home. I remember thinking that in certain ways I had far more in common with a black Ugandan, for example, who spoke English than with this White South African woman, who evidently did not know how to communicate with me in English and with whom I couldn't communicate in Afrikaans. It's so important to have those transformative experiences where you say, "Hey! This isn't at all how I thought it was going to be." It's like transformative learning theory, where Mezirow (1991) says you encounter a dilemma that kind of contradicts your previous assumptions. Then you learn through critically examining that dilemma. I assumed I would more easily connect with someone who looks like me than someone who doesn't. But it was clear that my assumptions were skewed. And it's interesting because at one point in your story about India, you said that you felt terrified because this was so new to you and kind of alien, and then you said you felt like you fit in more than you ever have. There is an interesting dynamic between feeling like you fit in and looking like you fit in. It's a beautiful feeling to feel like you fit in, right?

Sonia: Yeah. And you become a part of it, but at the end of that trip—and this is more about the second time I went to India—you are very much Canadian in your family's eyes when you go back there. We are coming from a more privileged standpoint. We have jobs that are secure, we have a police system that you can be comforted by instead of being suspicious of, for example. But yeah, you feel safe.

I remember coming back to Canada the second time I traveled to India, and I had had a really horrible experience: My sister-in-law passed away. I remember coming back to Canada from India and being so glad that I was home, and I didn't have to see the different ways that we mourn or go through things that I had never experienced before. I felt out of place in a lot of ways and frustrated because it was implied that, "Well you don't understand this because you're Canadian" or "You don't know what this is or how it's done." I found myself getting frustrated by it and so embedded in grief that by the time I got back to Canada, it was the best feeling to be around people like me . . . there were second-generation Indo-Canadians who could relate to what was going on. I could talk to them about that fine balance between Canadian and Indian culture. And I would never voice my questions or critical thoughts with anyone outside of the household or cultural group because I don't want or need people judging my culture.

Kari: I think you just brought up a really important point, which is how different nationality and culture can be. You have the Indo-Canadian culture, but part of that culture is Canadian, right?

Sonia: Absolutely.

Kari: I just had a fleeting thought of my cousin's daughter, who visited from Norway. My cousin, who is Norwegian, adopted her from China. Since she was six months old she has been growing up in Norway. Now she's seven years old, and she came to visit us in Canada. At the time, she could speak very little English, and . . . when she starts speaking her own language, you expect Chinese or Mandarin, right? And out comes this Norwegian language that my blue-eyed grandmother speaks. It just felt like such a contradiction because my first instinct said, "You look like you should be speaking Mandarin." It can be confusing when people defy what you expect of them. It was really refreshing experience for me because it confused me and led me to reflect on my understanding of the world in a broader sense. Mezirow (1991) would call it a disorienting dilemma, which leads to a change in meaning perspectives.

Sonia: I can imagine. Do you think we are always trying to categorize and position people in relation to us? I think that's a part of self-identifying, right? It's especially noticeable in Canada, where we may be used to seeing more visible minorities, and yet their identity is still a "hyphenated identity" that categorizes them as part of an immigrant group. And when that clean-cut categorization is challenged, in that case, for example, everything gets thrown up in the air because you wonder, "Am I trying to label you?" How do I relate to them . . . like that perception piece, right? When that's challenged, in that case, for example, it's really . . . everything kind of gets thrown up in the air because you're like, "Wait a minute; am I going to localize you?"

Kari: I think it was less so for me than for others because I knew her story, whereas a lot of people didn't. I took her to the lake with a bunch of White Canadian kids, and I would tell their parents, "This is my cousin, Nina. She's from Norway." I could see their wheels turning because it doesn't look like she's from Norway, and people can't fathom that you can be from somewhere but not necessarily look that way. It's such an anomaly. Most people can't really conceive of the fascinating narrative that Nina has so far.

Sonia: I wonder how many people within this country and around the world perceive how a "Canadian" looks. I'm interested to know how she's going to self-identify as she gets older.

Kari: Well, do you know what? We were playing Wii, and you can build your own person that looks like you. It was kind of informative because I watched as she built her Wii character. This was after she had started to pick up the language. So she started building her Wii character named Nina, and she was going to give her blue eyes. I asked, "Nina, what color eyes do you have?" She understood basic English at that point, and she said, "Brown." I responded, "Yeah, so maybe choose some beautiful brown eyes?" I don't know. Maybe I didn't have the right to tell her how to identify herself, but I wanted her to feel proud of her racialized identity rather than feeling as though she . . .

Sonia: . . . should fulfill that stereotype. We've talked about that feeling of fitting in somewhere. I wonder: When will her time come to identify with others around her? I think that speaks to globalization and how the world is moving. I mean, if you look at people who are of mixed race or have parents from different backgrounds, we live in a different world than before.

I have another friend who also traveled in India with me, and we had many conversations around how her perceived identity compared to how she self-identified. One of her parents is Italian and the other Indian. She found it very frustrating because she looked East Indian, even more so than I did, but she didn't speak the language that was expected from her. She found it so frustrating, and she was tired of . . . being looked at in a certain way. Like, for example, what if she wanted to smoke a cigarette? An East Indian woman smoking in public?! It doesn't happen! At least, it doesn't happen without some potential negative attention. We guessed that the possibility of someone saying something to her was probable.

Kari: So are you saying that you couldn't do it either?

Sonia: I don't know . . . but probably not. Maybe because that speaks of a gender issue, and the intersections between gender and race are difficult to separate (Ng, 1995). In this case, my race could be questioned because I'm fair skinned; however, I still look more or less Indian in that context. So I probably would also be questioned or perceived negatively because I am an East Indian woman smoking.

Kari: Interesting, but doesn't your visual identity shift from setting to setting, location to location, context to context, time to time?

Sonia: In some key ways, yes. It's an issue that follows us everywhere: the preconceived notions of how your identity markers are perceived. Himani Bannerji (1993) really explores this idea. I remember reading one of her works about how popular images of South Asian women are on the margins of Canadian society, such as when you look and compare commercial advertising to the woman who cleans at the airport. But, you know, it's the space in which we can self-identify and not be grouped as a homogeneous whole, a group based on some shared characteristics (Mohanty, 2003). It's okay to be in between, right? Or taking the context of a situation . . . this is what I mean by it being so complex.

Kari: Oh yeah, absolutely. It's interesting talking about societal pressure because it's tough to put our finger on exactly who or what pressures us to fulfill a certain cultural role. Afrocentric ideas always criticize the hegemony of Western perspectives that are based on the Eurocentric way of being (Graham, 1999; Okafor, 1996). It doesn't mean you have to identify yourself in relation to that, but it's so easy for me to say that as a White person.

But if we go back to the context of teaching, how much does identity affect who listens to us, and what messages they take from our teaching? As a woman, could I walk into a carpentry class as a teacher, for example, and be taken seriously by the—presumably—largely male student body? Alternately, how might a scruffy, bearded man wearing a plaid shirt be perceived by the carpentry students? In a similar way, it can be intimidating to walk into a room to talk about diversity when my skin color might suggest to an onlooker that I don't know the first thing about diversity. I know you've told me a lot of interesting stories about teaching in a classroom where a lot of the parents feel like they can identify with you and talk to you in private.

Sonia: Yes, people have mentioned that to me, parents and other staff members. That's been empowering when parents say to me, "It's really great that you're teaching here and that I can speak to you." They can ask questions that are related to the classroom or the student system, or even joke around in a certain way and say things that I understand. They don't have to explain certain things about their child's behavior. It brings up that question, again, of who *can* and *should* do this work in a diverse and multicultural setting (James, 2007). This question even extends into the classroom when you and I have spoken about teaching or facilitating conversations around race and racism. Does ethnicity matter? (Housee, 2008) In this case, yes, it does because it brings forth language, culture, and identification with a social group.

But, at the same time, who listens to you? On one side, the parents are very respectful in the community. But if I go back to the family example, some people look at you as being too Canadian, even as a teacher in a Canadian setting. I know there's one parent whom I've worked with in particular, who says that the Canadian education system is not what it should be. It's not good and lacks key qualities found in schools in India, the main issue being that we do not assign enough homework (worksheets). My experiences or professional expertise in how I can help their child doesn't count anymore because it's "too Canadian."

Kari: On one hand, we can be the bridge and assist in coming to an understanding of . . . collaborating with those families. But there is that sense where you can't because you've been shut out . . . just for being who you are, right?

Sonia: Yeah. Having been born in Canada, I'm not ever going to be enough in that person's eyes, which is sad. It's disempowering at some point. It makes me feel isolated because I very much identify as an East Indian person, speaking the language, and I am proud of it. But when it's that close in the context and it's implied, "Oh sorry, you don't get it," that is when I think, "Wow, I don't get it? If I was born in India . . . then I would?" Our identity and the way it's perceived by others really impacts the way we work and interact with others. It has also allowed me to understand the complexity of how we identify ourselves. Am I too "Canadian" in some ways and absolutely "Indo-Canadian" the rest of the time? I think so. This curriculum of defining ourselves with these varying identity markers is very challenging when they seem to conflict with each other.

Kari: I sometimes get told by other Canadians—mostly White Canadians—that by going and "helping" in other countries, I'm abandoning Canadians who need help. And that's a really interesting comment, I find, because helping is helping. I don't even want to get into the complexities of the word *help* and the colonialist attachments to that concept and the fact that I'm the one who is helped by those experiences. But, regardless, when you're doing what you think is right, does it matter where in the world you do it? And does it have to be just for Canadians? I find that a confusing stance. Without a doubt, there are Canadian children who live in poverty, and there are Canadian women who are victims of violence, and I support people who work for these causes. There are also Rwandan children, for example, who live in poverty and Rwandan women who are victims of violence, and I feel that people should support those who work for such a cause. Yes, we are Canadian citizens, but we are also global citizens, and it's interesting that some people get upset by this.

Sonia: That's very common. You know, people get very upset when there's fundraising going on for another region of the world when there are homeless children in [a Canadian city].

Kari: It's a great argument in the sense that we should help people here and address those issues that are problematic in our own city and country. But why is it a question of either/or? It's about where I choose to expend my energies. Just to go back to the disadvantages of our identity, when I taught in Ghana, there was that element of . . . everyone thinks you are infinitely rich and infinitely knowledgeable, and if they can just learn everything that you know, then maybe they could do better. That can be embarrassing and frustrating. Earlier this year, I was visiting a rural school in Uganda, and the principal had me in front of the class and said: "Kari is going to teach you maths today!" He handed me a math book, and everyone cheered. I was horrified! Ha ha! I haven't done math in years, and I wouldn't have any clue where to start!

Particularly in Africa—because that's where I've spent a lot of time—some people have unrealistic views about Whites. I felt that many Africans assumed I was smart and educated and rich, among other things. But this automatic admiration that White people are given in Africa I don't feel entitled to, and I'm not deserving of it. Sure, I go there to try and "help," but I go for myself and for the learning.

Sonia: No, I get where you're going with it, and it truly is hard to articulate. It's an assumption based on who holds privilege and power, a reality for our global context. Sometimes it is applied in ways that make you uncomfortable and ways that force you to question being "White."

Kari: Exactly. There is so much research out there that supports that feeling of discomfort when you are confronting Whiteness and forming your antiracist "White identity" (Carr and Lund, 2007; Kendall, 2006; Lund, 2008; Wihak, 2007).

Sonia: It's funny. When I complain about the hegemony or inequity in Canada, my dad would say something along the lines of: "Get over it. Stop complaining about things. It's the reason that you're in this country and that that you're able to be educated and you have a better life." That privilege of being able to come to Canada contradicts what I critically analyze about being "Canadian." I'm essentially a part of it now, the Canadian lifestyle, which almost means that I could/should stop?

If you go back historically and argue that we wouldn't even be in this position perhaps if it wasn't for colonialism so on—I have heard the argument, stating: "Don't be ridiculous. The past is the past. Now you keep going forward, and remember you're here for a reason. We came here for a reason. You have a job you never would have had that before. Life is the way it is. Get over it, Sonia." I know my dad is proud of me in the work that I do, but at the same time, you know, he makes me question my own perspectives in how I perceive being a Canadian and what constitutes success.

Kari: Again, there's an entire curriculum that our parents teach us. Your dad thought: "Go make your millions . . . go make your millions and be happy about it."

Sonia: Yes. Why did you come here, right? Why aren't we satisfied with being in a secure and prosperous country? I know I've been frustrated when I've heard criticisms of Canadian life, especially about those parents, the kind I mentioned before. I hear myself saying: "Well, why did you come then if everything is so wrong here?" But we're all economic slaves at some one point or another, right? And it is a better standard of life in many ways.

Kari: Sure. That's the interesting thing about it. I keep using countries in Africa as an example. In many developing nations, I have reflected on the fact that it's great to be here because it's healing, but guess what? I also get to leave. I get to go home, go to the doctor, and have my mom's turkey dinner at Christmas. To be Canadian is in many ways to be privileged. And on my end, I can add the fact that I'm White to the level of privilege I receive. I think some White people feel like if they talk about being White or their perspectives as White people, they will automatically be viewed as racist or, even worse, they will discover that they are racist in many ways. It's easy to have your guard up in that way; it's easier not to talk about it.

Sonia: I can imagine. It's difficult to work in this field being a visible minority and one who is minoritized. I think if there were more opportunities to engage is self-reflexive analysis like the one we've initiated today, there would be more opportunities to disrupt the status quo and address issues that impact how we perceive each other in our country. That's the other part of identity rights: The ability to sit here and talk to this academically and in a casual conversation is at the same time something we are very privileged to do.

Kari: Yes, and I think this would only help us further our work in a field as complex as diversity. Whether it is in Canada or another part of the world, we need to continue recognizing how imperative the reflection on identity is to the work that we do. I think it's essential. It makes me think of Freire (1970) and his insistence that individuals who are truly committed to social justice have to reflect and reexamine themselves.

Sonia: This process and conversation captured a lot of key points in how we came to think about and perceive our work.

Kari: It's so nice to know that someone else experiences these frustrations and these critical thoughts, even if it is from a totally different identity perspective. It's been refreshing for me to feel like I'm not so isolated and to have some of my views surfaced and challenged.

Sonia: It's been a change for me as well to really listen and take in the challenges that you've experienced as a White person in this field. This shared duoethnographic experience will definitely inform what it means to be "Canadian" and the ambiguities and complexities of identity politics. Our conversation has really made it poignant that the complexity of identity markers and how we and others perceive them really form *who* and *what* we are. My reasons for entering the field of education and working around issues of multiculturalism is resultant of the experiences I have shared with others, including our relationship as colleagues and friends. This is a continuous journey, and our interactions with the world and others will add to how I speak to and for the curriculum of diversity. How I navigate and negotiate my own identity will always impact my work and learning.

Kari: This conversation has in many ways been cathartic for me because I'm beginning to realize how much these stories, which I thought were random, have actually been quite pivotal in the formation of my worldview. It's helping me understand how I have created my idea of normalcy or even just my idea of who I am. A lot of these stories we've shared—and I don't know how it is for you, but for me, I felt quite vulnerable talking about a few of these topics. But because we're friends and this duoethnographic format has been fairly casual, I feel comfortable sharing these narratives and tracing my learning to certain moments and specific types of curriculum. I hadn't really thought of travel as a type of curriculum or my experiences with bullying as a type of curriculum until now. And through these very different types of curriculum, I've formed my idea of social justice and identity and racism, among other things. It's almost as if talking about it with you has pulled those past experiences into the present and repositioned them in my adult frame of reference. Then to juxtapose all of this with your narratives of learning . . . it's kind of enlightening.

REFERENCES

Bannerji, H. (1993). *Returning the gaze: Essays on racism, feminism and politics.* Toronto: Sister Vision Press.

Bhabha, H. K. (1994). *The location of culture.* New York: Routledge.

Carr, P. R., and Lund, D. E. (2007). Introduction: Scanning Whiteness. In P. R. Carr and D. E. Lund (Eds.), *The great White north? Exploring Whiteness, privilege and identity in education* (pp. 1–18). Rotterdam: Sense.

Dei, G. S. (2007). Foreword. In P. R. Carr and D. E. Lund (Eds.), *The great White north? Exploring Whiteness, privilege and identity in education* (pp. vii–xi). Rotterdam: Sense.

Dunlop, R. (1999). Beyond dualism: Toward a dialogic negotiation of difference. *Canadian Journal of Education, 24*(1), 57–71.

Fraser, N. (2003). *Redistribution or recognition? A political-philosophical exchange.* London: Verso.

Freire, P. (1970). *Pedagogy of the oppressed.* New York: Continuum.

Frideres, J. (2007). Being White and being right: Critiquing individual and collective privilege. In P. R. Carr and D. E. Lund (Eds.), *The great White north? Exploring Whiteness, privilege and identity in education* (pp. 43–56). Rotterdam: Sense.

Graham, M. (1999). The African-centered worldview. *Journal of Black Studies, 30*(1), 103–123.

Handa, A. (2003). *Of silk saris and mini-skirts: South Asian girls walk the tightrope of culture.* Toronto: Women's Press.

Headland, T. N. (1990). A dialogue between Kenneth Pike and Marvin Harris on emics and etics. In T. N. Headland, K. L. Pike, and M. Harris (Eds.), *Emics and etics: The insider/outsider debate* (pp. 13–27). Newbury Park, CA: Sage.

Honneth, A. (2003). *Redistribution or recognition? A political-philosophical exchange.* London: Verso.

Housee, S. (2008). Should ethnicity matter when teaching about "race" and racism in the classroom? *Race, Ethnicity and Education, 11*(4), 415–428.

James, C. (2007). Who can/should do this work? The colour of critique. In P. R. Carr and D. E. Lund (Eds.), *The great White north? Exploring Whiteness, privilege and identity in education* (pp. 119–134). Rotterdam: Sense.

Kelly, J. (1998). *Under the gaze: Learning to be black in White society.* Halifax, NS: Fernwood.

Kendall, F. (2006). *Understanding White privilege: Creating pathways to authentic relationships across race.* New York: Routledge.

Lund, D. E. (2008). Harvesting social justice and human rights in rocky terrain. *The Ardent Anti-Racism & Decolonization Review, 1*(1), 64–67.

Majhanovich, S., and Rezai-Rashti, G. (2002). Marginalized women: Minority women teachers in twentieth century Ontario. *Education and Society, 20*(2), 61–72.

Mezirow, J. (1991). *Transformative dimensions of adult learning.* San Francisco: Jossey-Bass.

Mohanty, C. (2003). *Feminism without borders: Decolonizing theory, practicing solidarity.* London: Duke University Press.

Ng, R. (1995). Teaching against the grain: Contradictions and possibilities. In R. Ng, P. Staton, and J. Scane (Eds.), *Anti-racism, feminism, and critical approaches to education* (pp. 129–152). Westport, CT: Bergin & Garvey.

Norris, J. (2008). Duoethnography. In L. M. Given (Ed.), *The SAGE encyclopedia of qualitative research methods* (pp. 233–236). Thousand Oaks, CA: Sage.

Norris, J., and Sawyer, R. (2004). Null and hidden curricula of sexual orientation: A dialogue on the curreres of the absent presence and the present absence. In L. Coia, M. Birch, N. J. Brooks, E. Heilman, S. Mayer, A. Mountain, and P. Pritchard (Eds.), *Democratic responses in an era of standardization* (pp. 139–159). Troy, NY: Curriculum and Pedagogy.

Norris, J., and Sawyer, R. (2008, October). *Duoethnography: A dialectic form of inquiry.* Paper presented at the International Institute for Qualitative Methods Conference, Banff, Canada.

Okafor, V. (1996). The place of Africology in the university curriculum. *Journal of Black Studies, 26*(6), 688–713.

Sawyer, R., and Norris, J. (2009). Duoethnography: Articulations/(re)creation of meaning in the making. In W. Gershon (Ed.), *Working together in qualitative research: A turn towards the collaborative* (pp. 127–140). Rotterdam: Sense.

Sheth, A., and Handa, A. (1993). A jewel in the frown: Striking accord between India/n feminists. In H. Bannerji (Ed.), *Returning the gaze: Essays on racism, feminism and politics* (pp. 45–99). Toronto: Sister Vision Press.

Waterfall, B., and Maiter, S. (2003, May). *Resisting colonization in the academy: From indigenous minoritized standpoints.* Paper presented at the Canadian Critical Race Conference, Vancouver, Canada.

Wihak, C. (2007). Development of anti-racist White identity in Canadian educational counselors. In P. R. Carr and D. E. Lund (Eds.), *The great White north? Exploring Whiteness, privilege and identity in education* (pp. 95–106). Rotterdam: Sense.

CHAPTER 10

A Curriculum of Beauty

Nancy Rankie Shelton and Morna McDermott

PROLOGUE

Duoethnography creates a research context for its participants to expose and examine underlying patterns of enculturation and indoctrination in relation to societal norms. Norms operate as internalized rules that frame our behavior and ways of perceiving self and others. With its focus on self as site, not topic, of research, duoethnography promotes researchers' access not only to their beliefs and values but also to the unfolding histories of those beliefs and values within societal and cultural contexts. It also presents both to researcher and reader, participants' narratives of experience in relation to those beliefs and values.

Morna McDermott and Nancy Rankie Shelton's study on beauty illustrates how duoethnographers can critically bring their beliefs and values to the surface and, in the process, experience and reconceptualize their perceptions of them. Central to this process are questions, dilemmas, and even emergent contradictions that occur to them as they write. Some examples of these questions for Shelton and McDermott are:

- *How to negotiate dilemmas arising from both rejecting and buying into beauty stereotypes?*
- *How does language frame perspectives of beauty?*
- *How do views of curriculum intersect with a curriculum of beauty?*
- *How do relationships among beauty, intellectual drive, and achievement intersect?*
- *How do perceptions of social class and beauty intersect?*

They then explore these questions and issues in depth through multiple perspectives, including their stories as well as their reflections about those stories at different time periods. For example, McDermott discusses actual quotes about beauty she finds in her teenage diary, an activity that takes her into the past from her current vantage point. Additional perspectives include photographs, which develop a counternarrative in their study, creating intertextual dialogue. And they include views of beauty from their students. They allow themselves to digress and play with their data, processes that move their text forward.

Their study contributes new understandings both to the topic of beauty and to qualitative research itself. As an example of how language in duoethnography reflects a new research paradigm, their study does not present conventional "findings" but rather contributions to their topic under consideration. As duoethnographers, we don't find something that has existed before the study. Rather the "finding"—the presentation of their stories and their accompanying conceptual change—is the process. In this study, McDermott and Shelton make their new understandings explicit.

—Richard D. Sawyer

INTRODUCTION

The term *beauty* is a loaded and complex one, but, then again, if we are to examine this topic from a critical stance, even terms like *loaded* and *complex* themselves become, well, loaded and complex.

According to *Webster's Dictionary*, Beauty is defined as:

1: the quality or aggregate of qualities in a person or thing that gives pleasure to the senses or pleasurably exalts the mind or spirit : loveliness
2: a beautiful person or thing; especially: a beautiful woman
3: a particularly graceful, ornamental, or excellent quality

The point is that we do not deconstruct the various philosophies of beauty across the centuries from Plato to Kant to Foucault, although we reference a few (e.g., Hamermesh and Parker, 2005; Montell, 2003) as we move across the landscape of our intertwined journeys, or *currere* (Pinar, 1994), self-reflecting and dialoguing on how we each developed our own personal curriculum of beauty. We are not arguing for what might be a right or wrong definition but, rather, to consider the implications of the definitions that were shaped around us and by us through our life journeys. Through the duoethnographic process, our individual histories are rewritten; the exhumation and reexamination of our memories are layered with alternative meanings through the eyes of another.

We found ourselves balancing within ourselves, and with each other, contradictory definitions of beauty as they play out in our histories. We focus specifically on beauty within the context of the "feminine"—feminine beauty—and how our multiple experiences with various understanding of this concept intersect with generational and class issues. Layered within our individual histories and within our friendship as adults is our struggle between the desire to resist dominant narratives taught to us by family, media, and society, yet we cannot completely untangle ourselves from it and wonder if complete rejection of this grand narrative curriculum of beauty is even possible. According to Norris and Creswell (2007),

We take control over our own conceptualizations by bringing them in question. Through the juxtaposition with another's stories, we see ourselves differently, and through the sharing of our stories and their reconceptualizations we enable others to juxtapose their meanings with ours and learn the process of dialogic thinking. (p. 1)

In addition to the process for doing this duoethnography, our friendship has led us both to reexamine our life histories as they reflect our current assumptions and expectations about beauty. We have lived each other's pains and triumphs intimately over the past eight years. Our shared present moments have transformed our prior interpretations of our individual pasts, so this duoethnography brings together our individual lives and represents a slice of our ongoing, shared, lived currere. We live our duoethnography every day of our friendship.

Nancy: What really has shaped my impression of beauty? I know I really do not think it's a stylish nose, which I never had; feminine features, which will never be mine because I look so much like my father; or an hourglass figure that works against everything that I am. I'll never pluck my eyebrows or get a manicure. I even think, in a way, that Joe has stolen a part of my mind by inviting me into this study because I am the one of

Figure 10.1 Nancy and friend, 2007.

the two of us who studies language, and if this isn't a study of how language shapes our beings, nothing ever was or will be.

This research has made me realize that I am a *victim* (and not just product) of my family in many ways. The males in my family contributed greatly to my sense of womanhood. Before this project, I had attributed my sense of beauty to the media. I blamed the media and never let my family take credit for their contributions. By not letting my family take credit for the construction (and destruction) of self, I never took credit for it myself because I did not see it as something I can control; I didn't accurately locate the source of the problem. *I have come full circle.* It's really a pleasure to me because I can wear jeans again and a t-shirt, and I can wear my old shoes and look in the mirror and feel good about myself. I do not think I would be able to stand in front of the mirror this morning knowing I look okay to me and love myself without doing the duoethnography . . . having realized the role my father played in this was important. He's been saying this shit my whole life. Things he has said about my looks/weight: I would not have heard those things as a distant voice if I had not done this duoethnography, and I would not have been able to reject them. I didn't know the source of the problem.

Morna: The biggest contributor to my conception of beauty, in terms of people as beautiful, is my sister. She is three years older than

Figure 10.2 Morna with Conor, 2006.

I, and since my adolescence, I remember her being the prettier one. I strived to find the right shoes, makeup, and hairstyle to meet her approval because I knew somehow that approval meant that I was "okay." Our mother always faithfully reminded both of us that we were each beautiful. She never criticized the way I looked.

I also remember around the age of thirteen getting reinforcement from men about my appearances. If I walked down the street and got honked at, I took that as a compliment. So, on the one hand, I was getting a lot of male attention that suggested I was beautiful, and yet with my sister around, I would suddenly feel not pretty enough.

One thing this study has done is force me to critically articulate how I can have a foot in both camps; one, that I perpetuate the stereotype about myself a lot—the way I dress, I want to fit into the stereotype of beauty—but at the same I want to critically deconstruct myself and reject this stereotype, trying to buy into it at the same time. How do I do that? To pretend that

Figure 10.3   Morna and sister Megan, 1990.

I don't is a flat-out lie. And it's funny because my academic self is something nobody can take away, but when I find myself in a situation where I am not feeling smart enough, I do feel reasonably comfortable with falling back to my appearances for reinforcement. It has always been a sense of security for me, reinforced by society. At the same time, it was my insecurity about my appearance that made me want to pursue my intellect because it distinguished me from my sister and other people because if I didn't measure up, I could at least say that I was smart. So I just contradicted myself . . . I always thought maybe I was secretly a hypocrite, but I realize now that contradiction *is* part of who I am . . . both/and . . . I have always liked the in-between.

BEAUTY AND SEXUALITY

One evening I sat Beauty on my knees—And I found her bitter—And I reviled her. Arthur Rimbaud (1854–1891)

Nancy: Beauty in me was taught by my mother. She constantly worked to make me feel beautiful. Of all the things that Claudette did, this is the one thing she tried to do right. She used to tell me all the time that "you are only as pretty as you feel" and that "someday your husband will be so lucky to have you for his wife." I used to ask why. Many times she repeated, "Because you can cook, sew, play piano, and you are smart" and other things I don't remember. I remember wanting to believe her—I remember wanting to believe her.

Morna: As I said, the biggest contributor to my conception of beauty is my sister, Megan. She is three years older than I, and since my adolescence, I remember her being the prettier one.

Other people, especially boys, reminded me of this constantly. I remember Mike T. coming to my house to be with me (to make out), and yet when he left, I discovered he had stolen a photo of my sister from the TV room! And so although I remember thinking of myself as attractive, I always suddenly felt ugly when I was around her. My self-esteem would shrink as we walk through a crowded place and men's heads would turn at the sight of her and me walking behind in her shadow. She used to critique my hair, my clothes, and something always seemed to be wrong with how I looked or dressed. I strived to find the right shoes, makeup, and hairstyle to meet her approval because I knew somehow that approval meant that I was "okay."

Figure 10.4   Megan with daughter Merrill, 2002.

Nancy: I took time to really gaze at your sister this weekend, and—*please* do not take this wrong—you are much prettier than she. I know you will argue this, but I think you have an unwarranted complex, which, I suppose, is why we both agreed to have this conversation. I think we both are uncomfortable with ourselves when it comes to judging beauty *in ourselves* but really work to make sure others do not have feelings that physical beauty matters more than internal goodness.

Morna: The beauty I impress upon myself in terms of my own self-image and the beauty I see in others are different. I don't look for, or judge people, for their beauty outside but what's on the inside, and yet I don't "see" myself in those same terms. The things I love—the beauty I see in you or my husband or my children—I view through a different "beauty lens." And yes, you *are* pretty (your clodhopper shoes notwithstanding)! Yet I judge *myself* according to those old standards set by my sister back when I was thirteen years old. But I also know that the superficial, stereotypical ideal of beauty is a powerful tool in our society, and I have used that power my whole life to control and manipulate.

Nancy: On a few occasions when cars did honk at me in a sexual communication, I shot back the finger. Passing car comments have always irritated me more than anything. That started when my sister Carol and I were young and we had to go out and pick blueberries on Saturday morning before we could be free from our mother's chores.

We went to the wild blueberries that grew along Route 8 in Speculator—the road that connected villages and towns and allowed tourists to head higher into the mountains. People in cars yelled out at us: "Berry pickers!" I was so embarrassed, I would squat as low as possible to try to hide my identity, but anyone who knows the size of wild blueberry bushes in upstate New York knows I was fully exposed.

Morna: Something I thought of at 5 AM related to what you've been writing—interesting as always how we share a mental wavelength—if beauty is how I *feel* versus beauty is how I *look*. You wrote about when you *felt* most beautiful. I *feel* beautiful when I am sitting in bed with Conor reading him a bedtime story,

Figure 10.5 Nancy and sister Carol.

when I can say or do something that helps a friend find strength or serenity, when I teach and get an "aha" moment from one of my students, and when Len says or does something warm and romantic when I least expect it.

Nancy: My sister was mad at me once when we were together, and she sold my picture to a really cute guy for fifteen cents and called me a whore. I remember where we were sitting when it happened. I was on the stairs inside one of the academic buildings. We were near the announcement board where we used to post our textbooks for resale. It's funny how you and I both have a sister/picture story that hurts. But they are very different stories. Carol is horrified that she did that—she was sorry immediately—but it's one more thing in life that you can't really take away once it's done.

Morna: This is beauty paired with sexuality, which to me is different than my sense of beauty when I look into nature or my newborn daughter's face. Somehow in my mind, they are separate.

Nancy: I don't know why we went to feminine beauty, but maybe it was the conversation we had when you came over with Molly to talk about this dialogue study. I have to write what I think right away because my writing and thinking change, and then I can't recollect the early thoughts. In fact, I have started reading the discourse analysis book so that I can continue to ground myself

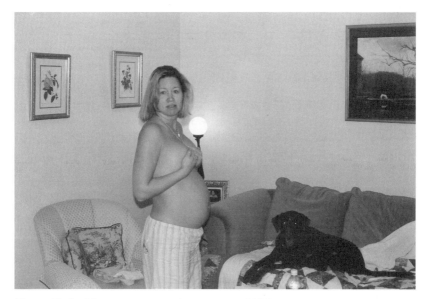

Figure 10.6 Morna seven months pregnant, 2005.

in the power of language as I see it for our Sugar Hill research, and all the time I read, I think about our/my thoughts solidifying and my finding what really has shaped my impression of beauty.

Morna: We both seem to be focusing on feminine sexuality and beauty—there must be a reason it was the first place we jumped to in this discussion. Unlike you, as you know, I did *not* feel beautiful during or after my pregnancy until I lost (or will lose) my baby weight. I see *other* pregnant women as beautiful, but I felt fat, bloated, double chinned, and gassy.

Nancy: I felt pretty during two stages in my life: just after Conrad was born and then again when I was in my late thirties after I had lost fifty-five pounds. Everywhere I went, I was complimented. Everyone I know told me I looked fabulous. After Conrad was born, I had a great figure. I was happy and a very proud mother. These are the only two stages of my life that I ever really felt feminine satisfaction with myself.

Morna: The changing of my body during this time really affected my identity since I have always banked a part of my identity in my appearances, especially my body image, I guess because it was so strongly reinforced into me for so many years. I was

Figure 10.7   Nancy with husband Jack and son Conrad, circa 1986.

complimented more on my looks than my mind or personality most of my life, and yes, I have admittedly used my looks to get things, as a source of power—to get free drinks at bars, to get out of speeding tickets, to get jobs—all before the age of twenty-five. After that is when I began to change and love who I am on the inside.

Nancy: My concept of worth—whether its beauty or not, I am not sure—is definitely linked to my mental power and my ability to break through the barriers of gender exclusion into a power-ful existence where my voice can be more influential than my brothers'. Wow, where did that come from? I talk a lot about my brothers, but has there always been this sense of drive to pass them intellectually? Hmmm. Where that came from is that *writing* is what helps us realize what we think. Writing gives words to what was previously unconscious, yet acted upon, parts of ourselves. Now that words have wrapped around this wondering about my drive, I will have to give it more thought.

Morna: Have to write this right now while it's fresh in my mind! Just this morning . . . Anne, my mother-in-law (a.k.a. Marie Barone)—a little pop culture reference—came over to do something with Conor. Anyway, she sits there in front of me, touching the lines around my mouth, telling me how I should start considering Botox and laser treatments for my face (I shit you not . . .), and how once I lose the baby weight and get my hair done, "within a year . . . I'll be a babe again" (that is a direct quote). I am stand-ing there in front of her (impeccably done up as usual), me with a big t-shirt on, twenty-five pounds of baby weight, unbrushed hair, four hours of sleep, and a huge zit on my chin . . . want-ing to shoot myself, or her . . . not sure which . . . I am thirteen again.

Nancy: I think we all (at least all women) have a serious double (if not triple) standard for beauty. I think we have one for ourselves, one for women we love dearly, and one for other women for whom we hold no close relationship. I have to think about that more. Okay, you opened the door. Dare we share our thoughts about sexual beauty? I'm not sure I'd want to open that door to the world beyond Jack! And alcohol: You opened that door, too. Surely it has had some role in our conceptualizations of beauty. I have not thought about that before either.

Morna: When I stopped drinking, I began to look more spiritually at things and to redefine my own worth. In fact, when it comes to other women, I find their beauty in their style, their strength, their uniqueness, their minds, their spirit . . . and I cannot "see" my own beauty through that same lens. I have a double standard for myself—a dual psyche, as it were—and I am stuck in my old thinking when it comes to how I see myself as beautiful and yet more feminist and open and less shallow when it comes to seeing others. By the way, what makes you beautiful on the outside, to me, is your fab style—yes, you have one! And it works.

Nancy: You identify my beauty in your eyes as style. I think what I see in you is: You are cute. You have a cute nose (I do not). You have a bold style. You know me, and you know, I think, we have to make statements. We have to be in someone's face. Your style does that with such grace. I am smiling now as I think about "Mr. X" telling you there is a dress code. But there is a very deep beauty in your kindness. There is something about you: You really feel for others in a way most people do not. From before I ever met you, you found time to help me make the transition to Towson. Here you were, planning a wedding, dealing with the loss of your first child, wrapping up the end of your first year as a professor at Towson, and you still took more time to answer my e-mails than any other single person at Towson. That is what I mean about a quality of kindness, empathy, real caring that is simply absent in most people but quite abundant in you. And, of course, my ultimate, necessary quality in any beautiful person: You are highly intelligent.

BEAUTY AND THE GENERATION GAP

Nancy: I think it's very important that we are not the same generation. I feel quite sure the media had a strong influence on you and a minimal one on me when it comes to decorating our bodies. Social norms and male dominance surely played more heavily on me than on you since my generation made it easier for your generation of women to be something other than "Suzie home-maker." But as I think about your struggle with pregnancy and how much more positive my experience was than yours, I wonder if what my generation gave you wasn't a mixed bag of confusion.

Morna: I grew up after the feminist movement, in the '80s Reagan era, with Madonna and MTV. I consumed *Teen Magazine*, *17 Magazine*, and *Vogue*, and those images really impacted how I saw women. I remember this one cover with Brook Shields on it and the photos of tanned women wearing turquoise jewelry and brocade bikinis. It was sensual, aesthetically pleasing—the colors, the lighting, all of it—and I wanted to be a part of that world. Using beauty to get what you wanted was reinforced in my community. Girls viewed it as a source of power, and it *was*, honestly. It protected you from ridicule, gave you status, got you in the right clubs.

Nancy: I never used my feminine self for any advantages. I think that might be related to the era in this country when I became socially conscious. Women were struggling to be recognized as equal contributors. Jobs were still not available to us, especially to me in the small-town environments where I lived. Everything was controlled by men. Even childbirth was controlled by the male-run institutions and not mothers: Lie on your back with your feet in the stirrups and take whatever drugs the doctors thought you needed. I refused that. I also refused to be a nurse or a teacher. I had to get to the point in my life where I knew I had other options before I let myself consider a career in education. When men tried to pick me up in a bar, they'd ask my name. I'd look at them and with a very flat voice say, "George," and I'd turn away. As I write this, I cannot think of a single time I let some stranger pick me up in a bar, but I had plenty of opportunities—I'm off track. This isn't about beauty; it's about construction of my feminine self.

Morna: This is from my personal journal entry from September 12, 1980:

> Christine S said that Kim K thinks I'm really pretty but why is she such a snob then? I don't consider myself totally ugly but I'm not much of a Cheryl Ladd either. Maybe she is nice but not to me. I don't like to make enemies so I'll be nice and if she snubs me one more time I'll beat the shit out of her.

BEAUTY AND SOCIAL CLASS

Morna: Your story of being called a slut reminds me of my friend Miriam M., who came from "the wrong side of the tracks" (if there even was such a thing in Chappaqua). Her family was very blue collar. They ran the local gas station and how she dressed (not preppy like the others, but skin tight jeans and heavy eyeliner) was an issue of social class, not sexuality. The "popular" girls would call her a slut. And she was a virgin. These same girls were definitely more promiscuous than she, but their social class protected them from being called sluts.

Nancy: But as you have forced me to think about social class and beauty, memories from high school flood my brain. Everything I had as "extra" by the time I got to high school was bought out of my own money. My parents didn't even spend money on shampoo.

I remember my eldest sister announcing my mother was horrible because she would not buy shampoo for her daughters. I was young (probably nine), and a bar of soap was all I ever knew. I am trying to focus on class and beauty, and my mind won't let me. Social class creates a tension in me, so nothing about it is really beautiful. The new house my sister has just purchased will never be as beautiful as the peaceful land around a shack. I think I need you to ask me more questions. These responses are coming in pieces. I wonder if money is associated with the kind of glamor that I hate: dyed hair, manicures, and thick makeup. I wonder if that is why I never aspire to be this kind of beautiful, and if that's why I find it all pretentious.

Morna: I remember going through the phase of rejecting where I came from, and a lot of that had to do with realizing how beauty is used to reject people. I then rejected the whole Chappaqua social scene. I was surrounded by "beautiful people" who were so ugly and cruel on the inside, and I wanted to disassociate from them by rebelling against those "norms." Yet, I have come back to it now in this duoethnography. Beauty is a form of cultural capital, and having that knowledge is power because it can determine how others see us. The issues of class clearly intersect with issues of sexual beauty. They are both forms of privilege too. Rich people usually look stereotypically

Figure 10.8a Speculator, New York.

Figure 10.8b   Whippoorwill Country Club.

"beautiful." Why? Because they can afford the good hair colorist, the caps on their teeth if they need them, the personal trainer, braces, manicures, etc. Standing in a crowd of people I have never seen before, I can tell you the socioeconomic status of most women by simply looking at their hair and their nails.

Nancy: Doing this research has made me think about my construction of self differently than what I have done in the past. I have examined my academic self. I have asked myself: Why I am the only PhD in my family? Why did I change my linguistic identity? Why did I disassociate myself from my upstate New York identity for so many years? But this duoethnography also made me realize that my conception of beauty is a different conception of self. It is completely different from my academic or linguistic self. Yet, I now see it as part of my drive to be who I am academically and linguistically. I think since I have always, deep down, felt a little less than "pretty," I have worked very hard to find a power in my brain, in my language (especially in writing), and in my career.

BEAUTY AND MORALITY

Morna: In 2008, I anonymously polled a group of twenty undergraduates using a questionnaire about their feelings on appearances and pedagogy. One of the responses included: "I often think fat people are lazy." We have a moral association with beauty. We see people as less if they are fat or "ugly." If you have a teacher who pisses you off and she happens to be fat, you find yourself calling her a "fat bitch." My students can't do that to me. They can call me a "bitch," but they can't use my appearances as a tool to take me down. That's why it becomes a defense. According to Montell (2003), referring to a study on appearances of professors in higher education,

> A glance at Web sites such as ProfessorPerformance.com and RateMyProfessors.com—where students rate their instructors on criteria such as coolness, clarity, easiness, helpfulness, and hotness (on RateMyProfessors.com, hot professors get chili peppers beside their names)—leaves little doubt about the viciousness of some students. Petty comments abound: "Someone fire this fat bastard" and "Looks like a hobbit, is not a nice person!" (n.p.)

Nancy: I have never thought about it from that perspective. If we already do not like someone for some nonbeauty reason, we dislike them more because we find them less attractive. It is something we use to take more—to put people down a peg.

Morna: We defer to beautiful people in this society all the time.

Nancy: I find it so amazing that the first time I have ever consciously thought about this.

Morna: Can you give an example?

Nancy: My father saying that he wishes that next time he sees me, I am thinner. I am not fat. I'm overweight, but I'm not fat, and I have to spend time telling myself that. I also came home and lost seven pounds in the first two weeks after seeing him.

Morna: How is that disassociated with your academic self?

Nancy: I know I'm smart.

Morna: So your academic self is where glean your confidence. No one can take that away from you.

Nancy: Yes, I can see its proven effects. I can see the papers, and I can look at the degree. I can enter doors that others cannot, using my intelligence.

BEAUTY AS POWER

Nancy: This is what Lisa Delpit (1996) calls the *culture of power*. Although her work is centered on dialects and teaching writing, we believe it is deeper than that. The culture of power is deeply entrenched in the power of beauty.

Morna: I have come to realize this is multidimensional; I can see how people use it, and now I know that being "cute" allows me to get away with things. I have gone back to what I learned as a child, to beauty and social class, and I turn it on its face. I know how the system works—I was raised in the system—beauty is currency. At first I rejected it in my own way, but I unconsciously use the tools of that system to fuck with the system. I can fuck with "Mr. X" because I use the fact that he perceives me as cute to get away with what I otherwise would not be able to. My subversiveness is to fly under the radar—it's how I operate.

Nancy: But when you do interact with "Mr. X," you can smile. I can't.

Morna: What does this have to do with beauty?

Nancy: I see it very connected. You can pull your punches that you have as part of your beauty toolbox.

Morna: He's never stared at my boobs, if that is what you mean.

Nancy: No it's fashion . . . flair.

Morna: When I wear my jeans, it's a big giant "fuck you" to him.

Nancy: No . . . it's more like you can *play* him; you can smile and know you are twisting his sick self. You know you are attractive, and he would have to see you as a woman and in some ways be deferential to you.

Morna: I never thought about it that way. I thought about it in another way, in that I always dressed unconventionally and cute as a form of pissing him off.

Nancy: When you piss him off, he still sees you as a woman.

Morna: More so than you? You think he defers more to women who are pretty?

Nancy: Yes. I see it as a toolbox . . . and . . . it's not a toolbox I carry.

Morna: The first time Len suggested I get away with saying things rather shocking or subversive simply because of my looks, I was really pissed at him. Don't my brains count for anything here? But maybe he was right. Subconsciously, what we think we can say or get away with and how we say it are determined in part by how we see ourselves and how others see us.

BEAUTY AS CURRICULUM

We reflect on studies such as the one by Hamermesh and Parker (2005). They found that "instructors who are viewed as better looking receive higher instructional ratings, with the impact of a move from the 10th to the 90th percentile of beauty being substantial" (p. 369). The authors invited anyone to write responses to this study, and what followed were two full pages of reactions, including these:

This works in both directions—being "too" attractive is as problematic as being "too" frumpy. Guess what? It is embarrassing to receive student evaluations that say, "I'd really like to _____ your _____," or "You're hot!" Why did I even open my mouth in class? Why didn't I just stand there and smile sweetly?

This issue is clearly one that for academics demands some level of self-examination. We consider how our own appearances affect how we teach. How do students' perceptions of our appearances shape how they listen to us? We also honestly examine how students' appearances affect our students–teacher relationships.

Nancy: I was raised to keep interactions with others at a business level. You were raised with a mother who taught you that interactions should be personal, fun (and flirty).

Morna: How we approach our students and begin a semester is inherently different based on these fundamental ways of interacting with the world. Perceptions of our own beauty further shape the styles with which we approach others.

Nancy: This is how beauty and teaching curriculum connect: our teacher selves.

Morna: I am the court jester/trickster, "cute" and funny but delivering honesty or truths you don't want to hear underneath. I can be many shapes or forms. I will always subvert who you expect me to be.

Nancy: I am businesslike and "in your face," the warrior. I tackle people and issues straight on. What you see is what you get.

Morna: How we are received based on our appearances (i.e., seen as pretty or cute) lends itself to openness. People respond more positively to attractiveness. Beautiful people get away with more. They're not afraid of being judged for how they look, so they are more open and unafraid with their personalities—to get away with saying more or being edgy/flirty. Social class also plays in here. We make lower class people feel ugly. It's a lack of entitlement.

Nancy: How we teach or how students perceive us relates to physical beauty because of how they hear us *and* how we hear them. What do we invite them to do in our classrooms? How do we establish what we allow our students to say or be in our teaching?

Morna: Referring to the questionnaire I passed out to twenty undergraduate students in 2008, one questionnaire respondent wrote, "Of course being a male, an attractive female teacher will always have my attention."

Nancy: It is this connection that I think is one of the more important
          for me to understand as a professor. My students come to
          me with the identities formed by their families. How they see
          themselves is closely linked to how their families shaped and
          molded them as women (or men) to be appreciated and/or to
          be unnoticed. I'm not presuming that there is a profile of "if/
          then" youthful experiences that will result in specific outcomes,
          but there is, in each of us, a curriculum of beauty.

Morna: Another questionnaire respondent wrote, "I had a teacher at
          ____ who was Arab and wore a trepan (sic) on his head. He
          was very rude and his appearance was very. . . ."

Further Implications

Nancy: I think, if nothing else, we begin to see how language runs
          through the course of race, class, and gender, and how
          this implication of beauty runs through everything. It has
          unbounded implications.

Morna: I also think about children's sense of identity. I think our col-
          lege students are in denial of this, that good guys and bad guys
          don't look the same. They fight me on it. They don't want to
          go there when we talk about racism/class paired with beauty
          in Disney films. They find a million excuses or say I am read-
          ing too much into it. I discuss the whole Protestant ethic that
          God favors those of us who are better off. They don't want to
          believe we actually operate this way in our society.

Nancy: I think we do the same thing with beauty. Society favors people
          for their beauty, and this has serious implications on our own
          teaching. Whether we admit it or not, are conscious of it or
          not, we are influenced by our appearances. We respond to each
          other based on first impressions, which become the founda-
          tions for our relationships. It's impossible not to start in-person
          relationships this way, and when we interact with individuals
          for only fifteen weeks (or less if your semester is shorter) in
          a relationship already complicated by teacher–student power
          dynamics, we have to work very hard to get beyond judging
          others on their appearances. Maybe the need to develop a
          relationship with students isn't equally important for all disci-
          plines, but it certainly is for ours (teacher education).

Morna: This duoethnography has helped me articulate the point that
          to pretend that looks do not matter is like saying, "I don't see
          color." The implications of racism are, of course, far more seri-
          ous, but the denial is parallel. To paraphrase the saying, "using

the master's tools to tear down the master's house," I wonder about women (and men) who argue that they don't care about how they look, that they're somehow above that superficiality. Yet, it reminds me of the first time I finally acknowledged my Whiteness. Similarly, beauty and looks in our society are a form of privilege; to reject this idea is foolish, and to deny it is naïve. We have to analyze critically its role in our life/curriculum in order to dismantle it.

REFERENCES

Delpit, L. (1996). *Other people's children*. New York: New Press.

Hamermesh, D., and Parker, A. (2005). Beauty in the classroom: Professors' pulchritude and putative pedagogical productivity. *Economics of Education Review*, 24(4), 369–376. Retrieved from https://webspace.utexas.edu/hamermes/www/Beautystuff.html

Montell, G. (2003). Do good looks equal good evaluations? *Chronicle of Higher Education*. Retrieved from http://chronicle.com/article/Do-Good-Looks-Equal-Good/45187

Norris, J., and Creswell, J. (2007, October). *The curriculum of health, hospitalization, suffering and mortality*. Paper presented at the Curriculum and Pedagogy Conference, Balcones Springs, TX.

Pinar, W. (1994). *Autobiography, politics and sexuality: Essays in curriculum theory 1972–1992*. New York: Peter Lang.

Rimbaud, A. (2008). *Arthur Rimbaud: Complete works*. New York: Harper Perennial Modern Classics.

Webster's Dictionary S.v., "Beauty." Retrieved from http://www.merriam-webster.com/

CHAPTER 11

Professional Boundaries:
Creating Space and Getting to the Margins

Kathleen Sitter and Sean Hall

Prologue

Expanding upon Berthoff's belief that "writing as a way of knowing lets us represent our ideas so that we can return to them and assess them" (1987, p. 11), duoethnography is a way of talking oneself into meaning. Duoethnographers use conversation as a means to generate data (stories) and analyze them through conversation. As Sitter reports,

> *as a result of this process and our ongoing conversation, I've developed a heightened awareness of how my past has influenced how I've taken up boundaries in my professional work. Our dialogue and reflection also opened up a space to journey through and within this topic and brought me to a deeper understanding of how I conceptualize boundaries. (p. 258).*

The duoethnography, itself, is a reconstructed artifact of those theoretical and storytelling sessions.

Although many duoethnographers make the methodology implicit throughout their writing, Sitter and Hall, like Breault, Hackler, and Bradley (Chapter 5) make the process a bit more explicated and transparent. They write that

> *when we began this dialogue eight months ago, we initially came together and recorded a two-hour face-to-face conversation. After transcribing our meeting, we've revisited our discussion through e-mail and continued to build, rework, edit, and add to our ongoing dialogue on boundaries. Guided by the metaphorical hermeneutic circle, our process of engaging in the conversation through cycling back and forth between our past, what we know, and how we might understand our meanings of boundaries. . . . (p. 258)*

However, this explanation does not appear at the opening of the piece. Rather, it is blended into the conversation as they reflect on their journey. Duoethnographies seldom follow the linear progression of traditional research. Each takes its own stylistic direction as the conversations unfold naturally. Building upon to Nietzsche's (1966) critique of the constructed linearity of cause and effect, duoethnographies do not impose a predetermined structure. Each finds their own progression.

This chapter also nicely blends in theoretical discussion about boundaries that apply to their work both as counselors and as researchers. They explore issues of privacy and the degree of public disclosure, Sitter reports that she "remember[s] being more willing to share" (p. 249), but she recognizes that others may not be so willing. Duoethnographers, autoethnographers, and all researchers who employ personal stories are implicitly reminded of the problems of telling their stories. They do not have anonymity and, by default, neither do the other people within their stories. This chapter makes ethical stances problematic and has implications for all duoethnographers.

—Joe Norris and Richard D. Sawyer

Kathy: I remember when we met last year through the visual work that we do within the community. Although our experiences are similar in that we have been involved in different participatory visual media projects, what I found intriguing was that in many of our discussions, the topic of boundaries kept coming up. I'm excited that we're exploring this topic and trying out duoethnography, a new method created by Rick Sawyer and Joe Norris (Norris, 2008). I learned about this approach from Darren Lund, who has also published on the topic (Lund and Evans, 2006; Lund and Nabavi, 2008). From my understanding, the idea is that we learn about a topic through a conversation (Lund and Nabavi, 2008). The approach builds on the traditions of narrative and storytelling and expands on William Pinar's concept of *currere*, where individuals explore their personal perspectives by employing multiple voices in dialogue (Norris, 2008).

I'm wondering where we should begin? Prior to immersing ourselves in a conversation about boundaries, it may be helpful to start with discussing our different educational backgrounds. I've often found myself wondering how I ended up in social work but as a filmmaker?! My education has taken me on so many different journeys. After receiving an undergraduate degree in public relations, I went to work in corporate sales and research for almost ten years. But it was in my volunteer work outside of the office where I found my passion. I eventually decided to make the career change into social work because many people I had developed relationships with through my volunteer work were social workers and doing the type of work I wanted to be involved in. They also spoke about the holistic approach of a biopsychosocial model, which really made sense to me. So I made the leap and went back to school. I'm curious: What attracted you to psychology versus social work or another profession?

Sean: Many colleagues have asked me similar questions over the years; I've been told that I am a psychologist that works like a social worker. When I look at the "bigger picture," I realize that looking at the individual within his/her environment is key; we don't live in a vacuum, so why would we work with people as if they were? I have also come from a much more clinically focused, medical model of care to one of prevention, promotion, community, and impacts of environment. These include things like social determinants of health and the impact they have on our development, attachment, personality, emotional well-being, and overall mental health. Interestingly, as I was engaged in course work to complete my master's of counseling psychology, and then again through community development work, I realized that many of the concepts that resonated with me are the same. For instance, a social justice approach to counseling is also utilized within community development work insofar as working towards equality, the distribution of power, focusing on advocacy-related interventions, encouraging self-determination, and the sharing of both opportunities and resources (Arthur and Collins, 2005).

Kathy: Have you ever faced challenges in your work as it relates to boundaries? The term *boundary* is such a widely used term in our fields of psychology, counseling, and social work. Although boundaries involve setting limits between persons (Dickson-Swift, James, Kippen, and Liamputtong, 2006), I find that boundary issues hold a number of different meanings. For example, in the context of qualitative research on sensitive topics, Dickson-Swift and colleagues identified various boundaries issues based on context, including relationship boundaries between friendship and research, research and therapy, and professional boundaries of the researcher. However, Reamer (2003) defines boundary issues as conflicts of interests that arise due to "dual or multiple relationships" that requires thoughtful consideration to both intended and unintended consequences of the risk to blurring boundaries (p. 121). The National Association of Social Workers' (NASW) *Code of Ethics* also explicitly states that social workers should not engage in "dual or multiple relationships with clients or former clients in which there is a risk of exploitation or potential harm to the client" (2010, para. 3).

Sean: That's an interesting point about the various types of boundary issues. I also find that balancing different approaches is always challenging, especially when there are those that are particularly dogmatic or married to a particular theoretical position. I remember speaking with my supervisor about an eclectic approach to counseling, and he asked if this type of approach meant no rules or morality, as eclectic can mean to pick and choose what fits in the moment. Does this mean that there is no moral compass? I don't believe this to be the case. Instead, I believe that awareness is key here. If I am aware of a variety of theoretical positions and I am aware of what these positions imply, given a specific situation, then there truly are rules and a moral compass. These various eclectic positions have to fit with the situation, but, more important, to avoid situational ethics, these positions have to fit with one another. Robertson, Crittenden, Brady, and Hoffman (2002) note that cultural norms do impact the ethical decisions that people make, so it appears that there does need to be flexibility when making ethical choices.

Kathy: Do you have any example you can share that speaks to your position?

Sean: I recently saw an individual who reminded me of the trickiness of setting and keeping professional boundaries. The fellow I saw was a client with whom I worked for over seven years; we initially worked in a vocational setting, followed by an evening and weekend recreational capacity. In hindsight, I question whether we would have developed the relationship that we did, and worked together as long as we did, if I utilized the professional boundaries that I currently employ in working relationships. Various boundary issues included completing flyer routes and other vocational opportunities, helping his family move, introducing him to my family and some of my friends, and going on a number of trips out of the city and even across the border into Montana at one point. A more clinically focused approach would indicate meeting at a clinic or other professional office or building. Working in a community setting, combined with a recreation focus, building relationships with his family and extended family, and having no professional supports or supervision from the organization employing me at the time all led to a more relaxed approach to boundary and limit setting.

Kathy: Your story speaks to me about addressing power in the relationship and attempting to mitigate that to a certain degree.

Sean: I've come to recognize that I was attempting to even out power differentials, even though I had no idea that that was what I was attempting to do. That said, though, I do recognize that there is still an incredible amount of power that I held in this relationship, including that I was paid to work with this individual, that I was the "professional" and was treated as such by others in our interactions in the community, and that I ultimately "called the shots" when it came to days and times for our meetings and activities.

Kathy: That's a good point; based on our positionality, we are given a certain level of power that also plays an important role in the work that we do. You've reminded me how the challenges of blurring professional and personal lines surface in boundary issues, and yet our lived experiences can also inherently shape the ideological lens through which one takes up boundaries. I'm wondering how your personal experiences growing up influenced how you've approached boundaries in your work.

Sean: I've been reflecting on your question for a while, wondering how much the personal and the professional were impacted by my family and my experiences throughout life. For example, to this day, I can still recall my mother teaching me that discussing family differences should always occur within the privacy of the family, not in front of dinner guests or out in public. On one such occasion, I had gone to visit my parents in Banff; they had gone there for the Easter weekend. While they were away, I had a party at their home, and they found out about it. A natural response could have been to scold or question me at the Easter brunch table, in front of their friends. After all, they had just found out about a prohibited high school party at their home a couple of nights before. Instead, "pleasantries" and decorum were enforced, and we discussed the party once we were all home. The lack of damage was observed, and calm cooler heads prevailed all around!

Perhaps these past experiences growing up have affected my own perceptions on boundaries. How often I have felt uncomfortable witnessing public disputes, or what a colleague calls "domestics," at the local shopping mall, in a restaurant, or in the countless other places that these disagreements invariably occur. In fact, I once was invited for dinner at a friend's home, and his entire family became involved in one heated dispute after another. All the while, I felt uncomfortable and embarrassed. "I shouldn't even be here," I thought. I never liked conflict, and to this day, I still consider myself a peacemaker and a problem solver.

Kathy: It sounds like your family experiences have also impacted your approach and perspective on conflict resolution. But how do you think your role as "peacemaker" influences your professional practice and implementation of boundaries?

Sean: Well, that is the question, isn't it? I often wonder if I was drawn to counseling because of the inherent privacy and personal nature of the therapeutic relationship. This could also explain some of the discomfort that I feel when parents ask after a session about the personal and private disclosures of their children. Is this discomfort the voice of my mother rearing its head, stating, "This should be discussed in private"? Obviously, there is a need to balance the wishes of the parents with the needs of the child, but setting and enforcing this boundary can often be uncomfortable for me, especially when parents are adamant.

Coming back to your initial question, I think as a counselor that there are professional boundaries that are required, but they are also needed for the health of all involved. One boundary that also comes readily to mind is the invaluable lesson learned regarding the difference between taking responsibility for the concerns of others versus supporting them to make their own decisions. What a freeing and relieving feeling, to let go of what is not mine. Simultaneously, I realized that this is also much more respectful to those that I work with. These are their decisions; who am I to believe that I can swoop in and save the day? These boundaries are appealing, but there are also my own personal boundaries that come up within the work environment.

I'm curious if you have ever considered how your history influences how you've taken up boundaries in your own work.

Kathy: I've been wondering about that lately. Growing up, I was always taught to respect my elders, and with that there was a level of inequality that was well established through different titles of authority. For example, the adults I was introduced to through family or school functions always had title caveats, such as *Mr.*, *Mrs.*, *Ms.*, or *Miss*. This distinction of authority readily marked with these labels was also coupled with boundaries I had on personal expression, such as the classic: Speak only when spoken to. In retrospect, I think, both impacted how much I shared with authority figures at a young age.

These experiences were also tempered with events in my teenage years that challenged this perspective, to a degree. At my first job in a pharmacy, I remember the owner telling me to call him by his first name. I was so surprised by this request as this was the first time an adult had afforded me a certain level of consideration I was not accustomed to. When I graduated from high school, I was also granted with the "privilege" of being able to finally call my teachers by their first names. It sounds foolish, but this simple gesture minimized certain unspoken power differences, which also opened up new spaces for building rapport with a number of teachers. Not only do I remember being more willing to share, but I felt a level of reciprocity in this action, and to this day, I have high school educators who I consider to be close friends.

I think these experiences have influenced my own struggles with some of the governing rules in my profession's standards of practice, specifically in maintaining professional boundaries and mitigating power differentials. In my role as a social worker, there is an inherent element of power. So even in attempts to minimize that in order to create some shared notion of power, I ultimately hold a privileged position in making certain decisions associated with the people I work with. And although I recognize the importance of setting up various boundaries with the amount of information I share about myself, I find that boundaries take on a different role in community-based settings and especially with community-based research. So if I'm really trying to minimize power differentials, there is a level of sharing about myself that is not only expected but done out of respect. And at times, I wonder if I'm sharing too much or too little.

Sean: It sounds like some of the challenges you have with boundaries are similar to those described by Dickson-Swift and colleagues (2006), where issues with blurring boundaries in qualitative research involve attempting to build rapport with participants, but that may or might also include creating an expectation that the research relationship is more so a friendship. Again, similar to the client that I told you about earlier, relationships are key, but it is likely perceived very differently from each side.

Kathy: I agree with your comment about the article, which I found valuable in considering protocol around disclosure, rapport, and strategies for ending the research relationship. However, perhaps there is also a need to consider how power takes shape and unfolds in the process, and the extent to which potential tensions of boundaries are tethered to the inequitable distribution of power. Starhawk's (1987) three dimensions of power—power-over, power-from-within, and power-with—may be helpful in this discussion. Power-over is linked to individual and groups enforcing control. Power-from-within is linked to abilities and potential and arises from our sense of connection with people and the environment whereas power-with is social power and entails the willingness of others to listen and be listened to (Starhawk, 1987).

With reference to Starhawk's (1987) theory of power and in your own work experience, have you been able to embrace the power-from-within while concurrently striving toward power-with?

Sean: I've never considered that before. Your question brings up an incident I had facilitating a women's group therapy session with this one woman who had years of experience. She asked me if I participate in the check-in and check-out process, and I said: absolutely. If I'm sitting in the room, I'm part of the group. But at the same time, I feel I have to disclose when it makes sense therapeutically. I'm also the only male in the group because it's a women's group, and I'm sitting there as a cofacilitator. So in many ways, this example brings forth a whole bunch of questions about power. The last thing I want to do is come across as some guy, where the ladies in the group say: "Okay, here's another guy who's trying to control me, telling me what to do." We had this very conversation during a recent group. I said that I really wanted to give positive feedback to the group members about their strength, assertiveness, determination, and resiliency, but I also noted that I did not want this statement to come across as condescending, patronizing, or more meaningful than from another group member just because I am the only man in the group or I am one of the cofacilitators rather than a group participant.

Kathy: You mentioned that through sharing, you attempt to even out power differentials, but your male voice in that context might overpower what it is you're trying to do. Is that right? Do you think there is something to be said about holding on to an awareness of how power and boundaries intersect differently based on situational contexts?

Sean: These questions of power are always there, but I just wonder if awareness of them is enough. But I'm also reminded of that story you shared during our first meeting about your encounter with a photograph and how your heightened awareness impacted how you approach your career. Tell me more about that.

Kathy: That experience I shared with you did influence how I situate myself in my work. It had to do with a photovoice project I'd been involved in for over three years. In the midst of the project, I remember one of the peer researchers saying she didn't own her photographs anymore, that they now belonged to the audience. But it wasn't until the following year where I actually felt implicated in what she said.

At that time, I was also working part-time at a homeless shelter, where people living there took me on a guided tour of downtown. At one point on the tour, we turned into an abandoned alleyway.

I felt like I had been there before, but I knew that was impossible because I had never been to that part of the city. It took me a few seconds to understand why this road felt so familiar, and I finally realized it was from a photograph taken by this woman in the project. When I started walking down this alley, it was a surreal experience where I felt like I was walking in her photograph. That experience reminded me that my role isn't just about staying behind the picture, so to speak, but involves stepping into the frame and being engaged in community work that might sometimes ruffle feathers or blur professional boundaries. So that photograph means something very unique for me.

Sean: Is it because you've been to that specific location, or is there something more to it?

Kathy: I've been there, but how I took it up and continue to reflect on this experience is also influenced by her story. She took that photo to communicate something about her life, yet I can't empathize with what she had gone through because I haven't experienced that myself. And her words about how she no longer owns her photos continue to echo in my mind when I think about that incident with her photograph.

Sean: Given the way that we met via our mutual interest in visual projects, haven't we previously discussed the questions, Who owns the visual work once it's finished? Is it the funder? Is it the university (in the case of research)? Is it the partnering agencies? Is it the client? Or is there some sort of shared ownership now?

Kathy: Yes, in our earlier conversations, we've spoken about physical ownership associated with ethics in using visual media, but there's also that aspect of symbolic ownership with this type of work. I think that symbolic transferring of ownership is part of sharing it publicly so that society hears voices that often aren't heard in the dominant discourse. But I wonder how sharing these personal photographs in public spaces impacts the people who take the pictures, knowing that the images are out there and live on and on and on.

Sean: You were saying how the story gets out there and how it morphs and changes. That's that whole idea of that narrative piece, right? So you say something, and that means something, definitely, to you. And now I've heard it and respond back. How does that change it? Now we've built something together.
         This reminds me of Glenn and Nelsen's (2000) work on perceptions. Perceptions are individual, cumulative, and unique, so no one has ever seen the same picture, read the same book, or heard the same story. We filter the picture, the

book, or the story through our own perceptions so they can never be exactly the same as the perceptions of others, or even of the photographer, author, or storyteller. But when we create the space to discuss our perceptions, then there is something created that is new and different from what initially came from the individual parts. This appears to be a very constructivist process combining a collaborative effort by participants—listeners, viewers, and tellers (Duffy and Jonassen, 1992)—while also taking into account experiences and backgrounds of these participants (Wertsch, 1985). This seems to fit nicely with your example of the alley and how individuals can start, add, change, enter, and exit the conversation at different times, ultimately altering the original perception, the original picture, for all involved.

But I'm wondering if you wouldn't mind unpacking your experience a little more. How did you take up your role prior to the encounter with the photograph?

Kathy: Before my encounter, I worried about thinking that part of my role in this community project was to "protect" the photographers, wanting to somehow make sure the "authenticity of the photograph" and meaning that people arrive at was based on the photographer's point of view. How self-righteous is that? So much for mitigating power!

But that encounter made me realize how impossible that was, and I felt like I actually experienced that paradox of social photography. It reminds me of what Susan Sontag said about a photograph also being evidence of a trace of something "stenciled off the real, like a footprint" (1977/1997, p. 154). Yet when our notions of reality change, the meaning of a photograph also changes (1977/1997). So now this photograph means something new to me, influenced by my own experiences but also shaped by the peer researcher's personal story. It also reminds me of Reason and Hawkins' work on storytelling, where "when we listen deeply to the stories of others and the responses of the group members, we become aware of how quickly a story moves from belonging to an individual, to being part of a collective" (1988, p. 93).

Sean: What you said about stories and the transferring of ownership really makes sense to me. I actually had a friend tell me a story; I wrinkled my brow, realizing: "Wait a second, I told you this story five years ago! That's not you! That's me!" But in his head, he's twisted it around, and it's *him* in the story.

Kathy: That's hilarious! Does he know that he did that?

Sean: Oh, I'd say to him, "I told you that story about five years ago about me and some friends on a trip, and you weren't even there." But in his mind, he twisted it around somewhere and made it his own. What is really intriguing to me now is how to use this twisting for "good" rather than evil! Subtly planting the seeds of future ideas and how these seeds bloom in the minds of others is anyone's guess!

Kathy: It reminds me of Clandinin and Connelly's work on narrative inquiry and the ways "people live stories and in the telling of these stories, reaffirm them, modify them, and create new ones" (2000, p. xxvi). You've mentioned storytelling a few times in our conversations. Were you always attracted to storytelling as a child?

Sean: Ironically, not really! I've always enjoyed reading and storytelling, insofar as I can read great stories. Many of my favorite books are from the ten- to thirteen-year-old period of my life. I still have many of the books, and I have read most of them multiple (or even dozens of) times.

When I started in my position three years ago, I went to a workshop about developmental assets and resiliency. The person presenting showed a video, and he had a couple of PowerPoint slides in the background that he briefly spoke to, but it wasn't a formal presentation; it was his relating stories and storytelling. He even spoke to his style. This was how he presented: He was a storyteller. I thought: "Wow this is absolutely who I am. Whenever I teach, I teach with metaphors." So yes, I thought, this absolutely made sense for me.

More recently, I attended a workshop in which the use of storytelling in counseling, via creative means (i.e., poetry, song, dance, and the visual arts), was discussed. I came to realize that my brain, my ways of thinking, my personality, and my learning style all fit with the use of metaphor, often realized through storytelling! In your work, you often use visual media to tell stories. I'm curious: What has drawn you to using arts in the community work that you do?

Kathy: I think that with storytelling, like film, poetry, or all these different creative forms of expression, there is this room to just "be." You can express yourself through various media and appreciate each other's presence in different ways. For me, in this type of work, it's a place where we can celebrate our tacit knowledge. One of the most amazing projects I've even been involved in was a film workshop where I worked with people with disabilities. We collaboratively worked on preproduction, production, and postproduction processes that involved storyboards, acting, directing, and editing. And the final films were wonderful! I remember two people mentioning that they took the workshop because they wanted to learn about filmmaking, and it wasn't about talking about their disability. That's what I love about the work. It's not about trying to "fix" someone; it's about being in a space where people can just express themselves.

Sean: And wouldn't it be great if you didn't even notice? You're just in that space where it's like: do-do-do. Often when I work with people, if they have a diagnosis of schizophrenia for example, it's so easy for people to say, "Oh, you're schizophrenic." It's funny because sometimes you'll hear people say, "Oh, you're diabetic," but do you ever hear someone say, "Oh, you're a heart attack" or "Oh, you're high blood pressure" or "Oh, you're cancer"? No. Those may be things that are going on in your body, but they're just one small part of you. But how does having high blood pressure speak to your ability to be a writer or an artist? Maybe it does, if it has something to do with your lack of exercise of something, I guess it speaks to it in that sense. But why do we constantly look for these labels that are so limiting? However, I think that we can find ways to connect with each other even when we come from different backgrounds.

Kathy: I'm curious if you've ever experienced any connections that really surprised you, that made you stop and really think about the reasons behind feeling that some type of connection actually took place?

Sean: That's an interesting question. You know, I saw the Dalai Lama recently. I think one of the reasons why he's such an amazing person is that here I am with more than 12,000 of my "closest friends" in the arena, up on the third level, and you couldn't imagine a more nonspiritual place. And yet he had this ability, for me anyway, to reach out from this little tiny speck that was him, and there I was looking at him and looking up at the big screen to see his facial expression. But he had this ability to connect. I felt connected to him through his words despite this huge immense space, with all of the other people present. I'm guessing that other people felt the same way as well. I think it's because he spoke to "universals." He said: "I want to have a good life. I want to be happy in my life. Other people want to be happy in their lives. That's what we need to concentrate on. We can't have a happy society, we can't have a peaceful society, until we have peace within ourselves. And from there, from peace, we can be compassionate towards others. We can be happy."

I'm paraphrasing what he said, but it's these things that are universal. His message is so simple but so utterly profound.

Kathy: It's amazing that you felt that level of connection to him! I also find hope in your comments about universal themes of humanity, where we can all relate to some of these powerful messages.

Sean: It's funny because I consider myself spiritual but not religious at all. I was raised Anglican, so I went through all of that rigmarole as a kid and with my family. But I don't feel religious, and I certainly don't believe in organized religions in many ways. I certainly work with many organized religions in Calgary, with the collaborative work that I do. There's some real good that's happening and being done by organizations, but there's also the opposite side of the spectrum. I wouldn't call myself Buddhist or anything. That's the other thing the Dalai Lama said yesterday, that he wasn't speaking from a position of religion: "Yes, I'm a Buddhist monk—that's my belief, and I hold strongly to that belief—but I'm speaking about compassion, and I think compassion is a trait of humanity. It's not of this religion or that religion." It's interesting because he said: "Some of the things I'm speaking to—'Be nice to one another, let's be compassionate towards one another'—what religion wouldn't say?" When he spoke of secular ethics, he wasn't talking about lack of religion but that this is *outside* of religion and that it doesn't preclude religion. I thought that this was very intriguing because so often we seem to get into the discourse of or/but, this/that, black/white; it's never about this *and* that.

Kathy: I can relate to what you're saying about religion and spirituality. I was raised Catholic, enrolled in Catholic school, Sunday school, and attended Mass every week. But I've always struggled with the institution and the different roles of men and women. I remember a priest at my high school making this comment, and it stayed with me for a long time until I decided to move away from the religion. He said something like: "You know, I look at Catholicism as being a member of my family, like a brother or sister. And even though I might not agree with everything they do, it doesn't mean I'm going to abandon them." For a while, his comment made sense to me, and I was able to justify some of the issues I was having with the church. And then it got to a point where there was such a disconnect for me on the messages being communicated in homilies—everything from homosexuality to the role of women in the church—and it just didn't make sense. In my twenties, I felt like the life I was living and my own values and beliefs weren't the same as this church's.

Sean: Using that same type of metaphor, I could see you saying: "You know, I'm not going to invite that brother to dinner anymore."

Kathy: No kidding! But at the same time, it was difficult because it was such a big part of my childhood and my early adult life. It took time to find certain spaces or moments where I felt a level of inner peace that the church did provide from time to time. And it was through the arts and these artistic modes of expressing myself where I found that comfort. Simple things, like listening to the whispers of a painting, hearing jazz, playing the piano, or even collaborating on a film. . . . In these spaces, I feel connected to myself.

Sean: How do you see this experience being connected to the topic of boundaries?

Kathy: You know, I've never thought of that before. Perhaps it has to do with calling into question reasons for setting up certain boundaries and holding on to that awareness we spoke about earlier and how I choose to approach my professional practice.

Sean: I see us being very much the same with spirituality. I feel so connected with myself and the universe and others when I'm in the mountains or hiking. Tomorrow I have the day off, and I can't wait to take my dogs on a walk and watch the sunrise and the city waking up. For me, that's a way to feel connected. So I'm guessing there are people who meditate or pray who are getting that same feeling that I get when I'm walking the dogs or hiking or listening to certain music.

There were a number of times last year where I was working as a therapist in the Catholic School Board. I remember in the middle of the first meeting I attended, someone said it was time for a reading or a prayer, and I must have looked stunned: "We're doing a prayer?" Out of the corner of my eye, I see everyone making the sign of the cross, and I thought: Oh. It wasn't something that I was used to, and after a couple of other meetings I attended, it was something I did start to expect. I didn't have to do it because it wasn't something that I believe in or that I do, but you respect other people and give them that space at the beginning of the meeting.

Kathy: Your story reminds me of a creative workshop I facilitated with a First Nations community. At the beginning and end of every day, we would do a prayer. It was in a different language, and I didn't know what was being said, but it was a very calming experience, and it set the tone for the day.

But I often wonder why I have more patience for religions that I actually don't know very much about. Where I'm familiar with the background of Catholicism, I find myself impatient with certain traditions. Like, when I'm visiting certain family members, they always say grace before dinner, or during the holidays we attend Mass. I only go through the actions out of respect to them, but sometimes I find that I don't have much tolerance.

Sean: I feel the same way. "Hey, should we do a smudge before the meeting?" someone asks. "Sure!" But if we were going to hand out the Communion and the wine first or something similar, I'd probably say: "Come on! What are we doing?" I wonder if it also has something to do with tradition, culture, or family tradition, if it feels like it's being forced down your throat versus if it's something new, the thought is: "This is really interesting, and I want to learn more."

Kathy: I wonder if in this discussion that has led to all of these topics about power, ownership, storytelling, labels, universals about humanity, connections, religion, and tolerance, if somewhere in all of our experiences, we have actually implicitly drawn on these concepts to try to make sense as to what constitute "boundaries" in our work. At times, I wonder if my own struggle with boundaries is about "keeping someone out" or away from certain spaces. This goes against some of the core concepts that we have talked about. Or maybe it is about creating new spaces that respect differences?

Sean: I think that one reason that we started discussing the topic of boundaries when we initially met was about the confusion that you speak of: Are they tools of "keep away," sharing, creating new spaces, or something else entirely? For me, I think that they are all of these things, with perhaps some of the "hard edges" sanded off so that they are much more connected with one another. What I mean by this is the ability to speak of boundaries as all of the aforementioned without it sounding paradoxical! Protective but also inclusive? Creating new spaces but limiting as well?

Kathy: Taking up the term *boundary* in that sense also speaks about support: supportive spaces around and within us.

Sean: The image I really appreciate is one shared with me by an individual in a group that I facilitate; she noted that boundaries are like a brick wall to her. When asked about flexibility, she stated that her boundaries could be flexible when needed as she could "take down" a layer of bricks or she could "put in a window"! In my work within domestic violence circles, boundaries are often referred to as protective tools of "keeping someone out."

We don't often speak to the creation of new space: I am going to set a boundary on what I am willing to accept, on whom I am going to share my story with, and which supports I am going to choose to assist me in my journey. This sounds like the creation of a new path, new experiences, and a great amount of new potential!

Kathy: I agree and have really enjoyed our conversation about boundaries. Exploring our experiences through duoethnography has also been extremely insightful. When we began this dialogue eight months ago, we initially came together and recorded a two-hour face-to-face conversation. After transcribing our meeting, we've revisited our discussion through e-mail and continued to build, rework, edit, and add to our ongoing dialogue on boundaries. Guided by the metaphorical hermeneutic circle, our process of engaging in the conversation through cycling back and forth between our past, what we know, and how we might understand our meanings of boundaries also required that we put our assumptions and understandings into play (Gadamer, 1975/2004). We've attempted to explore our preconceptions with an attunement to our understandings of personal experiences of the past and how our histories are at play with the present in the context of professional boundaries.

As a result of this process and our ongoing conversation, I've developed a heightened awareness of how my past has influenced how I've taken up boundaries in my professional work. Our dialogue and reflection also opened up a space to journey through and within this topic and brought me to a deeper understanding of how I conceptualize boundaries in different spaces and settings. For example, in relation to visual media and taking up creative forms of expression in the work that we do, boundaries evolve and unfold in dynamic ways. And often it's in the midst of the "messiness" where we learn from and with individuals, groups, and communities. In the process, we even discover more about ourselves. Thank you for agreeing to participate; I found our conversation to be a wonderful learning experience.

Sean: Thank you, Kathy! I truly believe boundaries are similar to our conversation; they are constantly in motion: constant change, fluidity, proposals, rejections, and within all of this the creation of some new thoughts, new ideas, and maybe even some new space. And isn't it interesting to see where this dialogue has taken us? I often wonder what it would be like if we all participated in our daily lives with real-time, running transcriptions!

I think that I would certainly be looking for more profound notions to express, but, more seriously, I would continue to be very interested in examining how my conversations start in one place and then meander throughout the forest of collected ideas and knowledge, before finally meeting up again with the original stream of consciousness.

One thing that struck me when having this discussion was the notion of boundaries as some sort of fixed or defined entity. As our discussion progressed, it really reaffirmed for me the idea that boundaries truly are unique to the time, place, and topic of discussions and specific relationships. At first glance, this might be taken to mean boundaries are merely situational or conditional, but I think that this is not the case at all; it is much more than this. Boundaries can and do change, but this seems much more about that space created between participants than some other outside force.

It's been great talking with you, Kathy! I truly feel that we have created some new space, and perhaps some new boundaries just outside the margins, on boundaries!

Thanks: Kathleen Sitter would like to thank the Social Sciences and Humanities Research Council for its generous support of this research.

REFERENCES

Arthur, N., and Collins, S. (Eds.). (2005). *Culture-infused counselling: Celebrating the Canadian mosaic.* Calgary, AB: Counselling Concepts.

Berthoff, A. (1987). Dialectical notebooks and the audit of meaning. In Toby Fulwiler (Ed.), *The journal book* (pp. 11–18). London: Boynton/Cook Publishers.

Clandinin, D. J., and Connelly, F. M. (2000). *Narrative inquiry: Experience and story in qualitative research.* San Francisco: Jossey-Bass.

Dickson-Swift, V., James, E. L., Kippen, S., and Liamputtong, P. (2006). Blurring boundaries in qualitative health research on sensitive topics. *Qualitative Health Research, 16*(6), 853–871.

Duffy, T. M., and Jonassen, D. (Eds.). (1992). *Constructivism and the technology of instruction: A conversation.* Hillsdale, NJ: Lawrence Erlbaum Associates.

Gadamer, H.-G. (2004). *Truth and method* (2nd ed.; J. Weinsheimer and D. G. Marshall, trans.). London: Continuum. (Original work published 1975)

Glenn, H. S., and Nelsen, J. (2000). *Raising self-reliant children in a self-indulgent world: Seven building blocks for developing capable young people.* Roseville, CA: Prima.

Lund, D. E., and Evans, R. E. (2006). Opening a can of worms: A duo-ethnographic dialogue on gender, orientation and activism. *Taboo: The Journal of Culture and Education, 10*(2), 55–67. Retrieved from: http://www.freireproject.org/taboo-journal-culture-and-education

Lund, D. E., and Nabavi, M. (2008). A duo-ethnographic conversation on social justice activism: Exploring issues of identity, racism, and activism with young people. *Multicultural Education, 15*(4), 27–32.

National Association of Social Workers. (2010). *Code of ethics of the National Association of Social Workers*. Washington, DC: Author. Retrieved from http://www.socialworkers.org/pubs/codeNew/code.asp

Nietzsche, F. (1966). *Werke*. Munich: Hanser.

Norris, J. (2008). Duoethnography. In L. M. Given (Ed.), *The SAGE encyclopedia of qualitative research methods* (Vol. 2, pp. 233–235). Thousand Oaks, CA: Sage.

Reamer, F. G. (2003). Boundary issues in social work: Managing dual relationships. *Social Work, 48*(1), 121–133.

Reason, P., and Hawkins, P. (1988). Storytelling as inquiry. In P. Reason (Ed.), *Human inquiry in action* (pp. 79–101). London: Sage.

Robertson, C. J., Crittenden, W. F., Brady, M. K., and Hoffman, J. J. (2002). Situational ethics across borders: A multicultural examination. *Journal of Business Ethics, 38*(4), 327–338.

Sontag, S. (1997). *On photography*. New York: Picador. (Original work published 1977)

Starhawk. (1987). *Truth or dare: Encounters with power, authority, and mystery*. New York: HarperOne.

Wertsch, J. V. (1985). *Vygotsky and the social formation of mind*. Cambridge, MA: Harvard University Press.

CHAPTER 12

Dangerous Conversations:
Understanding the Space between Silence and Communication

Deidre M. Le Fevre and Richard D. Sawyer

Prologue

Personal disclosure has always been problematic for qualitative researchers. Although they can bestow anonymity on others, what researchers traditionally told about themselves, by bracketing out (Donohoe, 2007; Spradley, 1980; Thorne, 2011) their own perspectives, revealed part of who they were. Such disclosure potentially made their personal lives vulnerable, as some of their relevant personal details became part of the research documentation. Duoethnographers disclose much about themselves but rather than trying to bracket personal information out, to achieve a mythical higher degree of objectivity, they bracket in (Norris, 2008, p. 234), recognizing that the researcher's lens or point of view is part of the research. Or as McLuhan (1967) puts it, "the medium is the massage." In duoethnographies, because researchers are the sites of the studies, they are, therefore, within them. Bracketing in, though a strength of duoethnographies, can be risky. Sawyer reflected, "I have written a number of pieces in the past where I have championed the rights of others but rarely did I write anything that created a risk for myself. There is one exception . . ." (p. 271). Sawyer recognizes that all writing involves a professional risk, but that duoethnographies increase the risk due to personal disclosure.

Norris, Higgins, and Leggo encourage personal disclosure, claiming that it is a necessary political and epistemological act.

> *Agency is as much about responsibility as it is about right. In this age of accountability many things have been marginalized, silenced and made invisible. In our small way we want to sabotage the oppressive measurement machine by throwing our wooden shoes or sabots into the cogs of the wheel to enhance the visibility of other research orientations. One orientation alone tells very little. Credibility comes with both breadth and depth and autobiography is part of that picture.*

But while risky, agency also brings with it a sense of making a difference. Le Fevre reported,

> *Conducting a duoethnography is, in itself, empowering. For example, I'm going to con-tinue my conversation with the graduate women that I silenced thirteen years ago. This methodology of duoethnography has given me the space and direction to consider the complexities of that conversation and, perhaps most importantly, energized me to pick up the pieces and carry on the conversation, eventually taking it into the more public domain. (p. 283)*

Both Le Fevre and Sawyer take pride in knowing that their research and its dis-semination has the potential of making positive change in the lives of others.

—Joe Norris

INTRODUCTION

Rick: To investigate the difficulties encountered as well as the ben-efits gained when disclosing personal stories in research and teaching, we have chosen duoethnography as our research methodology. Duoethnography potentially promotes an exami-nation of narrative and a deepening of intersubjective, relational ways of knowing. Other duoethnographies have shown the interlocking nature of form and content, as it were, underscor-ing the critically generative nature of the relationship between the duoethnographers. In duoethnography, the content or focus of the conversation may change and deepen as the relation-ship between the participants builds and changes (Sawyer and Norris, 2009).

To explore our *currere* (Pinar, 1975), we used dialogue in a variety of ways. We began by discussing the meaning of the concept *dangerous conversations*: What did the topic mean to us, and how could we locate ourselves and our research ques-tions in it? After that, we told and interpreted our stories to each other about when we first began to encounter this topic. We also introduced and analyzed as cultural artifacts earlier examples of "written conversations" that we considered at the time we produced them to be dangerous in some way. We used the notes and transcripts from our conversations together as the basis for more individual, self-contained pieces of writing. Although these are formed in relation to dialogue, they do not contain dialogue. Identifying and discussing emergent themes, we tried to surface and then deconstruct the sociocultural contexts surrounding our narrative ways of knowing to promote a transformative process.

Deidre: Yes, duoethnography is a conversation, and whenever we reveal ourselves, we become vulnerable. Such conversations can be both difficult to disclose and challenging to articulate. They are potentially dangerous, and if the danger is considered too great, they may be silenced out of fear.

Both: As the above discussion suggests, when we first began to write this duoethnography, we thought the topic was going to be the difficult conversations that educators have about change in the workplace (see, e.g., Robinson and Le Fevre, 2011). However, the topic quickly morphed from difficult professional conversations to include dangerous conversations, silenced ones, problematic self-disclosures, daring publications, and unfettered electronic communications.

In this duoethnography, we juxtapose our substantially revised and edited transcribed dialogue with written prose to compose a text that is accessible to the outside eye. The transcribed dialogue is presented in script format, whereas the prose is presented in traditional expository paragraphs. Navigating the logistics of Rick's being in North America and Deidre's being in New Zealand meant our primary modes for engaging in this duoethnography were via Skype and e-mail. It was summer in New Zealand and winter in the United States when we began this project; by the time we completed it, the seasons had reversed. The opportunities for communication via Skype enabled us to both see and hear each other in "real time" across the world. It wasn't quite as if we were in the same room, but Skype did promote a synergy found in the immediacy and flexibility of our conversations. This was not without challenges; sometimes the Skype connection would be intermittent, creating a delay in audio and video, resulting in our seeing each other either "frozen" or "blinking in slow motion." However, this gave ideas time to settle, a moment for pause, and time to reflect in the midst of the conversation.

Deidre: My interest in difficult conversations began with my professional and academic work supporting educational leaders in developing the confidence and skills needed to engage in productive and respectful conversations about difficult issues, such as a principal who needs to discuss a performance issue with a staff member. Empirical evidence suggests that though of critical importance, such conversations are either avoided or less effective than intended (Bryk and Schneider, 2002; Robinson and Le Fevre, 2011). In this duoethnography we began by drawing on the theoretical work of Argyris and Schön (1974,

1996) and the idea that conversations can be difficult and have negative outcomes. Negative outcomes include damaging a relationship, avoiding talking about a problem that needs to be discussed, or talking in such a way that the other party is "shut off" from contributing. Argyris and Schön claimed that within any conversation there is the task of progressing the issue or the problem and there is the task of progressing the interpersonal relationship with the person with whom you are having the conversation. Often we sacrifice one at the expense of the other. For example, we might go all out for the issue and the relationship suffers, or we put all our energy into maintaining the relationship but we don't get to the point of discussing the actual issue . . . we just dance around the important issue that needs to be discussed. Neither of these approaches tends to result in effective conversations wherein people feel respected and problem solving is progressed. We might refer to this as the relationship-versus-task dilemma. Getting past this dilemma involves adopting an alternative pattern of interaction discussed by Argyris and Schön (1974). This interaction demands attention to both the relationship and the task in ways that enable people to share and examine ideas and interpretations within a relationship of respect. These productive conversations have been referred to as open to learning conversations (OLC) (Robinson and Le Fevre, 2011) and are characterized by a number of core values, including the pursuit of valid information so that decisions are based on quality information and reasoning. Respect is an important value in OLCs and implies an essential relationship between the parties in the conversation so that one another's views are treated with the same care and there are opportunities for reciprocal influence. Both this theoretical work and our recent experiences were the motivators for focusing on difficult conversations.

Both: This duoethnography retraces some of our past experiences to generate new meanings about the nature of difficult or dangerous conversations.

Emerging Conversations . . . Emerging Challenges

Deidre: When I was a young child, a dangerous conversation for me was one in which I had to talk with my parents about something I shouldn't have done: "Had I ridden my bike on the road at age six when I was supposed to stay on the footpath?" "Yes, I had." The repercussions of my honesty were a verbal reprimand. The motivation for this reprimand was my parents' love for me and their concern that I might be hurt.

As I grew older, the context for what made a conversation dangerous grew from the concentrated and direct influence of my family to the larger contextual sociocultural influences of school. I entered elementary school as an excited, curious, talkative child bursting to both learn new things and share what I already knew. I wanted to talk and talk. However, I soon learned that conversations could be dangerous. At elementary school it became dangerous to raise my hand and answer a question. My answer might be skipped across and ignored by the teacher or, worse still, corrected and revealed as "wrong." I learned not to talk, and my conversations became silenced.

Rick: Deidre, your words take me back to Grade 3. The assignment in class was to write a fictional short story. I don't think that we were instructed in how to do this. We somehow just had to know. So I wrote one and, to complete the assignment, had to read it out loud in front of the class. I stood there as a seven-year-old, very proud of what I had written. In the story, I was trapped on a tropical island somewhere and had to get off. I had a car, but it wouldn't help with the water. So in the story, the car magically turned into a plane, and I flew to safety. Oddly enough, I wanted the little story to be conventional and have a happy ending. The teacher offered immediate, insensitive, almost mocking criticism. It was impossible for a car to turn into a plane. The story was very bad. I was embarrassed and didn't want to repeat that experience. However, on another level, this event has served as a weird rallying call for me ever since. Basically, the teacher was using conventional writing structures as the basis for her criticism. As someone with a conventional education, I could see that students could write papers showcasing "American know-how" in trade and commerce (on which paper I received an "A" in the same class) but not about fantasy on taboo tropical islands. Back then I had an abnormally heightened sense of "fairness" and equity, and I wondered where was the justice in an assignment in calling for but not valuing creativity. You can select beautiful colors for your drawings—but stay within the lines. In some ways, this realization was empowering, that I could begin to "read the system." However, this awareness grew from an experiential context—from my thoughts expressed in activity. I'm sure that I would have been happy with a little praise. Instead, I was confused and became more guarded: I had put a tentative foot on the path of righteous discontentment.

Deidre: Rick, the importance of voice in writing is so critical, and yet you were in effect silenced through the "curriculum" in your school at the time. This act of silencing one's "voice" leads me to think of how the integrity of your contributions was compromised. As you sensed, you could not communicate your actual contribution, you could not stand proud of the story you wanted to tell. Interestingly, one of the values open to learning conversations is the value of "internal commitment," or, in other words, holding a sense of the importance about the value of your message (Argyris and Schön, 1996).

Your writing about being "trapped on a tropical island" and consideration of this as a metaphor for where you were in class leads me to think about my own experiences about learning to write . . . and my early writing as a form of conversation. I am six, maybe seven years old. I sit in Mrs. Cowper's class. It is about half past nine in the morning. As is the same routine every day we have storywriting time. I sit down with my paper and pencil . . . a mix of anticipation and trepidation fills me as I begin to write furiously. I have a story in my mind, and I want to tell it . . . to get it finished. I've had it in my mind for about nine days now. Every morning I sit down and begin at the beginning of the story: "Once upon a time there was a little girl who had a pet lamb. The little girl and the lamb. . . ." Each day I get to about the same place . . . maybe a little further if I am lucky . . . but I never get to tell my story. I am reprimanded by Mrs. Cowper because my handwriting becomes messier and messier each day as I desperately try to get a little further, striving to reach even the middle of my story. After a few days, I decided it was too hard, gave up, and began another story . . . unfortunately repeating the same process . . . never getting to tell my precious stories . . . holding them in my mind . . . that is where they remained. Nobody suggested that I might continue on the next day where I left off the previous day . . . the teacher never questioned why an eager, bright, and interested child might persistently write the same thing day after day . . . that is how I learned to write.

Rick, your experiences at high school of "some topics being normal and acceptable and others not" resonate with my experiences at high school. My reluctance to talk continued through high school; 1987 was my last year at high school. New Zealand was on the brink of becoming nuclear free.

Feeling I had nothing to lose and sensing a need to be active in the world, I took on fighting the proposed visit of the U.S. nuclear-powered *Truxtun* military ship. "Truck off Fuxtun," I plastered around my school on large banners in bold writing. This was the beginning of my public conversations. The world and context that moved from silenced conversations to dangerous ones broadened, beyond my parents and my school and into the larger global context. A safe place to begin was visually, with banners, but I was also willing to talk, and I did. I was promptly ushered into the deputy principal's office and told my actions were inappropriate and the banners would be removed. Conversations were not only precarious in terms of teachers' potentially negative responses; they were dangerous in terms of the much higher stakes of my peers' impressions. But this censorship backfired and only served to fuel my energy and willingness to engage in dangerous conversations. I sensed that what was to be gained was worth more than what I had to lose. I decided that now was my time.

Rick: Your courage is impressive. Let me think about some of the conditions surrounding my becoming more outspoken—at least temporarily—as a student. I was bused to a junior high school in a rich neighborhood in Seattle. One morning I was heading to school on the city bus when a deadly earthquake struck. I clearly recall looking out the window and seeing the earth roll across the crest of a hill like a tsunami, heading towards my school. Class was canceled on that particular day.

    It was at about this time that my view of school suffered its own tectonic shift. At about this time, I was amazed to detect—in a bizarre role reversal—that some of my teachers actually tried to be certain students' pets. I was embarrassed to see some teachers shamelessly curry favor with the "in" crowd, consisting of beautiful students from privileged families (or so it seemed to me at the time). I remember thinking how these teachers were fixated on their unsuccessful junior high school lives and their unglamorous jobs! And I began to realize that the things I was interested in and wanted to learn about—the war in Vietnam, pop art and clothing, the literature of alienation, and the British music scene—didn't connect in any way with my educational setting. To talk about any of these things, even with most of the students and almost all of the teachers, almost always led to your being labeled a range of things, from a communist to a "fairy" (and this by the teachers). I started to become outspoken, or, rather, "inspoken," in that my criticism about inequities in the system went underground—in my mind. Outwardly, I began dressing in pop clothing—blue-and-yellow polka dot shirts, minstrel caps, green slacks with the wide corduroy. I may not have engaged my teachers in debate, but I was a sharp dresser.

The times became more political, and at my high school in the early 1970s, I took part in an all-school walkout. I was in the twelfth grade and attended a relatively conservative school. On the day of the demonstration, I put on a black armband to commemorate the thousands of innocent deaths in Vietnam. I then walked through the halls of my school in the shadow of the Space Needle, cut class, and joined a larger demonstration in downtown Seattle. I remember only one of my friends actually joined me in this cause (and only a handful of students from the entire school joined the protest). He showed real courage to take part in the demonstration. He was terrified that he would get arrested and his parents would find out. Nothing happened to us (although people were clubbed). But the next day, we discovered (to my delight and his shock) a close-up picture of his face in the tangle of the demonstration on the front page of the leading Seattle daily. For some reason, I saved a copy of this picture and just looked at it again. Before looking at it, I imagined him smiling in the photo. But in the actual picture, he has a terrified look on his face. And it is only now, as I write this with Deidre, that I begin to understand the meaning of dangerous conversations in a new way: This topic added to a nascent but growing theme in my life at that time of things I shouldn't talk about. These missing conversations come from many sources. As I was unable to even begin to articulate my anger and outrage both over the war and my school's acceptance of it, and as this was not a topic for "consciousness raising" at my school, I began to shut down. I felt alienated and silenced by my school and then by myself for being silent.

And now, thinking about Deidre's words, I can place my sense of alienation into a greater context of family, love, and commitment to the improvement of society. I wasn't alone, and my views didn't spring from a vacuum. They came from a place of meaning and security, from my mother's living belief in justice and fairness. I was glad not to get a protest photo of me in the local paper, but I think now that she would have been proud of me. My alienation, which sprang from my socialization into a school system at odds with what I knew and believed in, put what was important to me into a "null curriculum" (Norris and

Sawyer, 2004). A tension developed between publicly sanctioned but hostile perceptions and silenced but hopeful perceptions, marginalized and absent from the public discourse, yet central to who I was.

This tension makes me think of an excerpt from the poem "A Dream Deferred," by Langston Hughes (1994):

> What happens to a dream deferred?
> Does it dry up
> Like a raisin in the sun?
> Or fester like a sore—
> And then run?

How do we internalize a deferred dream? In my case, I got lost in the null curriculum (Flinders, Noddings, and Thornton, 1986) and became a good student.

Reflective Summary Discussion

Deidre: I was struck by the notion of "silencing" in this last conversation . . . we hadn't really talked about that previously. Well, we had talked about it but perhaps not named it? Making transparent the way these "conversations," whether written or spoken . . . or painted . . . were silenced as a result of perceived risks in continuing to try to "voice" is important to me. The silence is significant in terms of compromising our capacity to challenge existing power structures and limiting the possibilities to bring about change. On the other hand, evidence that we have and continue to voice our difficult conversations in small but safe(ish) circles . . . broadening these circles over time seems empowering.

Rick: Silencing . . . yes, this is interesting. Donna Krammer and Rosemarie Mangiardi's duoethnography, also in this book (Chapter 2), discusses the hidden curriculum of their learning to write—of becoming writers—and examines their lived experience throughout their student days. Examining the context of their writing now and what is valued and not valued, they describe many of the same issues we discuss. What I find interesting here is the ways that I became an accomplice to the power structure. A difference between you and me was that you had a voice—creating strong messages—but I used symbols: an armband, a school walkout, and a demonstration. It was visual. And I was glad my photo didn't make the paper. What does it mean that it was visual? In my own personal mythology,

I cast myself as a rebel with a cause. But there has clearly been a split between my private world (where this happened) and the public, where it didn't so much.

Deidre: This continual widening or broadening of the context (like a camera's lens) from the private to the public seems significant. It seems to happen throughout our paper and throughout our conversation that we . . . go in and out.

Rick: I was thinking about the private and the public, and I've focused on some relatively negative things. But then it occurred to me that it really has not been all negative. I think that when I was young, I started with the premise that trust and change are possible. You mentioned that integrity was possible, and I realized that I received much motivation to promote justice and integrity from my parents. Their friends (and my babysitters) were of different ethnicities (almost unheard of back then), and they also helped people on an individual level who were in need. They thought this was the normal way to live. I learned to be decent from them. My private space and my actions promoted peace; my school promoted war.

I found school lacking integrity. I didn't experience the curriculum as being motivated by larger principles, such as justice and love—things that my mom stood for—and I realized that integrity really wasn't there. The extrinsic motivation that came from my schooling wasn't about honesty or authenticity. I sensed then and believe now that teachers used normative structures to justify their beliefs, projecting hostility through these structures. At some point for me, there was a breakdown in trust: If you were authentic but deviated from the normative, you were a target. It was confusing to bring a social cause—protesting the Vietnam War—into my school, which was thick with conformity. At this time, teachers viewed me as being if not subversive then at least out of the norm. And I think that I decided just to wait until a different time and place to become active again. The question that I pose to myself now is, To what extent was I implicated in structures of silencing?

Written Artifacts: The Spaces Between Our Words

Both: Over the years, we have each broadened the contexts in which we engage in conversations, beginning within our families and moving out to the contexts of "formal schooling" and, ultimately 0, out into the wider world. Over time, we have also expanded the audience with whom we have conversations and changed the medium through which we have these conversations. In our professional lives now, many of our conversations are situated in published texts: conversations and texts for whom our audience is not necessarily known. In this section, we each examine an earlier piece of writing, one that we considered dangerous at the time that we wrote it.

Rick: I would like to think that I have published dangerous conversations throughout my professional life, but as I examine my publication history, I see that this really isn't true. In the past, I limited these conversations to actual conversations with friends or presentations. It's as if I wanted the "evidence" to be ephemeral.

I now ask myself, What stands out for me as something I consider a controversial piece of writing? I have written a number of pieces in the past where I have championed the rights of others, but rarely did I write anything that created a risk for myself. There is one exception. Joe Norris and I wrote the first duoethnography that explored aspects of our lives where our identities had crossed into a range of sexual identification territories. What made the paper complex and scary for me was not my drawing parallels between myself and sexual orientations but, rather, simply the honest discussion of my own life. I found that I had great difficulty writing about myself directly. Instead, I wrote between the lines and discussed myself in relation to the lives of friends. I wrote, for instance,

> I [have] decided to tell my story through the stories of two good friends, both departed. In the gay world, your friends are your family. As we need social acceptance to grow as individuals, gay identity is formed in relation to the intertwined lives of friends. My worldview—both personally and professionally—has been shaped by my friendships with other gay people.
> (Norris and Sawyer, 2004, p. 142)

In another paper, I wrote an interpretation of the photography of one of my friends, including the following:

> His photography also hints at ways that he saw the world. Steve took the following pictures in his twenties and early thirties. To understand him a bit, it is possible to begin to identify illustrative themes and patterns from his art. What are some themes that these photos share?
> (Norris and Sawyer, 2003, p. 6)

I continue:

> His photography presents disembodied images—with people often lost in a decontextualized or jarringly framed world.

He gives a hand, a leg, a foot a visual weight one would not normally assign to them and freezes them in all their blemishes. Commercial photography now has jarring edges and abrupt cuts, but 20 years ago, this style came from a vision, not a catalogue. Characteristics of Steve's photography include animated surfaces, amorphous shadows, sharp edges, and radiant light. And his eyesight was nearly gone. Sometimes his shapes are actively sinister and threatening, like scenes in the short story "Symbolism," by Nabokov, in which the symbolic meanings of objects become a pronounced sign of schizophrenia by a particular character in the story. Even at the time period these images tended to disrupt the narrative unity, to force the viewer to see them outside a story. Looking back three decades, I'm struck by how much I have to pull the images outside the frame of the story. I'm startled by their unique beauty. (2003, p. 6)

Figure 12.1 Under the hood.

Figure 12.2 Legs on the beach.

Figure 12.3 Boy gazing through picket fence.

Figure 12.4   Shaving in the shadows.

What I couldn't do is say that this discussion of my friend was a profound starting point for my own critical perspective of the world. This framing of the world is very consistent with queer and other forms of critical theory that promote a critical insider analysis of life and society in order to promote their change. This was difficult for me to do then, as it is now.

Deidre: Rick, your reflections on how you limited your conversations to actual conversations with friends or wrote abut 'the other' in an effort to keep the "evidence" ephemeral causes me to think further about the impact our perceptions of our audiences' interpretations and responses have on our willingness to make public conversations that feel "risky." Over a decade ago I undertook a study of the ways in which women in graduate school at a large North American research-focused university experienced their position and identity within the academy. Informed by critical perspectives around work/life issues within feminist practice (Acker, 1990; Fletcher, 1998; Tompkins, 1996), I sought to understand how women viewed their position in relation to the norms of the institution, and how they thought about their academic work within the larger picture of their lives. I interviewed several female graduate students and reported in my paper that these women were disillusioned with the lack of work/life balance that prevailed in academia, they lacked images or mentors of "successful" academic women with whom they could identify, and their personal values in and for education rubbed against the values they saw as key to the institution. My interest in this work was sparked by an awareness that women graduate students were experiencing competing demands in their academic work and personal lives and did not have role models within academia they valued in terms of how to do things differently. At the time I wrote, "The interviews roller-coasted between outbursts of raucous laughter, solemn talking tinged with anger, animated excitement, and tears of frustration."

I was invited to publish this work in a journal of women's studies. One would think I would have jumped at this opportunity as in the actual paper I had written, "This research has revealed both positive and negative aspects of the experiences of these women, and we need to think carefully about constructive ways to communicate these to a wider audience." However, I declined publication. It felt too dangerous to make these conversations (both the conversations with the women and my overarching analytical conversation) public. I could not find a way that felt safe enough for me to communicate my findings. Although fully aware of the currency of publication for my own future in the academy, I declined the invitation. Now, thirteen years later, the sense of risk seems less significant. The writing seems more benign now, but there remain traces of a sense of danger. I ask, "What made it feel so dangerous in 1998?" Perhaps it was that I was critiquing the very institution from which I was trying to get my "ticket" for my own academic career? That I might offend academic women who were my mentors? And why has the sense of danger subsided (though not completely gone)? The concept of risk is about the fear of possible future loss, damage, or threat (Zinn, 2008). Yates and Stone (1992) identify the three main elements of risk as (a) loss, (b) significance of the loss, and (c) uncertainty. Perhaps my perception of what there is to lose has changed now I am no longer a graduate student, now I am in a different location . . . a different country (with tenure), though this is an irony, for my findings could likely apply to women in almost any research institution of higher education in any country or state. Perhaps I have accepted to an extent that I need to have these conversations and am a little more willing to take such a risk, hence this chapter. It is a way of coming to terms with my silencing of self.

Summary: Reflective Discussion

Rick: When I read what you just wrote, I sensed your dilemma. First of all, you wanted to explore the topic of women's perception of the workspace. This topic was important both for the sake of the research and for you as a member of academia. And then, in the process of doing the study, you realized that that there was too much congruence between the study and life. And you chose not to publish it.

Deidre: That's interesting, actually, I think it was more: "Yes, this is congruent with life . . . and this very life makes it too dangerous to make this public."

And here I am now doing a piece of work with you . . . it's taken until now to reconnect with this work . . . but what we are doing here still remains beyond the mainstream.

Rick: Well, that's that other part that really struck me, that there is pressure in our work to stay within mainstream scholarship. And we can be faced with the task of bracketing out our identity from our work (or our work from aspects of our lives). Our identity is always reflected in our writing, so this process contributes to a sense of insecurity.

Are you thinking about resurrecting that article?

Deidre: Yes . . . I want to add to it and publish it. While I don't know where I'd publish it, I now do care about people reading it. For me, with this particular piece, it is not about the need to publish (though indeed I live within this reality) but more about finally honoring these and other women's stories, and recognizing that these stories of disjuncture are as recognizable and important to examine today as ever. So this artifact was the first thing that came to mind when you suggested we examine one. It is one that to some extent has been bugging me for years . . . the fact that I never made it public seemed dishonoring to the women I interviewed.

Rick: That's really interesting. There's this sense of trust that because . . . the one thing that you wrote that I thought was so wonderful. . . . Your quotation, from above: "The interviews roller-coasted between outbursts of raucous laughter, solemn talking tinged with anger, animated excitement, and tears of frustration." I love that quote. The world deserves to hear this and many other things that you have to say.

Deidre: I've recently located all those women. Conversations with you made me decide to see if I could find them. I found them all, and they are all doing different things related to education; some are academics and some are not. I corresponded with them all because it would be so interesting to juxtapose their stories thirteen years on when I finally publish this work, so this conversation with you has motivated me to resurrect it.

Rick: Wow . . . that's amazing. So you just e-mailed them. . . .

Deidre: Yes, I found them all by searching on the Web. I want to hear their stories now.

INTO A CYBERSPACE

Deidre: Now, several years later . . . a source I could not have previously predicted impacts my sense of danger in having some conversations. There is perhaps not necessarily new material to make my conversations dangerous. The same patterns continually reemerge . . . revealing the personal, the fear of retribution, the drive to take on the larger political system. But now, a new challenge enters the stage. Actually, it doesn't so much enter the stage as it underlies the stage: information and communications technologies (ICT). Now my conversations somehow become permeable, public, and permanent. I write a message, it is on e-mail and has the potential to go to anyone at any time, and the receiver inadvertently forwards my message on to someone it was not intended for. This unintended audience suddenly makes what was a "safe" conversation "dangerous." It is out of my control. I give a talk; it is recorded and put up on the Web for faceless people, unknown others with unknown motives, to listen to and "use." I teach a class; it is online, and I must contribute to conversations between students that are recorded and public. My contributions are permanent; I cannot erase them. We are all nervous, students don't come forward, and I don't have the capacity to show them why they should. Conversations that were already dangerous now have the overlay of being permeable (almost anyone can access them), public, and permanent. I continue to think about the role of technology in all of this. It promotes a blurring of boundaries between the public and private (though one might debate that this separation never actually exists).

But I'm also thinking that, at the same time, cyberspace—and we haven't really talked about this—provides a platform for the growth of other perspectives that can empower fringe groups and become normative views within online communities. When I was back in high school and I put a "Truck off Fuxton" banner on the wall, I didn't have some activist online community to go home to and talk with about what had happened . . . I was fairly much alone. Now, the empowering side of the technology means the Web can provide an international community. The Web has provided the capacity for people to engage in conversations across the world. It brings the opportunity to engage in global conversations to our fingertips.

Rick: I'm also nervous about technology. I recently woke up feeling anxious about a short presentation that I gave recently. The talk was partly about how globalization was impacting life and education in Mexico. My goal was not to try to understand what was happening in Mexico from a Mexican perspective but, rather, to establish parallels between what is happening in Mexico and the United States in relation to forces of globalization and neoliberalism.

   After the talk, I had a good conversation with the audience. What made me nervous was that the presentation had been videotaped to be put on a website. Thus, technology would change the time and place of my talk. Instead of just speaking to a relatively small group of people at noon in the auditorium of my campus, my talk would be available online 24/7 for anyone who is obsessive enough to find it (by doing a word search on the topic). When I woke up feeling anxious, I realized that I had engaged in a "dangerous conversation." With this realization, I went back to try to isolate what made me feel uneasy— what made the conversation dangerous for me. First, there was the topic. In this current climate in the U.S., you run a risk if you are critical of business and/or government. And this risk is magnified by technology; being online, the conversation is not bounded just by the moment I spoke but will be available at different times and through different social/political climates. Technology adds an unknown element to this situation that is already anxiety provoking for me. With technology I totally lose control of my words. What I might say in a spontaneous conversation that evolves in the moment is definitely not how I would present myself in writing. So the process connects to the topic in a more complicated way. In a way, with technology, one is putting once transitory messages out as permanent records.

Reflective Discussion

Deidre: There are, of course, multiple ways of thinking about the relationship between the capacity provided through new information and communications technology and our perceptions of dangerous conversations. The Internet can magnify a sense of danger in terms of the public, permeable, and permanency issues it layers on conversations. However, at the same time, the opportunities for communication these new technologies offer are also powerful and liberating. So it's important to hold on to the big picture, including the positive aspects of ICT for communication. After all, you and I wouldn't even be having this [Skyped] conversation without the Internet!

Rick: And the Internet contributes to democracy and the layered, fluid identity that younger people have because they are on the Internet (e.g., Matus and McCarthy, 2003), and they're living, as it were, in different places at the same time. They are living in a cyber-world.

Deidre: It's complex, and it has these multiple sides. So it's opportunities for democracy, on the one side, and yet it's still dangerous on whole other level because possibilities for misinterpretation and surveillance are amplified.

Because of our conversation, I've started reading about the creation of Facebook. One of the criticisms of Facebook has been that it blurs the public/private spheres of people's lives, and the founders of Facebook said, "Well, what about integrity?" What does it mean if we have to hold separate public and private lives? It's an interesting challenge.

Rick: Yes, the use of technology blurs the boundary between the private and the public. When you are talking to people, you have a better sense of where the boundaries are, and the boundaries give comfort. But when you don't know where the boundaries are and you're writing or saying something controversial, when you realize that the boundaries stretch almost to infinity, you become anxious. This adds a new dimension to consider. I was originally more inclined to engage in dangerous conversations in person than in writing, and then that flipped, and I felt that engaging in writing gave me a safe space. But with technology, the ease of access of what you write complicates and threatens this safe space.

Talking to you right now, I am realizing something new. Instead of directly discussing topics with a direct connection to my own life, that of social justice for gay youth, for example, I have written about social justice issues more detached from my own identity. To the extent that I am exploring personal topics, I am doing so through the use of proxies. Still, feelings of anxiety continue to surface through these topics. And those feelings—due both to the lack of personal connection and to the use of technology—have grown.

The other thing that you mentioned in an earlier e-mail and we didn't really follow up on was that we've been talking about things from the perspective of the speaker and not the listener.

Deidre: Yes, I was driving to pick my son Eli up from kindergarten today, and it dawned on me that most of our talk about dangerous conversations has been from the perspective of the "talker," the writer, the presenter, the one communicating the message, in other words from the position as giving out a message . . . not interpreting or receiving it. This is an interesting bias given that conversations are so very much an interactive process. While we have focused on interpretation, it has still tended to be from the perspective of what this means for us as the communicator and not of ourselves as interpreters of other people's communications. Is this one-sided bias a possible artifact of some of the immediate challenges we face in our work? Yes. I was driving along and found it quite fascinating that most of the discussion you and I have had about dangerous conversations has been about what it means about getting the message out and others interpreting it, but we haven't been thinking about ourselves as interpreters of others' messages, which is fine. But I guess that it reflects what we think is most dangerous about our jobs at the moment.

We have been talking about issues of safety in dangerous conversations from our perspectives as speaker or writer more than as the listener or interpreter. But this ignores a critical part of the interaction. Stories can lead us into a serious sea of enormous social issues (Behar, 1996). Boler contends that "listening is fraught with emotional landmines" (1999, p. 179), so the act of listening can in itself be perceived to be as dangerous as talking. We misinterpret; we misunderstand. I remember having a class of around twenty school leaders. Somebody said something, and I could tell when I responded that I had completely misinterpreted what she had said, by her face, by her gestures . . . but she didn't say anything. But I knew, and from that moment the conversation didn't move forward. So I went to talk to with the person after the class, and, sure enough, I had completely misinterpreted what was said, thus making it a dangerous conversation for her. I had misinterpreted her contribution publicly in front of her and her colleagues. It was an academic class, and as such, I was the person in the potentially damaging role as teacher misinterpreting her contribution. This is what I am thinking about when I say that for a good part of our conversations you and I have been thinking about ourselves as the speaker and not of ourselves as the interpreter making conversations so-called dangerous for other people.

Rick: We're in these roles of so-called power as teachers, and then people do say things in class and we filter what we hear with all the baggage that we are talking about.

Deidre: I'm teaching an educational change class, and what I've noticed is that—while I don't normally do this, I sometimes include one of my papers as a core reading, and they refer to it in their own writing. And it's quite mind-boggling to me how many people say, well, "Le Fevre says da-da-da-da-da-da-da," and it isn't actually what I'm saying at all. It's very easy to see it when it's your own, but how often do we do that to other people's writing?

Rick: We construct arguments in our writing, and then we just take someone's quote to support what we are saying.

Deidre: And it was this that occurred to me while I was driving after one of our conversations. When we write, we expose ourselves as interpreters of other people's contributions.

Rick: It's interesting also that you mention that it was when you were driving to pick up your son, Eli, from kindergarten when you thought of that. Does that come into play in some way?

Deidre: It does. Walking into a kindergarten, which is an early childhood setting for three- to five-year-olds here, can be one of the most phenomenal places in the world. They have the most incredible teachers. They notice, recognize, and respond to the lives of the children. It's a very creative place. When I walk in there, I always feel somehow liberated, like I can think better. It's much better than the "ivory tower." So it'd definitely relate to the early childhood setting and the freedom of expression and the empowering place that it is.

Rick: So it's about the paradigm, too, that in really good early childhood settings, the curriculum is built on the active interest and the curiosity of the child.

Deidre: And when the teacher doesn't get it right . . . when they are trying to understand what the child is saying, the child will just tell them: "No, that's not what I mean." Whereas once we grow out of early childhood, we just pretend that it was what we meant, and we'll just go away seething that they misinterpreted it, they didn't get it.

Rick: So they listen. It's a different paradigm. Is it impossible to have a place like that where people really do listen to each other and try to understand what they say, and if they interpret something and it's wrong, the other person can say, "No, that's really not what I meant"? That would change things. It would actually change how I view a lot of things.

It is about integrity, which has emerged as a large theme in our paper. Integrity and motivation and trust and where someone is coming from, the private area or the public sphere in terms of whether or not I trust the audience and feel safe, determining whether it is dangerous or not dangerous. And even if . . . it's sort of like Eli's kindergarten class . . . if there is integrity and I'm saying something that is dangerous, the other person can listen and then paraphrase and I can say, well, "That's what I meant" or "That's not what I meant."

Deidre: So it's about being able to check understandings and interpretations with the other person. That's actually from the theoretical work of Argyris and Schön (1974, 1996) that I have recently used with a colleague in aiming to describe the nature of open to learning conversations between educational professionals. It is about the importance of checking for understanding and seeking confirmation from the other person in relation to our interpretations. This has much to offer the academy. Duoethnography is a move in this direction. Rather than being monologic, it is dialogic, making explicit the searching for meanings rather than reifying a fixed solo metanarrative (Sawyer and Norris, 2009).

Rick: In this piece, we are continually conducting perception checks; we are not looking for universal truths but rather are trying to deeply listen to and respond to the Other. This is where these notions of diversity and normativity come in.

Deidre: Yes, this is particularly important in unequal power situations.

Rick: In your paper from 1998, you wrote about a power differential. Combine this with the notion of integrity. The intersection of the lack of integrity and great power is a scary place.

Deidre: Listening to you talk about integrity takes me back to thinking about how we learn to communicate in the first place. Perhaps all conversations are dangerous in some way. You were talking earlier in our work about your mother and about love and safety. We learn to talk with our families, with our mothers. And they are always looking to confirm and to understand and to make sense of our early utterances. All our utterances are accepted if not celebrated when we are learning to talk no matter how closely they resemble the normative language.

Rick: And in schools all over the world, a new global curriculum is becoming much more normative, standardized, and test driven, with the intent of sorting people into categories: the managers, the producers, and the elite . . . and all as shoppers. And with the spatial scale growing, so goes the message. If you speak out in one scenario, you are heard and debated; in another, ignored and made irrelevant; and in another, imprisoned even before being charged with anything.

Deidre: Yes, as we conclude, I'd like to focus on empowerment. Conducting a duoethnography is, in itself, empowering. For example, I'm going to continue the conversation that I silenced with the graduate women all those years ago. This methodology of duoethnography has given me the space and direction to consider the complexities of that conversation and, perhaps most importantly, energized me to pick up the pieces and carry on the conversation, eventually taking it into the more public domain.

Rick: Yes, this is empowering. It's about dialogue, about opening up perspective. It's about creating safe spaces in solidarity where we can look at how our narratives have been inscribed by ideas and beliefs that we, on an intentional level, don't want to engage or believe in. Duoethnography is always about transformation of the duoethnographers and, potentially, the readers of their documents, who witness and take part in the shifts of meaning as the dialogue unfolds.

Deidre: Even just acknowledging that conversations can be dangerous, silenced, difficult—whatever we want to call them—can be empowering. And if people can recognize that, then they can start thinking about why and work through that. As in my talking with the student I almost silenced in my class last week, if I hadn't gone to her afterwards and said, "You know, I'm sorry, I think I completely misinterpreted what you said," she may have come back to class the following week and not have said anything. So I can talk about that. It's a little clearer after these conversations with you. I'm sure she's going to talk a lot next week, and I'll probably misinterpret her again!

Rick: For me, as our voices are silenced, so are our identities. And if we come from diverse or impoverished backgrounds—in terms of culture, language, sexual orientation, poverty—we are at risk of not being heard. And if we can't communicate, then our epistemologies and ways of seeing the world start to vanish and leave the world.

Deidre: Yes, it is about ways of being in the world.

Rick: And a lot of what has made these conversations dangerous has been related to my personal identity, and if it's happening to me, I need to recognize, then, that it is happening to others. And as schools become more normative and as textbooks become more abstract and authoritative (with no clear author), then conversations will become more dangerous for a lot of people.

Deidre: Yes, and earlier you said something about research involving the continuous interpretation of others: "Duoethnography provides a critical platform to understand what happens in the process of research." For example, when you interpret someone else's life, the interpretation is really about yourself, like Rosenblatt's (1978) reader's response theory.

Rick: What we've talked about has implications for curriculum, for research, and for the value and recognition of diverse cultural epistemology. If fear of danger silences, we have a huge null curriculum (Flinders, Nodding, and Thornton, 1986) within the research community.

CONCLUSION

Rick: Deidre, seeking to gain an increased understanding of different contexts influencing my perceptions of dangerous conversations, I have followed this investigation down unexpected paths. Together, we have opened the definition of dangerous conversations to include those both in the private and the public spheres, those in speech and in writing, those that are bounded by time and space, and those that exist in a cyber-world. Investigating these emergent contexts, we have examined different examples of writing from different times in our lives. In this process, I have experienced my memories not as discrete linear images but, rather, as recursive thoughts. My earlier memories influenced my more recent memories and my more recent memories influenced my earlier one—as I thought about them from my current moment in time.

The tension that this interaction created—as well as that from our dialogues, usually conducted with clumsy interactive Internet software—encouraged me to see and reconceptualize once deeply veiled memories of dangerous events with a greater clarity and range of perspective. In tracing the contours of my current life backwards, forwards, and then backwards, I recognized that I have perceived conversations as dangerous not so much because of their content but, rather, because of how my words have intersected with my early childhood life of integrity, the cultural contexts of my conversations, and my perceived level of reception (based partly on the match between my perceptions of selves and "the norm"). Authentic but controversial content can take the fall for problematic norms, becoming themselves labeled and censored as problematic. In elementary school, the censorship may come from the teacher. By middle or high school, it may be internalized and come from the student, who has internalized the external censorship. If lucky, the student can search for himself or herself in adolescent idealism and then adult integrity. Through this study, I have become encouraged to reopen once closed work and gain closure on anxiety-producing work. Excommunicated conversations can be recommunicated. Risky disclosures can be revisited, reimagined, and reanimated to promote praxis and societal change now and in the future: The "aha" moments that I've experienced in this study will continue to present themselves to me.

Deidre: Now, having had time for pause since our last conversation, I ponder on my learning throughout this methodology. It feels empowering in itself to recognize that while conversations can feel "dangerous," there is a bigger context to them than just our own. Rick and I had an ongoing awareness of the potential for this duoethnography to become dangerous. At the beginning of our process, we agreed to talk about anything; it would have been ironic not to, given our focus—dangerous conversations! However, to free ourselves in order to do this, we first agreed on a process of openness, and later we would intentionally make decisions about what material we both felt comfortable to include for publication and that we would still censor. We continually navigated the public/private tension within our own process.

This duoethnography had been empowering for me. Recognizing that we don't need to internalize responsibility for a conversation being difficult is liberating. Conversations exist in the larger cultural and political realms. They exist within unequal structures of power and privilege. At the same time, having the courage to open up conversations that have been silenced gives us the opportunity to voice important issues and continue necessary conversations. An awareness of these issues helps me understand why I am continually confronted with a desire for my online teaching contributions to be ephemeral rather than so public, with a permeable permanence.

And what of the probable or preferred future? Dangerous conversations make us feel vulnerable—and vulnerability isn't for everyone (Behar, 1996). What will comprise dangerous elements of conversations that we are yet to perceive? Perhaps it is enough to try to understand that our current conceptions of conversations are influenced by our cultural and political contexts, power relations, interpersonal capabilities, and emerging capacities of electronic media. One challenge is to continue to voice our silenced conversations in ever enlarging circles of relative safety. Another is to face a degree of discomfort and be courageous in our conversations, for

> we are more likely to learn something from people who disagree with us than we are from people who agree. But we tend to hang around with and over listen to people who agree with us, and we prefer to avoid and under listen to those who don't. (Fullan, 2001, p. 41)

References

Acker, J. (1990). Hierarchies, jobs, bodies: A theory of gendered organizations. *Gender & Society*, 4(2), 139–158.

Argyris, C., and Schön, D. (1974). *Theory in practice: Increasing professional effectiveness*. San Francisco: Jossey-Bass.

Argyris, C., and Schön, D. A. (1996). *Organizational learning II: Theory, method and practice*. Reading, MA: Addison Wesley.

Behar, R. (1996). *The vulnerable observer: Anthropology that breaks your heart*. Boston: Beacon.

Boler, M. (1999). *Feeling power: Emotions and education*. New York: Routledge.

Bryk, A. S., and Schneider, B. L. (2002). *Trust in schools: A core resource for improvement*. New York: Russell Sage Foundation.

Donohoe, F. W. (2007). *Personality, perception, perseverance and peers—managing the transition from year 10 general education to a residential agricultural course in the upper secondary years*. Unpublished doctoral dissertation, The University of Notre Dame, Sydney.

Fletcher, J. (1998). Relational practice: A feminist reconstruction of work. *Journal of Management Inquiry*, 7, 163–186.

Flinders, D. J., Noddings, N., and Thornton, S. J. (1986). The null curriculum: Its theoretical basis and practical implications. *Curriculum Inquiry*, 16(1), 33–42.

Fullan, M. (2001). *Leading in a culture of change*. San Francisco: Jossey-Bass.

Hughes, L. (1994). *Collected works of Langston Hughes*. New York: Alfred A. Knopf.

Matus, C., and McCarthy, C. (2003). The triumph of multiplicity and the carnival of difference: Curriculum dilemmas in the age of postcolonialism and globalization. In W. Pinar (Ed.), *International handbook of curriculum research* (pp. 73–84). Mahwah, NJ: Lawrence Erlbaum Associates.

McLuhan, M. (1967). *The medium is the massage*. Toronto: Random House of Canada.

Norris, J. (2008). Duoethnography. In L. M. Given (Ed.), *The SAGE encyclopedia of qualitative research methods* (Vol. 1, pp. 233–236). Los Angeles: Sage.

Norris, J., and Sawyer, R. (2003, October). Null and hidden curricula of sexual orientation: A dialogue on the curreres of the absent presence and the present absence. Paper presented at the 4th Curriculum and Pedagogy Annual Conference, Decatur, GA.

Norris, J., and Sawyer, R. D. (2004). Null and hidden curricula of sexual orientation: A dialogue on the curreres of the absent presence and the present absence. In L. Coia, M. Birch, N. J. Brooks, E. Heilman, S. Mayer, A. Mountain, and P. Pritchard (Eds.), *Democratic responses in an era of standardization* (pp. 139–159). Troy, NY: Educator's International Press, Inc.

Norris, J., Higgins, C., and Leggo, C. (2004, April). *"Shh stories": The problematics of personal disclosure in qualitative research*. Paper presented at the Annual Meeting of the American Educational Research Association, San Diego.

Pinar, W. (1975). Currere: Toward reconceptualization. In W. Pinar (Ed.), *Curriculum theorizing: The reconceptualists* (pp. 396–414). Berkeley, CA: McCutchan.

Robinson, V. M. J., and Le Fevre, D. M. (2011). Principals' capability in challenge conversations: The case of parental complaints. *Journal of Educational Administration. 49*(3), 227–255.

Rosenblatt, L. (1978). *The reader, the text, the poem: The transactional theory of the literary work*. Carbondale: Southern Illinois Press.

Sawyer, R., and Norris, J. (2009). Duoethnography: Articulations/(re)creation of meaning in the making. In W. Gershon (Ed.), *Working together in qualitative research: A turn towards the collaborative* (pp. 127–140). Rotterdam: Sense.

Spradley, J. (1980). *Participant observation*. New York: Holt, Rinehart and Winston.

Thorne, S. (2011). Toward methodological emancipation in applied health research. *Qualitative Health Research, 21*(4), 443–453.

Tompkins, J. (1996). *A life in school: What the teacher learned*. Reading, MA: Addison-Wesley.

Yates, J. F., and Stone, E. R. (1992). The risk construct. In J. F. Yates (Ed.), *Risk taking behavior* (pp. 1–25). Chichester, UK: John Wiley.

Zinn, J. O. (2008). Introduction: The contribution of sociology to the discourse on risk and uncertainty. In J. O. Zinn (Ed.), *Social theories of risk and uncertainty: An introduction* (pp. 1–17). Malden, MA: Blackwell.

CHAPTER 13

Why Duoethnography:
Thoughts on the Dialogues

Richard D. Sawyer and Joe Norris

In a recent Roman Polanski (2010) film, Ewan McGregor's character is hired as a *Ghost Writer* for a retired politician who is writing his memoirs. A ghostwriter writes a book for a credited author while remaining invisible and unnamed in the process. As the thriller unfolds, the Ghost discovers that he is writing in the first person about a possible war criminal. The politician in question is hoping that "his" book will tell a persuasive cover story of himself as a romantic husband and dedicated public servant. Very quickly, the Ghost learns that he has become implicated in a corrupt narrative. Although the Ghost is never in danger of assuming the identity or narrative of the politician in question, he does become a possible object of assassination because he "knows too much."

This film has two implications for duoethnography. First, we find that during our lives we internalize historical and cultural scripts, even those that are harmful to us. These internalized narratives operate, in effect, as ghostwriters in our lives. For example, I (Rick), as a gay man, grew up internalizing many hateful narratives and perspectives about gay and lesbian identity spun by people who knew too little. I am now trying to understand the extent to which they still shadow my life. Second, unlike the person in the film hiring someone to do his writing for himself, duoethnographers study and write about themselves: They are firmly situated within their work. They are visible because they are engaged. By claiming that our research is "value free," we distance ourselves from it and its impact on our actions. Duoethnography has provided us (and other researchers in this book) with a research language to (a) expose and engage internalized scripts, (b) present these revealed scripts to other people as a basis for their reconceptualizations of thought and action, and (c) reconceptualize and restory our own narrative perspectives. Intertwining perception and creation, duoethnographers then both examine and create experience. Third, the duoethnographies themselves have defined the methodology. This book creates a recursive bottom-up, top-down dialogue. As the tenets help frame the studies, the studies assist in redefining, questioning, and expanding our understanding of the methodology. This chapter, then, is not a conclusion. It is a dialogue with the chapters.

In reading the eleven studies in this book, we find that the other inquirers have also—in dialogic relationships—explored, exposed, reconceptualized/restoried, and shared narratives of experience. We have all examined the relationships between our personal narratives and enculturating discourses. We have done this by exposing and examining—by learning to "read"—the pedagogy of our lived curriculum, our currere. Krammer and Mangiardi (in this volume) describe how this process of exposure and engagement may be focused on the hidden scripts within our currere, which they have named the "cryptic curriculum":

> How, then, do curricula teach these ideological "truths"? They do so by concealing them in customary practices and reinforcing them through regulation and routine. We have elected to refer to this process as *encoding*. In other words, the researcher who successfully uncovers the content of a hidden curriculum must still contend with—and decipher—an encrypted "lived" curriculum, a *cryptic curriculum*. The encoding of ideological "truths" occurs in the embodied interactions between students and teachers. If we are to successfully decode a cryptic curriculum we must enter into "the 'messy' details of actual lives [lived] through *talk and interaction*." (emphasis added; Gubrium and Holstein, 2000, p. 17, cited in Krammer and Mangiardi, 2012, p. 68)

As we have examined our cryptic curriculum, we have all framed our inquiry with the human voice. Read separately, these studies offer unique emic perspectives on pressing issues of our day. Read together as a collection, they communicate intertextual themes. Although these themes are all found in the individual studies, as a group their collective resonance expands, deepens, and changes them. As readers transacting with these studies (Rosenblatt, 1978), we have constructed a number of intertextual themes. These themes include identity and agency in contingent spaces, identity and curriculum, and landscapes of health. In the following discussion, we draw from the preceding studies in this book to offer a few illustrative examples of these themes. We then suggest why such research matters.

IDENTITY AND AGENCY IN CONTINGENT SPACES

In a recent keynote address, Janet Miller discussed a new vision for research focused on meaning made within "contingent communities without consensus." These research communities are grounded in the intersection of narrative and post-poststructuralism. Narrative within this research context is a means to engage in "the ethics of self-accounting" and to unpack autobiographically interpreted stories. Through dialogue, one allows one's story to be "refracted through the story of the other," promoting a sense of praxis. The concept of post-poststructuralism in this context refers to an interrogation of contingent spaces as text in order not only to interrogate meaning within that space (as in poststructuralism) but also to evoke, interrupt, and create new, uncertain spaces. These spaces promote new perceptions, the "imagining of alternate versions of self and work" (Miller, 2011). These are the contingent spaces created in the new global postmodernism, in the mixing and overlapping of cultures, epistemologies, families, and transborder Internet communications (Sawyer, 2010).

In such work, researchers think relationally and contextually and recognize the "vital porosity that exists between and among human groups in the modern world" (Matus and McCarty, 2003, p. 77). As Matus and McCarty stated,

> Postcolonial writers and critics such as Hommi Bhabha, Stuart Hall, Octavio Paz, and Gyatrii Spivak have . . . [argued] that culture and identity are the products of human encounters, the inventories of cross-cultural appropriation and hybridity, not the elaboration of the ancestral essence of particular groups. Within this alternative framework, culture and identity are conceptualized as the moving inventories and registers of association across narrowly drawn boundaries of group distinction. In his important essay, "Cultural Identity and Diaspora," Hall (1990) maintained that within any given community there are several other hidden or alternative communities wrestling to come to the surface. (p. 77)

Not only are the tools for such research different from those of more traditional qualitative research (Creswell and Miller, 2000) but so is the language (Sawyer and Norris, in press). The challenge is for a researcher to be open to the new language of this research. It comes not from the outside (e.g., formal English) but, rather, is generated as a transaction between the research texts and the researchers. It comes from the "ontology of narrative" (Morris, 2002, as cited by Clandinin, 2011), from researchers finding a new voice on the process of their working in a collaborative key.

Many of the researchers in this book have engaged in the "ontology of narrative" within their inquiries. They have, in reference to Clandinin's description of narrative inquiry, "not work[ed] with narrative as a tool, but rather let narrative work with them" (2011). Their themes resonate with what Foucault (1980) called subjugated knowledge—knowledge generated in counternarratives and expressed in local and subcultural ways of knowing and acting. Such knowledge, embedded in our lived experiences, often remains oppressed, repressed, or liminal. These narratives of experience unfold in contrast to recognized and reinforced mainstream narratives. Subjugated knowledge exists in Krammer and Mangiardi's discussion of the "cryptic curriculum" as a site of daily socialization from grade to graduate school. It exists in McClellan and Sader's investigation of the rhetoric of equality manifested in unequal academic work spaces. And it exists in Nabavi and Lund's duoethnography about "living in a multicultural nation in an era of borderless identities."

A reference to Nabavi's story about her student who became involved in the Green Party helps to illustrate the complexity of narrative within these studies:

> Her story, like many others in the study, sheds light on how young immigrants, while they are "multicultural," are caught seeking a space to express their multiculturalism in a way that is meaningful for them. In other words, she was not interested in expressing her Iranian identity through the superficial dimensions of the multicultural; rather, she wanted to be aligned with others fighting for rights. I think this is largely because the discourse and practice of multiculturalism is not speaking to the nuances of her national and political affiliations. In this context, I think it's not only useful but necessary to interrogate how the articulations and on-the-ground manifestations of multiculturalism in Canada inform our subject location and how, in effect, we can advance discussions about the multicultural nation using our diverse subject locations. (p. 188)

And it is these complex and diverse subject locations—these intertwined and contingent narrative identities in a land of "borderless identity"—that duoethnographers seek to explore, expose, and recreate. In their study, McClellan and Sader examine dialectic tensions found within contingent spaces and then apply them to leadership education. As they state,

> [Our goal in this duoethnography] is to uncover invisible barriers (such as fear of betrayal, feeling protective of family and friends, concerns about the proper role of self-disclosure, and students' resistance) that impacts honest discussion of diversity and social justice issues in leadership education (p. 138).

As part of this interrogation, they examine stories of socialization:

> We also learned from our families values about life (espoused and in use) and interactions with others (verbal and nonverbal cues). Through our socialization processes, we picked up coping strategies that continue to help and those we continue to unlearn (p. 141).

Their socialization process is nested within larger sociocultural patterns. Their parents' experiences reflect their own. The recurrence of this transnarrative echo underscores the need of analyzing self within cultural-historical contexts—including intergenerational contexts. Among other things, what is exceptional about their study (to us) is that they emphasize, again in Miller's (2011) words, the "ethics of self-accounting." Instead of distancing themselves from their inquiry through claims of objectivity, they state that "there is no such thing as value-free facts." They seek to let their students

> walk away from our courses with a new understanding of how race, power, and privilege play an integral role in the daily lives of leaders. We also want the knowledge blockers of privilege to be removed so that they can learn through the discomfort. Learning about one's privilege is challenging, emotionally taxing, and unnerving. (p. 150)

Nabavi and Lund in their study of social justice, identity, and racism present another example of how narratives can be contingent and contrasting. Exploring their own narratives of power in relation to dominant discourses, they create a critical dialectic. Maryam states that her goal "is to explore the 'messy' intersections in the context of the tensions that arise for immigrant youth living on the margins of a multicultural state; I explore this in relation to their non-national experiences and specifically how that informs their location in relation to the margin." Lund uses Maryam's words as a means to self-reflect. He states,

> As a member of the dominant group of White Canadians whose actions helped script these negative experiences for you, your stories lead me to question how I positioned myself then. Our family had its own narratives and rituals that placed us in the center of our community, and "foreign others" at the margins. Through some very direct teaching, I learned that I belonged here, and "they" didn't. From so many around me as a child, I learned a lot of negative lessons about specific ethnic groups such as Chinese, Pakistani, and Black people that I am not comfortable repeating here. (pp. 179–180)

Lund examines how he personally is situated within the cultural landscape of Canada—as a person seeking to deconstruct his mainstream position and offer new possibilities of action. Although his narrative cannot solve social injustice, it does support a personal vision of social justice and offers a "counterpunctual narrative" (Said, 1993), a new way to imagine cultural worlds within the tension of oppressive discourses and national metanarratives. Said discussed the connection between narrative and the internalization of the social imagination:

> The power to narrate, or to block other narrative from forming and emerging, is very important to culture and imperialism, and constitutes one of the main connections between them. Most important, the grand

narratives of emancipation and enlightenment mobilized people in the colonial world to rise up and throw off imperial subjection, in the process, many Europeans and Americans were also stirred by these stories and their protagonists, and they too fought for new narratives of equality and human community". (1993, pp. xii–xiii)

In their direct dialogue and discussion, Maryam and Lund construct their emergent intersubjectivity in practice within the narratives they express. In an earlier draft of their study, Maryam stated,

> I work to reclaim my multiple identities and become more aware of both the challenges and advantages that I carry. Finding a middle place to the extremes, as constructed by dominant rhetoric, is an ongoing process that I embrace through transformative approaches to social change and always being counter-hegemonic. (Lund and Nabavi, 2008, p. 27)

These multiple identities emerge in contrasting contingent spaces. For example, the straight/gay difference between Norris and Sawyer (2004), the different views of power and privilege between McClellan and Sader, and the different attitudes of reading and writing between Norris and Greenlaw increased the range of perspectives experienced by the researchers in relation to their narratives. In these pieces, the researchers focused their quests on both their similarities and differences, on the specific and the general.

IDENTITY AND CURRICULUM

As the inquirers in this collection examined their currere, curriculum itself emerged as either a text or subtext in many of the studies. Some of the writers focused explicitly on curriculum. In some of these studies, the formal curriculum became a context for the analysis of socialization processes that promote dominant discourses: As Krammer and Mangiardi ask, "What injustices and abuses of power have become so naturalized within the institution's hidden curriculum of schooling . . . ?" Examining this question, they investigate "the bureaucratic and managerial 'press' of the school—the combined forces by which students are induced to comply with the dominant ideologies and social practices related to authority, behavior and morality" (McLaren, 1989, pp. 183–184, as cited in Krammer and Mangiardi, 2012, p. 42).

As much of the learning process is embodied, Jim and I (Joe), by examining what inspired us to write throughout their lives, examine the underlying learning process. Creating two contrasting narratives of learning to write, our study underscores the complexity of the writing process and its connection to identity. We go back and unpack our meaning-making processes in earlier pieces of writing, such as journals, poems, and prose. To examine this writing in a more critical way, we use art—images and photos of their writing—to give them different perspectives. The rich, almost tactile texture we create with the interplay of written artifacts, images, and ongoing discussion promotes a process of reader response and transaction (Rosenblatt, 1994) and thus the creation of new texts.

This theme of the hidden and the crypted curriculum unfolded in nearly every study in this book. The study by Krammer and Mangiardi actually on the hidden curriculum of public education surfaced and named this process in this book. Amplifying the hidden curriculum subtexts in the other chapters, they begin to delineate a compelling intertextual dialogue among the chapters. However, as a stand-alone chapter, their study is important in its own right, given the increasingly politicized and regulatory nature of classroom curriculum. Theirs was possibly the first study that examined the relationship between how we internalize the hidden curriculum as part of our identity ("structured within [our] lives") and how we are socialized and influenced by it. As a learning case for methodology in duoethnography, their study highlights the uniqueness of inquiry focus, its frame for personal positionality (in relation to the hidden curriculum and its influence), and its potential space for self-awareness and reflexivity. Furthermore, as mentioned earlier, their study contributes to the literature on the hidden curriculum by their discussion of the "cryptic curriculum." This concept here refers to the pedagogy of curriculum, our learning to decipher and read curriculum as an emergent and layered dynamic.

In their imaginative and creative study, they begin by mentioning the complexities of the topic: "When the 'object' of study is a hidden *curriculum*, the task is particularly challenging. Here, the researcher must go in search of attitudes, values and routinized practices, none of which are easy to 'find'" (p. 66). They thus attempted to examine curriculum within a context of the underlying assumptions and meanings inherent in its "routinized practices." Given their normativity and regularity, these routinized practices as cultural artifacts are elusive yet potentially rich sites for investigation. Krammer and Mangiardi state provocatively: "Given this messy context, one so inclined can easily disguise and perpetuate self-serving beliefs and practices. Many are deeply invested in doing just that, for hidden curricula perform ideological work" (p. 66). They then act to restory their own narratives within this charged ideological context by moving their analysis (their currere) into the "lived present" and then by discussing the "metanarrative" of their study. Although the topic is highly conceptual (metanarrative as a means to decipher the hidden curriculum), their treatment is descriptive and concrete.

The concept of the hidden curriculum was central to my study with Tonda Liggett as we revisited and revised our views of the colonial foundations of our curriculum as teachers in the United States. We, Sawyer and Liggett, examined specific artifacts from our lives—photos from elementary school, high school yearbooks, and our own lesson plans as K to 12 teachers—in an attempt to discover colonial patterns of interaction that inscribed our lives and permeated our work. As a site for personal interrogation, we partly focused on the pedagogy of place, the process of learning from meanings embedded within specific physical locations (Greenwood, 2010). In this book, Liggett deconstructs her own stance toward culture, power, and personal identity. Discussing the time she spent in Kenya, she states that it "marked the beginning of an awareness about colonization, its legacy, and the ways that post/decolonization was apparent not only in my own personal identity but also in my teaching and in language arts curriculum" (p. 75). Our purpose in the study was to identify these patterns in order to engage in more self-reflexive and ethical teaching. We found that as an interactive, intersubjective experience, duoethnography carried the same moral obligation as daily life. In our study, we did not represent our lives; rather, through the presentation of our dialogic engagement, we tried to show ways of becoming more conscientious of how our curriculum reflected historical patterns of colonial domination. In this way, the duoethnographic process promoted decolonialism (and postcolonialism) but not colonialism. The meaning of the study laid in the unfolding process of, to again refer to Freire (1970), conscientization.

LANDSCAPES OF HUMANITY: PERCEPTIONS OF BECOMING

Duoethnography is not therapy, but as a methodological stance, it can promote its inquirers' sense of narrative awareness, how we frame the meanings we give to our lives. Premised on a postmodern notion of identity, it promotes a view of identity as hybrid, layered, recursive, multicultural, and shifting (Sawyer, 2003). Personal agency in cultural worlds is foregrounded, as "the media around which socially and historically positioned persons construct their subjectivities in practice" (Holland, Lachicotte, Skinner, and Cain, 1998, p. 32). A reconceptualized view of identity suggests that we recognize and examine the many identity boundaries within our lives and between Others and ourselves. Duoethnography holds that the layers of our identity can be in opposition to each other—often locked or in tension. In duoethnography, we seek to untangle our perceptions of our narratives and reform their proportional impact on our lives.

As we have mentioned, the concept of currere frames this reconceptualization process (Pinar, 1975). In a simplified form, duoethnographers draw from currere and work with self as text to restory their curriculum of life. This process is not about "revising history" but, rather, about being critically repositioned back into one's stories of experience. As we discuss and write about them, we expose and at times disrupt our perceptions of our lives (or gain a greater awareness of them). This happens by our weaving ourselves into the fabric of our inquiry, making such inquiry an embodied process. Instead of distancing ourselves from our work, in duoethnography we engage who we are. The collaborative method promotes a grounded and organic, yet conceptual process in duoethnography. Its researchers can lose the layers of defense found in other forms of research—the objectivity, claims of content neutrality, decontextualization of detail, deductive reasoning, and abstract framing. Instead, as they conduct their work, they position themselves within educative dialectics. These are the dialectics between, among others, self and other, the present and the past, cultural artifacts and self, stories from one researcher to another, and storytelling and critical summary reflection. In duoethnography, these dialectics are vocal and active participants in the process.

An example of one of the first duoethnographies that promoted researcher reconceptualization and self-reflexivity is found in Rankie Shelton and McDermott's investigation of the curriculum of beauty. "Beauty" as both a hidden and manifest curriculum goes to the core of North American culture and not only deeply shapes perception of self and others but also frames motivation and meaning in nearly aspect of our lives. These authors thought that autoethnography as a method of investigation offered them a way to examine how they were individually situated in relation to this topic. However, this topic by its very nature is layered, interactive, contextual, and lived. Thus they wanted to create a collaborative and dialogic study, to discover not commonalities so much as the many and contradictory perspectives of this topic—the varied ways in which it is contextually bound, institutionalized, and internalized.

They wove a critical discussion into their stories, making them both descriptive and analytical. Here McDermott expresses an analytical insight:

> We both seem to be focusing on feminine sexuality and beauty; there must be a reason it was the first place we jumped to in this discussion. Unlike you, as you know, I did not feel beautiful during or after my pregnancy until I lost (or will lose) my baby weight. I see other pregnant women as beautiful, but I felt fat, bloated, double chinned, and gassy. (p. 232)

Rankie Shelton also weaves description with insight:

> My concept of worth—whether it's beauty or not I am not sure—is definitely linked to my mental power and my ability to break through the

barriers of gender exclusion into a powerful existence where my voice can be more influential than my brothers'. Wow, where did that come from? I talk a lot about my brothers, but has there always been this sense of drive to pass them intellectually? Hmmm. Where that came from is that writing is what helps us realize what we think. Writing gives words to what was previously unconscious, yet acted upon, parts of ourselves. (p. 233)

They place these insights into sociocultural contexts, critiquing processes of enculturation while creating a transaction between self and perceptions of cultural milieu. McDermott's description in her study of a memory of a magazine cover presents a uniquely emic view of the culture surrounding her as a child:

I grew up after the feminist movement, in the '80s Reagan era, with Madonna and MTV. I consumed *Teen Magazine*, *Seventeen Magazine*, and *Vogue*, and those images really impacted how I saw women. I remember this one cover with Brooke Shields on it and the photos of tanned women wearing turquoise jewelry and brocade bikinis. It was sensual, aesthetically pleasing—the colors, the lighting, all of it—and I wanted to be a part of that world. Using beauty to get what you wanted was reinforced in my community. Girls viewed it as a source of power, and it *was*, honestly. It protected you from ridicule, gave you status, got you in the right clubs. (p. 233–234)

Rankie Shelton's reply presents a transgenerational dialectic:

I think it's very important that we are not the same generation . . . as I think about your struggle with pregnancy and how much more positive my experience was than yours, I wonder if what my generation gave you wasn't a mixed bag of confusion. (p. 234)

Their comparisons of differing time periods allow them to examine their own lives in slightly different imagined cultural contexts. The process of historiography promotes a changing view of self within an expanded social imagination.

As a curriculum of health, duoethnography presents opportunities for researchers to examine and restory how they construct meaning around culturally charged symbols. This is important because these symbols often form a backdrop to our lives. As we saw in Francyne Huckaby and Molly Weinburgh's exceptional study of privilege and entitlement in the southern United States, we have deeply embodied associations to music, which can trigger profound emotions. And, of course, these were the associations that Huckaby and Weinburgh investigated in relation to *Dixie* and *Lift Every Voice*. Juxtaposing these songs, they delineated their overlaps, differences, and gray zones. In their study, these two songs create a dialectical structure as a context for analysis. The research topic itself—patriotism within a landscape of complex inequities—is relatively inaccessible to many other research methods. On one level, they explored in various contexts the meanings they have made and are continuing to make in relation to the songs. For example, Huckaby shares these thoughts:

> I responded to *Dixie* as though it were an attack or at least a potential attack on my person—my Black, Southern person. The song created a visceral and emotional self-protection response for me. The option of considering what the person mentioning it, singing it, or honking it might mean did not enter my considerations. (p. 162)

Weinburgh, discussing with Huckaby how the meaning of the song *Dixie* may have shifted to become a de facto flag for the Confederacy, states:

> The shift can be gut wrenching for some. You can hear where I am— with both sides I become insecure because either threatens who I am and where I'm positioned. I do NOT want White supremacy. I don't want this supremacy thing to take on any force and potential at all. Though I side with the other way more intellectually, my gut says: But where does that leave me? I'm in that unusual position where I certainly don't want to go where the song *Dixie* seems to be leading. But it is unsettling to think about all of the things that I have taken for granted, things that would change if we restructure. Even if we restructure the way I'd like us to restructure, life's not going to be the same way it was, or is, or would continue to be. (p. 173–174)

As the above passage suggests, duoethnography can involve researcher dedication to honesty and at times destabilizing disclosure. Personal contradictory meanings emerge from the fabric of these embodied disclosures.

And on another level, as the song *Dixie* is loaded with shared local and national cultural meanings, Huckaby and Weinburgh use their personal analysis as a lens for a broader survey of the racial landscape in the United States from the Civil Rights Movement to the present. Furthermore, as they deconstruct their relationship to the historical, racial, and geographic contexts of these songs that are well known at least throughout the United States, they encourage the readers to do so as well.

Huckaby and Weinburgh's study suggests that duoethnography promotes a level of personal catharsis through a greater awareness of our symbolic landscape. This happened to Rick when Deidre Le Fevre's stories in our duoethnography on dangerous conversations evoked a realization that my adolescent sense of social justice stemmed in part not from my rebellion from my parents as a teenager but, rather, from the values of justice and fairness that they passed on to me. Although this insight might appear obvious and even a little trite, to me it was profound. Le Fevre also reconceptualized her perception toward her earlier study about how women students and faculty members experienced their position and identity within the academy. After doing the duoethnography, she wrote:

> I've recently located all those women. Conversations with you made me decide to see if I could find them. I found them all, and they are all doing different things related to education; some are academics and some are not. I corresponded with them all because it would be so interesting to juxtapose their stories twelve years on when I finally publish this work, so this conversation with you has motivated me to resurrect it. (p. 276–277)

Duoethnography created a space and a dialectic for us to imagine new possibilities for ourselves and our work.

A process of self-reflexivity is present in (and generated by) Rick Breault, Raine Hackler, and Rebecca Bradley's dialogue about the role of gender among male elementary teachers. This change in perception leading to current or future action is evident in each of them. Here it is reflected in the juxtaposition of thoughts Raine presented in different places in his study:

> Across the rolling prairie foothills of southern Alberta, Canada, in the shadowy lap of the Rocky Mountains, a twelve-year-old boy writes, "I live in a town that's two blocks wide. Two blocks wide and who am I?" . . . He knows that the only way to combat the boredom of a small prairie town is to escape into a world of creativity and invention, music and dance, truth or dare, hide and seek. Little does he realize that the path he has constructed before him will not run parallel to any he will cross in his life. (p. 120)

> As I sit here now, in a newly unwrapped "principal's" chair for the first time in my life, I catch myself carefully constructing opportunities for my brand-new staff to explore, encouraging them to question and challenge the processes they have become a part of before, rather than after, they consider replicating such perspectives, behaviors, values and paradigms in their daily professional and personal lives. (p. 133)

> As I listened to the stories, reflections, and questions of the two of you, I began to understand and validate the relevance of events in my own professional and personal journey. This was particularly signified by the focused exchange about our impact on our students (and our students on our own lives) through the lens of our sexualities, social identities, and deeply rooted philosophies. (p. 132)

In these thoughts, Hackler is examining the past from the present and projecting himself into the past to consider the present. As he does so, he makes connections between the experiential research process he has engaged in and the active and deeply contextualized ways of learning ("the lens of our sexualities, social identities, and deeply rooted philosophies") and his own professional and personal journey (Clandinin and Connelly, 1995). He then applies this insight to his work as a principal in considering ways to make his school setting more humane.

On more of a metalevel, given that their professions are in the mental health field, Kathleen Sitter and Sean Hall in their study of professional boundaries in the mental health field examine issues of health and wellness and the ethics surrounding them. Through the lens of their own lived professional experience, they examine a number of dilemmas in mental health/social work. A central dilemma involves the relationship between the codified, defined nature of professional boundaries (the rules of the road) and the more organic, fluid, relational, holistic, and emergent nature of community-based therapy. Their stories of interactions between self and client—with specific examples and rich detail—center on power and authority issues. In the following exchange, Kathleen speaks first and then Sean:

Kathleen: I wonder if in this discussion that has led to all of these topics about power, ownership, storytelling, labels, universals about humanity, connections, religion, and tolerance, if somewhere in all of our experiences we have actually implicitly drawn on these concepts to try to make sense as to what constitute "boundaries" in our work. At times I wonder if my own struggle with boundaries is about "keeping someone out" or away from certain spaces. This goes against some of the core concepts that we have talked about. Or maybe it is about creating new spaces that respect differences?

Sean: I think that one reason that we started discussing the topic of boundaries when we initially met was about the confusion that you speak of: Are they tools of "keep away," sharing, creating new spaces, or something else entirely? For me, I think that they are all of these things, with perhaps some of the "hard edges" sanded off so that they are much more connected with one another. What I mean by this is the ability to speak of boundaries as all of the aforementioned without it sounding paradoxical! Protective, but also inclusive? Creating new spaces but limiting as well? (p. 257)

Their tools as therapists include peoples' epistemologies and ways of meaning making. Part of their discussion examined metaphoric and nonverbal ways of knowing. They ask, What happens when we cross a boundary from words to photography and art? Sitter makes this provocative statement:

> My role isn't just about staying behind the picture, so to speak, but involves stepping into the frame and being engaged in community work that might sometimes ruffle feathers or blur professional boundaries. (p. 251)

And Hall shares this thought:

> This [the dynamic narrative nature of art] seems to fit nicely with your example of the alley and how an individual can start, add, change, enter, and exit the conversation at different times, ultimately altering the original perception, the original picture, for all involved. (p. 252)

Hall then asks, "Who owns the visual work once it's finished?" An alley in a photo becomes a metaphor for emergent pathways stemming from dialogic imagination. And then they bring this particular topic back to that of boundaries—of visual work and of collectively generated and shared stories. Their study builds on the tension they identify in shifting boundaries: The location of a boundary in any relationship that involves story and image is jointly created, changeable, uncertain, and even at times elusive. Hall states:

> One thing that struck me when having this discussion was the notion of boundaries as some sort of fixed or defined entity. As our discussion progressed, it really reaffirmed for me the idea that boundaries truly are unique to the time, place, and topic of discussions and specific relationships. At first glance this might be taken to mean boundaries are merely situational or conditional, but I think that this is not the case at all; it is much more than this. Boundaries can and do change, but this seems much more about that space created between participants, rather than some other outside force. (p. 259)

In Sitter and Hall's study, as well as the others, much of the value of the inquiry is found within its embodied process, its personal contextualization. This is generated as researchers explore their subject positions, clarify their epistemological beliefs, and tell stories with rich details. Furthermore, as they dialogically disrupt their narrative perceptions, they begin to relive and restory the events of their lives, reframing their views of their own narratives.

FUTURE DIRECTIONS

Duoethnographers have proposed a range of future research projects. Many of these topics include their following existing methodological ways of working to examine new inquiry themes and questions. Some of these include graffiti and resistance art, sustainability and place-based education, health, cleanliness, time, learning, emotional safety, and justice. These topics have the potential to promote knowledge and reflexivity. They are also, however, elusive, conceptual, and difficult to access with other forms of qualitative research.

In addition to considering new themes for duoethnography, its researchers are continuing to experiment with its emerging methodological boundaries. One possible direction involves duoethnographers working in new ways with nonacademics as research partners. For example, one academic researcher who has not yet worked with duoethnography is considering doing a duoethnography with his elderly father to examine transgenerational differences and similarities. His father, an African American, grew up in the southern United States in the 1930s and 1940s, whereas he grew up in the northwestern part of the country in the 1970s and 1980s. He would like to examine the relationships between the contexts of time and place on their socialization. Another researcher has been considering organizing a duoethnography with students, such as ethnic or sexual minority youth, who are often marginalized with other forms of research. Instead of being the objects of someone else's research, these students would become self-researchers, gaining research skills, voice, community, and empowerment as they contribute to readers' understandings of contexts of influence in their lives. A third future and perhaps counterintuitive direction is represented by individual researchers conducting duoethnographers on themselves. Tina Rapke, for example, has been actively exploring contrasting sides to her academic identity, a mathematical and an educational side. With duoethnography, she has been exploring this dialectic within her identity.

CONCLUSION

Duoethnography has emerged as a nascent research methodology in response to researchers seeking to work in a new key. Similar to other qualitative researchers, those working with duoethnography examine interpersonal experience within systems or cultures. However, unlike other forms of qualitative research, duoethnographers do not bracket themselves out of their research; rather, they bracket themselves in: They focus their inquiry with the subjectivity of their voices and identities. For the initial duoethnographers, part of what was missing in other forms of research was a dedication to the collaborative coconstruction and deconstruction of their topic of investigation. They each wanted to collaborate on the research and even have the process of collaboration be an explicit part of the investigation. Positioning themselves within polyvocal texts, they created nuanced, liminal, and unique questions. These questions appear in contingent and intersubjective spaces.

As they examine these questions, duoethnographers address fundamental issues within qualitative research. One of these is the issue of representation: How do you represent the Other if you believe that knowledge formation is an active intersubjective construction, thus changing through the act of representation? Duoethnographers, building on the work of autoethnographers, are the researcher as well as the object of their research. This process undermines the Western notion of ethnography as being a way to examine the Other as subject or object (Latour, 1993). It also directly allows its inquirers to address a second issue in qualitative research, that of self-reflexivity and trustworthiness of the inquiry. To many duoethnographers, research that does not lead to praxis or social improvement is not "valid" or trustworthy. Instead, the inquiry goal is to promote researcher/reader self-reflexivity and social justice: Duoethnography does not just "uncover findings" but, rather, promotes more complex and inclusive social constructions and conceptualizations of experience.

The eleven studies in this volume illuminate human experience in new ways. They offer new images of justice and equity and contribute to a cultural reservoir of the social imagination. As these researchers deconstructed their narrative unities, they reconstructed them to gain a new imaginative capacity for social justice. Their narratives suggest new and ethical ways of living not only for the researchers, but also for the readers of these studies. It is a new way of conducting research in which meanings are represented as fluid, not fixed, changing through dialogic interaction.

REFERENCES

Clandinin, J. (2011, January). *Narrative understandings of transitions: Site of inquiry.* Keynote address presented at the meeting of the Narrative, Arts-based, and "Post" Approaches to Social Research, Arizona State University, Tempe.

Clandinin, J. D., and Connelly, F. M. (1995). *Teachers' professional knowledge landscapes.* New York: TC Press.

Creswell, J. W., and Miller, D. (2000). Determining validity in qualitative inquiry. *Theory Into Practice, 39*(3), 124–129.

Foucault, Michel (1980). *Power/knowledge: Selected interviews and other writings 1972–1977* (C. Gordon, Ed.). London: Harvester.

Freire, P. (1970). *Pedagogy of the oppressed.* NY: Seabury Press.

Greenwood, D. (2010). A Critical Analysis of Sustainability Education in Schooling's Bureaucracy: Barriers and Small openings in Teacher Education. *Teacher Education Quarterly, 37*(4), 139–54.

Hall, S. (1990). Cultural identity and diaspora. In J. Rutherford (Ed.), *Identity: Community, culture, difference.* London: Lawrence & Wishart.

Holland, D., Lachicotte, W., Jr., Skinner, D., and Cain, C. (1998). *Identity and agency in cultural worlds*. Cambridge, MA: Harvard University Press.

Krammer, D., and Mangiardi, R. (2012). A duoethnographic exploration of what schools teach us about schooling. In J. Norris, R. D. Sawyer, and D. Lund (Eds.), *Duoethnography: Dialogic methods for social, health, and educational research*. Walnut Creek, CA: Left Coast Press.

Latour, B. 1993. *We have never been modern*. Cambridge, MA: Harvard University Press.

Lund, D. E., and Nabavi, M. (2008). Understanding student anti-racism activism to foster social justice in schools. *International Journal of Multicultural Education, 10*(1), 1–20. Retrieved from http://ijme-journal.org/index.php/ijme/issue/view/4.

Matus, C., and McCarthy, C. (2003). The triumph of multiplicity and the carnival of difference: Curriculum dilemmas in the age of postcolonialism and globalization. In W. Pinar (Ed.), *International handbook of curriculum research* (pp. 73–84). Mahwah, NJ: Lawrence Erlbaum Associates.

Miller, J. (2011, January). *Autobiography on the move: Poststructuralist perspectives on (im)possible narrative representations of collaboration*. Keynote address presented at the meeting of the Narrative, Arts-based, and "Post" Approaches to Social Research, Arizona State University, Tempe.

Morris, D. (2002). Narrative, ethics, and pain: Thinking with stories. In R. Charon and M. Montello (Eds.), *Stories matter: The role of narrative in medical ethics* (pp. 200–223). New York: Routledge.

Norris, J., and Sawyer, R. (2004). *Null and hidden curricula of sexual orientation: A dialogue on the curreres of the absent presence and the present absence*. Paper presented at the Democratic Responses in an Era of Standardization Conference, Troy, NY.

Pinar, W. (1975). Currere: Toward reconceptualization. In W. Pinar (Ed.), *Curriculum theorizing: The reconceptualists* (pp. 396–414). Berkeley, CA: McCutchan.

Polanski, R. (Director). (2010). *The ghost writer* [DVD]. United States: Summit Entertainment.

Rosenblatt, L. (1994). *The reader, the text, the poem: The transactional theory of the literary work*. Carbondale: Southern Illinois Press.

Said, E. W. (1993). *Culture and imperialism*. New York: Alfred A. Knopf.

Sawyer, R. D. (2003). Situating Teacher Development: The View from Two Teachers' Perspectives. *International Journal of Educational Research, 37*(8), 733–753.

Sawyer, R. D. (2010). Curriculum and International Democracy: A Vital Source of Synergy and Change. *Journal of Curriculum Theorizing, 26*(1), 22–37.

Sawyer, R. D., and Norris, J. (in press). *Understanding qualitative research: Duoethnography*. Oxford, UK: Oxford University Press.

Index

About the Authors

Sonia Aujla-Bhullar is a Master of Arts student in the Faculty of Education at the University of Calgary. She teaches public school in Calgary, and her current work centers on issues surrounding experiences of visible minority teachers in the school system. Previously, she has held positions including youth facilitator and community liaison with the Calgary Immigrant Women's Association, working with diverse communities, and programs for first and second-generation immigrant women. Sonia has also served in the Punjabi-Sikh community as a youth liaison, a position geared toward building awareness and cross-cultural understanding in Calgary. As an educator, she works both within and outside the school community with the diverse and growing population comprised of students, teachers, and families. Sonia aspires to develop her critical insights around social justice education and practice in the community and public sphere through her academic and professional work.

Rebecca Bradley is a doctoral student in the Bagwell College of Education at Kennesaw State University. She formerly taught science in rural and suburban elementary schools in the state of Georgia. In that role, her focus has been on guided and purposeful inquiry, an emphasis that she carried into her doctoral studies by inquiring into her own practices. Rebecca is also interested in the aesthetic dimensions of curriculum and has participated in seminars with teaching artists at Lincoln Center and with Maxine Greene. In her dissertation, Rebecca explores the use of aesthetic ways of knowing and observing in the self-study of teaching practice as a way of nurturing more imaginative thinking, critical reflection, and teacher change. She considers the opportunity to participate in duoethnography as pivotal in enhancing her understanding of qualitative research, where narrative exploration aids in the extension of perspective, understanding, and transformation.

Rick Breault is visiting professor of teacher education in the Department of Curriculum & Instruction/Literacy at West Virginia University. In his research, he seeks to integrate diverse interests in theology, the arts, history, and social foundations of education into ways of looking at curriculum and the classroom, and to improve his teaching. Rick also continues to experiment with arts-informed pedagogy to promote imagination and creativity in teachers and the students with whom they work. More recently, he has begun examining the role of geography and sense of place in the success or failure of school/university relationships such as Professional Development Schools. It was a serendipitous conversation with Joe Norris in which Rick shared a recent unfocused attempt at linking personal history, cultural and geographic place, and early gender development experiences to later effectiveness as an elementary school teacher that led him to duoethnography as one way to systematically explore those questions.

Kari Grain is Manager of the After School Program at the Calgary Bridge Foundation for Youth, which aims to help immigrant children bridge the journey to Canadian life. She leads a diverse staff of forty people, all of whom provide quality educational and recreational programming to students who are adjusting to new lives in Calgary, Alberta. Kari approaches education, work, and life with a focus on critical reflection as an avenue toward cross-cultural understanding. Her interest in duoethnography is rooted in her belief that curriculum is something we *live* and therefore something we learn; every experience is a tool with which we transform our perspective on what we "know" to be true. Kari's recent duoethnographic research on the transformative learning of white educators in Rwanda reinforced her view that critical reflection on topics such as racialized identity and privilege can serve to alter one's view of self and the world and thereby serve as powerful topics in a silent curriculum. She recently completed her Master of Arts in the Faculty of Education at the University of Calgary, with the support of the Ron Ghitter Award for Human Rights, the Queen Elizabeth II Scholarship, and the Richard Hirabayashi Award for Multiculturalism. Kari's Master's thesis won the national 2010 Michel Laferriere Research Award for the outstanding thesis in comparative and international education.

Jim Greenlaw is Dean of the Faculty of Education at the University of Ontario Institute of Technology. He has taught English education, curriculum theory, and computers in education courses at the University of British Columbia, the University of Regina, and St. Francis Xavier University. He has also taught writing at Changsha Railway University in China. Jim served as Director of the Royal University of Bhutan's Educational Leadership Graduate Program that was sponsored by the Canadian International Development Agency. He is also the Chief Editor and principal author of an English-as-a-Foreign-Language textbook series titled Project English that middle school students throughout China use. His research interests include literary theory, multicultural education, English as a foreign language, cultural studies, philosophy of education, and computers in education. His life-long reflections concerning the teaching of writing drew Jim to collaborate with Joe Norris on their chapter in this book.

Raine Hackler, a native of Alberta, Canada, is currently principal of the Main Street Academy Charter School in Atlanta, Georgia. Prior to this, he taught Grades 1–5 in Canada for twelve years, serving on numerous national curriculum committees. After several years of traveling and teaching in Southeast Asia and Africa, Raine settled in Atlanta and spent ten years in Atlanta Public Schools as an elementary school teacher, computer lab instructor, and professional development presenter. During that time, he was the recipient of a variety of awards, including Atlanta Public Schools System Wide Teacher of the Year, 11 Alive News "Class Act" Teacher of the Week, EdTech Tinfoil Star Award, and Atlanta Families Teacher of Excellence.

Sean Hall is a registered provisional psychologist, working as a family counselor with Alberta Health Services. He also holds a Master of Counselling Psychology and an after-degree in Education. Currently, he is working with clients of all ages but with a focus on children and youth. Previously, he worked as the mental health promotion representative for Alberta Health Services within a community collaborative as a Community Development Coordinator, focusing on children aged five through twelve and their families. It was within the scope of this position and as a domestic violence prevention group facilitator with the YWCA Sheriff King Home that he concentrated on promoting hope, via projects such as Hope Art and creative art tools such as producing Hope Trees and gardens. Sean is interested in promoting mental health via stigma reduction; let's start and continue conversations to shed light on the margins.

M. Francyne Huckaby, Associate Professor of Curriculum Studies at Texas Christian University, believes established knowledge and tacit ways of knowing complicate each other. Conceptualizing education broadly, she values critical analysis entwined with sensitivities to people's histories with interests in pedagogical sites where divergent worldviews coexist. Such sites are ripe with possibilities and dangers. Duoethnography extends these interests through critical exploration of the processes, products, and effects of knowledge, and creates openings and spaces for antioppressive discourses. Her work appears in *International Journal of Qualitative Studies in Education, Educational Philosophy and Theory; The Journal of Curriculum Theorizing;* and *Handbook of Public Pedagogy,* and also *Women and Pedagogy: Education through Autobiographical Narrative.* Her honors include Outstanding Dissertation (2006 American Educational Research Association, Qualitative Research), Straight for Equality (2007 PFLAG), and Mortar Board Preferred Professor (2009 TCU). As a Peace Corps volunteer in Papua New Guinea, she helped six South Foré villages develop primary schools.

Donna Krammer is currently a doctoral student in the Faculty of Education at the University of Alberta, Edmonton, Canada. Her autoethnographic dissertation is an account of the critical role that images—mental images of self and others, as well as image-based family artifacts—came to play in her quest to reclaim an ethnic Hungarian identity. Her scholarly interests include contemporary relational theory, specifically relational psychoanalysis. She believes that duoethnographic researchers can benefit from a study of the analytic process as contemporary theorists and clinicians have reconceived it—analysis as thoughtful and disciplined conversation.

Deidre M. Le Fevre is a senior lecturer in Education at the University of Auckland, New Zealand. She teaches courses in Educational Leadership and Educational Change. Her research focuses on how people learn, and she is particularly interested in innovative approaches to adult professional learning. Deidre has worked in universities, businesses, and schools in the United Kingdom, The United States, and New Zealand.

Tonda Liggett is Assistant Professor of English Language Learning in the Department of Teaching & Learning at Washington State University, Vancouver. Her research focuses on the intersections of race, language, culture, and gender in identity construction for teachers and English language learners. She also studies the broader political and social influence of immigration on the education of bilingual and multilingual students. Through this lens, she works to problematize the complex and dynamic knowledge frameworks that inform student learning as well as teachers' thoughts about teaching diverse populations. Her work with duoethnography extends this inquiry, adding a collaborative and reflective component that presses for better understandings of her own identity in relation to her teaching.

Darren E. Lund is a Professor in the Faculty of Education at the University of Calgary, where his research examines social justice activism in schools and communities. Darren earned his Ph.D. at UBC, and his duoethnographic work is an extension of his ongoing inquiry into topics around identity, sexual orientation, youth activism, and social justice pedagogy. Darren is a former high school teacher and is currently "Welcoming Communities" Domain Leader with the *Prairie Metropolis Centre*. He enjoys working collaboratively and has two coedited books (with Paul Carr): *The Great White North? Exploring Whiteness, Privilege and Identity in Education* (Sense Publishers, 2007) and *Doing Democracy: Striving for Political Literacy and Social Justice* (Peter Lang Press, 2008).

Rosemarie Mangiardi is a doctoral candidate in the Faculty of Education at the University of Alberta. Her doctoral research, *Youth Take Action to Improve their Sex Education*, concentrates on working with youth as they explore and express their views about and visions for school-based sexual health education. By employing Youth Participatory Action Research, Rose worked with a team of youth to call attention to students' experiences of the teaching and learning of sexual health. This participatory work culminated in the construction of an action plan aimed at initiating dialogue with educational decision makers centered on what can be sex education, were it to address and satisfy youth's expressed sexual health needs. Rose's duoethnographic exploration with friend, colleague, and mentor Donna Krammer emphasized for her the degree to which dialogue about the past finds place and purpose in changing the present so influence can be felt in the future.

Patrice McClellan (Ed.D.) is Assistant Professor and Director of the Masters of Organizational Leadership Program at Lourdes College. She teaches Leadership Foundations, Organization Development, Diversity and Social Justice, and Capstone Research. Her research foci include Leadership Preparation with a focus on culturally relevant pedagogy; Diversity and Leadership, exploring how race, gender, class, sexual orientation, and ability affects leadership practice; and Leadership Development with a focus on critical servant leadership and cultural competence. Dr. McClellan has also published in various journals with the most recent article titled "Toward Critical Servant Leadership in Graduate Schools of Education: From Theoretical Construct to Social Justice Praxis." In addition to journal publications, Dr. McClellan is coauthor of the book *Herstories: Leading with the Lessons of the Lives of Black Women Activists* (2011).

Morna McDermott is an Associate Professor at Towson University, where she teaches various theory and methods courses in the College of Education. Her scholarship and research interests focus on democracy, social justice, and arts-informed inquiry in K-post secondary educational settings, and working with beginning and experienced educators. She explores how the arts serve as a form of literacy that challenges traditional classroom learning and dominant narratives. She is the author of various publications including "Outlaw Arts Based Research" in *Journal of Curriculum and Pedagogy*, 7 (1); "Using Children's Literature and Drama to Understand Social Justice" (2010), coauthored with N. Rankie Shelton for *Teacher Development*; and "(De)constructing Fragments: Arts-based Inquiry as Passion Pieces," in J. G. Knowles et al. (Eds.), *Creating Scholartistry: Imagining the Arts-informed Thesis or Dissertation* (Backalong Books). Current and recent duoethnographies with friend and collaborator Nancy Shelton have illuminated how the complex layering of time, space, voice, and memory play powerful roles in creative inquiry. She currently lives in Baltimore with her husband and two children.

Maryam Nabavi is a Ph.D. candidate in Educational Studies at the University of British Columbia. Her interest in duoethnography furthers her commitment to exploring the ways in which social identities are defining makers of social, cultural, political, historical, and spatial inclusions and exclusions. Her doctoral research, which explores identity, belonging, and the nation from the lens of citizenship learning for young immigrants in Canada, is informed by her commitments to social justice research, policy, and activism during the past ten years. She has published in the areas of youth activism, citizenship education, and anti-colonial education.

Joe Norris is professor of Drama in Education & Applied Theatre in the Department of Dramatic Arts, Marilyn I. Walker School of Fine & Performing Arts at Brock University. He advocates the arts as ways of knowing, doing, and being. His book, *Playbuilding as Qualitative Research: A Participatory Arts-based Approach* (Left Coast Press, 2009), purports that playbuilding is a legitimate research methodology and received The American Educational Research Association's Qualitative Research SIG's Outstanding Book Award in 2011. The book documents how data generation, its interpretation, and its dissemination, all can be mediated through theatrical means. Using forum theatre, he invites audiences to reconceptualize the issues and themselves after the performance. His work with duoethnography furthers his interest in designing dialogic qualitative research methodologies that assist in the reconceptualization of the world and of the self. Driving his research agendas is the belief that an unreflected life is a life half lived and that we need the Other to assist us in understanding that which we cannot comprehend alone.

Jennifer Sader is an Assistant Professor in the Master of Organizational Program at Lourdes College. She has taught Leadership Foundations, Interpersonal Issues in Leadership, Research Methods, Quantitative Tools for Leadership, and, of course, Diversity and Social Justice. Her research agenda focuses on the development issues of graduate students and junior faculty. She earned her Ph.D. in Higher Education Administration from Bowling Green State University in 2007, and a chapter based on her dissertation work appeared in Spring 2011 as "The Influence of Gender: Women Doctoral Students in Computer Science" in P. A. Pasque and S. E. Nicholson (Eds.), *Empowering Women in Higher Education and Student Affairs: Theory, Research, Narratives, and Practice from Feminist Perspective* (Stylus Publishing, 2001).

Richard D. Sawyer is an Associate Professor of Education at Washington State University, Vancouver. He chairs both the Ed.D. Program in Teacher Leadership for Washington State University and the MIT Secondary Certification Program at Washington State University, Vancouver. The focus of his research is on the pedagogy of change and praxis, specifically within the contexts of duoethnography, international democratic education, teacher decision making, and curriculum theory. In terms of international education, he has recently conducted research in Oaxaca, Mexico, and Palestine. The applied context of curriculum theory is a key focus of his work. He is currently completing an additional book with Joe Norris: *Understanding Qualitative Research: Duoethnography* (Oxford University Press).

Nancy Rankie Shelton is an Associate Professor of Literacy Education at UMBC. As a critical literacy researcher, Nancy's work challenges the claims made by current federal reform movements that reduce literacy instruction to narrow, product-based performance measures. She seeks to help teachers understand the unintended consequences of approaching literacy learning as mastering a set of basic skills. Her current efforts are focused on supporting teachers to enable them to create the conditions in their classrooms that help students develop the proficiencies needed to participate in a critical democracy. Nancy's work in duoethnography provides the foundation for understanding how individuals create and re-create themselves within a larger sociohistorical environment and how these "personal curriculums" play out in our roles as public educators.

Kathleen Sitter is a doctoral candidate in the Faculty of Education at the University of Calgary. She also holds a Master of Social Work and a Master of Communication Studies. For the past decade, her creative work with marginalized communities draws on collaborative representational practices of visual media. Drawing on a social justice approach and a Freirean pedagogical framework, her doctoral research involved working with a disability advocacy group *Right to Love*, where members created a series of videos exploring the supports, barriers, and personal stories of love and relationships in the disability community. Her dissertation explores the strengths, ethical complexities, and "afterlife" of video advocacy. Her research interests include community-media and human rights, social justice research, and collaborative inquiry. She is also a recent recipient of the Social Sciences and Humanities Research Council Joseph-Armand Bombardier Graduate Scholarship for her doctoral research.

Molly Weinburgh, William L. & Betty F. Adams Chair of Education and the Director of the Andrews Institute of Mathematics & Science Education, is professor of science education at Texas Christian University. She is an active member of numerous science education societies. She directs the Ph.D. in Science Education, teaches courses in science education in the College of Education, and teaches the Honors section of a nonmajor biology course. Her first work with duoethnography is found in *Re-visioning Science Education from Feminist Perspectives* (Sense Publishers, 2010). Her research interests include equity issues in science education, inquiry science in K-12 classrooms, and professional development for teachers of science.